Martial Law and English Laws.

John M. Collins presents the first comprehensive history of martial law in the early modern period. He argues that, rather than being a state of exception from law, martial law was understood and practiced as one of the king's laws. Further, it was a vital component of both England's domestic and imperial legal order. It was used to quell rebellions during the Reformation, to subdue Ireland, to regulate English plantations like Jamestown, to punish spies and traitors in the English Civil War, and to build forts on Jamaica. Through outlining the history of martial law, Collins reinterprets English legal culture as dynamic, politicized, and creative, where jurists were inspired by past practices to generate new law rather than being restrained by it. This work asks that legal history once again be reintegrated into the cultural and political histories of early modern England and its empire.

John M. Collins is a lecturer in History at Eastern Washington University.

Cambridge Studies in Early Modern British History

Series editors

JOHN MORRILL

Professor of British and Irish History, University of Cambridge, and Fellow of Selwyn College

ETHAN SHAGAN

Professor of History, University of California, Berkeley

ALEXANDRA SHEPARD

Professor of Gender History, University of Glasgow

ALEXANDRA WALSHAM

Professor of Modern History, University of Cambridge, and Fellow of Trinity College

This is a series of monographs and studies covering many aspects of the history of the British Isles between the late fifteenth century and the early eighteenth century. It includes the work of established scholars and pioneering work by a new generation of scholars. It includes both reviews and revisions of major topics and books that open up new historical terrain or which reveal startling new perspectives on familiar subjects. All the volumes set detailed research within broader perspectives, and the books are intended for the use of students as well as of their teachers.

For a list of titles in the series go to
www.cambridge.org/earlymodernbritishhistory

Martial Law and English Laws, c. 1500–c. 1700

John M. Collins

Eastern Washington University

CAMBRIDGE
UNIVERSITY PRESS

CAMBRIDGE
UNIVERSITY PRESS

University Printing House, Cambridge CB2 8BS, United Kingdom

One Liberty Plaza, 20th Floor, New York, NY 10006, USA

477 Williamstown Road, Port Melbourne, VIC 3207, Australia

314-321, 3rd Floor, Plot 3, Splendor Forum, Jasola District Centre, New Delhi - 110025, India

79 Anson Road, #06-04/06, Singapore 079906

Cambridge University Press is part of the University of Cambridge.

It furthers the University's mission by disseminating knowledge in the pursuit of
education, learning and research at the highest international levels of excellence.

www.cambridge.org
Information on this title: www.cambridge.org/9781107469488

First published 2016
First paperback edition 2020

A catalogue record for this publication is available from the British Library

Library of Congress Cataloging in Publication data
Collins, John M., 1983–
Martial law and English laws, c.1500-c.1700 / John M. Collins,
Eastern Washington University.
New York : Cambridge University Press, 2016. | Includes bibliographical
references and index.
LCCN 2016008913 | ISBN 9781107092877 (alk. paper)
LCSH: Martial law – England – History. | Law – England – History.
LCC KD4442 .C65 2016 | DDC 342.42/062809031–dc23
LC record available at http://lccn.loc.gov/2016008913

ISBN 978-1-107-09287-7 Hardback
ISBN 978-1-107-46948-8 Paperback

[N]otwithstanding the length of time which we have taken ... we are apprehensive that we shall not be able to report any very satisfactory opinion. Indeed the time has been employed in the endeavour to procure information which we have not attained, and with respect to that which we shall state, if we could have foreseen that our researches would have been so unsuccessful, the following opinion might certainly have been communicated in much less time.[1]

Spencer Perceval to C.P. Yorke, 23 January, 1804 on the law of martial law

---

[1] BL, Add. Ms. 38,240, fos. 117v–18.

Contents

Table

Acknowledgments

I would first and foremost like to thank the University of Virginia and in particular the Corcoran Department of History for supporting this project while I was a PhD student. I would also like to thank Eastern Washington University for giving me the opportunity to continue my career as a lecturer in History. In particular, I thank Professors Bob Dean, Ann Le Bar, Edward Slack, and Liping Zhu for supporting me and my research. I am also very grateful to the Jervoise family of Herriard Park, who allowed me to examine their manuscript collection that is deposited at the Hampshire Record Office. I would also like to thank the Interlibrary Loan and Summit librarians at EWU's John F. Kennedy Library for their professionalism and kind assistance in obtaining often difficult-to-find books that range from the thirteenth to the twentieth century.

This work was made possible by the generous funding of multiple institutional bodies. These include the Dumas Malone/Albert Gallatin Fellowship from the University of Virginia, fellowships at the Lilly Library at Indiana University, the Henry E. Huntington Library, the Colonial Williamsburg Foundation, and the William Andrews Clark Library at UCLA, as well as the North American Conference for British Studies' Dissertation Year Fellowship. Without this funding, I would not have been able to conduct the manuscript research that is the foundation of this book.

Numerous forums have allowed me to work out my ideas. Parts of this book have been presented at two meetings of the Mid-Atlantic Conference for British Studies in 2011 and in 2012, the North American Conference for British Studies in 2012 and in 2014, the Southern Conference for British Studies in 2011, the Sixteenth Century Studies Conference in 2011, the Tudor-Stuart Seminar at the Institute of Historical Research in 2011, the University of Virginia Law School's Legal History seminar in 2012, and the British Legal History Conference in 2015. I thank the participants at all those venues. I published part of Chapter 5 as "Hidden in Plain Sight: Martial Law and the Making of the High Courts of Justice, 1642–1660" in the *Journal of British Studies*. Many thanks to the editors and anonymous reviewers of *JBS* for their comments and for allowing me to reprint some of that article in this book. I would also like to thank the editors of this series for their generous support of this project. Further, I would like to thank the editorial team at Cambridge University Press, including Jeevitha Baskaran, Srilakshmi Gobidass, Elizabeth Friend-Smith, Rosalyn Scott, and Rebecca Taylor for their hard work on this manuscript.

Sage counsels of many have saved me from making the grievous errors that so commonly accompany summary judgments. I would like to thank the late Christopher Brooks, Jordan Downs, Billy Graczyk, Rebecca Green, Paul Griffiths, Joel Halcomb, Paul Halliday, John Harrison, Simon Healy, Alec Hickmott, Krista Kesselring, the late Mark Kishlansky, Noah Millstone, Joseph Miller, John Morrill, Caitlin Morris, Jason Peacey, Stephen Roberts, Sophia Rosenfeld, Philip Stern, David L. Smith, John Terry, and Robert Tittler. I want to thank my colleagues at Eastern for their support over the last two years, including Georgia Bazemore, Larry Cebula, Michael Conlin, Bob Dean, Laura Hodgeman, Kathleen Huttenmaier, Ann Le Bar, Joseph Lenti, Edward Slack, J. William T. Youngs and Liping Zhu. In particular, I would like to thank Joe Lenti for his help and friendship. I would also like to thank my students at Eastern Washington University for patiently enduring the many errors (always committed on purpose, to see if you were paying attention) of a novice instructor. In particular, I would like to thank Tanya Blakely, Michael Edwards, Casey Hagan, Keegan Hovda, Kurtis Johnson, Michael Longwill, Kayla Miller, Michael San Miguel, Anastasia Utke, Jay Williams, and David Windham.

My greatest debts are to my teachers, who have been unfailingly generous with their time and patience. Sarah Fenton, one of my first mentors, provided remarkable enthusiasm, encouragement, and support to me even though my interests fell well outside of her area of expertise and though I suffered from an almost crippling shyness. Sophia Rosenfeld and Joe Miller, who both read through the dissertation version of this book, provided thoughtful, helpful, and encouraging comments on the work. I have had the pleasure to TA for both, and I have learned so much about teaching from their examples. John Morrill, who supervised my MPhil thesis in 2008, has provided constant support and encouragement. It was under John that I first fell in love with early modern English history. He has overseen multiple drafts of this work and has always given extremely thoughtful advice on its progress. This work could not have been completed without the support of Paul Halliday. Anyone aware of his work will know how much I am indebted to it. Every time I thought I had come up with a great idea, I subsequently realized, to my chagrin, that mine was but a half-baked imitation of a much better idea found in *Habeas Corpus*. Professor Halliday, better than anyone I know, balances encouragement with criticism. His guidance has made this work so much better than what it would have been.

This book is dedicated to the memory of Joseph Cure, a great man who befriended a flawed one.

Note on the text

All dates before 1752 are given in old style, though the year is taken to have begun on 1 January rather than 25 March. Dates after 1752 are given according to modern usage.

Abbreviations

A&O	*Acts and Ordinances of the Interregnum, 1642–1660* ed. C.H. Firth 3 vols. (London, 1911) accessed on British History Online February 2013-September 2015, www.british-history.ac.uk
BL	British Library, London
Bodl.	Bodleian Library, Oxford
BRO	Berkshire Record Office, Reading
CALS	Chester and Cheshire Archives and Local Studies Service, Chester
CJ	*Commons Journals* (London) accessed on British History Online February 2013-September 2015, www.british-history.ac.uk
CPR	*Calendar of Patent Rolls* (London)
CSPD	*Calendar of State Papers, Domestic Series* (London)
CSPF	*Calendar of State Papers, Foreign Series* (London)
CSPI	*Calendar of State Papers, Ireland* (London)
CUL	Cambridge University Library, Cambridge
CWTM	*Complete Works of Thomas More* 21 vols. (New Haven, CT)
DRO	Derbyshire Record Office, Matlock
DROE	Devonshire Record Office, Exeter
DUL	Durham University Library, Durham
EHR	*English Historical Review*
FSL	Folger Shakespeare Library, Washington, D.C.
GA	Gloucestershire Record Office, Gloucester
HEHL	Henry E. Huntington Library, San Marino, CA
HH	Hatfield House
HHC	Hull History Centre, Hull
HJ	*Historical Journal*
HMC	*Historical Manuscripts Commission*
HRO	Hertfordshire Record Office, Hertford
IWRO	Isle of Wight Record Office, Newport

JBS	*Journal of British Studies*
JSAHR	*Journal of the Society of Army Historical Research*
L&P	*Letters and Papers, Foreign and Domestic, of the reign of Henry VIII* (London)
LJ	*Lords Journals* (London) accessed on British History Online February 2013-September 2015, www.british-history.ac.uk
LL	Lilly Library, Bloomington IN
LPL	Lambeth Palace Library, Lambeth
NLI	National Library of Ireland, Dublin
NRO	Northamptonshire Record Office, Northampton
ODNB	*Oxford Dictionary of National Biography* (Oxford, 2004)
Old Bailey	*The Old Bailey Proceedings Online, 1674–1913* (www.oldbaileyonline.org, version 7.0, 24 March 2012), accessed 2011–15
P&P	*Past and Present*
PA	Parliamentary Archives, London
PN	*The Principal Navigations, voyages, traffiques and discoveries of the English nation* 12 vols. (Glasgow, 1903–05)
SHC	Surrey History Centre, Woking
SRO	Staffordshire Record Office, Stafford
SRP	*Stuart Royal Proclamations* ed. Paul Hughes and James F. Larkin 2 vols (Oxford, 1973-83)
ST	*Cobbett's Complete Collection of State Trials* 33 vols. (London, 1809–28)
Sutcliffe	Matthew Sutcliffe, *The Practice, Proceedings, and Lawes of Armes* (London, 1593)
TNA	The National Archives, Kew
TRP	*Tudor Royal Proclamations* ed. Paul Hughes and James T. Larkin 3 vols. (New Haven, 1969)

Introduction

William Fleetwood, the sixteenth-century lawyer and recorder of London, was not puzzled by martial law. He did not think it was a "legal black hole" where the sovereign possessed unlimited power.[1] Nor did he think martial law to be particularly exceptional. Instead, Fleetwood thought that martial law was one of the king's laws.

He made this clear in his perhaps fictional discussion with the poet and administrator Thomas Sackville, Lord Buckhurst, and Queen Elizabeth's favorite, Robert Dudley, the Earl of Leicester, which he claimed to have taken place in 1575.[2] The topic of the conversation was of grave importance. Could the queen apply England's penal laws given that the statutes that legalized them specifically used the word "king?"[3] The answer was ultimately yes. Fleetwood proved that Elizabeth could apply the laws of England because the Crown was not simply a living body but also an immortal corporate one. Its rights and privileges withstood any mortal deviation in gender. Thus, the concept of the "king's two bodies" allowed for a female king.[4] But before Fleetwood could prove this seeming contradiction, the lawyer first needed to establish what comprised the laws of England. Ever the systematic thinker, Fleetwood listed all of the means through which the king's "dome is conducted."[5]

---

[1] David Dyzenhous, "The Puzzle of Martial Law," *University of Toronto Law Journal* 59:1 (Winter, 2009): 2.

[2] William Fleetwood, *Itinerarium ad Windsor*, BL, Harley Ms. 168, fos. 4v–5. This tract has recently been printed with an important scholarly introduction. *The Name of a Queen: William Fleetwood's Itinerarium ad Windsor* ed. Charles Beem and Dennis Moore (New York, 2013), 24–9. For his systematic thinking, see Christopher W. Brooks, "Fleetwood, William," in *ODNB*.

[3] By penal laws, Fleetwood was referring to parliamentary statutes that regulated the economy. J.G. Bellamy, *Criminal Law and Society in Late Medieval and Tudor England* (New York, 1984), 90–114.

[4] Cynthia Herrup, "The King's Two Genders," *JBS* 45:3 (July, 2006): 493–510.The classic book on this concept is Ernst Kantorowicz, *The King's Two Bodies: A Study in Medieval Political Theology* (Princeton, 1957).

[5] *The Name of a Queen*, 27.

It began with God's laws written into the Old and New Testament.[6] Then Fleetwood moved on to the canons of the Church of England. Third were matters of marine causes heard and determined by the procedures of the Roman Civil Law. Fifth were the king's forest laws; sixth were the laws relating to merchants. Then Fleetwood listed the laws of wardonry, which had jurisdiction in the marches of Scotland. Eighth were the laws of the cities and boroughs; ninth were the laws of the king's steward. Tenth on his list was the "Highe Court of Parliament," which heard and determined cases as well as made law for the realm. Eleventh was the common law. Twelfth was the secret law of the Crown, which heard special cases. Fleetwood casually named martial law fourth in a list that also included common law and statute law. It was one of many laws.

The king's power was divided and channeled through a complex network of jurisdictions. Each was circumscribed by typological, geographical, and temporal boundaries. The king used forest laws to handle legal problems relating to venison and "vert": presumably those legal cases related to the trees in the forest. He used spiritual laws to address legal business relating to tithes and "thinges testamentary." He used merchant's law to resolve disputes relating to "assurances," or insurance. His other courts had both temporal and topical boundaries. The lord warden punished "Lymers," (rogues or scoundrels), but only in the marches of Scotland. Finally, according to Fleetwood, the king used martial law to punish offenses relating to "matters of armes and offences committed in the kinge's campe or battailes."[7]

Fleetwood's inclusion of martial law as one of the many laws of England was not unusual.[8] Almost all common lawyers in the late sixteenth and early seventeenth centuries recognized its place within England's jurisdictionally pluralistic legal apparatus. These jurists, the Crown, delegated authorities, as well as ordinary subjects disagreed about martial law's procedures. They disagreed about its substantive law. And they disagreed about its jurisdiction.[9] They nevertheless maintained that martial law was one of the king's laws.

---

[6] *Ibid.*, 27–9.   [7] *Ibid.*, 27.

[8] See Paul Halliday's analysis of Sir Francis Ashley's 1616 list of English laws. Paul Halliday, *Habeas Corpus: From England to Empire* (Cambridge, MA, 2010), 145–7.

[9] For the jurisdictional disputes within England in the seventeenth century generally, see David Chan Smith, *Sir Edward Coke and the Reformation of the Laws: Religion, Politics and Jurisprudence, 1578–1616* (Cambridge, 2014), 19–58; Christopher W. Brooks, *Law, Politics and Society in Early Modern England* (Cambridge, 2008), esp. 93–161; Louis Knafla, *Law and Politics in Jacobean England: The Tracts of Lord Chancellor Ellesmere* (Cambridge, 1977); Halliday, *Habeas Corpus*, 137–76. For English jurisdictional pluralism in its imperial context see Ken MacMillan, *Sovereignty and Possession in the English New World: The Legal Foundations of Empire, 1576–1640* (Cambridge, 2006). For jurisdictional plurality in its global contexts, see Lauren Benton, "Introduction" in the

This work follows Fleetwood's lead and argues that martial law was understood as one of the king's laws. Further, it argues that the parliaments of the seventeenth century maintained it as one.

II

This fairly intuitive argument – that the name of a concept reflected its nature – needs to be made because scholars subsequent to the seventeenth century have conceptualized martial law as a form of unmitigated power or rule and not one of the king's laws. In doing so, they have separated martial law from the military law that governs the standing armies of modern states. Further, many have insisted either that martial law was only the common law right of repelling illegal force with force or that it was the will of the general. In either case, martial law did not have a procedural or substantive tradition of its own. Beginning in the twentieth century and continuing into the twenty-first, scholars have conceptualized martial law to be a state of exception from law, where the sovereign utilizes unlimited discretion in order to save the polity from disaster. Fleetwood and other early modern jurists understood martial law to be one of the king's many laws. Subsequent traditions have removed martial law from the English legal tradition.

Those who have sought to exclude martial law have frequently cited the writings of Sir Matthew Hale. The seventeenth-century jurist famously claimed that martial law was "not a law, but something indulged, rather than allowed, as a Law."[10] As this book will show, Hale meant that martial law should only be indulged in wartime. He did not mean, as many have subsequently interpreted, that martial law was a synonym for arbitrary or extralegal power.[11] But scholars beginning with Sir William Blackstone have not understood Hale in this way. Instead, Blackstone claimed that martial law had "no settled principles."[12] This claim has been subsequently expanded to the point where scholars in the twentieth century began to argue that martial law was a misnomer: it should actually

---

American Historical Review's "Law and Empire in Global Perspective Forum" 117:4 (October, 2012): 1092–1100; Benton, "The Legal Regime of the South Atlantic World, 1400–1750: Jurisdictional Complexity as Institutional Order," *Journal of World History* 11:1 (Spring, 2000): 27–56; Benton, "Historical Perspectives on Legal Pluralism," *Hague Journal on the Rule of Law* 3:1 (February, 2011): 57–69; Benton, *A Search for Sovereignty: Law and Geography in European Empires, 1400–1900* (Cambridge, 2010).

[10] Sir Matthew Hale, *The History of the Common Law with an Analysis of the Civil Part of the Law* ed. Charles Runnington (4th ed., corrected, London, 1779), 34.

[11] For my analysis of Hale, see pages 249–53.

[12] Sir William Blackstone, *The Commentaries on the Laws of England in Four Books* ed. Edward Christian 2 vols. (London, 1818), 1: 412–3.

be martial rule and not law.[13] Historians down to the present day insist that martial law is not really law.[14] Its association with extra-legality has had a strong hold on the imagination of many political and legal scholars.

Some less noteworthy but better informed historians beginning in the eighteenth century vigorously protested this view. Both Stephen Payne Adye and A.F. Tytler, two judge advocates, argued for martial law's place within the English legal universe.[15] Both claimed that it derived from the medieval courts of the constable and the marshal. And both stated that martial law had all of those components that together comprised law. A small number of scholars have followed this school of thought. But these works are far from comprehensive and most, like Tytler and Adye, focus exclusively on the disciplining of soldiers.[16]

Jurists coming after Tytler and Adye began to argue for a strict division between martial law and military law, making a historical

---

[13] Charles Fairman, *The Law of Martial Rule* (2nd ed., Chicago, 1943).

[14] J.V. Capua, "The Early History of Martial Law in England from the Fourteenth Century to the Petition of Right," *Cambridge Law Journal* 36:1 (April, 1977): 152–73; Frederic William Maitland, *The Constitutional History of England: A Course of Lectures* ed. H.A.L. Fisher (London, 1955), 267; Joseph Minattur, *Martial Law in India, Pakistan, and Ceylon* (The Hague, 1962). The claim that martial law had no substantive tradition was very influential during the debates over Governor Eyre's use of martial law on Jamaica as well. R.W. Kostal, *A Jurisprudence of Power: Victorian Empire and the Rule of Law* (Oxford, 2005), 200.

[15] Stephen Payne Adye, *A Treatise on Courts Martial: Containing I. Remarks on Martial Law, and Courts-Martial in General II. The Manner of Proceeding against Offenders* ... (London, 1769); A.F. Tytler, *An Essay on Military Law and the Practice of Courts-Martial* (Edinburgh, 1800), 1–29. For a similar treatise see Sir Richard Sullivan, *Thoughts on Martial Law: And on the Proceedings of General Courts Martial* (London, 1779); and E. Samuel, *An Historical Account of the British Army, and of the Law Military as Declared by Ancient and Modern Statutes* ... (London, 1816).

[16] W.S. Holdsworth, "Martial Law Historically Considered," *Law Quarterly Review* 18 (1902): 117–32; Lindsay Boynton, "Martial Law and the Petition of Right," *EHR* 79:311 (April, 1964): 255–84; Boynton, "The Tudor Provost Marshal," *EHR* 77:304 (July, 1962): 437–55; Stephen J. Stearns, "Military Disorder and Martial Law in Early Stuart England," in *Law and Authority in Early Modern England: Essays Presented to Thomas Garden Barnes* ed. Mark Charles Fissel (Newark, 2007), 106–35; C.G. Cruikshank, *Elizabeth's Army* (2nd ed., Oxford, 1968), 159–73; Cruikshank, *Army Royal: Henry VIII's Invasion of France, 1513* (Oxford, 1969), 94–105; C.H. Firth, *Cromwell's Army* (3rd ed., London, 1961), 276–310; John Childs, *The Army of Charles II* (London, 1976), 75–89; Childs, *The Army, James II, and the Glorious Revolution* (Manchester, 1980), 92–3; Childs, *The British Army of William III 1689–1702* (Manchester, 1987), 84–99; G.A. Steppler, "British Military Law, Discipline, and the Conduct of Regimental Courts Martial in the Later Eighteenth Century," *EHR* 102:405 (October, 1987): 859–86. Arthur N. Gilbert has provided numerous articles on eighteenth-century military justice. See, for example, "Military and Civilian Justice in Eighteenth-Century England: An Assessment," *JBS* 17:2 (Spring, 1978): 41–65. There have been even broader works on the history of military jurisdiction. See Captain David A. Schlueter, "The Court Martial: An Historical Survey," *Military Law Review* 87 (1980): 129–66; James Snedeker, *A Brief History of Courts-Martial* (Annapolis, 1954), 1–19.

understanding of early modern martial law all the more difficult.[17] By the middle of the nineteenth century, scholars had separated the two concepts completely. Indeed, this was the one thing jurists agreed upon in regard to the law of martial law when they debated it in response to the acts of the governor of Jamaica, Edward John Eyre, who had declared martial law in 1865 before summarily executing hundreds and torturing hundreds more.[18] Scholars of the eighteenth century have generally recognized the lateness of the distinction between martial law and military law and have avoided making a clear-cut distinction between them.[19] Scholars of the seventeenth century, however, continually apply an anachronistic distinction between military and martial law.[20]

---

[17] John McArthur, *Principles and Practice of Naval and Military Courts-Martial, with an Appendix Illustrative of the Subject* 2 vols. (4th ed., London, 1813), 33–8. R.B. Scott follows McArthur in his *The Military Law of England (with all the Principal Authorities) Adapted to the General Use of the Army, in its Various Duties and Relations, and the Practice of Courts Martial* (London, 1810), 18–21. It is worth noting that in his first edition, published in 1793, McArthur makes no distinction between military law and martial law. Thomas Frederick Simmons, *The Constitution and Practice of Courts Martial: With a Summary of the Law of Evidence as Connected Therewith* (6th ed., London, 1873), 15–16. C.M. Clode, *The Administration of Justice under Military and Martial Law* (2nd ed., London, 1874), 4–9, 178–91; S.C. Pratt, *Military Law, its Procedure and Practice* (19th ed., 1915), 265–74. William Winthrop, *Military Law and its Precedents* 2 vols. (2nd ed., Boston, 1896), 47–50. For the transformation of martial law in the late eighteenth century, see George M. Dennison, "Martial Law: The Development of a Theory of Emergency Powers, 1776–1861," *American Journal of Legal History* 18:1 (January, 1974): 52–79.

[18] For these debates, see the excellent work of R.W. Kostal, "The Jurisprudence of Power: Martial Law and the Ceylon Controversy of 1848–51," *The Journal of Imperial and Commonwealth History* 28:1 (2000): 1–34, and Kostal, *A Jurisprudence of Power*. Also see, Charles Townshend, "Martial Law and Administrative Problems of Civil Emergency in Britain and the Empire, 1800–1940," *HJ* 25:1 (1982): 167–95. For understandings of martial law in America in this period, see Matthew Warshauer, *Andrew Jackson and the Politics of Martial Law: Nationalism, Civil Liberties, and Partisanship* (Knoxville, 2006), 177–96.

[19] Frederick Bernays Wiener, *Civilians under Military Justice: The British Practice since 1689, especially in North America* (Chicago, 1967); David Engdahl, "Soldiers, Riots and Revolution: The Law and History of Military Troops in Civil Disorders," *Iowa Law Review* 57:1 (1971): 1–73; Douglas Hay, "Civilians Tried in Military Courts, 1759–64," in *Canadian State Trials, Volume One: Law, Politics, and Security Measures, 1608–1837* ed. F. Murray Greenwood and Barry Wright (Toronto, 1996), 114–28; Jean-Marie Fecteau and Douglas Hay, " 'Government by Will and Pleasure instead of by Law': Military Justice and the Legal System in Quebec, 1775–83," in *Canadian State Trials*, 129–71.

[20] Clode, *Military and Martial Law*, 1–29; Barbara Donagan, "Codes and Conduct in the English Civil War," *P&P* 118 (February, 1988): 82–3. Donagan recognizes that "[c]ontemporaries referred to the articles of war indiscriminately as martial law or military law ... " Donagan, *War in England, 1642–1649* (Oxford, 2008), 171. Yet she still applies the modern distinction between military and martial law. Micheál Ó Siochrú, "Atrocity, Codes of Conduct and the Irish in the British Civil Wars, 1641–53," *P&P* 195 (May, 2007): 57–9; Wayne E. Lee, *Barbarians & Brothers: Anglo-American Warfare, 1500–1865* (Oxford, 2011), 83–9.

Adding to the confusion, jurists of the late nineteenth century argued that martial law was unknown to England.[21] Instead, there was a common law right of self-defense in times of extreme necessity. Jurists made this claim most strongly in the same controversy of 1865–6. Rebels might need to be violently suppressed – they were committing treason after all – but they could not be prosecuted once taken prisoner by a non-common law court.[22] As we shall see, this line of argument had strong early modern antecedents. Eventually, this conceptualization of martial law received the approval of some of the most famous constitutional scholars in English history.[23]

In the twentieth century, political theorists have claimed that martial law was a synonym for the state of exception – a time where law was abandoned so that the sovereign could take decisive actions that would save the polity. This association began with Carl Schmitt himself, who wanted to return discretion into the hands of a unified sovereign in times of crisis.[24] Schmitt believed that martial law was the Anglo-American variant of this exception. In his reading of martial law, its only relationship to the legal order was that it could determine the sovereign's martial law jurisdiction.[25] But once jurisdiction was properly claimed, there were no rules to martial law. In order to make this claim, Schmitt separated martial law from courts-martial, as Schmitt believed those to be a "return to legal form."[26] "The real core" of martial law, for Schmitt, comprised sovereign actions in an emergency that possessed no "legal form." These were decisions to destroy property, put down riots or rebellions with force, or kill enemies.[27] Giorgio Agamben and other recent political theorists have followed Schmitt's claims on martial law.[28]

---

[21] McArthur, *Principles and Practice of Naval and Military Courts-Martial*, 35.

[22] Kostal, *Jurisprudence of Power*, 40–55, 209–28.

[23] William Forsyth, *Cases and Opinions on Constitutional Law: and Various Points of English Jurisprudence, Collected and Digested from Official Documents and Other Sources; with notes* (London, 1869), 551–63. Maitland, *The Constitutional History of England*, 491–2. Maitland made similar but more extensive arguments in his 1890 notes on constitutional history. See CUL, Add. Ms. 7002, f. 105 and CUL Add. Ms. 6998, fos. 212–17. A.V. Dicey, *Introduction to the Study of the Law of the Constitution* (3rd ed., London, 1889), 262–71. Clinton L. Rossiter, *Constitutional Dictatorship: Crisis Government in the Modern Democracies* (Princeton, 1948), 142; Kostal, *Jurisprudence of Power*, 457–9.

[24] Carl Schmitt, *Political Theology: Four Chapters on the Concept of Sovereignty* trans. George Schwab (Cambridge, MA, 1985), 5–15.

[25] Carl Schmitt, *Dictatorship: From the Origin of the Modern Concept of Sovereignty to Proletarian Class Struggle* trans. Michael Hoelzl and Graham Ward (Cambridge (Polity Press), 2014), 149.

[26] *Ibid.*, 151.

[27] His examples were from nineteenth-century America, with *ex parte Milligan* looming large in his thinking. *Ibid.*, 150.

[28] Agamben, *State of Exception*, 4, 18–19; Nasser Hussain, *The Jurisprudence of Emergency: Colonialism and the Rule of Law* (Ann Arbor, 2003), esp. 99–118; Dyzenhaus,

The politics of martial law from the eighteenth century onward have made its early modern history difficult to recover. As R.W. Kostal has noted, the law of martial law in 1865 was "dauntingly complex, perhaps utterly incoherent."[29] With the notable exception of several scholars, twentieth- and twenty-first-century historians have fared little better than their mid-nineteenth-century counterparts.[30] The subject has produced confusing statements and anachronistic divisions in no small measure because many scholars of martial law have often been more interested in its future than in its past. In order to avoid future atrocities like the ones on Jamaica, many jurists thought it better to comprehend martial law as only common law actions of self-preservation based on extreme necessity. The politics of others have led them to argue that it was the will of the general on the battlefield. For others, it was a variant of the state of exception. This politicization was likewise present in the early modern period. Because of these subsequent interpretations, our understanding of martial law is now far removed from William Fleetwood's conceptualization in *Itinerarium ad Windsor* that was as one of the many laws the king used to cast doom and judgment upon his subjects.

III

While many historians and theorists subsequent to the seventeenth century have attempted to remove martial law into the sphere of "policy," "exception," and "military rule," this book argues that martial law was understood, debated, and practiced as law. By including martial law into English legal history, particularly in the sixteenth century, this work

"The Puzzle of Martial Law," 1–64; Mark Neocleous, "From Martial Law to the War on Terror," *New Criminal Law Review: An International and Interdisciplinary Journal* 10:4 (Fall, 2007): 489–513.

[29] Kostal, *The Jurisprudence of Power*, 10.

[30] The best are Boynton, "Martial Law and the Petition of Right"; Stearns "Military Disorder and Martial Law in Early Stuart England"; John Bellamy, *The Tudor Law of Treason: An Introduction* (London, 1979), 228–35; Krista Kesselring, *The Northern Rebellion of 1569: Faith, Politics, and Protest in Elizabethan England* (Basingstoke, 2007), 118–43; and the works by David Edwards. Edwards, "Beyond Reform: Martial Law & the Tudor Reconquest of Ireland," *History Ireland*, 5:2 (Summer, 1997): 16–21. Edwards, "Ideology and Experience: Spenser's *View* and Martial Law in Ireland," *Political Ideology in Ireland, 1541–1641* ed. Hiram Morgan (Dublin, 1999), 127–57; Edwards, "Two Fools and a Martial Law Commissioner: Cultural Conflict at the Limerick Assize of 1606," in *Regions and Rulers in Ireland, 1100–1650: Essays for Kenneth Nicholls* ed. David Edwards (Dublin, 2004), 237–265; Edwards, "The Escalation of Violence in sixteenth-century Ireland," in *Age of Atrocity: Violence and Political Conflict in Early Modern Ireland Age of Atrocity: Violence and Political Conflict in Early Modern Ireland* ed. David Edwards, Pádraig Lenihan & Clodagh Tait (Dublin, 2010), 34–78; Edwards, " 'Some Days Two Heads and Some Days Four' – Head Taking in Tudor Ireland," *History Ireland* 17:1 (January/February, 2009): 18–21.

paints a darker picture of England's laws: one with judicial terror through speedy trials and mass executions. However, by including law in the history of martial law, particularly in the seventeenth century, this work also paints a much lighter picture of martial law: one that includes legal professionals who cared deeply about evidence.

Because it was law, martial law should not be reduced to power; nor should it be reduced to violence. As John Fabian Witt has so succinctly summarized a generation of legal theory on this matter, "[t]he choice between law and power is a false dichotomy."[31] This statement is true in part because as Robert Cover and many subsequent legal theorists have rightly noted, those who come before courts stand on a "field of pain and death."[32] In this study, those who stood most often on the field of pain and death were the poor, both as the intended audience of martial law's violence and as its victims. But martial law was not simply violence. Nor was violence unique to martial law.

Indeed, this work argues that the best way to understand martial law is first through its procedure, second, through its substantive law, and third, through its jurisdiction. It is important to think in those terms because jurists and commanders in the early modern period often understood martial law as process and divided variant martial law practices through their differing procedures. While jurists often made a distinction between summary and plenary martial law, they did not make a military versus martial law distinction.

These constitutive parts of martial law were dynamic but not arbitrary. They changed because those who used martial law were informed by their surrounding environment, their ethnicity, their politics, and their understanding of history. Indeed, well before Fleetwood began writing his tract, martial law had already been made and re-made by Crown authorities who sought solutions to various legal dilemmas. Further, different variations of martial law were made in England, Ireland, and British dominions in Africa, Asia, and North America. Because of its dynamism, there was no essence to martial law.[33] But understandings of martial law were

---

[31] John Fabian Witt, "Law and War in American History," *American Historical Review* 115:3 (June, 2010): 770.

[32] Robert Cover, "Violence and the Word," *Yale Law Journal* 95 (1986): 1601–29; Austin Sarat and Thomas R. Kearns, "Introduction," in *Law's Violence* ed. Austin Sarat and Thomas R. Kearns (Ann Arbor, 2003), 1–21.

[33] Quentin Skinner, "Meaning and Understanding in the History of Ideas," reprinted in *Meaning and Context: Quentin Skinner and His Critics* ed. James Tully (Princeton, 1988), 29–67. For the application of Skinner's ideas to the history of religion see *Seeing Things Their Way: Intellectual History and the Return of Religion* ed. Alistair Chapman, John Coffey, and Brad S. Gregory (South Bend, 2009). For its application to legal history, see Halliday, *Habeas Corpus*, 2.

not limitless, either. Indeed, the creativity of those who re-made martial law was more in the way they combined, rethought, or adapted preexisting practices than in complete and total innovation. There were enough common jurisdictional claims, procedures, and substantive laws that made variant martial law practices across English dominions similar to one another even if they were never identical. Martial law was both durable and flexible.[34]

This dynamism is at odds with traditional views of English legal culture. While many historians have recognized the creativity of sixteenth-century jurists, historians of the seventeenth century since John Pocock's seminal work *The Ancient Constitution and the Feudal Law* have told us – over and over again – that English legal thinking in the seventeenth century was conservative, unimaginative, and insulated from continental legal developments.[35] This view has recently been challenged by scholars of English legal practice and discourse who have argued that it was more dynamic than previously supposed.[36] Further, scholars of transatlantic legal culture have in numerous contexts noted the adaptability of English laws in new world contexts.[37]

This work builds on these more recent traditions while also arguing for an interplay between England's legal culture and those of its dominions. Martial law is an ideal subject to better understand such an interaction because unlike some of the other laws on Fleetwood's list, the English Crown by the seventeenth century almost always granted martial law powers to its overseas authorities. As English social, political, and legal practices went global, so too did martial law. At the same time, central institutions, like the Privy Council, the Board of Trade and Plantations, and parliament desired to supervise its use. While these bodies believed it important, indeed essential, to delegate martial law jurisdiction, they also believed it needed to be monitored. Both the use and the monitoring of the use of martial law played important roles in imperial governance.

---

[34] My language here is inspired by Anthony Grafton's important discussion of astrology in *Cardano's Cosmos: The Worlds and Works of a Renaissance Astrologer* (Cambridge, MA, 1999), esp. 5–6.

[35] J.G.A. Pocock, *The Ancient Constitution and the Feudal Law: A Study of English Historical Thought in the Seventeenth Century: A Reissue with a Retrospect* (Cambridge, 1987). Christopher Brooks has provided the most balanced criticism of the Ancient Constitution in his study of early modern English legal discourse. Brooks, *Law, Politics and Society*.

[36] See for example, Brooks, *Law, Politics and Society*; Halliday, *Habeas Corpus*; Smith, *Sir Edward Coke and the Reformation of the Laws*.

[37] Daniel J. Hulsebosch, *Constituting Empire: New York and the Transformation of Constitutionalism in the Atlantic World, 1664–1830* (Chapel Hill, 2005); Mary Sarah Bilder, *The Transatlantic Constitution: Colonial Legal Culture and the Empire* (Cambridge, MA, 2004); John Ruston Pagan, *Anne Orthwood's Bastard: Sex and Law in Early Virginia* (Oxford, 2003).

No one, not even the MPs in the Petition of Right Parliament, wanted to eliminate martial law. Instead, they attempted to restrain martial law to wartime. In both concept and practice, wartime served as a jurisdictional boundary and not as the boundary between law and arbitrary power. In this tract of time, courts-martial still sat. They followed procedural rules and heard evidence. Further, actions undertaken in wartime were reviewable by civilian courts or by state institutions. As Lauren Benton has noted for a later period, even in wartime, sovereignty was not absolute.[38] This work, in other words, argues that theorists of the state of exception are wrong. Martial law, even when all other laws went into abeyance, was law.

Martial law remained one of the laws of the realm through parliament. The 1628 Parliament bound martial law to wartime but this had the unintended consequence in some dominions of transforming martial law from a complementary law into an all-encompassing one. Further, other parliaments ignored the temporal requirements altogether. In the end, various parliaments both during the English Civil War and after the Glorious Revolution overturned many of the restrictions seventeenth-century jurists had placed upon martial law, allowing eighteenth-century statesmen to use it more often than their seventeenth-century counterparts.

IV

This book traces the making and remaking of martial law across the early modern period. It begins with a prologue in the Middle Ages in order to examine some of the key jurisdictional and procedural debates that informed later thinking on martial law. The first section of the book, "A Jurisprudence of Terror," traces how English monarchs began to use martial law in innovative ways in the sixteenth century in order to quell religious and economic uprisings.

By the middle of the sixteenth century, delegated authorities in Ireland and, to a lesser extent, England, used summary martial law process to convict vagrants, traitors, and notorious wrongdoers. These wide-ranging powers led to abuse, and eventually the English Privy Council circumscribed the delegation of summary martial law. The section concludes by examining the transformation of martial law. By the end of the sixteenth century, commanders and martial jurists used the practices of continental and classical armies as rough guides in order to transform the substance and procedures of martial law.

---

[38] Benton, *A Search for Sovereignty*, 290.

The second half of the book traces the relationship between martial law and English parliaments beginning in 1628. Jurists in the seventeenth century attempted to confine martial law to wartime. The Petition of Right, however, often had unintended consequences overseas as colonial administrators adapted the law of martial law to make public rights claims. Further, subsequent parliaments both in the English Civil War and in the aftermath of the Glorious Revolution authorized martial law, overturning some of the Petition of Right's restrictions. Parliament, while closely monitoring its authorization, allowed for permanent martial law jurisdictions in eighteenth-century England. But before we can understand MPs' relationship with martial law, we first need to understand the medieval ideas they used to re-make the law of martial law.

Prologue

On 22 March 1322, the day of his execution for treason, it is unlikely that Thomas of Lancaster was contemplating the procedures Edward II had used to condemn him. The hereafter was probably instead in the forefront of his mind. Yet outside of the pilgrims who made their way to Pontefract Castle to pray with his surviving hat and belt in hopes of headache relief, Thomas has been chiefly remembered for the controversies surrounding his conviction.[1] For twelve peers had not convicted him of treason. Instead, Edward II, as the fountain of justice, convicted Thomas upon his record because his treason was "notorious": so well known that the king did not need to rely on witnesses or the aid of counsel. In 1327, in the first year of Edward III's reign, Parliament reversed Thomas' conviction, and declared that convictions upon record could only take place during wartime, which it defined as being either when the Court of Chancery was closed or when the king had raised his banner.[2] At first thought, it seems simple to draw a line between Lancaster's trial, conviction, and execution, and the early modern law of martial law.[3] After all, Sir Edward Coke and Sir Matthew Hale cited Lancaster's reversal when they claimed

---

[1] J.R. Maddicott, "Thomas of Lancaster, second Earl of Lancaster, second Earl of Leicester, and Earl of Lincoln," in *ODNB*. For an overview of the politics of the reign, see J.R. Maddicott, *Thomas of Lancaster, 1307–1322: A Study in the Reign of Edward II* (London, 1970), and Seymour Phillips, *Edward II* (New Haven, 2010).

[2] The reversal can be found in *Rotuli Parliamentorum; ut et Petitiones, et Placita in Parliamento Tempore Edwardi R. III* (Ann Arbor, 1984), 3–5. For the background to Edward III's first year in power, see W. Mark Ormrod, *Edward III* (New Haven, 2012), 55–66.

[3] Several historians have argued for this. J.V. Capua, "The Early History of Martial Law," *Cambridge Law Journal* 36:1 (April, 1977): 152–73. J.G. Bellamy is more cautious than Capua, but he does see sixteenth-century martial law as the inheritor of medieval treason convictions by notoriety tradition. *The Law of Treason in England in the Later Middle Ages* (Cambridge, 1970), 212. Bellamy, *The Tudor Law of Treason: An Introduction* (London, 1979), 228–9. The best narrative of the fifteenth-century trials comes from the work of Maurice Keen. Keen, "Treason Trials under the Law of Arms," in Maurice Keen, *Nobles, Knights, and Men-at-Arms in the Middle Ages* (London, 1996), 149–66; Keen, "The Jurisdiction and Origins of the Constable's Court," in *Nobles, Knights and Men-at-Arms*, 135–48.

that martial law was only legal when the courts of Westminster were closed.

There was, however, a far more complicated relationship between medieval precedents and early modern martial law practice. Martial law commissioners in the sixteenth and seventeenth centuries only selectively and occasionally applied the procedures used against Thomas to convict suspects of treason and other offenses like vagrancy, resisting arrest, and various felonies. Its reversal was likewise only selectively and occasionally applied throughout the early modern period, oftentimes in ways that would have shocked the MPs who had crafted it in 1327. And Thomas' case illustrates just one – albeit a very important one – of the many medieval practices relating to war that future jurists would find useful in shaping and reshaping the law of martial law.

The legacies of the Middle Ages did not bind early modern jurists. Instead they provided them with a wellspring of ideas. Let us explore the three medieval practices that were most influential upon later practices and debates: the governance of the king's hosts, treason trials during wartime, and the jurisdiction of the High Court of Chivalry.[4] There was no proto-martial law, but there were many laws related to war that would later inform it.

The Court of the Verge in war and peace

Let us begin by examining the growth of the use of process by information for wrongs that had taken place within the king's host. These more informal arraignment procedures in all likelihood began in the king's great ambulatory Court of the Verge and were transferred to itinerant courts of the constable and marshal by the early fourteenth century.

The king's government in the late Middle Ages was "one in perpetual movement, a government of the roads and of the roadsides."[5] At the front of the great host rode the marshal. In his hand, the marshal carried the wand of peace, often called the verge wand, which signified to all those

---

[4] Both Holdsworth and Stephen Payne Adye understood martial law to be a descendant of this court. Holdsworth, "Martial Law Historically Considered," *Law Quarterly Review* 18 (1902): 117–18. Adye, *A Treatise on Courts Martial: Containing I. Remarks on Martial Law, and Courts-Martial in General II. The Manner of Proceeding against Offenders* (London, 1778), 9–12.

[5] J.E.A. Jolliffe, *Angevin Kingship* (London, 1955), 140. Because of its ambulatory nature, the king's household was important to the running of his government, although even by the thirteenth century the Crown had stationary servants who also helped run the administration. See T.F. Tout, *Chapters in the Administrative History of Mediaeval England* 6 vols. (Manchester, 1920–33); J.H. Johnson, "The King's Wardrobe and Household," in *The English Government at Work, 1327–1336* ed. J.F. Willard and W.A. Morris 3 vols. (Cambridge, MA, 1940–50), 1: 206–49.

within sight the presence of their lord. It also signified justice.[6] Anyone within a 12-mile circumference of the wand could obtain a hearing from the king in the court of his hall, usually convened by the king's steward. The king's marshal meanwhile supervised all the king's prisoners, and executed all judgments made in the court of his hall. While historians of the common law have focused their attention on the courts that eventually sat down at Westminster, this ambulatory court continued to have jurisdiction over all members of the king's household, and over cases within the "verge" of "wherever the king may be in England."[7] It was thus often referred to as the Court of the Verge.[8] In more turbulent times, the marshal still rode at the head of the king's host. But instead of waving the wand of peace, he carried the king's banner that signified war. In these times, the king's army became "awake."[9] Members of the host were in all likelihood supervised by the court of the king's constable.[10] His jurisdiction was temporal. We can well imagine that on the ground this distinction became blurred as most of the king's host held both civil and military responsibilities.[11] In all likelihood, at times both the steward and the constable supervised the discipline of the king's host.

These positions were not unique to the household but instead could be found in many of the king's courts. All three of these offices were held by nobles.[12] But more often than not, the steward, the constable, and the marshal of the household, or of the king's camps, were delegates of these powerful men. Thus, many different marshals and constables operated

---

[6] *Fleta*, ed. H.G. Richardson and G.O. Sayles 4 vols. (London: Selden Sociey, no. 89, 1972), 2:109, 112–14.

[7] *Fleta*, 2:109. Historians have usually focused on the making of King's Bench and Common Pleas in their stories on the making of the Common Law to the neglect of the Court of the Verge. R.V. Turner, *The King and His Courts: The Role of John and Henry III in the Administration of Justice, 1199–1240* (Ithaca, NY, 1968); Turner, "The Origins of Common Pleas and King's Bench," *American Journal of Legal History* 21: 3 (July, 1977): 238–54. S.F.C. Milsom, *Historical Foundations of the Common Law* (London, 1981).

[8] W.R. Jones, "The Court of the Verge: The Jurisdiction of the Steward and the Marshal of the Household in Later Medieval England," *JBS* 10:1 (November, 1970): 1–29; Tout, *Chapters in Administrative History*, 1: 201–5, 2: 251–3; Marjorie McIntosh, "Immediate Royal Justice: The Marshalsea Court in Havering, 1358," *Speculum* 54:4 (October, 1979): 727–33. For examinations of the court for later periods, see W. Buckley, *The Jurisdiction and Practice of the Marshalsea & Palace Courts* (London, 1827); and Douglas Greene, "The Court of the Marshalsea in Late Tudor and Stuart England," *American Journal of Legal History* 20:4 (October, 1976): 267–81.

[9] *Fleta*, 2: 114.

[10] J.O. Prestwich, "The Military Household of the Norman Kings," *EHR* 96: 378 (January, 1981): 7–9.

[11] Michael Prestwich, *Armies and Warfare in the Middle Ages: The English Experience* (New Haven, 1996), 176–7.

[12] Jolliffe, *Angevin Kingship*, 191–2. For the history of the Steward, see L.W. Vernon-Harcourt, *His Grace the Steward and Trial by Peers: A Novel Inquiry into a Special Branch of Constitutional Government* (London, 1907).

within the king's dominions at any given time. The office of the marshal in particular became associated with all English law courts. In King's Bench, in Exchequer, and in the King's Eyre, the marshal provided the same services. He was a jailer. He executed the judgments of the court. And in itinerant courts he set up and supervised camp.[13]

This relationship between the Court of the Verge and the host helps us better understand the surviving plea roll of the army – *placita exercitus* – that dates from Edward I's campaign against Scotland in 1296.[14] The fact that the recorder – the deputy marshal of the army, John Lovel – titled it "the army plea roll" signifies he thought it to be distinctive from other plea rolls – the king's pleas, for example. And there is a discernible difference in procedure between how soldiers were adjudged on the army plea roll and common law trials that opened with a presenting jury. While soldiers came before petty juries for various offenses, a presentment or indictment was not necessary to start an action. Instead, an information from the marshal was all that was required.[15]

An information or plaint (*querela*) was an accusation, often made by one person to a magistrate. It was, in other words, an "untried bill." No grand jury had inspected it. The magistrate on his own discretion decided the veracity of the plaint. Along with this increased discretion given to the magistrate, the informer often did not have to reveal him or herself publicly.[16] While associated with the Inquisition, English kings had also adopted the procedure in the Middle Ages. Edward I allowed his subjects to use plaints to charge Crown officials with malfeasance.[17] In all likelihood, the Court of the Verge used this same informal plaint system in

---

[13] Thomas Madox, *The History and Antiquities of the Exchequer of the Kings of England in Two Periods* (London, 1711), 725, 728; Helen Cam, "The Marshalsy of the Eyre," *The Cambridge Historical Journal* 1:2 (1924): 133–37. In the late sixteenth and early seventeenth centuries, histories of the marshal and steward of England were written. See for example, BL, Cotton Vespasian Ms. C.XIV, fos. 385–415; BL, Cotton Titus Ms. C I. In general, historians have neglected the office of the constable. See a manuscript history of the office in TNA, WO 93/5.

[14] TNA, E 39/93/15. The roll has been calendared in *Calendar of Documents relating to Scotland* ed. Joseph Bain 5 vols. (Edinburgh, 1881–88), 2: no. 822. It has been briefly examined by Michael Prestwich. Prestwich, *War, Politics, and Finance under Edward I* (Totowa, N.J., 1972), 107. It was also found by John Selden, see Chapter 4.

[15] John Bellamy, *The Tudor Law of Treason: An Introduction* (London, 1979), 230.

[16] J.G. Bellamy, *Criminal Law and Society in late Medieval and Tudor England* (New York, 1984), 90–114.

[17] Gordon Leff, *Heresy in the Later Middle Ages: The Relation of Heterodoxy to Dissent, c. 1250–1450* 2 vols. (Manchester, 1967), 1:44–7. Bellamy, *Criminal Law and Society*, 90–1. Alan Harding, "Plaints and Bills in the History of English Law, Mainly in the Period 1250–1350," *Legal History Studies* ed. Dafydd Jenkins (Cardiff, 1975), 65–86. Edward I invited his subjects to submit informations in 1289 about his law officers who had governed England during his absence. See T.F. Tout, *State Trials of the Reign of Edward the First, 1289–93* (London, 1906).

all of its criminal proceedings against members of the king's household: a jurisdiction it possessed until the early fourteenth century.[18]

Process by information did not end with the circumscription of the Court of the Verge. Commanders were still allowed to use procedure by information or plaint to discipline their soldiers from at least the early fourteenth century.[19] In all likelihood, the itinerant courts of the constable and marshal utilized this same informal procedure in cases involving discipline. We only have small hints relating to the procedure of these itinerant courts. The prescriptive commands the king gave to his army commanders stated that one judge had powers to hear and determine cases relating to discipline. The ordinances of war for the army of Henry V, for example, declared that the king, constable, marshal, or another "judge ordinary" could judge cases involving life or death.[20] These great officers, the constable and marshal, stood in for the king, and possessed his legal powers abroad.[21] In important cases, the constables of the king's hosts empaneled knights to hear and determine cases. In 1367, for example, the Black Prince empaneled twelve knights to hear a treason case against the French Marshal D'Audreham, who had been captured after the battle of Najera.[22] While in 1425, after the English conquest of Le Mans, the army commander Lord Scales set up a special tribunal – with himself as president – to hear and determine cases relating to ransom.[23] The courts of the constable and marshal heard evidence, allowed the defendant to speak in court, and could on occasion acquit the defendant of the charges levied against him.

The constables and marshals of the itinerant courts focused most of their attention on enforcing the lengthy written ordinances that commanders proclaimed to their host before the beginning of the campaign.[24] Unlike the customary laws of war, which applied to the

---

[18] The Court of the Verge's ambit was restricted by *Articuli Super Cartas* (1301), c. 3 and the Statute of Stamford, Jones, "The Court of the Verge," 15.

[19] *Rotuli Scotiae in Turri Londinensi et in Domo Capitulari Westmonasteriensi asservati* ed. James Basire, George Eyre, Andrew Strahan 2 vols. (London, 1814–19), 1:137, 213.

[20] Francis Grose, *The Antiquities of England and Wales* 8 vols. (London, 1777–87), 1:43.

[21] Thus, the constable and marshal and their retinues were allowed to wear the king's liveries even when he was absent when others were barred from doing so. 1 Hen. IV. c. 7.

[22] Maurice Keen, *The Laws of War in the Late Middle Ages* (London, 1965), 33, 50–3. For the laws of war in this period, also see Theodor Meron, *Henry's Wars and Shakespeare's Laws: Perspectives on the Laws of War in the Later Middle Ages* (Oxford, 1994).

[23] *Ibid.*, 33.

[24] The medieval ordinances have been printed. See, for example, "Charter of Richard, King of England, for the government of those who were about to go by Sea to the Holy Land (1189)," *JSAHR* 5 (1926): 202–3; Grose, *Antiquities of England and Wales*, 1: 34–50; Grose, *Military Antiquities respecting a History of the English Army from the Conquest to the Present Time* 2 vols. (London, 1812), 2: 64–8. *Monumenta Juridica:*

military caste in general, the articles of war – variously called ordinances, constitutions, statutes, articles, martial laws, or military laws – outlined rules specific to the forthcoming campaign. The king with his chief ministers crafted its substance and ordered the promulgation of the martial ordinances, statutes, and constitutions. Every man in arms had a responsibility to uphold the constitutions. Punishments for transgressions were severe. The king prescribed death for almost half of the ordinances. Non-fatal punishments included fines, loss of wages, imprisonment, and the degradation of knightly honors. The Crown wrote rules in the constitutions relating to prisoners, ransom, and discipline in general. Among others, the ordinances stipulated that the Crown receive one third of the ransom payments for any prisoner taken.[25] The ordinances outlined duties for the soldiers while in the host. Leaving the host without permission, for example, was punishable by death.[26] The ordinances of war also addressed outrages committed by soldiers on civilians. Soldiers were forbidden from pillaging a church, or from taking "noe man nor woman of holy church, prisoner," unless they were armed.[27] The king also declared that no soldier slay or "enforce" any woman upon pain of death.[28] The ordinances were meant to inspire discipline through fear.

The king's constables and marshals by the late Middle Ages governed the king's hosts through their courts. They did so usually by the written constitutions of the army and by procedures that in all probability utilized informations or plaints – an inheritance from the Court of the Verge – instead of indictments where one judge or in greater cases a council of knights determined a verdict.

Wartime and treason

Along with the itinerant courts that disciplined the host, one of the most important intersections between law and war was treason. The king's

---

The Black Book of the Admiralty ed. Sir Travers Twiss, 4 vols (London, 1871–6), 1: 281–99. A list of surviving ordinances can be found in Barbara Donagan, *War in England, 1642–1649* (Oxford, 2008), 405–7. For analysis of the medieval ordinances, see Rémy Ambühl, *Prisoners of war in the Hundred Years War: Ransom Culture in the late Middle Ages* (Cambridge, 2013), 29–31; Maurice Keen, "Richard II's Ordinances of War of 1385," in *Rulers and Ruled in Late Medieval England: Essays Presented to Gerald Harriss* ed. Rowena E. Archer and Simon Walker (London, 1995), 33–48; Anne Curry, "The Military Ordinances of Henry V: Texts and Contexts," in *War, Government and Aristocracy in the British Isles, c. 1150–1500: Essays in Honour of Michael Prestwich* ed. Chris Given-Wilson, Ann Kettle, and Len Scales (Woodbridge, 2008), 364–88.
[25] Grose, *Antiquities of England and Wales*, 1: 38.   [26] *Ibid.*, 41.   [27] *Ibid.*, 34.   [28] *Ibid.*

constables possessed a treason jurisdiction, usually referred to as "the law of arms." This was rarely different in substance than statutory treason. Instead it differed by the procedures the king's constables utilized. They often convicted defendants based upon the record of the king because of the notoriety of their offenses. In order to understand the relationship between wartime and conviction upon record, we need to first go back to the late thirteenth century.

English monarchs in this period used treason law to punish nobles who had waged war against them more harshly than their predecessors. These treasons comprised the betrayal of the king "or of his army" by one or more of his subjects.[29] In Bracton, treasons were the compassing of the king's death, conspiring with the king's enemies, forging the king's great seal, or counterfeiting the king's money.[30] The army was included with the king because embedded in the idea of majesty was the older idea of *perduellio*, or "the bad soldier." Crimes related to *perduellio* included conspiring to betray garrisons, deserting the army to that of the enemy, furnishing the enemy with supplies or information, and breaking an exile.[31] The substance of treason law had always been intertwined with war and the army. Edward I successfully used these laws to instill order among the restive nobility in England, Wales, and in Scotland; his less successful son attempted to imitate him.[32]

But they did not do so according to trial by peers. Instead Edward I and his son convicted upon their record based upon the defendant's notoriety: the public's knowledge of his guilt. Monarchs utilized this proof throughout Western Europe in the fourteenth century, with French kings in particular using it to punish their rebellious nobles.[33] In Roman Law, magistrates likewise used manifest proofs both to convict suspects and to bring them to trial in lieu of an information or accusation. In England, manifest proofs like notoriety could be used to force painful imprisonment upon those who refused to plea.[34] But monarchs also used the

---

[29] *De Legibus et Consuetudinibus Angliae* (hereafter Bracton), ed. George E. Woodbine, trans. Samuel E. Thorne 4 vols. (Cambridge, MA, 1969), 2: 334.

[30] *Ibid.*, 334–38; Bellamy, *The Law of Treason in England in the Later Middle Ages*, 1–22.

[31] Floyd Seyward Lear, *Treason in Roman and Germanic Law: Collected Papers* (Austin, 1965), 6–7.

[32] Bellamy, *The Law of Treason in England in the Later Middle Ages*, 10–11.

[33] *Ibid.*, 23–58. For the French kings' use of this concept, see S.H. Cuttler, *The Law of Treason and Treason Trials in Later Medieval France* (Cambridge, 1981), 55–6, 85–7. John L. Barton, *Ius Romanum Dedii Aevi* (Roman Law in England) (Milan, 1971), 31–4.

[34] "The First Statute of Westminster," 3 Edw. I c. 12.

concept to convict men taken in arms against them of treason. Thomas of Lancaster, as we have seen, was convicted by this method. And as we have seen, MPs in 1327 attempted to confine conviction by record according to their definition of wartime. The nobles who clearly had an interest in constraining this power did so by using clause twenty-nine of Magna Carta, which stated that no freeman "shall be taken or imprisoned or disseised or exiled or in any way destroyed, nor will we go upon him nor send upon him, except by the lawful judgment of his peers or by the law of the land."[35] However, Parliament made an exception for wartime, which it defined as either the king's banner being raised or by the Court of Chancery being closed.[36]

What did a "time of war" mean? Here, medievalists provided multiple definitions. We have already seen that wartime could mean the constable's claim to jurisdiction in the itinerant host. For others, like Bracton, a time of war meant that either an individual or a group of individuals had abandoned the king's peace and engaged in criminality. For example, a time of war might mean that one was disseized "by force and wrongfully."[37] In these cases, wartime was specific to the actions of one or more individuals. It was irrelevant, in this definition, whether or not there was an actual declared war. What mattered was whether an action was performed legally or whether a person or persons simply seized money, goods, or lands by force of arms. If they had done so, they were in a time of war. As we shall see, John Selden was influenced by this interpretation of wartime in 1628.

However, this interpretation of wartime was likely not what the MPs in the 1327 Parliament meant when they referred to a time of war. Instead, they were probably referring to a more general wartime. What constituted a more general time of war? Hobbes, while admittedly writing much later, provided a succinct definition of general wartime that was in all likelihood similar to how medievalists conceptualized it. For Hobbes, war was "a tract of time: wherein the Will to contend by Battell is sufficiently known: and therefore the notion of *Time*, is to be considered in the nature of Warre."[38] Just as a period of bad weather meant more rain or snow than usual or just as a lamentable time meant more mourning or sadness than usual, so wartime meant more assaults, battles, and sieges than usual.

---

[35] Quoted in Anne Pallister, *Magna Carta: The Heritage of Liberty* (Oxford, 1971), 117.

[36] *Rotuli Parliamentorum; ut et Petitiones, et Placita in Parliamento Tempore Edwardi R. III*, 3–5.

[37] *Bracton*, 3: 57, 213; 4: 171 (quote at 4: 171).

[38] Thomas Hobbes, *Leviathan*, ed. Richard E. Flathman and David Johnston (New York, 1997), 70.

In all of these temporalities, adaptation of behavior was required. In times of bad weather, one stayed inside and built larger fires. In a time of mourning, one dressed differently than usual and attended church more often. In a time of war, at least as it pertained to law, jurists and military commanders most frequently argued that laws more specific to the needs of the host were required, more severe punishments than those prescribed in times of peace were necessary to maintain order, and shorter processes than those mandated by common law were allowable. English jurists did not in general argue that law evaporated in wartime. Certainly, at times, they invoked the famous maxim, *inter arma enim silent leges*. But in these instances, they were usually referring *only* to common law and not all law.

Finally, wartime was a time of solidarity. Here a distinction needs to be drawn between both medieval and most early modern jurists and Hobbes' much more famous depiction of wartime in *Leviathan*. Medieval jurists, like Hobbes, might very well have understood wartime to be atavistic, but unlike Hobbes, they would not have viewed it to be individualistic.[39] Wartime was not a free-for-all. Instead, the king or any superior magistrate could make claims on property or labor for the preservation of the host or kingdom. Or, and this would have been most important to the MPs in the 1327 Parliament, he could summarily execute traitors upon his record if he felt it necessary.

We have already seen the banner being used as a badge of war. What about the closure of Chancery? Here, the implication was that with Chancery closed, original writs could not be issued, making it impossible for the Court of Common Pleas to operate. In these instances, other procedures could be used instead of the common law ones that were in abeyance. MPs did not make clear whether the king himself could close the courts upon his discretion or whether they could only be closed as *an effect* of the surrounding chaos of war. In ancient Rome, magistrates did have such discretion. Like the English – who were probably modifying their ideas – the Romans understood the status of the courts to be badges of either war or peace. There, magistrates, upon a *tumultus*, proclaimed a *iustitium* (vacancy), which closed the courts and allowed them to mandate military duty for those who were normally exempt from it or to seize property in order to preserve the republic from its enemies.[40] English

---

[39] Cary J. Nederman, "Nature, Sin and the Origins of Society: The Ciceronian Tradition in Medieval Political Thought," *Journal of the History of Ideas* 49:1 (January-March, 1988): 3–26.

[40] Gregory Kung Golden, "Emergency Measures: Crisis and Response in the Roman Republic (From the Gallic Sack to the Tumultus of 43 BC) (unpublished PhD diss., University of Rutgers, 2008), 53–127.

MPs were now deploying a similar idea to bind the practice of conviction upon record.

Treason convictions by manifest proofs thus continued in wartime. As J.G. Bellamy has noted, the case against Lancaster and its subsequent reversal firmly "connected conviction on the royal record with trial for treason under the law of arms."[41] While wartime had been used as a jurisdictional boundary before, it was now mandated. The great treason statute passed in 1352 reinforced this restriction and set boundaries for the substance of treason. Edward III also agreed that he could not seize real property without a conviction by peers. In the immediate aftermath of the passing of the treason statute, the king and MPs overturned two convictions made in the 1320s by notoriety.[42] Through jurisdictional politics, MPs had removed treason trials that allowed manifest proofs to wartime. The only exception to this rule was that Parliament could on its own discretion use manifest proofs to obtain conviction and to seize real property through the practice of attainder.[43]

Kings in the fifteenth century often invoked wartime when they sought to punish their enemies through conviction upon record. Their badges of war were not always the same as those used in the 1327 reversal of Thomas of Lancaster. In 1405, for example, Henry IV's constable used manifest proofs to convict Henry de Boynton of treason. The jurisdiction of the constable and marshal was allowed because of wartime: this time defined as the firing of a gun at a fortress. Boynton was hanged, beheaded, and quartered.[44] Convictions such as this happened so often during the Wars of the Roses that Edward IV's enemies labeled Sir John Tiptoft, Edward's constable, the "butcher of England." When Henry VI briefly regained the throne, the Earl of Oxford, who had relatives executed by Tiptoft, presided as constable in his treason trial by law of arms.[45] Monarchs, in other words, were not particularly hindered by the 1327 Parliament's mandate that convictions upon record only take place in wartime. Further, if monarchs wanted to confiscate the lands of those

---

[41] Bellamy, *The Law of Treason in England in the Later Middle Ages*, 51.

[42] *Ibid.*, 59–101. 25 Edw. III stat. 5. c.2.

[43] T.F.T. Plucknett, "The Origin of Impeachment," *Transactions of the Royal Historical Society* 4th ser., 24 (1942): 56–63; Plucknett, "Presidential Address: Impeachment and Attainder," *Transactions of the Royal Historical Society* 5th ser., 3 (1953): 151–54. Bellamy, *The Law of Treason in England in the Later Middle Ages*, 177–205.

[44] Keen, "Treason Trials," 149–50, 158. By the fifteenth century, there were common "signs of war" used throughout Europe that lawyers could use at the Courts of the Constable and Marshal to either justify or condemn acts of violence. Maurice Keen, *Laws of War*, 101–18.

[45] Quoted in Keen, "Treason Trials," 154; Vernon Harcourt, *His Grace the Steward*, 362–415. Benjamin G. Kohl, "Tiptoft [Tibetot], John, first earl of Worcester (1427–1470) in *ODNB*.

they had convicted upon their record, they resorted to a posthumous act of attainder.[46]

Through politics, conviction upon record through manifest proofs and the governance of the king's hosts had become connected through the offices of the king's constables and marshals. However, the procedures of the two remained distinctive, and the king had delegate constables and marshals who oversaw different courts. No one jurisdiction was forged from the two.

War and geography: the High Court of Chivalry

Along with the courts of the host and treason trials by the "law of arms" by the middle of the fourteenth century, the Constable of England sat in the High Court of Chivalry to handle the legal business of war. The Crown created it to handle disputes relating to the "military commercialism" of the fourteenth and fifteenth centuries.[47] Although there is dispute over this, the Court of Chivalry probably had procedural and substantive consistencies with the itinerant courts of the king's hosts. However, it is almost certain that the itinerant courts were far more concerned with military discipline than the Court of Chivalry and in all likelihood employed from time to time swifter procedures than its more august counterpart.[48] Because of jurisdictional politics, the Court of Chivalry became restricted geographically and topically in order that it be restrained from hearing civil pleas.

The court heard and determined cases based on customs relating to conduct in war generally known as the "laws of war," or the "laws of chivalry." Along with customs relating to the soldierly profession, the law of nations and Roman Canon Law also informed the laws of war.[49] This common code of behavior was recognized throughout Europe. There was some overlap between the written ordinances of war and the laws of war, but the two traditions were not identical. The laws of war had developed special and often unique rules for some of the most pertinent areas of law relating to the soldierly profession. First, soldiers had a law of treason distinctive from that of English law. Treason by the laws of war was

---

[46] Keen, "Treason Trials," 156.

[47] It probably did so in imitation of the French. However, the French had a court of the Marshal that was separate from the Court of the Constable. J.H. Mitchell, *The Court of the Connétablie: A Study of a French Administrative Tribunal during the Reign of Henry IV* (New Haven, 1947), 7–13. Keen, *Laws of War*, 7–59.

[48] I follow Maurice Keen's critique of G.D. Squibb. Keen, "Origins of the Constable's Court," 135–48. G.D. Squibb, *The High Court of Chivalry: A Study of the Civil Law in England* (Oxford, 1959), 26–8.

[49] Keen, *Laws of War*, 7–22.

a knight's betrayal "to his faith and knighthood."[50] All members of the profession had a duty to uphold the laws of chivalry. Along with cases of treason, the laws of war had rules relating to the taking of plunder that allowed both soldiers and those civilians plundered to take action at a court of the constable and the marshal if they felt wronged.[51] By the end of the fourteenth century labyrinthine rules had been constructed for how spoil should be divided. Military courts adjudicated these disputes. They also adjudicated ransom claims. Finally, the laws of war had complex rules relating to armorial bearings.[52]

The Court of Chivalry utilized several procedures, none of them unique. It sometimes used Roman Law procedure. If a plaintiff wanted to pursue an action he would issue a "libel" or complaint. The court then commanded the defendant in the complaint to respond. Once the issue had been joined, the court would take witness testimony by commissioning certain members of the court to depose the listed witnesses in private. Ultimately, either the constable or the marshal delivered a verdict. They often did so upon the consultation of learned advisors who were usually lawyers trained in Roman Civil Law.[53] Second, a case could be heard upon the authority of the judge (*ex officio*). Finally, cases of treason or murder were often brought in upon an appeal. An appeal began when an appellor made an accusation in court against another. If both the appellor and the defendant were men, the outcome of the trial would be decided by battle.[54]

The Court of Chivalry's popularity among litigants caused concern. In the reign of Richard II, MPs successfully circumscribed it and several other courts that threatened the business of the Court of Common Pleas. In 1384, parliament demanded that no common law pleas be heard at the Court of Chivalry.[55] Apparently, this was ineffective. Five years later, MPs complained that the Court of Chivalry "daily doth incroach Contracts, Covenants, Trespasses, Debts, and Detinues, and many other Actions pleadable at the Common Law ... "[56] In order to restrain

---

[50] *Ibid.*, 53.   [51] *Ibid.*, 137–55, 251–3.

[52] *Ibid.*, 156–85. Squibb, *The High Court of Chivalry*, 162–90. Ambühl, *Prisoners of War*, 19–51; Adam J. Kosto, *Hostages in the Middle Ages* (Oxford, 2012), 99–121.

[53] Anon., "The Manner of Judicial Proceedings in the Court of the Constable and Marshal (or Court Military) touching the Use and Bearing of Coats of Arms; observed and collected out of the Records of the Tower of London" in *Collection of Curious Discourses* ed. Thomas Hearne 2 vols. (London, 1775), 2: 243–9.

[54] Squibb, *The High Court of Chivalry*, 22–6, 191–220. For trial by battle and appeal generally in the later Middle Ages, see J.G. Bellamy, *The Criminal Trial in Later Medieval England* (Toronto, 1998), 19–56.

[55] 8 Rich. II c. 5.

[56] 13 Rich. II. st.1 c.2. For background on the statute, see Squibb, *The High Court of Chivalry*, 18–20; Keen, "Origins of the Constable's Court," 136–7.

it, the MPs gave topical and geographical boundaries to the Court of Chivalry. The Court had "[c]ognizance of Contracts touching Deeds of Arms and of War out of the Realm, and also of Things that touch War within the Realm, which cannot be determined nor discussed by the Common Law … "[57] Ten years later, the Court received powers to hear all appeals "of Things done out the Realm."[58] The Court was thus circumscribed to a military and civilian cognizance abroad and to a military one at home provided it did not infringe upon common law. The MPs at the end of the fourteenth century were not primarily concerned with the trial of wrongs, military discipline, or with itinerant courts of war. They were concerned with civil pleas at the sitting Court of Chivalry.

The Court of Chivalry added yet another important judicial responsibility for the constables and marshals of England, with a jurisdiction that diverged from their wartime jurisdictions and that focused on litigation more than discipline.

Conclusion

At the beginning of Tudor rule, the sitting of Court of Chivalry fell into abeyance. The Constable of England likewise was becoming less important within the king's hosts. Further, popular support in certain areas of the country for the continuation of the Wars of the Roses led Henry VII to think on the relationship between his laws and war anew.

He and his successors would not need to invent martial law from scratch. Instead they could select from the many laws relating to war that had operated during the Middle Ages. Indeed, by the end of the fifteenth century there was not one clearly defined martial jurisdiction that was bounded, that had one substantive law, and that had one procedure. There was one set of officers – the constable and marshal – but there were many constables and marshals that operated in different courts. Procedure by information, trial by appeal, proof by notoriety, trial by battle, as well as jury trials were used in various courts at various times to handle the legal problems of war. Further, the ordinances of war, the "laws of war," customs relating to heralds, and common and statute law were all employed by these courts. The boundaries of courts of war were likewise intertwined with other courts. Further, by the end of the fifteenth century, jurists, commanders, and MPs had made various claims as to what signified wartime. Meanwhile, the Court of Chivalry was exempt

---

[57] 13 Rich. II st. 1 c. 2.   [58] 1 Hen. IV. c. 14.

from this temporal boundary, but was instead confined to the business of war that could not be determined by common law.

What would be true of the Tudors would likewise be true of colonial officials, MPs, commanders, and jurists over the next two centuries. Along with Roman and European sources, they would often look back to these medieval procedures, substantive laws, and discourses relating to wartime in order to try and resolve their own problems relating to martial law. The sheer variety of laws, procedures, and jurisdictions jurists granted to the constables and marshals during the Middle Ages allowed for creativity in later periods.

Part I

A jurisprudence of terror

The courts of the constables and marshals within the king's armies used procedure by information in certain instances to hear and determine cases against those in the king's host. By the 1490s, Henry VII delegated these procedures to commissioned officers who had powers to hear and determine cases according to the customs of the constable and marshal. In 1521, Henry VIII executed the Duke of Buckingham, the Constable of England, for treason. The tempestuous king did not find a replacement. The customs of the constable and marshal became the customs of the marshal. Soon, Crown officers began referring to these practices as the laws of the marshal. By the 1530s, they used the phrase "martial law."

The banality of the creation of the phrase "martial law" belied the innovation in legal strategy. Tudor monarchs tried the low-born by life and limb by martial law when they feared juries might not convict defendants. Instead, they either used procedures by information where a judge instead of a jury heard and determined a case or, and this was especially true in Ireland, a commissioner was allowed to convict upon manifest proofs like notoriety. Along with more assurances of conviction, the Tudors hoped that the terror inspired by these swift procedures would induce their subjects into obedience. As they would discover by the end of the sixteenth century, unsupervised martial law commissioners potentially posed as great a threat to order as hostile juries.

Commanders and jurists transformed these procedures at the end of the sixteenth century. New ways of fighting war on the continent challenged the Crown, its ministers, and its martial community to make transformations in their military apparatus so that they might keep up with their more potent European rivals. Along with attempting to update tactics and strategy, these ministers focused on improving the martial discipline of Crown forces. The product of this transformation was more laws, more rules relating to procedure, and more records. While still desirous of setting an example through corporal and capital punishment, courts-martial by the end of the seventeenth century possessed fairly normal legal procedures. Once known for their speed, courts-martial by the end of the seventeenth century had slowed down. By the end of the seventeenth century, English armies and navies possessed cultures of law.

1   Making martial law

It is not a coincidence that one of the earliest known usages of the phrase "martial law" came in a debate over process. The debate was between Sir Thomas More and Christopher St. German over procedures in the king's ecclesiastical courts.[1] They were controversial because ecclesiastical judges could arraign a suspect based upon secret information that was transformed into a formal accusation by an officer of the court through the power of his office (*ex officio*).[2] Further, judges, and not juries, determined the case. While in some ways unique, the ecclesiastical courts shared much in common with other courts that utilized procedure by information.[3] Heavily critical of it, St. German argued that "cruell iudges" might be able to punish innocents through these procedures because they granted them too much discretion.[4] More responded that

---

[1] For the debate see, John Guy, "Thomas More and Christopher St. German: The Battle of the Books," in *Reassessing the Henrician Age: Humanism, Politics, and Reform, 1500–1550* ed. Alistair Fox and John Guy (Oxford, 1986), 95–120. Guy, "The Legal Context of the Controversy: The Law of Heresy," *CWTM* 10: xlvii–lxvii. For heresy and the English ecclesiastical courts, see R.H. Helmholz, *The Oxford History of the Laws of England, Volume One: The Canon Law and Ecclesiastical Jurisdiction from 597 to the 1640s* (Oxford, 2004), 599–642. For St. German's legal thought see Alan Cromartie, *The Constitutionalist Revolution: An Essay on the History of England, 1450–1642* (Cambridge, 2006), 33–58.
[2] Guy, "Thomas More and Christopher St. German," 108–11.
[3] The 1487 Parliament passed the so-called Star Chamber Act that allowed councilors to hear cases brought by bill or information. 3 Hen. VII c. 1. Also see 11 Hen. VII c. 25, and 19 Hen. VII c. 12, 14. The 1495 Parliament authorized procedure by information for Justices of the Peace to prosecute riot.11 Hen. VII c. 3, 7. P.R. Cavill, *The English Parliaments of Henry VII, 1485–1504* (Oxford, 2009), 78–101. For other tribunals in Henry VII's reign that used procedure by information, see R. Somerville, "Henry VII's 'Council Learned in the Law,'" *EHR* 54:215 (July, 1939): 427–42, and M.M. Condon, "Ruling Elites in the Reign of Henry VII," in *Patronage, Pedigree, and Power in Later Medieval England* ed. Charles Ross (Gloucester, 1979), 133–4. Henry VIII set up more lasting conciliar courts. J.A. Guy, *The Cardinal's Court: The Impact of Thomas Wolsey in Star Chamber* (Hassocks, 1977). R.R. Reid, *The King's Council in the North* (London, 1921). Penry Williams, *The Council in the Marches of Wales under Elizabeth I* (Cardiff, 1958). For secret informers and the penal laws, see G.R. Elton, "Informing for Profit: A Sidelight on Tudor Methods of Law-Enforcement," *The Cambridge Historical Journal* 11:2 (1954): 149–67.
[4] Sir Thomas More, "The Apology of Thomas More,"*CWTM* 9: 3–172. Christopher St. German, "Treatise Concerning the Division between Spirituality and Temporality," *CWTM* 9: 177–212. The quote is at *Ibid.*, 191.

if clerics used the more elaborate procedures demanded by St. German, "the stretys were lykely to swarme full of heretykes."[5] Faced with yet another attack by St. German, More, in his *Debellation of Salem and Bizance*, continued his defense of ecclesiastical procedure by comparing it to the procedures the king used to punish treason.[6] While indictments were generally the best way to proceed, nevertheless sometimes "iudges myght procede and put felons to answere without endyghtementes/ as in treason is vsed in thys realme by the lawe marshall vppon warre rered."[7] More concluded his thought by stating that though it was good to trust juries, and that common law was in general better than martial law, sometimes "yet myght we truste the iudges as well."[8]

Martial law was the most drastic measure the Tudors used to control juries.[9] While St. German's position was in this moment on the side of Henry VIII, the king and his successors at various points throughout the sixteenth century agreed with More that judges alone should be entrusted with determining cases of treason and of felony. The reformations loomed large in their decisions to use these swifter and more controllable procedures. Wars with France, Spain, and Scotland, and rebellions in Ireland likewise contributed to further experimentation with martial law. In difficult cases involving potential blood sanctions where Crown authorities did not want the delay of common law procedure, when they worried that juries might refuse to convict defendants, or when they believed juries might be overzealous in their prosecutions of soldiers, they opted for procedure by written information or public suspicion instead of an indictment by grand jury where a Crown judge instead of a petty jury heard and determined the case and was allowed to punish by taking the life or limb of a convict: martial law. Before we see how martial law was used, let us first examine how the Crown delegated its jurisdiction.

---

[5] *Ibid.*, 130.
[6] Christopher St. German, "Salem and Bizance," *CWTM* 10: 326–92. Sir Thomas More, "The Debellation of Salem and Bizance," *CWTM* 10: 136.
[7] *Ibid.*   [8] *Ibid.*
[9] For Crown attempts at controlling juries in this period, see Cynthia B. Herrup, *The Common Peace: Participation and the Criminal Law in Seventeenth-Century England* (Cambridge, 1987), 158–64. J.S. Cockburn, *Calendar of Assize Records, Home Circuit Indictments, Elizabeth I and James I: Introduction* (London, 1985), 70–1, 113–17, 130–4. Thomas Andrew Green, *Verdict According to Conscience: Perspectives on the Criminal Trial Jury, 1200–1800* (Chicago, 1985), 105–52, esp. 150, n. 179; for contemporary criticism of juries in the sixteenth century, see J.S. Cockburn, "Twelve Silly Men? The Trial Jury at Assizes, 1560–1670," in *Twelve Good Men and True: The Criminal Trial Jury in England, 1200–1800* ed. J.S. Cockburn and Thomas A. Green (Princeton, 1988), 158–81. For jury nullification or lawlessness in the sixteenth century, see P.G. Lawson, "Lawless Juries? The Composition and Behavior of Hertfordshire Juries, 1573–1624," in *Twelve Good Men and True*, 117–57.

The first commissions

The similarities between a commission of martial law and a commission of *oyer and terminer* are striking. The differences are just as striking. Let us examine a commission issued to Sir Edward Bellingham, the new lord deputy of Ireland, in 1548 in order to better understand the relationship between martial law and common law.[10]

The commission was not unusual for its time. But because of the relative newness of the concept of martial law, the writer of the commission, who was probably the clerk of the Crown Office in Chancery, Edmund Martin, outlined in very specific terms what he believed constituted martial law.[11] The commission, written in Latin, gave Bellingham the power to hear and determine cases within the army.[12] Near the end of the commission, the Crown ordered Bellingham to "arraign the accused and compel witnesses to give evidence according to the law and custom of the marshalsea hitherto used in that realm, called martial law." Let us look again at the ending of this command in its original language. Bellingham was to arraign the accused and compel witnesses to give evidence according to the "legem & consuetudinem marescalcie ... vocat marciall lawe."[13]

How strange! In a commission written in Latin, Martin kept "marciall lawe" in English. He almost certainly did so because martial law had no classical Latin cognate. In discussing military discipline, Roman and continental sources used the phrase "*de re militari.*" This tradition emphasized military law more by its substance and by its jurisdiction than by its unique procedure.[14] But the phrase is not to be found in English legal documents. Nor did martial law derive from "*lex martialis.*"[15]

---

[10] TNA, C/66/812, m. 1d. A similar commission is calendared and translated in *CPR*, *Edward VI*, 1:133. For commissions of martial law similar to this one, see TNA, C/66/802, m. 33d; TNA, C/66/814, m. 2d–5d; TNA, C/66/830, m. 4d; TNA, C/66/831, m. 14d; TNA C/66/837, m.12d; TNA, C/66/897, m. 19d; TNA C/66/917, 22d; TNA C 66/1013, m. 4d–5d. Starting with Mary, clerks often wrote the commissions in English. English martial law commissions were the norm by the middle of Elizabeth's reign.

[11] For clerks of the Crown Office, see Cockburn, *Introduction*, 15–25 and Sir John Baker, *Oxford History of the Laws of England: Volume VI, 1453–1558* (Oxford, 2003), 440–2. The best evidence that the clerks of the Crown Office wrote these commissions is that they can be found in their precedent books. See following pages.

[12] TNA, C 66/812, m. 1d.   [13] *Ibid.*

[14] *The Digest of Justinian* ed. Theodor Mommsen with the aid of Paul Kreuger trans. Alan Watson, 4 vols. (Philadelphia, 1985), 4: bk. 49, ch. 16.

[15] This post-classical phrase means "law of war." Thus some scholars have attempted to conflate the laws of war with martial law. This is at best confusing as martial law was not substantively or procedurally consistent with the international laws and rights of war. This conflation can be found in W.F. Finlason, *Report of the Case of the Queen v. Edward John Eyre* (London, 1868), xii; and Finlason, *The History of the Jamaica Case* (London,

In particular, English clerks never used *lex martialis* in legal documents like commissions that delegated martial law to Crown servants. Martial law was new and it was English.

But just as we can understand the newness of the phrase "martial law" through Bellingham's commission, we can also understand the oldness of the phrases that surrounded the two English words. Martin had copied some of the Latin text from other legal documents. For example, the Crown commanded Bellingham to "hear and determine" all complaints within the army. This order was similar to Crown commands in commissions of *oyer* and *terminer*, which authorized itinerant common law justices to hear and determine cases at assize courts on their semi-annual circuits throughout England. Further the Crown's command to Bellingham to hear and determine all "treasons, felonies, rape, [and] murder" was similar to the lists of wrongs the Crown ordered its itinerant justices to hear and determine in commissions of *oyer* and *terminer*. For example, in a commission of *oyer* and *terminer* in 1622, the Crown ordered Robert Houghton, Ranulph Crewe, and others to inquire into the truth of matters "concerning whatsoever treasons, misprisions of treasons, insurrections, rebellions, murders, felonies, homicides, killings, burglaries, rapes of women" and a host of other misdeeds.[16] It was a longer list than that of the martial law commission, but the general idea was the same.

Other language within the commission can be traced to previous commissions that delegated legal power to military lieutenants. Some of the language can be traced back as far as the fourteenth century. But considering Martin worked in the Crown Office, we can come up with a more specific guess as to where he obtained his language. He probably found it in the precedent book of one of his predecessors at the Crown Office, William Porter, who had copied the commissions of the Earl of Shrewsbury, who had commanded a host against the Scots in 1513, and of Sir Thomas Lovell, who was to act as marshal in 1513 in the absence of the marshal of England. In both of these commissions, the Crown allowed the commissioner to hear and determine all complaints between and about soldiers within the host. Bellingham's commission likewise

---

1869), 299. Most scholars have understood that martial law does not derive from *lex martialis*. See for example G.G. Phillimore, "Martial Law in Rebellion," *Journal of the Society of Comparative Legislation* 2:1 (1900): 45. It appears that law dictionaries from around the eighteenth century started to conflate the two terms. F.O., *The Law-French Dictionary Alphabetically Digested* (London, 1701), "*Martial Law.*"

[16] Printed in Cockburn, *Introduction*, 218–21. For criminal proceedings under commissions of *oyer* and *terminer*, see J.S. Cockburn, *A History of English Assizes, 1558–1714* (Cambridge, 1972), 86–133.

contained such a clause. The commission of martial law was a new thing made from old things.[17]

Knowing where the maker of the commission obtained his language allows us to better understand what he believed to be the responsibilities of those empowered with martial law. He had borrowed from commissions of *oyer* and *terminer* in part because he recognized a similar function between that of Bellingham and of an assize judge. Granted, he circumscribed Bellingham's powers in different ways. Bellingham could only use his judicial power on soldiers in the army stationed in Ireland. But he clearly thought the two responsibilities – that of a commissioner of *oyer* and *terminer* and that of a martial law commissioner – to be similar. The Crown commanded Bellingham to be a judge.

The maker of the commission defined martial law through its procedure. While Bellingham was compared with common law judges in his responsibilities, he was contrasted with common law judges through the means by which he would execute those responsibilities. Laws associated with war – the laws of war, the laws of chivalry, and the ordinances of war – were not foremost on Martin's mind when he wrote the commission. It was the procedure of martial law that was important.

What was the key difference between martial law procedure and that of common law? Martial law commissioners were to hear all "*causas*" and "*querelas*" that arose within the army.[18] Martial law procedure, in other words, was allowed to operate by more informal plaints, complaints, or informations, and not by indictments. Martial law can thus in part be traced to the medieval itinerant courts of the hosts that in turn were likely adapted from the Court of the Verge. It can also be situated with other courts that used procedure by information. All of these courts did not require either grand or petty juries. The key difference between martial law and those other courts was that commissioners of martial law frequently utilized information procedure in matters where defendants could lose life or limb should they be convicted.

It was this difference that made martial law an alluring alternative to common law for the Tudors when they believed sharper measures were necessary or when they thought juries might be unreliable. Let us now look to how Bellingham might have used his powers of martial law on soldiers.

---

[17] TNA, C 193/142, fos. 98v–101. Baker, *Oxford History of the Laws of England: Volume VI*, 218.

[18] TNA, C/66/812, m. 1d.

Martial law: soldiers and sailors

In instances where they lived under martial law, soldiers present at a court of the marshal were supposed to learn that the commander both possessed severe powers of correction and was just. In order to teach these lessons, martial law commissioners tried to obtain proof before they convicted defendants. Martial law process was shorter than common law process. It granted more discretion to judges than common law. But it was not arbitrary.

Soldiers often but not always were disciplined by the customs of the marshal. Commanders of royal hosts usually had martial law jurisdiction over soldiers in pay. They also, by 1588, had martial law jurisdiction over rebels and enemy invaders.[19] In garrison towns, however, a complex network of jurisdictions supervised soldiers that only sometimes included martial law. Both the mayor of the town and the marshal of the garrison supervised the garrisoned soldiers. Soldiers in Berwick-upon-Tweed, for example, came before city courts in cases of felony. They were, however, usually exempt from prosecutions of debt at civilian courts. The infuriated townsmen instead had to petition the commander for redress. In Chapter 4, we will examine more closely the controversial "petitioning system" that regulated misdemeanor charges against soldiers. It suffices to say for now that multiple jurisdictions in Berwick clashed with one another over how to supervise soldiers.[20] In Ireland, on the other hand, the Crown exempted its soldiers completely from Irish common law only in 1543, when the marshal of the army complained to Henry VIII that he could not punish his own soldiers because of the interference of common law officers.[21] Soldiers in Scotland under Edward VI were likewise under the discipline of martial law.[22] When the king either thought his soldiers needed to be disciplined by a more severe process or worried about the interference of juries, he granted martial law jurisdiction to his commanders.

While many jurists in the seventeenth century employed the 1389 statute that restricted the High Court of Chivalry to claim that martial law should only be used in criminal cases outside of England, in the sixteenth century no such geographical distinction existed. In Edward's reign, during his war with France, the king commanded that the workers

---

[19] LPL, Ms. 247, fos. 5–7, 9–11v.   [20] TNA, WO 55/1939.

[21] Henry VIII to the Deputy and Irish Council, August 1543, TNA SP 60/11 f. 81v. Henry VIII to the Irish Council, August 1546, TNA, SP 60/12, 318. The 1550 instructions to Anthony St. Leger declared that soldiers had been troubled by too many vexatious lawsuits and therefore should only be governed by martial law. HEHL, El Ms. 1700, f. 5v.

[22] Edward VI to James Wilford, captain of Hadington, BL, Lansdowne Ms. 155 A, f. 320v.

on his fortifications in Cornwall be governed by martial law.[23] Meanwhile, in 1596, Elizabeth I granted the Earl of Essex, who was to lead a raiding expedition to Cadiz, powers of martial law over his host. A record of the regiments of the camp shows that Sir Francis Vere, the marshal of the army, had two men executed, one "a fugitive thother a mutinier."[24] A marshal's court banished one lieutenant Hammond from the army for corruption, while it detained another and released him from the army for "wordes" against the lord marshal. Further, it seems likely that martial law was practiced at the Tilbury camp in 1588.[25] Soldiers in England in the sixteenth century were not exempt from martial law. Nor were they always subject to it. The Crown, when it felt it expedient, used martial law to discipline soldiers.

This was also true of sailors and "soldiers on the sea." We know even less about when and for what purposes commanders utilized martial law on board ships in the sixteenth century.[26] In general, sailors were governed by the laws and customs of the sea, often referred to as the Laws of Oléron. Like the army these were ordinances that governed life on board ships.[27] Some of the laws and customs of the sea were similar to the ordinances of war. But what differentiated the laws and customs of the sea from martial law was that the death penalty was rarely handed down on board ships. And the records we have of trials that did involve a potential blood sanction – the most famous being Drake's prosecution of Master Thomas Doughty – often involved the impaneling of juries.[28] In general, the masters of ships had much less authority over their sailors. It was generally true that on board Crown ships, discipline was more strictly enforced. But even on these ships, capital punishment was probably rarer than in armed camps. Naval commanders only occasionally received martial law powers when the Crown felt it urgent to use more severe measures to discipline its sailors. On the other hand, generals on military expeditions almost always possessed martial law powers. In these

---

[23] "A Commission for Martial Justice in a towne of warre," BL, Lansdowne Ms. 155 A, f. 317v.

[24] "The Svall Regiments of the Army," SRO, D593/S/4/6/34. Another copy of this manuscript can be found in FSL, Ms. v.b.142, f. 20. A copy of Essex's commission can be found in TNA, SP 12/257, fos. 31–33v.

[25] Matthew Sutcliffe, a judge marshal, was paid for his services there. See page 39.

[26] David Loades, *The Tudor Navy: An Administrative, Political and Military History* (Aldershot, 1992), 199–200; N.A.M. Rodger, *The Safeguard of the Sea: A Naval History of Britain, 660–1649* (New York, 1997), 321–4.

[27] *The Naval Tracts of Sir William Monson* ed. M. Oppenheim, 5 vols. (London, 1902–14), 4: 200–1.

[28] W.S.W. Vaux, *The World Encompassed by Sir Francis Drake* (London, 1854), 165–74, 202–11. For this trial see Kenneth R. Andrews, *Drake's Voyages: A Re-Assessment of their place in Elizabethan Maritime Expansion* (New York, 1967), 63–8.

instances, martial law procedure was used to prosecute wrongs like mutiny.[29]

When they fell under martial law jurisdiction, soldiers and sailors were tried before a court of the marshal. Unfortunately, few full courts-martial records have survived from the sixteenth century.[30] Therefore we will have to rely on the prescriptive literature and a few descriptions of cases that commanders relayed to the Privy Council through correspondence.[31]

The martial law commissioner judged fact and law. They were in many ways perceived as a "fountain of justice" and could act as eyewitnesses and judges simultaneously if the wrong was committed before them. In the army, the Crown delegated martial law powers to its lord general and to its high marshal, the second in command. Either the lord general or more often the marshal – hence the "marshal's court" – possessed

---

[29] Sir William Winter was allowed to use martial law to discipline those in his fleet off Ireland in 1580. See the Irish Council to Sir William Winter, 13 May 1580, LPL, Ms. 597, fos. 357v–360v. An adapted articles of war for the 1596 campaign can be found in *The Naval Miscellany volume one* ed. J.K. Laughton (London, 1902), 51–8. Drake and John Norris received martial law powers in 1589. TNA, SP 12/222, f. 122. Drake prosecuted mutiny by martial law. M. Oppenheim, *The History of the Administration of the Royal Navy, 1509–1660* (London, 1896), Appendix B. Walter Raleigh likewise in 1592 possessed a martial law jurisdiction. *The Naval Tracts of Sir William Monson*, 1: 284. Matthew Sutcliffe included ordinances of war specifically for the sea. *Sutcliffe*, 333.

[30] The only actual surviving court-martial record from the army is so terse that it is barely helpful. "Court-Martial of Lt. Hudson, 21 Oct. 1591," HH, CP 168/54.

[31] The manuscript prescriptive literature on martial law in the sixteenth century is as follows: Thomas Audley (provost marshal of Guines), "A Treatise on the Art of War," BL, Add. Ms. 23,971, fos. 1–37; Audley, "An Introduction or ABC to the wars, dedicated to Edward VI ... " Bodl., Tanner Ms. 103, fos. 45v–7; "A Book directing the choosing and ordering of the Army and making war," BL, Harley Ms. 4191, fos. 74–75v, 112v; "Directions howe farre any mans office in an Army dothe Extende and what Duties the officer is to doe," BL, Harley Ms. 168, fos. 123–27v and LPL Ms. 247, fos. 129–35v; "The Institution & Dyssepline of a Souldier, etc.," BL, Harley Ms. 519, fos. 72v–80v; "Sir Francis Vere's Notes Concerning the Duty of Every Officer in the Army," BL, Harley Ms. 6844, fos. 77–82v; Sir Robert Constable (?), "The Order of a Camp Royall ...," BL, Harley Ms. 847, fos. 49v–53; "The Ordering of an Army and the duty of Every Officer," BL, Harley Ms. 6068, fos. 40–53v; "Directions both general and particular drawen by the Lord-Generall Essex for ... the government of the Army," BL, Harley Ms. 703, fos. 25–26; "Martial and Military Lawes of the Field etc." BL, Harley Ms. 5109, fos. 62–5; "Articles concerning the Lord Marshall of the kings highness' armye," LPL, Ms. 3470 fos. 1–2v. For a review of this literature see Major Evan Fyers, "Notes on Class Catalogue, No. 50 (Military) in the Department of Manuscripts, British Museum," *JSAHR* 4 (1925): 38–48. Printed sources are: *Sutcliffe*, 339–42; Barnabe Rich, *A Path-way to Military Practice ...* (London, 1587), sigs. D4–H; Charles Cruickshank has outlined the sixteenth-century procedure in his books on the armies of Henry VIII and Elizabeth. Cruikshank, *Army Royal: Henry VIII's Invasion of France, 1513* (Oxford, 1969), 94–104. Cruikshank, *Elizabeth's Army* (2nd ed., Oxford, 1966), 41–60, 159–73.

powers to arraign and then to hear and determine cases that fell under their jurisdiction.[32] Often, the general or the marshal subdelegated these powers to assistants or to subordinate commanders stationed in garrisons away from the army royal. Usually, their power was absolute, but in delicate cases, martial law commissioners sought advice from the Privy Council. They had the powers to convict and convey the death penalty. The lord general also possessed the power to pardon.

Arraignment procedure granted discretion to the martial law commissioner. According to Matthew Sutcliffe, an experienced martial jurist, those with martial law powers could use "all means of examination, and trial of persons accused dilated, suspected, or defamed."[33] The commissioner of martial law thus had flexibility when it came to the manner in which he brought suspects to trial. A formal accusation sufficed. A written information would have also worked. This was the most common way suspects were brought before a court in the seventeenth century. So too did "public fame" – where the public suspected that a person had committed a wrong – that triggered inquisitorial process.[34] All of these methods produced a charge that did not require confirmation from a grand jury.

The rules of evidence of martial law resembled those of common law: there were few formal rules of evidence. At common law, because the Crown assumed juries were self-informing, it developed few formal rules relating to proof.[35] This relative laxity contrasted with Roman Law, which had "laws of proof" that mandated that the judge either obtain a confession or receive testimony from two eyewitnesses to the crime.[36] Martial law commissioners, while they did not need to meet this high bar, still needed to obtain eyewitness testimony conducted upon oath or

---

[32] The commission to Edward Bellingham, for example, gave him and his marshal powers of martial law. TNA, C 66/812 m. 1d. Through the sixteenth century, the Ordnance Office was exempt from the court of the marshal, and the Master of the Ordinance held his own court, about which we know little, that disciplined ordnance officers according to the ordinances of war. Cruikshank, *Army Royal*, 100–1. The rules outlining the Ordnance Office's jurisdiction in the 1590s can be found in BL, Lansdowne Ms. 70/11.

[33] *Sutcliffe*, 339. For Sutcliffe's service see page 39 and Chapter 3.

[34] As R.H. Helmholz has noted, accusation based on public fame allowed "proof by notoriety, ejected by the canonists through the front door ... back inside through the rear." Helmholz, *Oxford History of the Laws of England: Volume One*, 607. For accusations at Roman Civil Law, see John Langbein, *Prosecuting Crime in the Renaissance: England, Germany, France* (Cambridge, MA, 1974), 131.

[35] For an examination of common law criminal procedure in the sixteenth century, see Langbein, *Prosecuting Crime in the Renaissance*, 5–125. As John Langbein noted, "[t]o this day an English jury can convict a defendant on less evidence than was required as a mere precondition for interrogation under torture on the Continent." Langbein, *Torture and the Law of Proof* (2nd ed., Chicago, 2006), 78.

[36] Langbein, *Torture and the Law of Proof*, 4–12 (quotation on 5).

a confession. Suspicion alone, while it could provoke detainment, was not enough to convict. Thus, occasionally drastic measures like torture were deemed to be necessary in order to acquire the proof necessary for conviction. According to Matthew Sutcliffe, a commissioner could use torture "where presumptions are sufficient, and the matter heinous, by racke or other paine."[37] Presumptions were a form of proof. Often they mirrored what we now describe as circumstantial evidence, and certain types of presumption could be used in common law courts as evidence in felony and treason trials. In general, they alone were not enough for a martial law commissioner to obtain a conviction.[38]

One of the few examples of martial law commissioners using torture comes from a report on treasonous activity in 1586 from Ostend, one of the cautionary towns held by the English during Elizabeth's war with Spain.[39] Thomas Wilford, the military governor of the city, uncovered a conspiracy by one "Joise Lews" and his son to take the city and deliver it to the Spanish. According to Wilford, the Spanish had promised Lews that he would "be made a great person."[40] Wilford had caught the man with "treasonous" letters written by the Spanish in his belt. Certainly this satisfied the requirement of presumption, if Wilford had been thinking along those lines. He ordered the son to be tortured after he had failed several times to get his father to confess under torture. There was nothing in the letter to suggest the son was involved in the conspiracy, although he may have been. Wilford made Lews watch, presumably to persuade him to confess so that his son might be relieved of his pain, and to see his reaction if the son implicated him. The son, who was blindfolded, finally confessed to his father's participation in the conspiracy. Wilford adjudged the father guilty and sentenced him to death, but because of the importance of the case relayed his actions back to his commander, the Earl of Leicester, before he proceeded to the sentence. In other words, martial law commissioners wanted to obtain evidence before they gave judgment. The bar was just not that high.

Martial law commissioners often had assistants who helped them obtain evidence and evaluate cases. These legal aids were dubbed judge marshals. The sixteenth-century prescriptive literature rarely described the position.[41] Nevertheless, enough sources exist to suggest

[37] *Sutcliffe*, 340.
[38] Barbara Shapiro, *Beyond Reasonable Doubt and Probable Cause: Historical Perspectives on the Anglo-American Law of Evidence* (Berkeley, 1991), 208–16; Michael R.T. McNair, *The Law of Proof in Early Modern Equity* (Berlin, 1999), 267–75.
[39] F.G. Oosterhoff, *Leicester and the Netherlands, 1586–87* (Utrecht, 1988), 40–7.
[40] Thomas Wilford to Leicester, 25 January 1586, *CSPF* 20: 321–2.
[41] *Sutcliffe*, 339; LPL, Ms. 3470 (Fairhurst), f. 1. Markham was one of the first authors to write extensively on the judge marshal. Markham, *Fiue Decades of Epistles of Warr* (London, 1622), 109–12.

it was a near constant office in the army by the end of the sixteenth century. Our first firm record of a judge marshal comes from the English chronicle of the 1547 campaign against the Scots. The chronicler William Patten recounted how he and William Cecil had been appointed judges of the "Marshalsea" and had executed several soldiers for misdeeds.[42] By the 1580s, these judge marshals were almost always Doctors of Roman Civil Law.[43] Matthew Sutcliffe, a trained Civil Lawyer, for example, served as a judge marshal in Leicester's army in the Low Countries and at Tillbury. Bartholemew Clarke, another trained in Roman Civil Law, also accompanied the Earl of Leicester in his campaign in the Low Countries.[44] Roman Law-trained lawyers were the norm by the end of the century.

The judge marshal was the oracle of the law for the army. He gave legal advice to the general or the lord marshal. He obtained and kept track of plaints, and he deposed witnesses. He recorded the wills of the soldiery. If they obtained a privy seal warrant from the marshal, the judge marshal could also hold court, and hear and determine cases. By the end of the sixteenth century, the judge marshal may have sat in the lord marshal's court in his stead almost all of the time.[45] This was certainly true in Ireland by 1598, when Adam Loftus was charged with hearing and determining all cases involving the soldiery before his marshal's court.[46] He was to prosecute all offenses against the written law code of the army. Ireland possessed a permanent judge marshal well over sixty years before there was a permanent judge advocate in England. This is not that surprising given that Ireland possessed a standing army so much earlier than England.

---

[42] William Patten, *The Expedicion into Scotla[n]de of the most Woorthely Fortunate Prince Edward . . .* (London, 1548), sig. P. IVv.

[43] For the Civil Law profession in England, see Brian Levack, *The Civil Lawyers in England, 1603–1641: A Political Study* (Oxford, 1973).

[44] One of the best ways to track judge marshals is through the accounts of the army. Both Clarke and Sutcliffe accompanied the army on the Leicester expedition: TNA, E 351/ 240. "A Brief Account of the 3000l received by Sir Thomas Sherley," *CSPF* 21 (pt. 3): 425. "Officers Serving in the Low Countries," *CSPF* 21 (pt. 4): 2. Sutcliffe was also paid for twenty- three days service, presumably at Tillbury, from 31 July until 22 August 1588. TNA, E 351/242.

[45] Markham, *Fiue Decades of Epistles of Warre*, 110.

[46] *Calendar of the Patent Rolls, Ireland, Elizabeth I* ed. J. Morrin (Dublin, 1862), 432–3. This document has received an unfortunate interpretation from David Edwards in "Ideology and Experience: Spenser's *View* and Martial Law in Ireland," *Political Ideology in Ireland, 1541–1641* ed. Hiram Morgan (Dublin, 1999), 153. Adam Loftus was not a "civil official." He was a doctor of *Civil* Law, the standard education for judge marshals in this period. And he was responsible for prosecuting offenses against the statutes of the army, not "the common law." *Ibid.* Also see, "Army in Ireland," *HMC, Salisbury* 9: 145, and "Memorials for Ireland," 16 October 1604, TNA, SP 63/216, f. 132v.

Other martial officers aided the lord general in his judicial responsibilities. By the late sixteenth century, colonels played important roles in judicial proceedings. The 2nd Earl of Essex, sometime in the 1590s, stipulated that all colonels had to "call together all his Captaynes & shall enquier of all officers in his Regiment and examine ye nature of and qualytye of such officers to prepare causes for a short and easy hearing in the Marshalls Court."[47] The attendance of the officers at the marshal's court is one of the few details revealed in Lieutenant Hudson's 1591 court-martial.[48] This order likely meant that the colonel helped organize depositions of complaints made within his regiment beforehand so the court could hear them quickly. Captains also at times played a role in advising the marshal on important judicial business.

The provost marshal of the army acted as jailer, accountant, and police. The provost marshal became a standard position within the English army by the early sixteenth century. Henry VIII probably incorporated it from seeing a similar position, the *prévôt*, in French armies.[49] The incorporation also took place at the same time as the demise of the constable. There was little, however, that was radically new about the provost: he performed duties that were previously assigned to the marshal. The provost marshal made arrests, kept prisoners, ensured the camp was clean, and kept accounts of victuals.[50] He was responsible for bringing all prisoners to court and making sure all witnesses were present. Finally, the provost marshal had to make sure ordinances and proclamations made by the king, lord general, or marshal were posted for all to read. The provost had several assistant provosts. To help the provost marshal, the army also employed executioners, clerks, and several tipstaves, who assisted the provost in making arrests, and were supposed to ensure that soldiers remained quiet and orderly in camp.[51] On occasion, the marshal commissioned his provost marshal to act in a judicial capacity.

Martial law commissioners also heard private plaints between soldiers. We know less about this procedure. But from the few descriptions of courts-martial that we have, the court operated as a great gathering of the army where soldiers probably could have leveled complaints in the hopes

[47] "Directions both generall and pticular drawen by ye lo: Generall Essex for the better instructing ye govment of ye army," BL, Harley 703, f. 25.

[48] "Court-Martial of Lt. Hudson, 21 October 1591," HH, CP 168/54.

[49] Lindsay Boynton, "The Tudor Provost Marshal," *EHR* 77:304 (July, 1962): 437–8. A. Vaughan Lovell-Knight, *The History of the Office of the Provost Marshal and the Corps of Military Police* (Aldershot, 1943). Also see, H. Bullock, "The Provost Marshal," *JSAHR* 7 (1928): 67–9, 129–32.

[50] BL, Harley Ms. 168, fos. 123v–124.   [51] BL, Harley Ms. 847, f. 53.

of receiving justice.[52] These meetings would have happened regularly during a campaign. The courts for the 1513 campaign in France, for example, heard complaints from soldiers three days a week.[53] It is almost certain that equitable principles guided the marshal or judge marshal in these hearings. Indeed, there were few written rules. The exception to this was that at the end of the sixteenth century, the army had adopted several rules relating to wills. If soldiers did not have a will, their moveable goods would go to their next of kin. If unclaimed for a year, the judge marshal would distribute the dead soldier's goods to the poor soldiers of the regiment.[54] But in everything else, the marshal or judge marshal had to use his conscience to resolve the particular dispute that came before them.

Very few official court-martial records survive but we can piece together how procedure actually worked from correspondence and other accounts. One of the clearest examples of martial law procedure comes from the Low Countries in 1586. In March of that year, several soldiers stationed in Utrecht approached the lord general and demanded their wages.[55] The Earl of Leicester, after conferring with his colonel-general, Sir John Norris, ordered the leader hanged for requesting pay, which was "contrary to martial law."[56] Distraught over the verdict, the mutinous soldiers broke their condemned colleague out of jail. Two companies of Welshmen arrived shortly after and helped the army leader-ship re-capture the condemned man and nine other chief mutineers. One of the imprisoned soldiers accused another named Roger Greene of participating in the jail break. The commander, John Norris ordered Greene arrested, and commanded his legal assistant, Bartholemew Clarke, and his provost marshal to interrogate Green, and to depose other witnesses.[57] Once the information was taken, Norris commissioned his marshal "for the [hangin]g of the three of them in the presence of the other seven, who were released the same day."[58] Evidence was gathered. Some kind of deliberation was made before sentencing. Nevertheless, the discretion given to the martial law commissioner was vast.

One of the most complete records comes from the seventeenth-century chronicle of Sir Thomas Gates' stay in Bermuda in 1609.[59] Gates had

---

[52] Sir Thomas Coningsby, "The Journal of the Siege of Rouen, 1591," ed. John Gough Nichols *Camden Miscellany* 1 (1847): 29–30.

[53] Cruikshank, *Army Royal*, 100.   [54] *Sutcliffe*, 339.

[55] "Account by Captain Crips of the Mutiny at Utrecht," 28 March 1586, *CSPF* 20: 495.

[56] Dr. Thomas Doyley to William Cecil, 16 April 1586, *CSPF* 20: 557.

[57] Captain Cripps, who related the story, was also a provost marshal. *CSPF* 20: 495.

[58] *Ibid.* The numbers in the account suggest that Green in the end was not charged.

[59] Samuel Purchas, *Hakluytus Posthumus, or Purchas his Pilgrimes: Contayning a History of the World in Sea Voyages and Lande Travells By Englishmen and Others* 20 vols. (Glasgow, 1905–07), 19: 30–2.

been sailing to Virginia but his voyage got sidetracked when a storm threw the ship off course. He landed in Bermuda, where he and his troops stayed for several days to gather supplies and fix their ships. In the course of their delay, problems of discipline arose among the sailors. Two sailors came forward to Gates and informed him that one of the men, named Stephen Hopkins, was plotting a mutiny against him. Gates brought the suspect before him and heard his entreaties: Hopkins claimed that he was innocent. Then he deposed two witnesses who claimed that Hopkins had indeed plotted a mutiny against Gates. In the end Gates decided with the two witnesses and declared Hopkins guilty of mutiny. He sentenced him to death. But then the other sailors petitioned Gates to grant mercy for the sailor. The commander obliged.

In these two examples, martial law commissioners had employed several practices worth further unpacking. First, the commander could act as witness as well as a judge. Leicester saw the wrong being committed – it was committed against him – took counsel, and then gave a verdict using his own senses as testimony. However, when the wrong was unknown to the martial law commissioner, he relied upon informations in the form of written depositions taken by his judge marshal and by his provost. Only then did he determine a verdict. In Gates' case, he likewise took depositions from two of his men and held a trial, where he heard an answer from the defendant before determining guilt. In both cases, mercy was employed for political and teaching purposes. Norris had the seven pardoned watch the hangings before they returned to camp. Gates, while stuck in Bermuda, probably desired to be perceived as merciful by his restless outfit. Both penalties and mercy could stay mutiny, both could terrify, and both reinforced hierarchy.

The most notorious way in which leniency and severity were intertwined was decimation, the practice of executing one tenth of all those who had committed a wrong. According to Machiavelli, commenting upon Livy, decimation was "the which punishment, was in such wise made, that though euery man did not feele it, euerie man notwithstanding feared it."[60] A brutal example of decimation came in Ireland in 1599, when the Earl of Essex held a court-martial that convicted a company of cowardice in the face of the enemy. After taking counsel, Essex had the officer who was second in command executed, all other officers cashiered and imprisoned, and every tenth soldier executed.[61] Those that had not been convicted were forced to see the penalty enacted so that they might learn not to commit a similar offense.

[60] *The arte of warre, written in Italian by Nicholas Machiavuel, set forth in English by Peter Withorne* (London, 1588), 84v.
[61] "Proceedings of the Earl of Essex," 22 June–1 July 1599, in *CCM*, 1589–1600, 308–12.

Essex's actions were brutal. But the mechanisms for this violence were not "extralegal." While the general, his high marshal, or another delegated authority like Sir Thomas Wilford, possessed an enormous amount of discretion, they still desired evidence in no small measure to maintain order and quiet within the army and to reinforce their position as the fountain of justice. Terror through executions was necessary but those executions needed to be justified through a conviction based upon evidence. Mutinies might arise, after all, from tyrannical superiors as well as undisciplined soldiers.

Martial law and treason

Much more infamously than disciplining soldiers, the Tudors used martial law to punish commoners who had risen against them. As we have seen, the use of the courts of the constable and marshal to punish treason had been quite common in the fourteenth and fifteenth centuries. However, the Tudors used this jurisdiction to punish members of the commons and not wealthy and important men like Thomas of Lancaster. Further, and most importantly, these courts-martial took evidence and even allowed answers. It does not appear that they used manifest proofs, like notoriety. These were not the treason trials by the law of arms of earlier periods.

This experimentation perhaps began in 1497 under Henry VII. In June of that year, the commons of Cornwall rose against Henry because of his new taxation policies. The revolt was short-lived. With the leaders of the rebellion, Henry adopted the policy with which we are now familiar. In March 1497, he issued a commission that authorized four men to call before them James Touchet, Lord Audley, one of the leaders of the rebellion, and to "execute the office of constable and marshal upon him."[62] Audley was convicted before the panel according to the law of arms. Perkin Warbeck, the Yorkist pretender, was likewise tried and executed before the constable and marshal.[63] However, prior to these more grandiose tribunals, Henry also sent two commissioners to Cornwall to try less important participants in the rising. In July 1497, the king issued a commission for Robert Clyfford and John Digby to

---

[62] *CPR*, 1494–1509, 115. For the trial of Audley see L.W. Vernon Harcourt, *His Grace the Steward and Trial by Peers: A Novel Inquiry into a Special Branch of Constitutional Government* (London, 1907), 397–99. The full patent roll that commissioned the trial of Audeley is printed in *Ibid.*, 414–15.

[63] Baker, *Oxford History of the Laws of England: Volume Six*, 216–17. Audley and some of his followers were attainted in 1504. I. Arthurson, "The Rising of 1497: A Revolt of the Peasantry?" in *People, Politics, and Community in the Later Middle Ages*, ed. Joel Rosenthal and Colin Richmond (Gloucester, 1987), 14–15.

"execute the office of constable and marshal of England with respect to the rebels who levied war in Devon and Cornwall."[64] A similar commission was issued in 1500.[65] These were some of the first instances that a king sent officers to use the procedures of the constable and marshal to prosecute commoners. Unfortunately we know little about what happened after the issuing of these commissions, although it seems that most of those implicated got away with their lives.

In 1536–7, Henry VIII used a similar policy much more violently during the greatest crisis of his reign.[66] In the autumn of that year large popular movements often collectively known as the "Pilgrimage of Grace" protested Henry's new religious and taxation policies.[67] Spurred on by rumors of future depredations, the commons, first in Lincolnshire and, more importantly, Yorkshire, became a substantial military threat to Henry's reign by that November. By the end of November, they had control of York, Hull, and Pontefract Castle, one of the key strategic Crown fortresses in the region, and had co-opted many of the gentry into their ranks. In December, Henry granted a general pardon, and mendaciously promised to convene a parliament in the north to hear the grievances of the pilgrims. Splinters of the pilgrims were unhappy with these agreements, and began to plot more uprisings. The rebellion was not firmly put down until the following spring.

Throughout the rebellion, the Crown faced tough choices on how to prosecute the pilgrims. In the autumn of 1536, the lord chancellor, Thomas Audley prepared special commissions of *oyer* and *terminer* for the lord general of Henry's army, the Duke of Suffolk. Likewise, in the aftermath of the rebellion, in the spring of 1537, the Crown used common law for most treason cases.[68] But some of the Crown's activities reveal that it was concerned about jury nullification. It should have been, as many of the juries, empaneled in counties where the rebellion had taken

---

[64] *CPR*, 1494–1509, 115. Mark Stoyle has described Henry VII's response to the rebellions as "comparatively restrained." Stoyle, "Cornish Rebellions, 1497–1648," *History Today* 47:5 (May, 1997): 25.

[65] *CRP*, 1494–1509, 202. John Bellamy, *The Tudor Law of Treason: An Introduction* (London, 1979), 229.

[66] It seems unlikely that Henry used martial law in the aftermath of the rebellions over the "Amicable Grant" in 1525. Surviving indictments suggest participants were indicted for riot. G.W. Bernard, *War, Taxation and Rebellion in Early Tudor England: Henry VIII, Wolsey and the Amicable Grant of 1525* (New York, 1986), 138–41.

[67] R.W. Hoyle, *The Pilgrimage of Grace and the Politics of the 1530s* (Oxford, 2001), esp. 93–157. For an innovative examination of the politics of the pilgrims, see Ethan Shagan, *Popular Politics and the English Reformation* (Cambridge, 2003), 89–128.

[68] G.R. Elton, *Policy and Police: The Enforcement of the Reformation in the Age of Thomas Cromwell* (Cambridge, 1972), 293–326.

place, refused to convict defendants of treason.[69] In order to eliminate this problem, Henry in certain instances brought caught rebels to London to be tried there instead of in the place of the rebellion. He also experimented with trying rebels by martial law.

Henry conceived martial law to be a verge jurisdiction delimited to a 12-mile circumference around his banner of war. In October 1536, the king rode with his army to Windsor with his banner raised before it travelled north to fight the pilgrims without him. In that period, according to the prominent and legally trained chronicler Edward Hall, the king heard information that a butcher expressed support for the pilgrims and that a priest declared them to be "Goddes people [and] did fight and defend Goddes quarrel." According to Hall, the two were only "v. myle of Winsore," well within the verge of the king's banner.[70] Both men were executed for treason by martial law.

In February 1537, the Duke of Norfolk desired this jurisdiction to try men for treason at Carlisle. Norfolk had advanced with a royal army upon the rebel splinter groups a month earlier. After putting down the risings, he began to prosecute caught pilgrims at York in the middle of February. Then he turned his attention to Carlisle, where a rebel army had just failed to take the city.[71] After he had entered the city, Norfolk demanded that all those who had participated in the post-pardon revolts submit to his authority. By his count, 6,000 men and women came and submitted themselves to him. Writing to the Council on 19 February, Norfolk wrote to Henry that he "must p[ro]cede by the lawe marciall" because "if I shold p[ro]cede by inditements many a great offender myght ... be fownd not giltie saying he was brought forth against his will."[72] Norfolk was clearly worried that the inhabitants of the north would be too sympathetic to indict participants of the risings for treason. Three days later, the king responded to Norfolk, approving of his plan to seek justice through martial law. The king declared that

We do right well approve and allow your p[ro]ceedings in the displaying of our banner/ And forasmuche as the same is now spredde and displayed by reason

---

[69] *Ibid.*, 314–15.

[70] Edward Hall, *Hall's Chronicle: Containing the History of England ... to the End of the Reign of Henry the Eighth* ed. H. Ellis (London, 1809), 823. The relationship between the banner and martial law jurisdiction has been noticed in passing by Elton, *Policy and Police*, 90, and R.V. Manning, "The Origins of the Doctrine of Sedition," *Albion* 12:2 (Summer, 1980): 107.

[71] Hoyle, *Pilgrimage of Grace*, 389–420; Madeleine Hope Dodds and Ruth Dodds, *The Pilgrimage of Grace, 1536–7 and the Exeter Conspiracy, 1538* 2 vols. (London, 1971), 2: 99–140.

[72] Norfolk to Council, 19 February 1537, TNA, SP 1/116 f. 83.

whereof tyll the same shalbe closed again the cours of our lawes must give place to thorden[a]nces and estatutes marciall/[73]

Once the banner was raised, Henry desired that Norfolk cause "dredfull" execution to be done upon the participants for the sake of terror to others living in the region so they might not attempt another rising. Henry required that Norfolk instill this fear by the "hanging of them vpp on trees" and by setting their heads and quarters where everyone would be sure to see them.[74]

On 24 February, Norfolk reported back to the king the product of his judicial undertaking. First, he attached the names of those he executed at martial law to his letter. They totaled seventy-four.[75] Again, Norfolk declared how common law procedure would have impeded justice: "And, surely had I proceeded by the trial of xii men, I thinke that not the fifte man of these shold haue suffered for the common saing is here 'I came owte for feare for my liff,' And 'I came forthe for feare of losse of all my goodes' . . . And a small excuse wilbe well beleved here."[76] Norfolk was not stating that he wanted to convict the innocent or convict those without evidence. Instead, he was concerned that a jury might acquit those who had, according to the Crown, broken the law. By circumventing the jury, Norfolk obtained his convictions, and crowed that "the like nomber hath not be herd of put to execution at one tyme."[77]

Norfolk seems to have received information from key members of his council in order to try the rebels. His council at this point included Sir Ralph Ellerker and Robert Bowes, both of whom had initially participated in the Pilgrimage of Grace in the autumn and had negotiated with Henry on the Pilgrims' behalf. They had received pardons from the king and had been joined with Norfolk, in part to prove their allegiance, later in the winter. Both Bowes and Ellerker eventually served in legal capacities during the trials. Norfolk named Ellerker as marshal and Bowes as an "attorney general" to prosecute the suspects.[78] He had narrowed the number of men to be tried from the supposed 6,000 down to seventy-four by their advice. We know few details, but given what prosecutors and marshals generally did in English courts, we can make a good guess as to the responsibilities of Ellerker and Bowes. Ellerker, as marshal, probably was in charge of detaining and supervising the suspects. While Bowes, as attorney general, probably was charged with taking down examinations of the prisoners, and probably drafted informal charges or informations so Norfolk could make a judicial determination as to their guilt. From this,

[73] Henry VIII to Norfolk, 22 February 1537, TNA, SP 1/116 f. 95.   [74] Ibid., f. 95v.
[75] Norfolk to Henry VIII, 24 February 1537, TNA, SP 1/116 fos. 108–11.
[76] Ibid., f. 108.   [77] Ibid.   [78] Ibid.

he decided which ones he wanted to execute for the sake of terror. As Madeleine and Ruth Dodds noted long ago, it is possible they held these positions as a form of humiliation for their past participation in the revolt.[79] But it is just as likely that Norfolk used them to generate informations based on their knowledge of the important participants of the rebellion.

The only clear example of the use of martial law to prosecute treason or sedition during the reigns of Edward and Mary comes from late January 1558, in the immediate aftermath of Mary's loss of Calais. Some feared a French invasion. The lord warden of the Cinque Ports, Sir Thomas Cheyney, reported to the queen and her council that the mayor of Canterbury had caught two men, Robert Cockerell and Francis Barton, and accused them of speaking seditious and traitorous words against her majesty. He also sent depositions of their acts. The warden reported that as per the instructions the mayor had received from the Privy Council earlier in the year, they could proceed by martial law.[80] We do not have the instructions the Crown sent to the warden or to the mayor and alderman of Canterbury, but apparently they could use martial law. The warden informed the Crown that they should proceed against Cockerell "by order of the marshall lawe without any length keeping of him" so that his fate would be a "terror to others." In the margins the recipient wrote that he should only be convicted "if the words in the deposition be dewly proved against him."[81] Proof was still required for conviction. We know little about why martial law jurisdiction was allowed in this case. It is possible that both Cockerell and Barton were soldiers. Canterbury housed around 100 Crown soldiers that winter.[82] Further, Cockerell was a Protestant. On his way to execution, the alderman of Canterbury asked him to repent and say a paternoster. Cockerell refused and, according to William Oxenden, the new lord warden of the Cinque Ports, blasphemed God before he died.[83] Barton was only sentenced to the pillory. Protestants swearing against Mary in a time of fear apparently needed to be executed by martial law.

The most illuminating example of the use of martial law in times of rebellion comes from the aftermath of the Northern Rebellions in 1570.[84]

---

[79] Madeleine and Ruth Dodds, *The Pilgrimage of Grace*, 2: 119.

[80] Sir Thomas Cheyney to Mary I, 23 January 1558, TNA, SP 11/12/32.   [81] *Ibid.*

[82] Peter Clark, *English Provincial Society from the Reformation to the Revolution: Religion, Politics, and Society in Kent, 1500–1640* (Rutherford, NJ, 1977), 104.

[83] William Oxenden to Mary I, 3 February 1558, TNA, SP 11/12/46 and 46 I.

[84] The Edwardian regime probably used martial law in both Kett's Rebellion in Norfolk and the Prayer Book Rising in the southwest but little is known about judicial prosecutions after the rebellions. Andy Wood, *The 1549 Rebellions and the Making of Early Modern England* (Cambridge, 2007), 71 n.4. We do know the Privy Council made plans during

By the fall of 1569, a combination of religious grievances and particular grievances by several of Elizabeth's great northern lords, the earls of Northumberland and Westmorland, led to what has now come to be called the "Great Northern Rebellion." On 14 November, the Earls with a small contingent rode into Durham and issued a proclamation that declared their loyalty to the queen and to the traditional faith but hostility to her "evil councilors."[85] In a move identical to the one her father made against the Pilgrims, Elizabeth issued a pardon on 19 November for all those who left the rebel camp by the 22 November.[86] Seeing their hopes of a successful rising fade, Northumberland and Westmorland fled into Scotland by December. Those who had followed the earls had to await the justice of the queen. She was not interested in granting them mercy. As Krista Kesselring has noted, "the Queen demonstrated a recognition that it was the many men who answered the earls' calls ... that had made the revolt a danger to her regime."[87] The queen and her council wanted to terrorize the inhabitants of these areas through public executions of a select number of participants of the rebellion. William Cecil, at the time Elizabeth's secretary of state, ordered to execute rebels "in every special place where the rebels did gather any people, and in every market town or great parish, there be execution by martial law."[88] Along with terror, fear of jury nullification probably influenced their desire.

Elizabeth's council focused more on economic status than on temporalities when it came to martial law jurisdiction. While some type of claim to "turbulent times" was probably made, the regime was clearer on the economic restrictions to martial law jurisdiction: no person of freehold was to be tried by martial law.[89] Cecil probably understood this bar from his readings of medieval precedent. We have seen that in 1352, along with passing a treason statute, parliament banned the alienation of property by any means except those that were qualified by chapter 29 of Magna Carta. This stricture forced the various kings of the fifteenth century to posthumously attaint those they had convicted upon record during war in order that they might obtain their property. The Elizabethans seem to

the rebellion to give local officers powers of martial law. See Chapter 2. Although there were rebellions and conspiracies against Mary, she did not seem to use martial law in these instances. See D.M. Loades, *Two Tudor Conspiracies* (Cambridge, 1965), 89–112.

[85] K.J. Kesselring, *The Northern Rebellion of 1569: Faith, Politics, and Protest in Elizabethan England* (Basingstoke, 2007), 56–61.

[86] *Ibid.*, 78.   [87] *Ibid.*, 90.   [88] Quoted in Kesselring, *The Northern Rebellion*, 122.

[89] Earl of Sussex to Cecil, 28 December 1569, TNA, SP 15/15, f. 229. "Memorandum of rebels appointed to be executed by martial law," 1570, TNA, SP 15/17, f. 45. Sir George Bowes' memorandum in 1573 also pointed to prosecuting the impoverished. BL, Harley, 6991 no. 33.

have understood this same boundary. Martial law commissioners in their view could not seize real property of convicts.[90]

In the same memorandum that advocated using martial law, William Cecil planned an extensive torture campaign where suspects would be "put to fear, and as need should require, pinched with lack of food and pains of imprisonment."[91] The plan was put into execution by the Earl of Sussex, the leader of the queen's army in the north, and his knight marshal, Sir George Bowes, who in all likelihood gathered evidence in order to find those they wanted to try and execute by martial law.[92] Sussex, as we shall see, had implemented martial law quite aggressively during his time as lord deputy of Ireland in the 1550s. And he implemented a variant that required only the senses for conviction: no information gathering was required and no answers by defendants were allowed. But in this case the Crown wanted to make sure it executed the right people: those who were guilty, yes, but also those like the constables who were important members of their community even though poor. Further, each town that sent men to the rebel armies needed to witness a portion of its men executed by martial law.[93]

Evidence was gathered. While the Privy Council warrants do not survive for this period, circumstantial evidence indicates that Crown officials used torture to obtain information on the rebels. Through this information gathering, the Earl of Sussex was able to make lists of men he wanted tried at courts-martial.[94] We also have an idea that the evidence gathered against those eventually convicted was more substantial than implication by another when under torture. Bowes reported in a 1573 memorandum that he had only convicted the "greatest offenders; for there was none executed by me, but such as did confess with their owne mouths that they were in the actual rebellion."[95] We do not need to fully accept Bowes' claims. But it is likely that he and Sussex

---

[90] Conviction of felons was quite lucrative for the Crown. K.J. Kesselring, "Felony Forfeiture and the Profits of Crime in Early Modern England," *HJ* 53:2 (June, 2010): 271–88. In the Northern Rebellion, the queen largely relied on an act of attainder to secure forfeiture. Kesselring, *The Northern Rebellion*, 130–1.

[91] TNA, SP 15/15 no. 139.

[92] A knight marshal was more important than a simple provost marshal. It was more similar to the eventual title of provost marshal general. He would have had responsibilities over discipline within the host.

[93] Sussex to Cecil, 28 December 1569, TNA, SP 15/15 f. 229; DUL, Bowes Ms. 534, fos. 2, 4–7.

[94] Kesselring, *The Northern Rebellion*, 124–5.

[95] This has been printed in the *Memorials of the Rebellion of 1569* ed. Sir Cuthbert Sharpe (London, 1840), 188. The original is "Account of the Northern Rebellion by Sir George Bowes Field Marshal," BL, Harley Ms. 6991, no. 33.

attempted through the examination of evidence to execute those who willingly marched against the queen.

Defendants were probably allowed to answer during brief trials. We know this because Sir George Bowes held judicial proceedings in January 1570 where he examined suspects and gave verdicts. Records for several of these tribunals have survived but they offer almost no details about the ways in which Bowes administered the proceedings. Bowes only listed the name of the suspect who came before the court, where he was from, perhaps what his occupation was if he was a constable or other local officer, and if he was executed or not. The top of the record reads:

Rebells convicted before Sir George Bowes knight mshall of the quenes matie Armye levyed in the north Pte At the sessions or mshals court holden at Allerton and Thyrske the xiiith xiiiith xxth & xxiith dayes of Jannuarye in the xiith yeare of the Reigne of or Souarigne ladye Elizabeth etc and executed as foloweth.[96]

The suspects had to be convicted before they could be executed. Nevertheless, they did not have much chance of survival. If we are to believe Bowes' later account of these trials, it was at this tribunal that defendants confessed to their participation. Only two seemed to have obtained acquittal. When one "Robert Peters" came before the court, his execution was "stayed at the earnest sugt of Anthony Wycleff."[97] Bowes also stayed the execution of another man named William Waller, at the suggestion of one Thomas Layton. Who was Thomas Layton? We do not know. The word "stay" suggests Bowes had reviewed evidence on Peters in advance and had planned on convicting him, but a petitioner whom he trusted convinced him otherwise. Through evidence, defendants either were pronounced guilty or were relieved.[98]

Through Bowes' tribunal we can see an adaptation from medieval tribunals that used notoriety as a form of proof to sixteenth-century courts that relied upon witnesses and confessions. It is not difficult to see why this adaptation occurred. Notoriety was more useful for the high born: those who had led and had gained public infamy for their actions. The exact extent of participation of the lower born was much more difficult to discover through public knowledge. More evidence was required to separate innocent from guilty and guilty from the "worse sort" who really needed to be executed for their participation.[99] Thus it

---

[96] DUL, Bowes Ms. 534, f. 6. There is also an account of a court-martial at Richmond, *ibid.*, f. 8.

[97] *Ibid.*, f. 6v.

[98] Similar stays of execution happened under Sussex who probably used similar methods as Bowes. Kesselring, *The Northern Rebellion*, 124.

[99] Kesselring, *The Northern Rebellion*, 124.

seems that either defendants were allowed to present witnesses on their behalf or Crown informants were present at the tribunals to provide testimony for the judges. These innovations saved few. The increased use of evidence ensured that the Crown exacted vengeance on those it believed most needed it.

Conclusion

While martial law was associated with war, with armed camps, with states of rebellion, and often with treason, the Crown defined it through its procedure. Each one of these procedures was not unique. Indeed, in many ways martial law was just one more jurisdiction that utilized procedure by information instead of by grand and petty jury. But those with martial law commissions could punish by life and limb where others that utilized process by information could not. Indeed, it was this power that separated it, in the minds of the Tudors, from the courts of the marshal that still periodically sat to hear and determine cases relating to prisoners of war and heraldry.[100] The Crown used martial law to prosecute its soldiers. Sometimes it used martial law to discipline sailors, or "soldiers on the sea." The Tudors also frequently used martial law to punish those who had risen in commotions against their religious and economic policies.

In the Elizabethan period, many still believed there were temporal boundaries to martial law. Most of the examples we have examined in this chapter still involved the royal host, and several claimed jurisdiction through the raising of the royal banner. As late as 1573, English ministers claimed martial law was still so restricted. For example, Elizabeth demanded a commission of martial law so she could execute an attempted assassin. The zealous puritan Peter Birchet had attempted to kill one of the queen's new favorites, Sir Christopher Hatton. Unfortunately both for Birchet and his victim, the person he attacked was not actually Hatton but Sir John Hawkins, the famed privateer. Hawkins survived the attack. But his luck did not assuage Elizabeth's wrath. After Birchet had been seized, Elizabeth wanted to execute him immediately. Many within the queen's council strenuously objected to her demands. William Cecil, who heard of the affair from a letter by the Earl of Sussex, noted that discreet councilors – including Sussex, who was apparently appalled by the queen's plan – told Elizabeth that martial law should not be used in times of peace when "ye procedings must be by forme of judiciary process

---

[100] G.D. Squibb, *The High Court of Chivalry: A Study of the Civil Law in England* (Oxford, 1959), 29–46.

wch put her by yt purpose."[101] Instead, according to Cecil, martial law should only be used in armed camps and in turbulent times. Martial law was controversial well before the Petition of Right, even for two of martial law's most notorious practitioners.[102]

But these protests hardly bound martial law. Procedures that bypassed grand and petty juries were too enticing. While the Crown authorized martial law for the governance of armed camps and for the prosecuting of sedition and treason during turbulent times, these only scratch the surface of how the Tudors experimented with martial law jurisdiction in the sixteenth century. Indeed, Cecil, as we shall see, was involved in authorizing martial law for other purposes beyond rebellion and disciplining soldiers in armed camps. These authorizations granted civilian authorities who were far away from the royal host powers of martial law. By Elizabeth's reign, Crown officers in Ireland had already expanded martial law jurisdiction and adapted its procedures to grant even more discretion to more and more martial law commissioners. These experiments did not always end with the desired results. While the Tudors at various moments were deeply concerned about trusting juries, by the end of the sixteenth century, Elizabeth began to seriously question whether it was indeed wise to put so much trust in judges.

---

[101] The Earl of Sussex to Sir William Cecil, 28 October 1573, BL, Harley MS 6991, no. 35.

[102] Combined, Cecil and Sussex executed far more people than the more controversial Governor Eyre in 1865 or the more boastful Duke of Norfolk in 1537. And this is not even including the unknown number of people who died because of Sussex's summary martial law policies in Ireland. See the next chapter.

2   Making summary martial law

In 1586, the queen and her council were worried about a variant of martial law that they believed was being abused in Ireland.[1] Her Irish kingdom in recent years had experienced unbelievable transformation. The Fitzgeralds of Desmond had lost their territories in two rebellions after the Dublin government had put them down in brutal fashion. Her government was now in the process of settling Protestants on the Desmonds' former lands.[2] Presidents in Munster and in Connacht were supervising areas of Ireland that the English had not controlled for centuries. Even the Gaelic lords in Ulster seemed for the moment to be acquiescing to English supervision.[3] Nevertheless, Elizabeth was concerned with the policy of granting summary martial law commissions, which allowed sheriffs, constables, mayors, loyal peers, provost marshals, and seneschals to execute vagrants, suspected felons of ill name, and traitors upon sight. This jurisprudence of terror was part of a larger reform program within English-controlled lands to help usher in law and order and end the rebellions, private wars, and raids that had hindered English settlement. Elizabeth believed the practice to be dishonorable. Yet, if it were properly modified and supervised, she and her council believed it still to be useful. By the end of her reign, she was using summary martial law practices more often in England.

---

[1] Their desires for its reformation can be found in the new instructions to Sir John Perrot, the lord deputy of Ireland. BL, Add. Ms. 37,536, fos. 14–15v; BL, Add Ms. 4,786, fos. 37–8.

[2] Michael MacCarthy-Morrogh, *The Munster Plantation: English Migration to Southern Ireland, 1583–1641* (Oxford, 1986).

[3] For an overview of sixteenth century Ireland, see Colm Lennon, *Sixteenth-Century Ireland: The Incomplete Conquest* (Dublin, 1994). The key narratives of this period, which often do not agree with one another, are Ciaran Brady, *The Chief Governors: The Rise and Fall of Reform Government in Tudor Ireland* (Cambridge, 1994), 72–300; Nicholas P. Canny, *The Elizabethan Conquest of Ireland: A Pattern Established, 1565–76* (New York, 1976); Canny, *Making Ireland British, 1580–1650* (Oxford, 2001). I tend to try and split the difference between the reform-minded governors of Ciaran Brady's narrative and the brutal "conquistadors" that dominate the narrative of Canny.

The variant they attempted to more closely monitor had been adapted from the process we have already examined in Chapter 1. In England's royal hosts, we have seen that process was usually begun by information and concluded by a martial law commissioner who determined verdicts based upon evidence after receiving legal counsel. Summary martial law commissioners, on the other hand, frequently tried and convicted suspects immediately through manifest proofs. While usually only threatened in England, summary martial law commissioners in Ireland frequently used notoriety or public infamy to execute defendants for felonies, treasons, and even vagrancy. They could do so due to the widespread perception that English commissioners could comprehend ethnic differences through name, dress, and speech that supposedly would allow them to only target the poor Irish. Without proper identification, these poor "idlers" were hanged.

David Edwards has rightly argued that martial law practice in Ireland, while related to that practiced in England, was far more widespread and produced far more violence than its English counterpart. One can also sympathize with the view that Irish martial law commissioners were simply private conquerors who did what they wanted.[4] Although the patchy survival of sources makes it difficult to argue anything definitively, it seems likely that commissioners executed by summary martial law more often in Ireland because the English valued Irish life less than they valued English life. The rhetoric of many English planters and officials suggests as much, as one of their stated beliefs was that force was required to bring the Irish into English "civilization."[5]

But it is equally important to note that martial law practice in Ireland and in England informed one another through the supervision of the English Privy Council. The English Privy Council first experimented with summary martial law in England. Further, by 1589 the English Privy Council brought aspects of Irish martial law practice into England. But given what had happened in Ireland, Elizabeth and her Privy Council had little desire to grant such overwhelming power unequivocally into the hands of her delegated authorities. It is true that the English state relied on government by commission. But, as Paul

---

[4] David Edwards, "Beyond Reform: Martial Law and the Tudor Re-Conquest of Ireland," *History Ireland* 5 (1997): 16–21.

[5] For this rhetoric, see Vincent P. Carey, "Icons of Atrocity: John Derricke's *Image of Irelande* (1581)," in *World Building and the Early Modern Imagination* ed. Allison Kavey (New York, 2010), 233–54. Brendan Bradshaw famously divided those who wanted to anglicize and reform by the sword from those who wanted to conquer through persuasion in his "Sword, Word, and Strategy in the Reformation in Ireland," *HJ* 21:3 (September, 1973): 475–502.

Halliday has shown, it also cared deeply about supervising those commissioners and reprimanding them when they abused their powers.[6]

The development and supervision of summary martial law in both kingdoms produced the first extended discussion on martial law jurisdiction in the early modern period. In the 1580s, Elizabeth and her council developed rules that restricted martial law long before the famous common lawyer MPs of the 1628 Parliament. While less elaborately constructed than the arguments made by Coke, Selden, or William Noy, they predicted seventeenth-century arguments on the law of martial law. Like those later arguments, the Privy Council was only partially successful in corralling summary martial law practice, which by the middle of the seventeenth century was usually only allowed for the execution of those who resisted arrest. In order to better understand why the Privy Council began to review Irish martial law practice, let us examine how it was constructed.

The dualism of martial law

Let us begin near the end. In 1641, Adam Loftus, Lord Ely, the judge marshal general of Ireland, arrived in Westminster to testify against his enemy, the lord lieutenant of Ireland, Thomas Wentworth, the Earl of Strafford, who was on trial for treason. He was to testify on Irish martial law practice because one of the articles of treason claimed that Strafford had employed martial law illegally while lord deputy of Ireland, thus subverting the king's laws.[7] The charge focused on Strafford's activities in the winter of 1635, when the then lord deputy called a council of war, which tried and convicted Lord Mountnorris, a captain in the Irish army, of seditious speech against his commander. A council of war sentenced Mountnorris to die, but Wentworth pardoned him on condition that he resign as vice-treasurer of the Irish government.[8] Wentworth had also hanged another soldier for desertion and theft in 1638. He defended his actions by claiming that it was customary in Ireland for the lord deputy to use martial law on soldiers in the army, and that he therefore was not subverting the king's laws by utilizing martial law in Ireland.

---

[6] This was true of every jurisdiction, not simply martial law. Paul D. Halliday, *Habeas Corpus: From England to Empire* (Cambridge, MA, 2010), 11–38.

[7] John Rushworth, *Historical Collections of Private Passages of State* 8 vols. (London, 1721), 8: 186–205. Accessed on British History Online February 2013–September 2015, www.british-history.ac.uk.

[8] Hugh Kearney, *Strafford in Ireland, 1633–41: A Study in Absolutism* (Manchester, 1959), 71–2.

In order to better understand the practice of martial law in Ireland and thus prove its case against Strafford, parliament deposed Lord Ely.[9] During his examination, Ely divided martial law into two separate jurisdictions: "plenary martial law" and "summary martial law." He dubbed the form Wentworth had used against Lord Mountnorris as "plenary." Plenary martial law for Loftus involved this procedure:

> The parties complained, the other appearing, an Information was drawn in writing, Witnesses produced, and reduced in writing, a Sentence given absolutely or condemnatory, and the Party punished or acquitted, and the Warrant directed to the Provost-Marshal to put the Judgment in Execution.[10]

We should by now recognize these procedures. While a council of war tried Mountnorris instead of one martial law commissioner, the other kinds of process involved in the trial were similar to the form of martial law that we examined in Chapter 1.[11] English officials in Ireland had developed fairly stringent boundaries for the jurisdiction of "plenary martial law." Commanders could only employ plenary martial law if three conditions were met: in a time of war, on soldiers in pay in the army, and only when those soldiers were "in the field" serving on a campaign. Thus, soldiers could not be tried at martial law during states when the army was dissolved or inactive, or when the kingdom was at peace.

Loftus contrasted plenary martial law with "summary martial law:" a variant that allowed immediate execution based on manifest proofs. No court proceedings were necessary. Provost marshals had these powers to prosecute "Rebels and Kernes that kept [to] the Woods."[12] When provosts caught these men they "[h]anged them on the next tree." Only the poor, those who held less than 40s in real property, could be tried at summary martial law. Sir Simonds D'Ewes recorded this testimony in his diary, noting that summary martial law could only be used on those rebels who resisted arrest.[13]

Let us for the moment abandon the highly restrictive jurisdictions Ely gave for both summary and plenary martial law. They did not exist in the middle of the sixteenth century. Nevertheless, these two variants of martial law that Ely described, while never as clearly differentiated as he and other jurists made them out to be, took shape by that period. Let us first explore authorizations for the use of martial law within the army before we contrast them with summary martial law commissions.

---

[9] W.N. Osborough, "Loftus, Adam, first Viscount Loftus of Ely," *ODNB*.
[10] Rushworth, *Historical Collections*, 8: 186–205.
[11] For the council of war, see Chapter 3.
[12] Rushworth, *Historical Collections*, 8: 186–205.   [13] BL, Harley Ms. 164, f. 144.

Multiple fiants, which were calendared in the nineteenth century, of martial law were exclusively concerned with the punishment of soldiers in Ireland dating from Edward VI's reign, although a unique martial law jurisdiction for soldiers probably began in the 1540s.[14] They all contain a clause similar to the one included in a 1560 commission to Sir George Stanley, the marshal of the army in Ireland. The Dublin government empowered Stanley to "hold the marshal's court for causes civil and criminal concerning soldiers."[15] Although no originals survive of these commissions, they were in all likelihood similar to the commission granted to Sir Edward Bellingham by the English Chancery in 1548 that we explored in the last chapter.

Now let us turn to a summary martial law commission which the Dublin government granted to a wide variety of officials from the 1550s until the end of Elizabeth's reign. We are going to examine one of the surviving original commissions granted to Sir Warham St. Leger, the provost marshal of Munster, in 1579.[16] We can be reasonably sure that this commission is identical to ones granted as early as 1560.[17] From this examination we can learn how summary martial law varied from plenary martial law. As we shall discover, it varied more by degree than by kind.

First, the commissioners were not concerned with soldiers but instead with the disciplining of "haughtie livers, idell vagabounds," and others who were uncertain in their allegiance in spite of being the queen's subjects. Because of their supposedly natural inclination to disobedience, the government needed to employ "speedie and sharpe meanes rather than by our common laws." Along with vagrants, if St. Leger discovered "fellons robbers or . . . notorious evil doers" he could proceed by the order of martial law. Discovery of such persons could be by "trial and search."

---

[14] Fiants were commands from the Irish Chancery to the Great Seal to make a commission. They were calendared before they were destroyed in the twentieth century. See Kenneth Nicholls, "Introduction," in *The Irish Fiants of the Tudor Sovereigns: During the Reigns of Henry VIII, Edward VI, Philip & Mary, and Elizabeth I* (hereafter Fiants) ed. K.W. Nicholls 4 vols. (Dublin, 1994), 1: v–xi. *Fiants, Edward VI*, no. 13; *Fiants, Mary*, no. 11. For Henry VIII's commands for martial law on soldiers in Ireland, see Chapter 1.

[15] *Fiants, Elizabeth*, no. 201. For similar fiants, in her reign, see *ibid.*, nos. 809, 4195, 6252. *Calendar of the Patent Rolls, Ireland, Elizabeth I* ed. J. Morrin (Dublin, 1862), 432–3.

[16] The commission is in LPL, Ms. 597, fos. 187–88v. Other original commissions can be found in LPL, Ms. 608, f. 68v; NLI, d. 3106; d. 2687; d. 2688–9; d. 3261; NLI, Ms. 8066/2; HH, CP 215/13. Along with powers of martial law, these commissions delegated extensive sovereign powers to its recipients, such as the ability to allow safe-conducts and treat with enemies that were generally reserved for monarchs or lord protectors in England. I will not discuss these powers in any detail here as Rory Rapple has already handled them well in his recent work. Rapple, *Martial Power and Elizabethan Political Culture: Military Men in England and Ireland, 1558–1594* (Cambridge, 2009).

[17] LPL, Ms. 597, fos. 187–8v. The fiant for the commission says "as in 218," which was a fiant issued in 1560. *Fiants Elizabeth*, no. 3595.

The commissioner was allowed to convict either through the evidence his senses had acquired or through the public knowledge of a suspect's guilt. No formal court of the marshal was required to convict them as it was for the disciplining of soldiers. However, if St. Leger felt himself to be unsure, he could make inquiries with other local law officers to verify the suspect's guilt.

The instructions attached to the commission explicitly granted St. Leger powers to convict through manifest proofs.[18] The first stipulation in the instructions reveals that he had to inform the populace of his commission through proclamations, which were supposed to be distributed widely. Eight days after the issuance of the proclamation, any low-born person of bad name was to be executed if they did not possess a pass, including "harpers rimers and bards." This was even true for those who traveled with an "honest man in English apparell" provided they were known to the provost marshal to be an idle person. Further, any man who resisted arrest by the provost could be executed by martial law. Along with notorious wrongdoers, martial law commissioners in Ireland could execute the poor Irish – known through their dress, occupation, or name – upon sight if they did not possess a pass.

The best evidence for how these commissions were used comes from a report of service prepared by Piers Butler Fitz Edmond of Roscrea in 1589. FitzEdmond had received a commission of martial law in February 1586 while sheriff of County Tipperary.[19] In 1589, he sought to secure a pension from the lord deputy and thought that by listing his services performed he might obtain his goal. In the document, FitzEdmond listed all of the Irish rebels he had either caught or killed while in the service of the Earl of Ormond and all those he had personally killed "then and there" by martial law. Because he prepared this list in the hope that he would be rewarded, we know it comprised actions FitzEdmond believed the lord deputy and the Crown wanted performed by martial law commissioners. All in all, FitzEdmond listed sixteen executions over the course of his three years as sheriff by martial law. Ten of those executed were supposed thieves. Three were "known" to have participated in rebellion. One had supposedly aided traitors. One was a suspected arsonist. One had spoiled and broken up a house. These were a range of wrongs not simply that of treason through open war against the Crown. Reputation provided the proof. FitzEdmond executed

[18] "Acts of the Privy Council in Ireland, 1556–71," *HMC Haliday*, 20–1; LPL, Ms. 597, fos. 189–91v; LPL, Ms. 616, 114–17; NLI, Ms. 18,768; NLI, Ms. d. 2688–89.

[19] "Note of all suche Good Seruyces and worthie exploytes w[hi]ch Piers Butler Fiz Edmond of Roscrea ... hathe done in her Ma[jes]ties Realme of Irelande ...," TNA, SP 63/149, f. 215. *Fiants*, Elizabeth, no. 4963.

suspects because they were "known," "notable," "common or vagrant," "notorious," or of "evil fame and name." As Edward II had executed Thomas of Lancaster due to the notoriety of his offense, so now Piers Butler of Roscrea executed suspects by manifest proofs in Tipperary.

We began this section by making a distinction between plenary and summary martial law. Let us end by blurring that distinction. In three of the cases, Piers Butler obtained a confession – in other words full proof – before he proceeded to sentence. In later instructions, the Irish Privy Council authorized Warham St. Leger to torture suspects, signaling a desire for more traditional proofs.[20] Further, by 1569 the "watchmen" on the highways were required to bring travelers before the commissioners. One can imagine a short hearing taking place on occasions such as these – provided that officers in the countryside actually followed their instructions.[21] On the other hand, we have already seen the Earl of Leicester convict by his senses in his host in the Low Countries, and at least on one occasion the Dublin government allowed army officers to make similar summary convictions on soldiers in Ireland.[22] On the ground, the differences between summary and plenary martial law were never as clear as later jurists made them out to be. Nevertheless, sheriffs like Piers Butler in all likelihood used manifest proofs more often than plenary martial law commissioners because of the nature of their instructions. The question is, why did someone as lowly as Piers Butler of Roscrea receive the power to convict and execute a suspect by manifest proof in the first place?

The Earl of Sussex and the making of the summary martial law regime

The answer lay with Thomas Radcliffe, the future third Earl of Sussex, and his plans for Ireland's reformation.[23] It would be Sussex, the same man who supervised the executions by martial law in the north of England in 1570, and who was apparently shocked by Elizabeth's desire to execute Peter Birchet by martial law in 1573, who would first implement the martial law policies that remained an important and extremely controversial component of Ireland's legal order through the end of the century. He and his successors did so for three reasons. First, they wanted to use

---

[20] LPL, Ms. 597, f. 446v.   [21] *Fiants*, Elizabeth, no. 1411.

[22] See the fiant issued for Thomas Lee's commission of martial law in 1597. *Fiants, Elizabeth*, no. 6135. Others made no distinction. See *Fiants, Elizabeth*, nos. 940, 961.

[23] For Sussex, see Wallace T. MacCaffery, "Radcliffe, Thomas, Third Earl of Sussex," in *ODNB*. Radcliffe did not become the Earl of Sussex until 1557, but for the sake of simplicity, I will just refer to him as Sussex throughout this chapter.

martial law to terrify the poor into acquiring passes. This was part of a larger policy of surveillance that had the end goal of eliminating private armies. Second, martial law commissioners were meant to complement common law officers who had been unable to catch and prosecute suspected felons. As we have seen, Piers Butler used his martial law commission most often to execute felons, not traitors. Nevertheless, third, martial law commissioners were to punish those who had actively fought against the Crown immediately by martial law to terrify others into obedience.

Sussex first proposed summary martial law in Ireland in 1556 in a treatise he wrote, entitled "A Present Remedy for the Reformation of the North and the rest of Ireland," which outlined how he would resolve the problems English governors faced there.[24] Ireland, while now a kingdom, was still mostly autonomous from Mary's rule. In the north, consistent military actions by Gaelic lords threatened the security of the Pale. In the south and in the west, the Crown claimed little authority over the strong Anglo-Norman and Gaelic magnates who ruled more or less as independent sovereigns. In the Pale, those who claimed English descent had been clamoring for reform for decades. They wanted a stronger central government to install a more regularized court system and to put an end to the private retinues and armies that consistently disrupted the peace even in county Dublin. As Ciaran Brady has rightfully noted, most of Sussex's plans to redress these problems were unoriginal.[25] But there was one notable exception. Sussex argued that marshals or provost marshals should be sent through the realm to search for "suspect p[er]sons, vacabounds & all other ydell and maysterles men" and to punish them by martial law.[26] Summary execution by martial law was a part of a larger attempt to reform Ireland.

Sussex's proposal provokes many questions as to where he got the idea to grant a martial law jurisdiction that used manifest proofs to convict vagabonds and suspect persons. Harsh measures were not unusual in the regulation of the wandering poor because, according to contemporary social theory, these masterless men naturally tended toward wrongdoing.[27] They were also frequently conceived of as lying outside the "commonwealth," or even being enemies to it because they produced nothing for its benefit.[28] Many commentators wanted these criminals in

---

[24] "A Present Remedy for the Reformacion of the north and the rest of Ireland," TNA, SP 62/1, fos. 50–2.

[25] Brady, *Chief Governors*, 52–69.   [26] "Present Reformacion," TNA, SP 62/1, f.52.

[27] Paul Slack, *Poverty and Policy in Tudor and Stuart England* (London, 1988), 91–107; A.L. Beier, *Masterless Men: The Vagrancy Problem in England, 1560–1640* (London, 1985), esp. 152–3; Roger B. Manning, *Village Revolts: Social Protest and Popular Disturbance in England, 1509–1640* (Oxford, 1988), 157–86.

[28] Raphael Holinshed, *The Firste [laste] Volume of the Chronicles of England, Scotlande, and Irelande* ... (London, 1577), 107.

waiting to be sent back to their county, town, or village where they would be supervised by local authorities. In order to accomplish this task, some statutes on vagrancy prescribed extraordinary punishments like slavery in the hope of terrifying vagabonds into acquiescing to Crown demands.[29] There were also continental examples of summary executions of vagabonds. Some monarchs on the continent in periods of war had given summary powers of execution to provosts for vagabonds, deserters, and highway robbers. We know that Sussex had traveled extensively on the European continent. By 1556, he had already served as an envoy to France, the Low Countries, and to Spain in the service of Phillip II. Unfortunately, there is no definitive proof that Sussex borrowed these practices so he could employ them in Ireland.[30] There are also examples within English law for the granting of conviction by the senses. The most common was for contempt. At times, conviction by the senses was also granted to prosecute riot.[31] During the 1490s, Justices of the Peace often possessed powers to convict men of being illegal retainers or liveries of lords upon sight.[32] Sussex may have thought of these examples, although none of them allowed for capital punishment.

Similarly, Sussex had a variety of different examples to choose from when it came to the use of public infamy and notoriety. We shall recall that in the Middle Ages kings could convict on their record notorious traitors. Certain continental courts also convicted strangers solely by their reputation.[33] Church courts similarly used manifest proofs frequently in the Middle Ages, and, although church courts in general used them less in the sixteenth century, the Marian Regime probably deployed notoriety as a form of proof in the infamous heresy trials of the reign.[34] Even at common law "notoriety" continued to be used for the purposes of

---

[29] 1 Edw. VI c.3.

[30] Lindsay Boynton, "The Tudor Provost Marshal," *EHR* 77:304 (July, 1962): 437–9; Georges Guichard, *La Jurisdiction des Prévots du Connétablie et des Maréchaux de France* (Lille, 1926), 27–65.

[31] In the case of riot, the JP was commanded to go to a place of the forcible entry. If the JP saw that anyone was currently holding a place forcibly, he could convict them upon sight. See, for example, 15 Rich. II c. 2. J.H. Baker has described these powers as conviction in open court "where knowledge of the offence was conveyed through their own senses." Baker, "Criminal Courts and Procedure at Common Law 1550–1800," in *Crime in England, 1500–1800* ed. J.S. Cockburn (Princeton, 1977), 24. J.C. Fox, The *History of Contempt of Court* (Oxford, 1927).

[32] These policies were an attempt by the Crown to circumscribe but not eliminate the military powers of the nobility. See S.J. Gunn, *Early Tudor Government, 1485–1558* (New York, 1995), 42–8.

[33] Laura Stokes, *Demons of Urban Reform: Early European Witch Trials and Criminal Justice, 1430–1530* (Basingstoke, 2011), 84–5.

[34] Eamon Duffy, *Fires of Faith: Catholic England under Mary Tudor* (New Haven, 2009), 105.

arraignment. By the Statute of Westminster, judges could forcefully imprison – and later practice *pein fort et dure* – notorious suspects who refused to plea, but they could not use those practices on those only lightly suspected.[35]

Finally, Sussex was likely influenced by summary martial law practices within England. However, as with the others, it is difficult to locate his practice with previous uses of martial law. The most likely influences are martial law proclamations in England. Henry VII commanded constables to "repress ... all manner of insurrections, riots, routs, unlawfull assemblies; and all other misdoers."[36] It is unclear if this proclamation granted them powers of execution. A clearer inheritance comes from Henry VIII's 1536 proclamation that ordered punishment for unlawful assemblies. He cautioned those currently assembling to go back to their homes. If they refused, he would destroy "them, their wives, and children, with fire and sword, to the most terrible example of such rebels and offenders."[37] The phrase "fire and sword" can be found in several Irish fiants to delegated authorities.[38] But Henry's threat in 1536 said nothing about vagrants. It is also unclear if he even understood "fire and sword" to be an identical practice as martial law.

The Edwardian government probably used a summary variant of martial law. In the summer of 1549, during the height of the rebellions against the regime, it issued a proclamation declaring martial law on any rioters.[39] The regime made this proclamation after it had issued pardons to all past rioters and after it ordered its magistrates to investigate the causes of the riots and punish those who had committed wrongs. In July, the regime issued a proclamation that declared that any rioter could be punished "upon pain of death presently to be suffered and executed by the authority and order of law martial, wherein no delay or differing of time shall be

---

[35] James Heath, *Torture and English Law: An Administrative and Legal History from the Plantagenets to the Stuarts* (Westport, CT, 1982), 254–5, n. 11; "The First Statute of Westminster," 3 Edw. I c. 12.

[36] The legality of proclamations will be discussed later in this chapter. *TRP*, 1: no. 19. There is also a proclamation from the time of Henry VII that demanded rebels to submit themselves, otherwise their lives were to be forfeit. *TRP*, 1: no. 8.

[37] *TRP*, 1: no. 168.

[38] *Fiants*, Mary, no. 228; *Fiants, Elizabeth*, nos. 828, 1452, 2445, 2997, 3601–2, 5428, 5891, 5932, 6020, 6111, 6116, 6290–1.

[39] *TRP*, 1: no. 341. The edition of Tudor Royal Proclamations is generally excellent. However, in certain instances the authors seem to have crafted their own titles for proclamations that were not in the original editions. For example, a June 1549 proclamation that threatened future rioters with punishment by the laws of the realm has been labeled by Hughes and Larkin as "Pardoning Enclosure Rioters; Ordering Martial Law against Future Rioters." *TRP*, 1: no. 334. However, there is no reference to martial law in the title of the original version of the proclamation and martial law does not appear in the body of the text. The same can be said for *TRP*, 2: no. 438.

permitted or suffered."[40] However, the sheriff could not actually execute the offender based on his own judgment. Instead, the officer had to attach them to jail and then notify the Lord Protector or his council. In the end they would be the ones who could order the execution. This command makes several stories from chroniclers of the rebellions of 1549 about the use of summary martial law difficult to verify.[41]

At the same time, the Edwardian government created county officers who had powers of martial law. At the height of the rising in 1549, Edward's council thought about creating county "marshals" to apprehend mutineers and rebels. The plan outlined that they would then bring the prisoner before a panel of four men of the county, two sheriffs and two gentlemen who would examine the defendant and adjudge guilt. If they decided the defendant was guilty, he or she was to be executed immediately on the next market day.[42] After they had quelled the uprisings, the king's council began to make plans for how these sorts of uprisings could be prevented in the future. One of their solutions was to create a lord lieutenant in every county of the realm during periods of turbulence. The lord lieutenant became the Crown's chief military officer of the county. The Edwardian government decided to give these lords lieutenants a martial law jurisdiction. A lieutenancy commission from 1552 allowed the lieutenant to "fight against the king's enemies and rebels and to execute upon them the martial law and to subdue invasions, insurrections, etc."[43] The Crown consistently put a clause that granted martial law jurisdiction over rebels and invaders in lieutenancy commissions. Provost marshals could be appointed by the lord lieutenant, but it seems that they could not execute martial law without the lord lieutenant's assent.[44]

---

[40] *TRP*, 1: no. 341.

[41] Richard Grafton, *Grafton's Chronicle, or History of England. To which is added his table of bailiffs, sheriffs, and mayors, of the city of London. From the year 1189 to 1558 inclusive* 2 vols. (London, 1809), 2: 519–20. There are some stories from 1549 of both London magistrates and county provost marshals using martial law. They may very well be true but are difficult to substantiate. For an analysis of the chronicle tradition, see B.L. Beer, "London and the Rebellions of 1548–9," *JBS* 12:1 (November, 1972): 27–30; Boynton, "The Tudor Provost Marshal," 440.

[42] "Ordre to be taken for repressing of commotions and vproars iff any suche shall happen," TNA, SP 10/8/9. For the creation of the lieutenancy, see Gladys Scott Thomson, *Lords Lieutenants in the Sixteenth Century: A Study in Tudor Local Administration* (London, 1923), 14–42; Neil Younger, *War and Politics in the Elizabethan Counties* (Manchester, 2012).

[43] Notice of Commission of Lieutenancy for the Duke of Somerset (5 May, 5 Edw. VI), reprinted in Thomson, *Lords Lieutenants*, 149–50. The commissions of lieutenancy under Mary commanded that they could kill any enemies or rebels by any means necessary. Thomson, *Lords Lieutenants*, 150–1.

[44] Provosts could only execute by martial law after the lord lieutenant had authorized it. See The Marquis of Northampton to William More, 30 June 1552, SHC, 6729/10, f. 12.

While he had plenty of examples to draw on, Sussex and his successors clearly adapted martial law in an attempt to resolve their perceived problems with governing Ireland. One of the key problems was the private armies of Gaelic and Old English lords. Proclamations of martial law were intended to help English legal officials keep track of the Irish poor so they would not end up raiding English settlements. Further, through fear and violence, English administrators hoped to show the poor that wealthy Irish lords could no longer protect them. As David Edwards has rightly noted, "[t]hreatening the peasantry was a guaranteed way to sever the ties binding the broad mass of ordinary people to their traditional local rulers."[45]

Sussex and his successors circumscribed these powers in two ways. First, the commissioner utilized martial law only on those who possessed less than £10 moveable property or 40s in real property. At times, these thresholds varied. As we have seen, the purpose was to prevent the wealthy from being tried by martial law because real property was not forfeit due to a martial law conviction and because martial law commissioners were allowed to keep one-third of all forfeited moveable property while the Crown only received two-thirds.[46] Second, martial law commissioners were supposed to keep track of all those they had executed, and every month they were supposed to send this list to the lord deputy. Presumably, he could punish his commissioners for malfeasance if they had executed someone illegally. These were not strong constraints.

In the instructions, Sussex and his successors mandated that martial law commissioners put forth proclamations stating their powers. The poor Irish were supposed to obtain passes so that the number of servants of any lord in Ireland could be tracked. It also seems likely that some English officials wanted to turn the poor Irish into sedentary farmers. We learn this from the one possible surviving proclamation from Munster, likely written by John Perrot in 1571 during the first Desmond rebellion.[47] The proclamation is disturbing: *every* landowner in the province could summarily execute any known criminals and rebels upon

---

[45] David Edwards, "The Escalation of Violence in Sixteenth-Century Ireland," in *Age of Atrocity: Violence and Political Conflict in Early Modern Ireland* ed. David Edwards, Pádraig Lenihan & Clodagh Tait (Dublin, 2009), 74.

[46] This rule is stipulated in the instructions to the commissioner. See *HMC, Haliday*, 21. This rule is probably derived from the penal laws, where informants were allowed one-third of the fine of those convicted because the Crown understood them to be acting prosecutors.

[47] "Laws and Ordinances proclaimed at Limerick by Sir John Perrott, Lord President of Munster," 1571, LPL, Ms. 614, fos. 229–36. It is also possible that these are (highly) adapted ordinances of war meant specifically for the civilian population in Munster. Carew dates this 1569, but Perrot was not lord president then.

sight. It was also preoccupied with reform. Like most English social commentators, the proclamation believed idleness to be the cause of criminality. In the Irish lordships, the practice of herding – while an occupation – supposedly produced too much idleness. In their downtime, they joined private retinues and created havoc. Thus, along with punishment, idlers needed to be taught to learn "tillage." Sons of farmers needed to continue the family's occupation.

Martial law was thus part of a plan of reformation that would transform a mobile herding society into something that more closely resembled English society. While more draconian, there are some similarities between this proclamation and previous vagrancy statutes. These since Henry VIII had demanded that local officers – sheriffs, mayors, constables and the like – maintain lists of all men within their jurisdiction that begged for a living. If the beggar was not from the region, the officer was to give them a passport to return to their home, where they could either apply for a license to beg or, if they continued to refuse to work and were able-bodied, would suffer imprisonment along with corporal punishment.[48] Summary martial law was a far more violent method of getting supposed idlers to work.

Along with the control and supervision of the poor, martial law commissioners were also supposed to act as auxiliary police officers in the aid of often overmatched local law officers. They were to investigate robberies and murders, detain the aiders of felonies for prosecution at law, and supervise the highways. With this last responsibility, martial law commissioners could upon sight punish at their discretion anyone wearing Irish dress, who did not possess a passport, and who was travelling at night unaccompanied. They could also execute resistors of arrest. It is probable that Sussex and his followers installed these more severe measures due to the inefficiency of the assizes and the relative ease by which wanted suspects escaped capture and trial.[49] Rather than use outlawry and the posse which were not all that effective in England, let alone in unsupervised Ireland, the Dublin government opted for summary martial law.[50]

Crown officers simultaneously pursued prosecutions of felony and treason by both martial law and common law. In 1566, for example, Sir

---

[48] 33 Henry VIII c.15 Ir.

[49] Regular assizes were not established until after the end of the nine years' war in Connacht and Munster. Jon G. Crawford, *A Star Chamber Court in Ireland: The Court of Castle Chamber, 1571–1641* (Dublin, 2005), 48–9.

[50] Susan Stewart, "Outlawry as an Instrument of Justice in the Thirteenth Century," in *Outlaws in Medieval and Early Modern England* ed. John C. Appleby and Paul Dalton (Farnham, Surrey, 2009), 51–4.

Henry Sidney, the lord deputy of Ireland, reported to the English Privy Council that he "caused sessions to be held" in all the counties of Leinster and in certain parts of Munster.[51] He claimed that he executed fifty traitors at common law, while he executed over twenty by "martiall order." He made a similar distinction in 1577, when he reported his judicial undertakings to the Crown.[52] The Earl of Ormond, writing to William Cecil in 1586, declared that "sword, the m[ar]shall law, and of late the common law" had gotten rid of treasonous and criminal people in the county of Kilkenny, where the earl resided.[53] Perhaps the "of late" referred to the increased usage of commissions of *oyer and terminer* at the expense of martial law jurisdiction, but nothing is certain. Martial law was a complement to both common law and military conquest.

These multiple paths were also available during the great rebellions of the period. William Fitzwilliam, the lord justice of Ireland, wrote in 1571 during the Desmond rebellion to Elizabeth that Irish rebels would be prosecuted by the "ordenarie tryall of lawe and those of the vyle and base sort by your marshall lawe." Those in the field and those fleeing were killed by the sword.[54] The Earl of Ormond likewise in 1570 reported that he had executed 200 traitors by martial law, and he had delivered "divers others" to be tried at common law.[55] In another account of the justice following the Desmond rebellion, Sir John Perrot, the lord president of Munster, reported that he had hanged 800 rebels, "by the Lawes of this Realme and also by the mershall lawe."[56] He did not say how these executions had been divided. Arthur Lord Grey de Wilton likewise reported that he had killed over 1,500 men and women in his attempt to put down the second Desmond rebellion. Some of this number were put to death by martial law.[57] Perhaps, courts-martial were used in these cases as they had been in England in 1570. In all likelihood, these mass executions involved both manifest proofs and more detailed investigations when English commissioners desired to separate wealthy traitors from poorer ones.

---

[51] Sidney to Privy Council, 15 April 1566, TNA, SP 63/17, f. 31.

[52] Sir Henry Sidney to the Privy Council, 27 April 1576, *Calendar of the Carew Manuscripts preserved in the Archiepiscopal Library at Lambeth, 1575–1588* ed. J.S. Brewer and William Bullen (London, 1868), 52.

[53] Ormond to William Cecil, TNA, SP 63/110, f. 125v.

[54] Sir William Fitzwilliam to Elizabeth, 29 September 1571, TNA, SP 63/34, f. 38. The jail record of Kilkenny was sent to Elizabeth. Suspects were hanged, executed by the sword, bailed, slain, or killed. *Ibid.*, f. 39.

[55] "Some Part of the Earl of Ormond's Service done since 13 August 1569 by virtue of his Commission and Instructions given to him by Lord Deputy Sidney and the Council," TNA, SP 63/39, f. 156v.

[56] Sir John Perrot to the Privy Council, 9 April 1573, TNA, SP 63/40, f. 57.

[57] Edwards, "Ideology and Experience: Spenser's View and Martial Law in Ireland," in *Political ideology in Ireland, 1541–1641* ed. Hiram Morgan (Dublin, 1999), 135.

Jurisdiction and summary martial law in Ireland

The Dublin government granted summary martial law jurisdiction widely in Ireland from 1558 until the early 1590s. By that time, delegated authorities throughout the island, including the colonizers of Ulster, received summary martial law powers from the Dublin government. Its jurisdiction became increasingly controversial. Palesmen bitterly protested abuses by martial law commissioners. English Privy Council members increasingly argued that the extensive and unsupervised delegation of martial law powers might in fact hurt their imperial project. With more and more complaints and with more transplanted Englishmen due to arrive in Ireland from the 1580s onwards, the English Privy Council wanted martial law jurisdiction circumscribed and supervised.

It was wary of the project from the beginning. When Sussex arrived as lord deputy in the summer of 1556, he commissioned summary martial law for delegates to use in Ulster. He and the Irish Privy Council granted the new "marshal of Ulster," George Stanley, powers to "execute the marshall lawe in all cases thought by him to be convenient."[58] In September, the Irish Privy Council gave identical powers to the new general of Ulster, Andrew Brereton.[59] By November, Sussex planned on issuing multiple commissions of martial law, and the Irish Privy Council accordingly drafted instructions that were to accompany the commissions.[60] However, Sussex stopped issuing commissions of summary martial law for a time after his initial authorizations.

His plans were probably stopped by the English Privy Council. Summary martial law during times of peace on vagrants was a new concept and one the council thought illegal. In September 1556, the Council sent Sussex a message thanking him for his service. However, they cautioned him on his proposal to punish vagabonds by martial law:

those lewde personnes do well deserve severe ponishment, y[e]t do they thinke it not best they be proceaded withall by the marshall lawe, but that whensoever he shall finde any suche notable offendours he do cause them to be ordered and ponisshed according to the laws of the realme.[61]

No martial law jurisdiction for the prosecution of vagabonds exists for the remainder of Mary's reign. Sussex instead only issued commissions to punish those in open rebellion by martial law.[62]

---

[58] "The Irish Privy Council Book 1556–71," in *HMC, Haliday*, 6–7.   [59] *Ibid.*, 10–11.
[60] *Ibid.*, 20–1.
[61] *APC*, 5: 349. Apparently, Sussex had reiterated his plans to the council in August 1556.
[62] *Fiants*, Mary, nos. 228–9, 242.

In 1559, under Elizabeth, Sussex began issuing more summary martial law commissions. By January of that year, he issued commissions that allowed commissioners in Wexford, Waterford, Meath, Louth, Carlow, and many other areas powers to "execute martial law . . . on all persons not having 20s hereditaments, found to be felons, rebels, enemies, or notorious malefactors."[63] What would become the paradigmatic commissions of martial law were issued in 1560.[64] Sussex probably issued these commissions – and was allowed to do so – due to the security concerns the Dublin government faced in Ulster as a result of the increased power and belligerence of Shane O'Neill as well as a change in policy from the Privy Council of the new regime.[65] Sussex led multiple expeditions into Ulster in an attempt to neutralize the threat Shane posed. In all probability, he issued the martial law commissions to delegates within the Pale out of a fear that Shane O'Neill might incite rebellion as a part of his military strategy.[66] The commissions were supposed to put down through fear any unwarranted gatherings and to eliminate those who English officials deemed to be "traitors in waiting:" the vagrants and idlers.

The martial law commissions became a normative component of the legal order from 1560–1582. Sussex, who retained his post until 1564, granted martial law commissions on a yearly basis to the commissioners who operated in the Pale and in the territories associated with the lordship of the Earl of Ormond. He also on occasion nominated a marshal of Ireland who possessed a martial law jurisdiction. Twice he gave them to delegates sent to the O'Byrnes and O'Tooles country south of Dublin in an attempt to obtain their obedience.[67] After his departure in 1564, subsequent lord deputies granted summary martial law commissions to several types of officers.[68] First, they granted them to their lord presidents

---

[63] *Fiants*, Elizabeth, no. 26. Also see, *Ibid.*, nos. 32, 39, 46–7, 53–7, 182, 193.

[64] *Ibid.*, no. 218.   [65] For Sussex's rivalry with Shane O'Neill, see Brady, 99–101.

[66] Sussex by 1560 convinced the English Privy Council that O'Neill might encourage tumult and rebellion within the Pale and elsewhere in Ireland and needed to be destroyed. Brady, *The Chief Governors*, 100.

[67] *Fiants*, Elizabeth, nos. 218, 230, 251, 264, 285, 304, 395, 443, 469, 502, 580, 581, 582, 590, 682.

[68] *Ibid.*, nos. 724-5, 819, 824, 828, 861, 896, 939–40, 953, 961, 979, 999, 1007, 1010–15, 1019–20, 1027, 1059, 1086, 1119, 1190–92, 1196, 1233, 1253, 1261–3, 1270, 1283, 1302, 1329–30, 1335–6, 1379, 1382–3, 1412, 1416, 1432, 1457, 1487–8, 1505–7, 1518, 1520, 1535, 1548, 1636–7, 1647, 1661, 1728, 1782, 1810–12, 1814–15, 1829–35, 1845, 1855–6, 2092, 2094, 2099–2100, 2104–5, 2114–5, 2119–20, 2123, 2133, 2139–40, 2143–4, 2150, 2152, 2162–3, 2174–5, 2181, 2183, 2195, 2200, 2220–2, 2292–3, 2326, 2351, 2359–61, 2364, 2374, 2379, 2390–1, 2404, 2430, 2437, 2456, 2461, 2484, 2521, 2529–31, 2536, 2544, 2553–5, 2751, 2757, 2766, 2772, 2775, 2807, 2814, 2815, 2821, 2824, 2829–30, 2841–2, 2844, 2851, 2863, 2868–70, 2899, 2905, 2907, 2912, 2916, 2918–23, 2933, 2937, 2945, 2949–50, 2952, 2958, 2975, 2979, 2991–3, 2997, 2999, 3001, 3019, 3051, 3061–2, 3143–5, 3168, 3178, 3188, 3190, 3233, 3482, 3486–8, 3517, 3523–4, 3528, 3588–96,

in Munster and then in Connacht, starting in 1569, who were supposed to bring all of Dublin's laws to these previously disobedient areas.[69] Second, martial law commissions were granted to English constables or "seneschals" in Irish polities.[70] Third, the lord deputy granted martial law powers to Anglo-Irish and Irish magnates. Fourth, the sheriffs, constables of English counties, and provost marshals assigned to regions like Munster received martial law powers. Even mayors of towns were also included in martial law commissions.

Given the sheer number of martial law commissioners who had discretion over life and limb, it is not surprising that protests began to emerge. The brutality of Arthur Lord Grey de Wilton's employment of martial law in the aftermath of the second Desmond rebellion also provoked outrage among influential and loyal lords in Ireland, who gained a hearing in England to voice their concerns.[71] The Catholic Old English of the Pale and of the port towns began to protest the abuse of martial law powers by commissioners who generally were protestant newcomers to Ireland. Some of those enraged by these new governors revolted in 1580 under the Viscount Baltinglass.[72] Some of their complaints were outlined in a short tract entitled "A Remembrance for Ireland."[73]

The tract complained that the commissions of martial law had been given to men of "meane calling," who used their discretionary power to make any law that they wanted. So terrified were the Old English of these martial law commissioners, according to the "Remembrance," that many had fled into Ulster in order to avoid their arbitrary power. The "Remembrance for Ireland" was only the first of several tracts decrying the abuse of power by martial law commissioners. Many claimed that the seneschals, sheriffs, and provost marshals used their martial law powers to extort Crown subjects. Provosts and sheriffs, after all, could claim the moveable property of those executed.[74] Martial law commissioners in all probability created protection rackets in their territories.[75]

3601–2, 3623, 3626–8, 3630–1, 3636, 3669–70, 3695, 3756, 3816, 3848–9, 3860, 4040–2, 4045–7, 4050–3, 4055, 4057–60, 4062–5, 4098.

[69] For these tribunals in Ireland, see Canny, *The Elizabethan Conquest of Ireland*, 93–116.

[70] Brady, *The Chief Governors*, 271–90.

[71] Edwards, "Ideology and Experience," 127–57.

[72] Brady, *The Chief Governors*, 204–7.

[73] "A Remembrance for Ireland," TNA, SP 63/90, f. 150.

[74] "Note of Matters to be laid to Captain Heron's Charge," TNA, SP 63/12, f. 37. The accounts date to 1558, but Heron first received a martial law commission in 1560. *Fiants*, Elizabeth, no. 218. Heron earned money from "fines" at martial law and from the moveable property of felons. For the actions of a provost marshal in Ireland, see M.D. O'Sullivan, "Barnabe Googe: Provost Marshal of Connacht, 1582–1585," *Journal of the Galway Archaeological and Historical Society* 18:1/2 (1938): 1–39.

[75] Rapple, *Martial Power and Elizabethan Political Culture*, 240–3.

Controversies over martial law erupted again in 1585, this time in Connacht. In 1585, Sir Richard Bingham, the lord president of Connacht, used his martial law jurisdiction to threaten Gaelic lords into submission. In 1585, the Irish government came up with a new composition scheme that allowed Gaelic lords to claim exemption from taxation on their demesne lands if they agreed to end practices like Coigne and Livery and submit disputes to the presidency courts. Some, like the Burkes of County Mayo, felt insecure about the increased supervision by the English president. The leadership of the Burke lordship also became personally hostile to Bingham, who had attempted to assert his authority over the province through demands of loyalty and through brutal common law sessions held in Galway. The Burkes refused to submit, and Bingham responded by executing several important members by martial law. A short insurrection followed, which forced the lord deputy to lead a host into Connacht: an expensive and undesirable measure.[76]

The complaints against Bingham continued well after he put down the Burkes' rebellion. By this point, Connacht was inhabited not just by the Irish but also by new English settlers and former inhabitants of the Pale who had traveled to Connacht and invested in land in the aftermath of the formation of the provincial council.[77] These families had come to the province in part on the assurance that it would be governed by English common law, which supposedly would protect them from the depredations of the Irish lords. But increasingly, these families were worried about the depredations of the English lord president. Much resentment grew about Bingham's style of rule. A revolt in Iar-Connacht, a province in the far west of the region, erupted in no small measure due to the president's brutality toward dissidents.

All of these problems with martial law inspired arguments at various moments for the restriction of its jurisdiction. In 1583, a former lord deputy of Ireland and member of the English Privy Council, Sir James Crofts, in two separate tracts made what would become common jurisdictional boundaries for martial law.[78] Crofts believed Ireland could

---

[76] Rory Rapple, "Taking up Office in Elizabethan Connacht: The Case of Sir Richard Bingham," *EHR* (April, 2008): 277–99. "A True Discourse of the Late Rebellion of the Bourkes," November 1586, TNA, SP 63/126, fos. 216–219. "A Discourse of the Services done by Sir Richard Bingham in the County of Mayo," October 1586, TNA, SP 63/126, fos. 146–153v.

[77] Bernadette Cunningham, "The Composition of Connaught in the Lordships of Clanrickard and Thomond 1577–1641," *Irish Historical Studies* 24 (1984): 1–14; Mary O'Dowd, *Power, Politics, and Land: Early Modern Sligo, 1568–1688* (Belfast, 1991), 35–40.

[78] Sir James Crofts, "Arte Militarye, Dec. 1583," NRO, Fitzwilliam MS. 67 (Irish), fos. 1–6; Crofts, "A Discourse for the Reformacons of Ireland [1583]," NRO, Fitzwilliam Ms. 67 (Irish), fos. 7–12v.

never be "reduced to obedience" unless the governors there cared more for the implementation of justice. He was, as Cecil would later be, deeply troubled that sheriffs either had to compete with provosts with martial law jurisdiction or had martial law powers themselves. He was concerned because he believed martial law to be "vnnaturall" and "vnseemly."[79] It created more disorder than it quieted. For Crofts, martial law needed to be doubly bound. It should only be used "in tyme of hostilitie" or a "tyme of warr." Further, it was to be used "in ye campe onelie." In other words, Crofts wanted martial law jurisdiction bound to the host. He also demanded that only the marshal and his delegates receive martial law powers. This highly restricted jurisdiction, which he may have obtained from Sir Thomas Smith's *De Republica Anglorum*, would become very popular during the Restoration.[80]

Along with Crofts' concerns, Elizabeth worried that unsupervised martial law commissions were hurting the imperial project. We have already seen that Elizabeth came to believe that martial law practice was "dishonourable."[81] Like Crofts, she wanted sheriffs stripped of their martial law powers. She also wanted to end the practice of clearing the jails through martial law and jurisdiction shopping in general: a practice that had clearly taken place in the past.[82] One of the largest problems in delegating such extensive jurisdiction was that traitors who possessed real property were being executed by martial law. These summary executions prevented the Crown from seizing real property and moveable goods because, as we shall recall, real property was traditionally only forfeited upon conviction by one's peers.[83] Further, martial law commissioners had the right to claim a portion of the moveable goods, preventing the Crown from fully profiting from the execution.

Indeed, Irish families successfully defended their titles to land by taking advantage of the fact that their ancestors had been executed by summary martial law. We do not know how many engaged in this strategy because legal records for the sixteenth century are so scarce. But there are at least two extant records that reveal the irony that martial law could hinder English imperial designs. Both examples are cases heard before

---

[79] *Ibid.*, fos. 11, 12v.

[80] *Ibid.*, f. 11. Sir Thomas Smith, *De Republica Anglorum* ed. Mary DeWar (Cambridge, 1982), 85.

[81] BL, Add. Ms. 37,536, f. 14v.

[82] The Irish government, with the full knowledge of Sir Francis Walsingham, executed Dermot O'Hurley by martial law after realizing that he might be innocent of treason at common law. For the story, see David Edwards, "Dermot O'Hurley," *ODNB*. Lords Justices to Walsingham, 7 March 1584, TNA, SP 63/108, fos. 25–6. Loftus and Wallop to Walsingham, 9 July 1584, TNA, SP 63/111, f. 27.

[83] BL, Add. Ms. 37,536, f. 14v.

commissions of inquest which the Crown, starting in the middle of the 1580s and continuing into the 1590s, commanded to operate in order to find concealed Crown lands – land held by tenants without legal title that the Crown could recover in order to sell it for a profit. The commissioners comprised the chief legal officers of each county. These men would impanel a jury, who in turn would hear information from local authorities into landholdings.

Unfortunately, the records of these two inquests are brief. The first comes from a hearing on 14 April 1591, when Crown officers in County Wexford obtained information on the lands and tenements of five men who had been executed in Dublin by martial law. Why were these landholders brought to Dublin and executed by martial law? At least one commentator, who was an English soldier and administrator, wrote that martial law commissioners took the land of prominent householders by arresting them, sending them to Dublin to be executed at martial law, presumably by the lord deputy or a prominent government official, and then divvying up their land.[84] They also might have been abettors of traitors, an offense that usually required the Dublin authorities for condemnation rather than simply a provost.[85] In any event, the jury found the information to be true, therefore "they find that all and singular which the aforesaid persons so hanged by Marshall Law or ought to have at the time of their deaths shall be and remain to their heirs and assignes."[86] Because the men had died by martial law, their real property descended to their heirs. A year later another family came before a similar commission to uncover concealed Crown lands in county Tipperary and used an identical strategy to recover their property. They secured title because they were the lawful heirs to a man who had been executed by martial law.[87]

In light of these concerns, the English Privy Council put forth yet another restriction on martial law powers. Because it was supposedly dishonorable, Elizabeth, like Crofts, wanted to eliminate martial law commissions to sheriffs. But more importantly, she wanted to transform

---

[84] Thomas Lee, "A Brief Declaration of the Government of Ireland Opening many Corruptions in ye same: Discovering Discontentments of the Irishry and the Cause of Moving these Expected Troubles," *Desiderata Curiosa Hibernica* 1: 87–114. For the career of Thomas Lee, see John McGurk, "A Soldier's Prescription for the Governance of Ireland, 1599–1601: Captain Thomas Lee and his Tracts," in *Reshaping Ireland, 1550–1700: Colonization and its Consequences: Essays Presented to Nicholas Canny* ed. Brian MacCuarta (Dublin, 2011), 43–60.

[85] *HMC Haliday*, 21.

[86] NLI, Ms. 29,711 (6). This inquisition does not mean, as David Edwards has argued, that the jurors thought "the state was guilty of murder." Instead, the jurors understood that the Crown could not escheat the property from those who had been executed at martial law. Edwards, "Ideology and Experience,"142.

[87] NLI, d. 3181.

summary martial law into a power only to be used on those in the act of committing a crime (*in flagrante crimine*). We have already seen that one of the powers of martial law commissioners in Ireland was that they could execute by martial law those that resisted arrest. In their revised instructions to Perrot, Elizabeth and her council wanted to completely restrict martial law to that power. According to her, martial law should never be used on any who "hath yeelded himselfe to Iustice."[88] It was only for the execution of those in rebellion or those who attempted to seize the queen's castles or forts. Even in those instances, according to the queen, Perrot needed to take counsel before authorizing martial law. Crofts wanted to restrict martial law to soldiers. Elizabeth wanted to restrict it to a power of execution upon rebels and outlaws.

In reality, throughout the 1580s, commissions of summary martial law were still granted with identical powers. But they were delegated to less and less people, particularly after 1586. The Earl of Ormond and his delegates in counties Kilkenny and Tipperary and the presidents of Munster and Connacht had martial law jurisdiction on rebels and invaders. The main region that was relieved from summary martial law commissions was the Pale. No summary martial law commissions were issued for counties Dublin, Meath, or Westmeath in the 1580s; only one commission, to the Earl of Kildare, was issued for county Kildare. In areas that still had a predominant Irish population, like King's and Queen's counties, the policy continued unabated.[89]

Nevertheless, there were further problems. In July 1589, the lord deputy wrote to Cecil about the problems of unsupervised delegated authorities. He had traveled to the west of Ireland in order to restore order to the province and to assert his authority over Bingham. After reviewing many of the "wicked" practices used by inferior officers, Fitzwilliam claimed he restored the country to order. He added that Connacht would remain in order if "wicked and inferior officers and ministers maie be restrained from their bloody part and extorcons and the Comon Lawe onlie vsed."[90] In the early part of the century, Palesmen and others desirous of expanding English rule demanded that if only the arbitrary exactions of Irish lords could be stopped, Ireland could be

---

[88] BL, Add. Ms. 37,536, f. 14v.

[89] Edwards, "Ideology and Experience," 136–7; *Fiants*, Elizabeth, nos. 4105, 4119, 4161, 4190–1, 4249, 4455, 4483–4, 4527, 4530, 4549, 4556, 4573, 4601–2, 4640, 4658, 4790, 4829, 4955, 4962–3, 4967, 5007–8, 5023, 5027, 5039, 5044, 5048, 5109, 5117, 5234, 5238, 5289–90, 5292–3, 5361, 5366, 5393, 5397, 5428.

[90] Fitzwilliam to William Cecil, 3 July 1589, TNA, SP 63/145, f. 111v. Bingham was outraged that his powers were being stripped. Bingham to Walsingham, 11 July 1589, TNA, SP 63/145, fos. 149–50.

pacified. Now this same argument was being used to restrain the provincial officials who had overseen the subduing of the Irish magnates.

What happened next is telling of what central authorities increasingly thought about martial law. It was useful for purposes of terror, but delegating its jurisdiction often caused unwelcome results. Thus, Fitzwilliam deprived Bingham of his martial law jurisdiction but only by "or seacret aduises and commaundemts."[91] Fitzwilliam still wanted the populace of Connacht to think that Bingham had powers of martial law so that they would be too scared to engage in rebellion or sedition. Useful only as a threat, martial law was too dangerous to actually delegate.

By the next year, the English Privy Council had made up its mind that martial law needed to be further controlled by the Dublin government. In January, Walsingham asked Robert Gardiner, the chief justice of Queen's Bench in Ireland, to draft a proclamation to call in the martial law commissions.[92] For Gardiner, the obedience of the population at large meant that the martial law commissions were no longer necessary. It had been but a step in a process of transforming those inclined to resistance into loyal subjects. Now it was dangerous because inferior officers – the senseschals, sheriffs, and captains – exploited their martial law commissions to extort the queen's subjects. Further, Gardiner was disgusted by the thought that commissioners could convict by suspicion of felony alone, even if the suspects were notorious.[93] His views were shared by William Cecil, who wrote two tracts aimed at restricting summary martial law practice in the early 1590s. They contained views similar to those already expressed by Crofts and the Privy Council throughout the 1580s.[94] His views, at least temporarily, were also those of the Privy Council. Only three martial law commissions, which were all issued in 1590, were made from 1590 until 1594.[95]

The desire to supervise and control martial law jurisdiction was part of a larger state-building project in Ireland. The English Privy Council increasingly demanded that the Irish government more closely monitor

---

[91] Fitzwilliam to William Cecil, 3 July 1589, TNA, SP 63/145 f. 111.

[92] Gardiner to Walsingham, 4 January 1590, TNA SP 63/150, fos. 6–7. Gardiner, "A Memorial for Ireland delivered by Justice Gardiner," 4 January 1590, TNA, SP 63/150, f. 14. Christopher Maginn, *William Cecil, Ireland, and the Tudor State* (Oxford, 2012), 105–6.

[93] "Draft Proclamation to Restrain Martial Law in Ireland," TNA, SP 63/150, f. 8v.

[94] "Burghley's Memorial," TNA, SP 63/156/65. He issued another report on Irish legal culture in 1592. "Articles containing things to be considered of by lord deputy and council in Ireland, and answered to Her Majesty," 31 May 1592, TNA, SP 63/164/49 (i). Maginn, *William Cecil, Ireland, and the Tudor State*, 160–2.

[95] *Fiants, Elizabeth*, nos. 5393, 5397. Both were issued in February 1590. Another martial law fiant, but with powers only to execute rebels by fire and sword, was granted to the Lord President of Munster in June 1590. *Fiants, Elizabeth*, no. 5428.

the actions of delegated authorities. Now that the Munster planation had been made, that Connacht had a lord president, and that the great Irish magnates of Ulster had submitted to Elizabeth, the various officials who had received discretionary powers needed to be restrained. Summary martial law would only inhibit colonization and perhaps lead to rebellion by previously loyal subjects. But even as the summary martial law commissions were being drawn in, no one thought of eradicating its jurisdiction altogether. Dishonorable, abused, and in certain ways ineffective in achieving the Crown's aims in Ireland, summary martial law was nevertheless considered to be an important tool of governance provided it was carefully monitored.

Summary martial law in England

We have already seen that the Irish variant of martial law was probably in some measure influenced by martial law proclamations issued in England in 1549. This practice was continued by Mary and Elizabeth who proclaimed martial law in England against heretics and owners of heretical books, pirates and abettors of pirates.[96] Both Mary and Elizabeth's governments considered using summary martial law to put down "stirs." Mary's government in the end did not authorize the jurisdiction, while Elizabeth's was only going to authorize summary martial law in the event of a Spanish landing in 1588.[97] In 1585, with war declared against Spain, Elizabeth's government once again created lords lieutenants who in all likelihood only possessed powers of martial law to slay rebels or invaders in the act of rebelling or invading the English realm. Particularly given what we know about the attempted restriction of martial law in Ireland in

---

[96] *TRP*, 2: no. 443, 699. In 1588, there is evidence that provosts searched for heretical books, but no evidence for executions by martial law. "Letter Book of the Earl of Huntington," HEHL, HM 30,881, fos. 112–113v, 177v. Pirates were perhaps the subject of martial law because juries, often comprised of those who profited from the practice, refused to convict them. The proclamation also perhaps was intended to placate the Spanish who were the targets of piracy. *TRP*, 2: no. 585; Mark Hanna, "The Pirate Nest: The Impact of Piracy on Newport, Rhode Island and Charles Town, South Carolina, 1670–1730" (unpublished PhD Dissertation, Harvard University, 2006), 2.

[97] R.R. Steele, *Catalogue of Tudor and Stuart Proclamations* (Oxford, 1910), no. 486. In August 1558, one of Mary's provosts, Sir Gyles Poole, attempted to put down a riot taking place in St. James' Fair in London. One of his men killed one of the rioters in the process. Mary's Privy Council ordered a coroner's inquest to hear and determine the matter. Presumably if they found a true bill, then the assistant to the provost would have been tried for murder. *APC*, 6: 370. This event has been completely misinterpreted by J.V. Capua. Capua, "The Early History of Martial Law in England from the Fourteenth Century to the Petition of Right," *Cambridge Law Journal* 36:1 (April, 1977): 164. For Elizabethan plans to use martial law in the event of an invasion, see "Council of War Minutes, 1588," BL, Harley Ms. 444, f. 114.

1586, the English Privy Council in all likelihood did not delegate to lieutenants powers to hold a marshal's court. They probably only possessed the power to execute those who were caught red-handed committing rebellion or invasion.[98] In the English variant, it is probable that the Crown and Privy Council only used proclamations for the purposes of terror until 1589. Supervision continued to be important after 1589, when the Elizabethan government expanded martial law jurisdiction to include vagrants, rioters, and those who resisted arrest.

The Crown and its council used proclamations to make laws as well as to communicate to its subjects. In the words of historian Frederic Youngs, proclamations were a "a royal command, normally cast in a distinctive format, which was validated by the royal sign manual, issued under a special Chancery writ sealed with the Great Seal, and publicly proclaimed."[99] Opinions on the jurisdiction of proclamations varied in the Tudor period, as the statutes that had defined their powers in 1539 and 1542 had been nullified in 1547.[100] However, legal status was not as important as the messages proclamations sent to subjects. Officials proclaimed the commands of the monarch in at least four market towns within every county. These proclamations were formal and probably well attended.[101] The chronicler Henry Wriothesley described the announcement of a proclamation of martial law in 1549:

The eighteenth day of Julie was a proclamation made in the cittie of London for mershall lawe, booth the sheriffes riding and the knight mershall with them in the middle with the trumpett and the common cryer afore them one of the clerks of the papers with him, which proclamation was made within the city in diuers places in the forenonne, and at afternonne without the gates of the city.[102]

We can see from this description that people in and about London would have had a difficult time not hearing about the proclamation of martial law.

---

[98] Thus, I agree with the interpretation of the lieutenancy commissions given by MPs in the 1628 Parliament. See Chapter 4. For the revival of the lieutenancy, see Younger, *War and Politics in the Elizabethan Counties*.

[99] Frederic A. Youngs Jr., *The Proclamations of the Tudor Queens* (Cambridge, 1976), 9–10.

[100] For the statute of 1539 see E.R. Adair, "The Statute of Proclamations," *EHR* 32:125 (January, 1917): 34–46; Joel Hurstfield, *Freedom, Corruption, and Government in Elizabethan England* (Cambridge, MA, 1973), 33–41. The most comprehensive examination of the statute comes from Rudolph Heinze, *Proclamations of the Tudor Kings* (Cambridge, 1976), 153–78. The acts have been printed in *TRP*, 1: nos. 545–54. For a general introduction to proclamations, see *TRP*, 1: xxi–xliii.

[101] Kevin Sharpe, *Selling the Tudor Monarchy: Authority and Image in Sixteenth-Century England* (New Haven, 2009), 344–7.

[102] Charles Wriothesley, *A Chronicle of England during the Reigns of the Tudors, from A.D. 1485 to 1559* ed. William Douglas Hamilton 2 vols. (London, 1875), 2:15–16.

In 1589, the Elizabethan Privy Council used this messaging with martial law to combat vagrancy after several statutes and proclamations had failed. Vagrancy, due to overpopulation, was an intractable social problem by the end of Elizabeth's reign. The problem had only gotten worse due to the return of soldiers from England's failed attempt to invade Portugal who were now loitering in port towns.[103] On 13 November, Elizabeth threatened vagrants with execution by martial law. She declared to those who would not return home that "in due course of policy cause the said ... provost marshals above mentioned to proceed out of hand to the punishment of the transgressors of the late proclamation."[104] Here was the threat of summary martial law. But it allowed vagrants two days to report to either a mayor or justice of the peace and receive a passport so they might travel back to their birthplace. Like other statutes relating to vagrancy, and like the summary martial law proclamations in Ireland, the Crown gave a time window for vagrants to self-correct their behavior.

The proclamation served three purposes. First, it publicly humiliated JPs. The first portion of the text harshly critiqued their performance in executing vagrancy statutes. Second, it established new county officers – the provost marshal – who would see that the statutes were executed and would in effect provide competition to the JP. Finally, it was meant to make subjects think that those provosts had powers of martial law. If vagrants refused to return home, the proclamation declared that they would be executed within the county or city in which they were caught "according to such direction as shall be given by warrant from her majesty in that behalf to be made."[105]

Precise directions were given from the Privy Council. The procedure actually envisaged was contained in a draft commission, written on 14 November.[106] In this draft, the queen and her council maintained control over martial law powers by mandating that six or more members of the Privy Council were required to sign a warrant before the lord chancellor actually issued a commission for martial law to a provost

---

[103] 14 Eliz. c. 5; 18 Eliz. c.3; *TRP*, 2: nos. 637, 692, 715. Youngs, *Proclamations of the Tudor Queens*, 73–4.

For England's foreign policy in this period, see R.B. Wernham, *After the Armada: Elizabethan England and the Struggle for Western Europe, 1588–1595* (Oxford, 1984).

[104] *APC*, 18: 222–4; *TRP*, 3: no. 716.   [105] *TRP*, 3: no. 716.

[106] "Form of Commission to be issued to the Lords Lieutenants of the several shires ... " TNA, SP 12/228, f. 64. "Warrant of Queen Elizabeth to the Lord Chancellor, authorizing him to issue commissions for appointing provost marshals," 14 November 1589, TNA, SP 12/228, f. 62; another copy of this warrant is in BL, Lansdowne Ms. 59, no. 80.

marshal in a given county.[107] This plan gave the Privy Council the ability to circumvent common law. But it also meant that the entire country was not put under martial law: only those places that received a commission with the assent of the Council were allowed to grant provosts powers of martial law. The proclamation itself, in other words, granted no martial law jurisdiction. These powers were restricted to three months, although they were extended in the spring of 1590. Sunset clauses, which would be an important device that parliaments in the seventeenth century would use to monitor martial law, were first used by the English Privy Council.

It seems as though provosts detained vagrants but did not summarily execute them. Sir Henry Cocke, Cecil's deputy lieutenant in Hertfordshire, informed his master of a special session to clear the jail of all the vagrants the Hertfordshire provosts had imprisoned. In his January reports to Cecil, Cocke claimed that he heard fifteen cases of vagrancy and issued passports to twelve of the men so that they might return to their home counties.[108] The other three were indicted as repeat offenders. If Cecil had desired to execute them by martial law, he probably could have gotten a commission to his lieutenant. But it is unlikely that he did. Another report from Surrey likewise reveals no executions by martial law.[109] Instead, the provost was more concerned about "horsemen" on the highways and the outrages that they had committed. The provost of Surrey only seemed to have granted passes to returned soldiers and vagrants so that they would return to the county of their birth. At least one "rogue" was not fooled by the proclamations. Cocke related to Cecil that he had overheard a conversation between an old rogue and a young masterless man.[110] The elder rogue admitted that "ther was great speeches about London, that ther sholde be provoste marshalles in every sheare, to hang them uppe." But he reassured the young man by stating, "they dare not doe it, for theie are as much afrayed of us, as we are of them, they know ther are manye of us, and ther are many Ennymyes abroad, and at home also, therfore I warrant thee, they dare not hurte us." Indeed, it appears that the only ones who were terrified in the winter of 1589/90 were the queen and her council.

---

[107] "A Letter to the Lord Chancellor of England," 17 November 1589, *APC*, 18: 224–5. Privy Council to sheriffs and justices of the peace of Surrey, 25 November 1589, SHC, 6729/10/78. Also see *HMC*, Finch, 1: 29; and LMA, Jour. 22, f. 347v. In London, it seems that the provost continued previous practices, which was to deliver them to the Bridewell where two aldermen were to examine them the following day and issue those not to be prosecuted for felony passports, *Ibid.*, f. 341.

[108] Sir Henry Cocke to William Cecil, 7 January 1590, BL, Lansdowne Ms. 62, no. 26 printed in Lindsay Boynton, "Tudor Provost Marshal," 449–50.

[109] "Memorandum of Sir George More," SHC, 6729/3/29, undated. SHC, 6729/3/30.

[110] Sir Henry Cocke to William Cecil, 7 January 1590, BL, Lansdowne Ms. 62, no. 26.

Nevertheless, in 1591, the Privy Council repeated its earlier strategy.[111] In November of that year, it issued yet another proclamation that threatened martial law. It declared that the lords lieutenants of the realm had "sufficient warrant by their Commissions to execute Martiall Law vpon such offenders against the publike peace and state of the Realme."[112] This was deceiving. The lords lieutenants only had martial law powers over invaders and rebels. They would have needed an additional commission of martial law to take action on vagrants. Then, in the very next line, the Privy Council declared that the lieutenants could appoint provost marshals to arrest and detain vagabonds, who would be punished "as by the Lawes of the Realm they shall deserve." No martial law jurisdiction was granted in this proclamation, but a less than careful reading or hearing of it might make English subjects think otherwise. That year, William Lambarde, in a charge to a grand jury, warned about the advancing jurisdiction of the provosts: "we are not peremptorily sentenced by the mouth of the judge . . . but by the oath and verdict of jurors that be our equals."[113] Certainly, Lambarde believed this to be true. But he was hardly working against the Privy Council's wishes. The 1591 proclamation had been made in part to spur competition between provosts and JPs. Lambarde was helping communicate this public threat that if workers of the common law did not do their duty better, they would be replaced.

On three occasions in the 1590s the Privy Council granted a limited martial law jurisdiction to provosts in London for the executing of those who resisted them as the city descended into economic crisis.[114] Due to riots by apprentices in the metropolis in 1591–2, 1595, and 1598, the Crown issued a proclamation that declared that all apprentices, vagrants, and idle and masterless men in London or in nearby counties should be detained by a newly appointed provost marshal. If any of these types of people resisted arrest or refused to be "readily reformed and corrected by the ordinary officers of justice" they were to be executed "without delay" by martial law.[115] No one was to go out at night except the justices of the

---

[111] Many counties chafed at the expense of keeping the provost marshal and his assistants. Steve Hindle, *The State and Social Change in Early Modern England, 1550–1640* (Basingstoke, 2000), 54.

[112] *By the Queen* (STC 8207).

[113] Quoted in Christopher Brooks, *Law, Politics, and Society* (Cambridge, 2008), 92.

[114] Due to near constant disturbances, and probably to its comparative wealth, London was far more interested in paying for marshals who acted as a police force. London aldermen seem to have paid for the provosts. In 1596, for example, all aldermen were ordered to pay 30s for the upkeep of the city marshals. LMA, Rep. 23, fos. 503, 511. For the city marshals and policing in general, see Paul Griffiths, *Lost Londons: Change, Crime, and Control in the Capital City, 1550–1660* (Cambridge, 2008), 291–432.

[115] *TRP*, 3: no. 740. The 1595 and 1598 proclamations contain similar language. *Ibid.*, nos. 769, 796. The Privy Council may have made these proclamations because it believed

peace or the provost and his officers. No assemblies were allowed. As with Ireland, we can detect dissatisfaction of outlawry process or that of the posse.[116] In 1595, anyone caught writing seditious pamphlets was subject to martial law, but the Privy Council alone possessed this jurisdiction. The mayor in the summer of 1595 encouraged the Council to summarily execute authors of pamphlets for example's sake, but there is no evidence it did so.[117]

The chief work of the provosts was to search for vagrants and put them before tribunals so they could be sent to their home county. After proclamations were issued in both 1591 and 1595, the Crown organized two tribunals to sit at Newgate. One was to handle vagrants and masterless men, the other to handle soldiers and those who pretended to be soldiers. They issued passports, usually after applying corporal punishment, so that these idlers might return home.[118] This process at least once generated a legal dispute between the provost and those he had attempted to arrest. In February 1596, the mayor committed John Read, one of the city's marshals, for an "vnseemly se[r]che."[119] Reed had apparently attempted to apprehend a "lewd woman" but was forcibly prevented from doing so by some men "of the temple."[120] Eventually, a writ of trespass was issued against Reed and damages were found for the plaintiff at the Court of Star Chamber.[121] Even the comparatively restricted powers of the provosts were supervised by other courts in England.

Nevertheless, these restricted martial law powers were still controversial. In 1598, for example, the Earl of Essex challenged the forthcoming martial law proclamation after the Privy Council sought his advice on a draft.[122] Essex was probably in part opposed to the proclamation because it originated from his rival Robert Cecil. But his statements are revealing in that they probably expressed common fears about this

---

previous attempts to put down riots by the mayor of London had been insufficient. *APC*, 22: 549–50; 23: 19–20, 28–9, and 242–3.

[116] On the dissatisfaction with the *posse comitatus* in general in this period, see Cynthia Herrup, *The Common Peace: Participation and the Criminal Law in Seventeenth-Century England* (Cambridge, 1989), 70–2.

[117] John Spencer, Lord Mayor of London, to William Cecil, 29 June 1595, BL, Lansdowne, Ms. 78, no. 64.

[118] "Names of Certain Officers, etc. appointed by the Queen for examining disorderly persons," BL, Lansdowne, Ms. 66, no. 94; BL, Harley Ms. 7018, no. 6 for 1592. For similar sessions in 1595, see "A Certificate of the examination of certain idle and masterless men and women at the Old Bailey, by Commissioners," BL, Lansdowne Ms. 78, no. 53.

[119] LMA, Rep. 23, f. 508v.

[120] It is not clear who these men were. LMA, Rep. 23, f. 532v. Apparently, the case was initially heard before the Court of Star Chamber.

[121] LMA, Rep. 25, fos. 36v, 46.

[122] Privy Council to the Earl of Essex, 6 September 1598, HH, CP 63/108.

adapted martial law jurisdiction. According to Essex, it would be against "her maties mercifull and excellent gouernt" to allow summary martial law to operate in England. Like William Cecil earlier in the 1590s, the Earl of Essex pointed out that temporal boundaries should not be violated: martial law should not be used as long as "her kingdom is free from inuasion and rebellion."[123] At the very least, according to Essex, vagrants and rogues should have the right to appear before a marshal's court, just like soldiers in his army. Indeed, Essex, like Lord Ely in 1641, had a clear understanding of the difference between martial law as supervised by a marshal's court and the "sans repliqué" variant authorized by the Privy Council in 1598.[124]

Summary martial law continued to be periodically authorized even after the crises of the 1590s died down. It was not confined temporally, although it was circumscribed to certain offenses. Reservations over its use, however, probably limited its jurisdiction. The Crown used summary martial law again in February 1601 when the Crown in an effort to clear London proclaimed that all loose and idle people found in the city would be executed by martial law.[125] These powers were granted to provosts during the rebellion of none other than Essex. James I continued to use summary martial law during times of riot both in 1607 and again in 1618.[126] In England, summary martial law fairly quickly became circumscribed to prosecute either riot or to execute those who resisted arrest. In general, provosts became policing officials, who were authorized in places where vagrancy was a problem.[127] Martial law commissioners never had access to multiple jurisdictions like they did in Ireland, and they were supervised by other legal officers. Through the experimentations with martial law by proclamation over the course of the sixteenth century in both England and Ireland, the Privy Council in England eventually created a controllable tool that in the end was used selectively to enhance policing powers.

Summary martial law in Ireland into the seventeenth century

Those in favor of more brutal and violent policies had fervently resisted the recall of martial law commissions. In 1594, with the outbreak of what would quickly become an island-wide revolt, the hardliners seemed to have been proven correct. From 1594 until the end of Elizabeth's reign,

---

[123] The Earl of Essex to the Privy Council [undated, 1598] HH, CP 64/67.   [124] *Ibid.*
[125] *TRP*, 2: no. 809.   [126] *SRP*, 1: nos. 72 and 177.
[127] Provost marshals should thus not be conflated with martial law. The provosts in Gloucester, for example, had no powers of martial law. GA, GBR/G3/SO7, fos. 105–7.

Ireland was engulfed in war.[128] Martial law commissions were reintroduced by 1596. However, the calls for restraint had not been completely forgotten. As David Edwards has rightly noted, some of the martial law commissions of the 1590s were only justified due to the suspension of common law.[129] After the war ended, increasingly pervasive assize circuits supervised martial law commissions. Summary martial law remained a tool for Irish governance, but one that was employed less often and that was supervised more closely.

The authorization of martial law during the Nine Years War was not a full return to martial law policies of earlier periods. Edmond Spenser and others wanted to rule the Irish by martial law because the Irish for Spenser would be unreliable jurors and needed to be terrorized into becoming more civilized.[130] This plan was not fully adopted. Beginning in 1594 and accelerating in 1597–8 during some of the darker moments of the war for the English, the Dublin government granted commissions of martial law to its delegates in Munster, the midlands, and even in the Pale.[131] However, the restraints argued for martial law jurisdiction in the 1580s were at times acknowledged. While many of the commissions were replicas of earlier summary martial law commissions, beginning in 1598, some contained sunset clauses intended to restrict martial law practice to two months, thereby allowing the central government to revisit martial law jurisdiction and, if necessary, restrain its delegated authorities.[132] Further, six martial law commissions were granted in 1598 for the purposes of jail delivery. These commissions argued that martial law was acceptable to clear the jails because "there can be no sessions held whereby the prisoners

---

[128] Hiram Morgan, *Tyrone's Rebellion: The Outbreak of the Nine Years War in Ireland* (Woodbridge, 1993). For the military history of the Nine Years War, see Cyril Falls, *Elizabeth's Irish Wars* (London, 1950), 202–339.

[129] Edwards, "Ideology and Experience," 151–3.

[130] Edmund Spenser, *A View of the State of Ireland* ed. Andrew Hadfield and Willy Maley (Oxford, 1997), 30. Also see Richard Beacon, *Solon his Follie (1594)* ed. and annot. Claire Carroll and Vincent Carey (Binghamton, 1996), 22–5. The best work on Spenser's views on martial law is Edwards, "Ideology and Experience," 127–58. There has been considerable debate over how original Spenser was as a thinker, and how influential he was among new English settlers. Ciaran Brady, "Spenser's Irish Crisis: Humanism and Experience in the 1590s," *P&P* 111 (May, 1986): 17–49; Nicholas Canny, "Debate: Spenser's Irish Crisis: Humanism and Experience in the 1590s," *P&P* 120 (August, 1988): 201–09; Brady, "Spenser's Irish Crisis: Humanism and Experience in the 1590s: Reply," *P&P* 120 (August, 1988): 210–15; Canny, *Making Ireland British*, 1–55.

[131] *Fiants* Elizabeth, nos. 5881–3, 5891, 5932, 6020, 6028, 6068, 6074, 6084, 6092–3, 6103, 6111, 6116, 6127, 6135, 6144, 6164, 6199, 6202–17, 6221, 6223, 6227–8, 6237–8, 6240–1, 6243–7, 6255–6, 6260, 6269, 6281–2, 6285, 6288, 6290–1, 6307–8, 6319, 6325, 6342–3, 6356, 6364, 6369, 6375–6, 6385, 6415, 6420, 6528, 6546–7, 6572, 6637, 6645, 6675.

[132] *Ibid.*, nos. 6202–13.

might receive their trial by ordinary course of law."[133] The Irish government did not always feel the need to make such claims. After 1598, through the end of the war in 1603, the government issued martial law commissions much as it had since 1560. But the notion that martial law could be justified when common law courts were inoperable, a common claim made by later imperial officials, was experimented with in the 1590s.

With peace, the new regime of James I made a similar decision to the one made by Elizabeth's government during the 1580s. In February 1605, James declared through a proclamation that due to the fact that many martial law commissioners had abused their power for private gain, they needed to hand in their commissions within forty days of the printing of the proclamation.[134] The mayors of the port towns, the great lords like the Earls of Ormond and Thomond, sheriffs who had already received commissions, and the lord presidents of Munster and Connacht all maintained their privilege to execute by martial law. Even the Earl of Tyrone, who only two years earlier had been in open warfare against the Crown, received a commission of martial law. But others lost their martial law powers. Summary martial law continued in Ireland.

Assize judges, at least more often, supervised these powers. In the aftermath of the Nine Years War, regular assize circuits began to operate throughout Ireland.[135] Many of these commissioners, following in the path of Crofts, Cecil, and Gardiner, sought to at least supervise summary martial law jurisdiction. One of martial law's most prominent opponents was Sir John Davies, a prominent legal theorist who became the Solicitor General of Ireland in 1603.[136] Davies also believed that the Irish needed to be civilized in order for the island to become obedient to the Crown. But from Davies' perspective, martial law was not the means to civilize Ireland. Instead, it was simply a continuation, now through letters patent, of the "plaine tiranny" that had existed in former times.[137] Davies' goal as solicitor general was to root out all those legal customs, both English and Irish, which he deemed to be repugnant to English law.

Davies claimed a right to supervise summary martial law jurisdiction in 1606.[138] That year, the provost marshal of Munster, Sir George

---

[133] *Ibid.*, nos. 6214–5, 6221, 6244–5, 6255. The quote is at no. 6214.

[134] BL, Add. Ms. 41,613, fos. 26v–29v.

[135] John McCavitt, "Good Planets in their Several Spheres – The Establishment of the Assize Circuits in Early Seventeenth Century Ireland," *Irish Jurist* 24 (1989): 248–78.

[136] For Davies' career, see Hans Pawlisch, *Sir John Davies and the Conquest of Ireland: A Study in Legal Imperialism* (Cambridge, 1985).

[137] John Davies, *A Discouerie of the True causes Why Ireland was neuer Entirely Subdued, nor brought vnder Obedience of the crowne of England ...* (London, 1612), 276.

[138] This story is beautifully told by David Edwards in "Two Fools and a Martial Law Commissioner: Cultural Conflict at the Limerick Assize of 1606," in *Regions and*

Downing, used his powers of martial law to summarily execute a "fool" who was traveling in county Limerick. The wrong was vagrancy, which meant that the "fool" was not a property owner and, if the provost had executed him legally, would not have been carrying a pass from a property owner. Unfortunately for the provost marshal, the fool had a pass on his body when he was killed. The Earl of Thomond, a powerful Irish magnate who had submitted to the Crown, had claimed the fool as one of his followers. Enraged by this wrongful execution, the Earl of Thomond demanded justice. In spite of the vigorous protests of the lord president of Munster, Sir Henry Brounker, Davies on his assize circuit agreed to hear the case – with Brounker presiding over the court. A grand jury found an indictment of murder to be a true bill. Then a petty jury initially convicted Downing of the offense after hearing evidence from the Earl of Thomond. But Brounker delayed the public reading of the sentence until the following day, to the dismay of the common law judges. In the meantime he threatened the jury that they should arrive at an alternative verdict or he would prosecute them at the Court of Castle Chamber.[139] The jury remained steadfast and convicted Downing.

In the end, this trial was about supervision. Davies and the other common law commissioners agreed that Downing should be pardoned. The Earl of Thomond was inconsolable; he believed his dead servant had been deprived of justice. Brounker was likewise inconsolable. Storming out of the sessions, he believed his authority and his honor had been undermined. Indeed they had. The point, from Davies' perspective, was not to make a spectacle by executing an officer of the Crown. Instead, it was that common lawyers had the right to supervise the Crown's other jurisdictions. As Davies put it to the Earl of Salisbury, he was not going to subvert the lord president's or his deputy's authority. But common law judges had the right to examine "whether he exceeded his authority maliciously or no."[140] Perhaps the most important aspect of this story was that reports about this contest over jurisdiction filtered back to the English Privy Council. This jurisdictional dispute between two of its delegated authorities gave the Council information about the operation of law in Ireland and allowed it to act as a referee in their disputes.

Rulers in Ireland, 1100–1650: Essays for Kenneth Nicholls ed. David Edwards (Dublin, 2004), 237–65. "A Copy of a Letter from my Lord President of Munster," TNA, SP 63/219, f. 67; The Earl of Thomond to the Earl of Salisbury, 16 April 1606, TNA, SP 63/218, f. 121; "Proceedings against John Downing," TNA, SP 63/218, f. 123v; Sir John Davies to the Earl of Salisbury, 4 May 1606, TNA, SP 63/218, f. 152.

[139] The Court of Castle Chamber was the Irish equivalent to the Star Chamber. For its history, see Crawford, *A Star Chamber Court in Ireland.*

[140] Davies to the Earl of Salisbury, 4 May 1606, TNA, SP 63/218, f. 152.

The Privy Council and common law judges continued to monitor martial law jurisdiction after 1606. Administrators more in line with Spenserian ideology, like lord deputy Sir Arthur Chichester, often wanted to use martial law more liberally than men like Davies would have wanted. And at times they did so.[141] But they often had to justify summary martial law to an English Privy Council that was increasingly opposed to its unrestricted use. This issue became sensitive after the foundation of the Ulster Plantation and the arrival of even more English and Scottish planters who had no desire to live under martial law.[142] In 1615, fearing plots for a new insurrection against the English government in Ulster, Chichester wrote to the Privy Council that he had authorized provost marshals to use summary martial law. However, they did not possess the power to "put any man to death without the consent and allowance of some justices of the peace."[143] Further, that justice of the peace had to take into account special examinations – in other words evidence was required before execution. Even these activities were closely monitored by John Davies, who reported in 1615 that he and other common law judges had overseen many indictments of provosts who had overstepped their bounds. This supervision probably led in 1617 to the issuing of several pardons of provosts for their use of martial law by the new lord deputy, Oliver St. John – a strategy that would also be used in England after the passage of the Petition of Right. By the end of James' reign, Irish administrators still used summary martial law, but they were forced to justify it.[144] As portions of Ireland became anglicized, summary martial law was used less often than in the sixteenth century.

Increasingly, summary martial law was a jurisdiction allowed for those policing fugitives and other dangerous criminals. It was still employed by 1628 because the Old English once again demanded its restriction. In the so-called Graces, a list of grievances the "Old English" subjects of Ireland submitted to Charles I in the spring of 1628, Irish subjects demanded that a reduced number of provost marshals in Irish provinces be allowed martial law powers only during times of rebellion or invasion.[145] As with other protests, the restrictions desired in the Graces only partially

---

[141] Canny, *Making Ireland British*, 187.

[142] Chichester in 1613 informed some of the most prominent Catholics of the realm that provosts had not been given powers of summary martial law in six years. *CSPI*, 1611–14, 415.

[143] Chichester to the Privy Council 18 April 1615, TNA, SP 63/233, f. 40. It seems that provosts actually recorded examinations of suspects. See "The Examination of Teage O'Lennon taken by Thomas Foster, gent., provost marshal of the county of Londonderrie, 9 April 1615," TNA, SP 63/233, fos. 44–5.

[144] *CSPI*, 1615–1625, 301.

[145] Aidan Clarke, *The Old English in Ireland, 1625–42* (Ithaca, 1966), 48, 249.

worked. Presidents in Munster and Connacht retained martial law powers "to prosecute those men that cannot be had into the Law that is Rebels and Fugitives."[146] Lord Ely, in his deposition, argued that summary martial law had been restricted to the execution of those who had resisted arrest as well as rebels and those who lived outside the law. But it seems as though in Connacht, summary martial law powers continued and were not supervised particularly well. For plenary martial law, he gave it a jurisdiction identical to the one given by Sir James Crofts in 1583. But perhaps this was too convenient, as it meant the Earl of Strafford, Ely's avowed enemy, had subverted the laws of the realm by executing a soldier for desertion in 1638.

Conclusion

In so many ways, the story of summary martial law is a synecdoche for the general history of martial law. It was made from other legal practices. It was adapted to meet specific political conditions. Ideas surrounding summary martial law circulated between England and Ireland, transforming martial law practices in both kingdoms in the process. Its jurisdiction was contested, with many fearing the brutality of martial law commissioners would lead to revolts, while others felt it necessary to maintain order. Its use and abuse in Ireland also produced some of the most lasting arguments on how martial law should be restricted but not ended. Many, like Crofts, would come to argue that martial law was only allowable in hosts during periods of war or tumult, while others, like Elizabeth in 1586, wanted to reduce martial law to a power of execution on those in the act of committing rebellion or invasion. These attempts were ultimately – over a long period – successful in restricting martial law practice in Ireland. Nevertheless, martial law survived albeit in circumscribed form.

The extended use of the summary variant in Ireland also produced a lasting duality in the way that jurists conceived of martial law. This division was first and foremost based on process. In other words, summary martial law was not military rule and plenary martial law was not military law. At various moments, even army commanders supervised their soldiers by summary martial law. Further, while jurists all the way through Matthew Hale would separate the powers of executing rebels and invaders *in flagrante crimine* from sitting courts-martial, on the ground, as we have seen, these distinctions were often blurred.

---

[146] Rushworth, *Historical Collections*, 8: 186–205.

Conviction through manifest proof became less and less important in the seventeenth century – with, as we shall see, one very important exception – as it was increasingly restricted to the execution of those who refused to yield and bring themselves before the law. The fights in the seventeenth century, while consistent with some of the jurisdictional arguments made over Irish martial law practice, would be over variants of martial law that in general used process by information where a court heard evidence through the aid of a lawyer. We have seen some of these procedures in the last chapter, but those were undergoing transformations as well as English commanders and jurists attempted to emulate the disciplinary mechanisms of the more powerful armies operating on the European continent.

3   Transforming martial law

Hatred and admiration of the Spanish can be found side by side in the writings of Thomas Digges. The military theorist, after spending the past several years serving the Earl of Leicester in the Low Countries, had updated his father's 1579 military manual *Stratioticos* in 1590. Both versions began by claiming that in England the "Militarie Lawes and Ordinances have been neglected." While England's armies enjoyed occasional successes since 1579, for Digges, they were still behind. In order to advance the discipline of the English armed forces, Digges in the 1590s version transcribed a translated copy of the ordinances of war of the Spanish.[1] In the preface to the ordinances, Digges argued that due to their discipline "small handfuls of that megre wretched Nation (onely by obedience to their officers, and reuiuing among them a few of those antique Romane customes) haue done things almost incredible, euen in these our dayes."[2]

Digges connected contemporary Spanish discipline with that of the ancient Romans. He was not alone. By the 1590s, many translations or partial translations of Spanish military texts were available in England, including a dialogue on military duties between the two great maestro de campos of the Spanish armies in the Low Countries, Sancho de Londono and Francisco de Valdés.[3] Meanwhile, others like Sir James Crofts, Roger

---

[1] Leonard Digges and Thomas Digges, *An Arithmetical Warlike Treatise named Stratioticos* (London, 1590), sig. Aii. For overviews of martial prescriptive literature in this period, see Henry J. Webb, *Elizabethan Military Science: The Books and the Practice* (Madison, 1965), and David R. Lawrence, *The Complete Soldier: Military Books and Military Culture in Early Stuart England, 1603–1645* (Leiden, 2009).

[2] Leonard and Thomas Digges, *Stratioticos*, 297.

[3] F. de Valdés, *The Serieant Maior. A Dialogue of the Office of Sergeant Maior* (London, 1590). Thomas Styward, *The Pathwaie to Martiall Discipline* (London, 1583). Styward claimed to have found a copy of a Spanish treatise of war in a fort in Ireland and translated it in his third book, which "Comprehendeth The Very Right order of the Spaniards . . . " *Ibid.* [title page]. However, the whole treatise, and not just the third book, was informed by continental practice. For example, Styward used continental names for officers like "maister of the campe" instead of marshal and "praetor" instead of judge marshal. *Ibid.*, 7, 31. Also see L. Gutierrez de La Vega, *A Compendious Treatise, Entitled De re Militari, Containing*

Williams, William Garrard, and Matthew Sutcliffe, while they hated the Spaniards, admired their discipline.[4] In order to improve, these military theorists believed that English armies needed at least selectively to imitate more successful armies like those of Spain and ancient Rome.

Indeed, the desire to improve discipline meant that jurists, commanders, and martial theorists were willing to look anywhere for better practices. Through selective imitation between 1585 and 1639, they transformed both the written laws of the army and its procedures.[5] In these efforts, they at times emulated historical and contemporary armies they perceived to be superior to their own. However, this process of attempted improvement did not simply mean that the English copied continental examples or those from Roman history.[6] Instead, commanders and their assistants thought deeply about martial lawmaking, applied examples from successful armies selectively, and combined those additions with laws designed for the perceived needs of specific campaigns, garrisons, or even plantations. Even the Virginia Company creatively deployed martial laws for the governance of its Jamestown plantation. The product of these attempts was a complex legal apparatus that has fortunately left behind far more records of its activities than its sixteenth-century predecessors.

The records of the councils of war in this period reveal a culture of law. Even for minor offenses, soldiers, sailors, or planters had their day in court. Oftentimes, lawyers and councils of war carefully examined evidence before they heard and determined cases. As Digges noted in another tract, harmony within the martial polity depended not just upon discipline but also upon a commander who "establisheth martiall lawes full of Equitie, and causeth them to be inviolablie observed."[7] For

---

Principall Orders to be Observed in Martiall Affairs ... (London, 1582); D. Bernardino de Mendoza, Theorique and Practise of Warre (London, 1597). Lawrence, The Complete Soldier, 231–3.

[4] Sir James Crofts, "Arte Militarye," NRO, Fitzwilliam Ms. 67 (Irish), f. 1; Roger Williams, A Brief Discourse of Warre (London, 1590), particularly 8–9, but the whole work is an examination of Spanish military practice. For Sutcliffe, see below. William Garrard claimed expertise on discipline from his service in the Spanish armies. Garrard, The Art of Warre (London, 1591).

[5] For continental influences on England's armed forces, see Roger B. Manning, An Apprenticeship in Arms: The Origins of the British Army, 1585–1702 (Oxford, 2006); Barbara Donagan, War in England, 1642–49 (Oxford, 2006), 33–62; David J.B. Trim, "Fighting 'Jacob's Wars.' The Employment of English and Welsh Mercenaries in the European Wars of Religion: France and the Netherlands, 1562–1610," (unpublished PhD dissertation, University of London, 2002).

[6] For this view in general, see Alan Watson, Failures of the Legal Imagination (Philadelphia, 1988).

[7] Thomas Digges, A Breife and True Report of the Proceedings of the Earle of Leycester for the Reliefs of the Town of Sluce (London, 1590), 31.

the most part, English officers attempted to follow this advice as well. Martial law was meant to balance the imperative of strict discipline with the equally important imperative of harmony through justice.

Transformations in the articles of war

Let us first examine how generals and jurists transformed the articles of war in this period. As we have already seen, Elizabethan statesmen had used martial law creatively. But the only substantive adaptation within martial law was to take wrongs that were not punishable by death, like vagrancy, and to turn them into capital offenses. As Barbara Donagan has rightly argued, it was not until the code of the Earl of Leicester, written in 1585, that English commanders and jurists began to think more critically about the potential of the ordinances of war.[8] Before that, the codes of Henry VII, Henry VIII, and Elizabeth had been roughly consistent with their predecessors.[9] Leicester's code was much longer than medieval codes, and it was far more concerned with duties in camp and with treasonable offenses. This is in no small measure due to transformations in war taking place in the Low Countries.

The late sixteenth century has become treacherous ground for military historians. Only a short time ago, it was renowned as the birthplace of the "military revolution" when the Dutch supposedly updated tactics in order to overcome obstacles to offensive warfare. Eventually, this military revolution was placed farther back in time.[10] According to Geoffrey Parker, it actually began with the invention of the *trace italienne*, a star-shaped fortress designed in Italy in the fifteenth century to neutralize heavier artillery fire, which allowed those in command of towns under siege to hold out against advancing armies for much longer than their predecessors. Further, he argued that the introduction of harquebuses and muskets led to the decline of cavalry.[11] There have been multiple other variations where scholars have put the revolution forward or backward

---

[8] Donagan, *War in England*, 143–6. The chronologies of my work on the ordinances of war and Donagan's are nearly identical. The difference between our interpretations is that I stress the importance of the 1590s and Spanish and Roman influences and she on the 1630s and what she believes to be a distinctively Protestant military law tradition. Leicester's code has been printed in C.G. Cruikshank, *Elizabeth's Army* (2nd ed., Oxford, 1968), 296–303. There are two manuscript versions in the British Library. BL, Add. Ms. 30,170, fos. 35–9, and 38,139, fos. 16–18.

[9] *Statutes and Ordynances for the Warre* (London, 1544); "Orders for the Soldiers in Newhaven, September 1562," *CSPF* 5: 326–7.

[10] See Michael Roberts, *Essays in Swedish History* (London, 1967), 195–225.

[11] Geoffrey Parker, "The Military Revolution, 1560–1660– a Myth?" *The Journal of Modern History* 48:2 (April, 1976): 195–214; Parker, *The Military Revolution: Military Innovation and the Rise of the West, 1500–1800* (2nd ed., Cambridge, 1996), 6–44.

in time, shifted its geographic location, and put forth different causes.[12] But in general, most agree that wars became longer in the early modern period. Armies got bigger. More tracts on military science and military discipline were written.[13] Most agree that there was an increased emphasis on infantry beginning in the late medieval period, and thus an emphasis on collective actions which required discipline.[14] Most of the arguments put forth by these scholars, although they diverge from one another, support the notion that discipline within the soldiery became a heightened concern in this period.

The conditions in the extended wars in the Low Countries, which were dominated by sieges where the defensive side held the advantage, made this desire for discipline especially strong.[15] Commanders, particularly on the Spanish side, needed to keep larger armies in the field for long periods of time. Because of this, they had an incentive to oversee a strict disciplinary regime and often employed jurists and clerks to make sure soldiers were kept in line. Because they were also humanists, many of these same men resolved to update their law codes by adapting Roman Law. Monarchs, administrators, town officials, and civilians in general shared the desires of commanders albeit for different reasons. Strict discipline meant that soldiers might stop pillaging their lands and cities.[16]

While historians of the military revolution have focused on the Dutch – and in particular the tactical innovations of Maurice of Nassau – it was the Spanish monarchs and their commanders that were initially the most innovative in terms of discipline and military organization.[17] The most

[12] David Eltis, *The Military Revolution in Sixteenth Century Europe* (London, 1995), 6–42; James Raymond, *Henry VIII's Military Revolution: the Armies of Sixteenth-Century Britain and Europe* (London, 2007). For a critique of Parker's chronology, see Jeremy Black, *A Military Revolution? Military Change and European Society, 1550–1800* (Basingstoke, 1991). For a critique of his emphasis on the *trace italienne*, see Bert S. Hall, *Weapons and Warfare in Renaissance Europe: Gunpowder, Technology, and Tactics* (Baltimore, 1997), 201–35.

[13] This is one of the major points made by Eltis, *The Military Revolution in Sixteenth Century Europe*.

[14] Wayne E. Lee, *Barbarians & Brothers: Anglo-American Warfare, 1500–1865* (Oxford, 2011), 85–9.

[15] Eltis, *The Military Revolution in Sixteenth Century Europe*, 16–21.

[16] Geoffrey Parker, "The Etiquette of Atrocity: The Laws of War in Early Modern Europe," in *Empire, War and Faith in Early Modern Europe* (London, 2003), 143–68; Eltis, *Military Revolution in the Sixteenth Century*, 60–1.

[17] Jan Glete, *War and the State in Early Modern Europe: Spain, the Dutch Republic, and Sweden as Military-Fiscal States, 1500–1660* (London, 2002), 67–139; Fernando González de León, "*Soldados Platicos and Caballeros*: The Social Dimensions of Ethics in the Early Modern Spanish Army," in *The Chivalric Ethos and the Development of Military Professionalism* ed. D.J.B. Trim (Leiden, 2003), 235–68; González de León, " 'Doctors of the Military Discipline': Technical Expertise and the Paradigm of the Spanish Soldier in the Early Modern Period," *Sixteenth Century Journal* 27:1 (Spring, 1996): 61–85.

important of these innovators came to be collectively known as the "school of Alba," who attempted to install greater discipline through emulation of the spirit of the Romans.[18] The desire for order and discipline among this group led to the making of the most influential treatise on the laws of war of the century, written by Balthasar de Ayala. It also led to Alba's maestro de campo, Sancho de Londono, writing a comprehensive military law code.[19] The school of Alba had reason to focus on discipline because the soldiers of the Spanish army of the Low Countries were notorious for mutinying.[20]

Most of the laws in Londono's code were not new; they were not supposed to be. One can trace most to Roman and other antique sources, the most important being the chapter in Justinian's Digest on *de re militari*.[21] Others can be traced to the unwritten "laws of war." What was innovative about Londono's code was not its originality but instead its comprehensiveness and level of detail. Much that had gone unwritten was now transmitted in writing from the commander to his lieutenants, who would then inform their soldiers. The code focused heavily on camp regulations like how, where, and when victuals would be brought into camp and where they would be sold. Regulations for pass systems, which authorized soldiers to leave camp, were written down. Rules that enforced the hierarchy of the army became more detailed. Soldiers needed to react to a variety of signals, trumpets, and drums in specific ways. Dueling was outlawed. Strict laws against rape and pillage were outlined. At least in theory, the soldiers of the Spanish armies lived under an extensive law code.[22]

The English code of 1585 was made in the context of these broader military changes.[23] The additions to Leicester's code included more

González de León, *The Road to Rocroi: Class, Culture, and Command in the Spanish Army of Flanders, 1567–1659* (Leiden, 2009), 107–43.

[18] Eltis, *The Military Revolution in Sixteenth Century Europe*, 60.

[19] Balthasar Ayala, *De Jure et Officis bellicis et disciplina militari libri III* ed. John Westlake 2 vols. (Washington, 1912). Part of Ayala's treatise was on military discipline, *ibid.*, 2: 205–40. A modern edition of Londono's work is available, Sancho de Londono, *Discurso sobre la forma de reducir la disciplina militar a mejor y antiguo estado* (Madrid, 1943); Digges' translation is reasonable (although truncated), *Stratioticos*, 283–97.

[20] For the mutinies of the Spanish armies, see Geoffrey Parker, *The Army of Flanders and the Spanish Road, 1567–1659: The Logistics of Spanish Victory in the Low Countries* (Cambridge, 1972), 185–206.

[21] *The Digest of Justinian* ed. Theodor Mommsen with the aid of Paul Kreuger trans. Alan Watson 4 vols. (Philadelphia, 1985), 4: bk. 49, ch. 16; C.E. Brand, *Roman Military Law* (Austin and London, 1968).

[22] Digges, *Stratioticos*, 283–97.

[23] Cruikshank, *Elizabeth's Army*, 296–303. Although it cannot be proven, it is likely that someone with more military experience on the European continent, like John Norris or Roger Williams, helped to write these ordinances given Leicester's inexperience in war.

articles on treason and treasonable acts, which is unsurprising given that sieges could be won or lost based on treachery. These included rules against conference with the enemy, sending messages to the enemy, divulging important information, spying for the enemy, leaving camp without authorization, or by a route other than the official entrance of the camp. The code included demands that soldiers pay strict attention to all of the trumpet signals of the camp and an increased number of articles related to religious observance. The omissions were just as important. From the Middle Ages onward, commanders had included numerous articles relating to the rules of ransom. By the end of the sixteenth century these were cut down significantly.[24] In keeping with an important theme, Leicester's code was not a carbon copy of either Roman disciplinary measures or those of the Spanish or any other army. But the changes to the code reflect the broader transformations going on at the time.

Calls for military reform increased by the 1590s. In part, this was due to lack of success in battle.[25] Most of the new works emanated from a group of men who depended on Robert Devereux, the 2nd Earl of Essex, for patronage.[26] Essex, who had been apprenticed in war during the Earl of Leicester's campaigns in the Low Countries, fashioned himself as one of the great Roman generals of antiquity. He led Elizabeth's forces in campaigns in France in 1590, Cadiz in 1596, and in Ireland in 1599. One of Essex's projects throughout the decade was to improve Elizabeth's war machine. This reforming impulse included attempts to improve military discipline both in Elizabeth's armies and among her recruits, who often failed to appear at muster. He often supported former soldiers and administrators who wrote tracts on military tactics and discipline.[27] Members of his circle collected and contemplated historical examples in order to improve Elizabeth's armies.

By the 1590s, these martial theorists called for disciplinary reform based on classical precedent but updated with examples from contemporary armies. The most important of these texts was the compendious treatise by the most experienced judge marshal of the period and a client of Essex, Matthew Sutcliffe, who we have briefly examined in Chapter 1. Sutcliffe hoped that his tract would train English martial men so that they would no longer have to worry about "either the malice, or power, or

---

[24] Donagan, *War in England*, 144.

[25] For one of these failures, see R.B. Wernham, *The Expedition of Sir John Norris and Sir Francis Drake to Spain and Portugal, 1589* (Aldershot, 1988).

[26] For the Essex circle, see Paul E.J. Hammer, *The Polarisation of Elizabethan Politics: The Political Career of Robert Devereux, 2nd Earl of Essex, 1585–1597* (Cambridge, 1999), 199–268.

[27] *Ibid.*, 238–42.

riches of the Spaniard, or other forreine enemie of this state."[28] In order to improve martial discipline, Sutcliffe provided the first comprehensive digest of ordinances of war. Drawing on classical, French, Spanish, Italian, as well as English sources, he listed all martial laws he thought beneficial for future commanders who could choose which laws they thought best for their campaigns. The most important classical examples, as one would expect, came from Rome, who, according to Sutcliffe, "deserued speciall commendation."[29] The most important recent examples were Philibert of Châlon, Prince of Orange, who commanded Charles V's armies before Florence in 1530, and Alba, who was, "though otherwise cruel, yet a man skilfull in matters of warre, for reformation of diuers disorders crept in among the Spanish soldiers, gaue order to Sacho de Londonno, to frame certaine statutes in writing."[30] By learning from these examples, he hoped the English armed forces, who according to Sutcliffe were backward in military discipline, might one day join Rome and Spain in splendid military successes.

Sutcliffe categorized his martial laws for the benefit of future readers. These nine categories were laws concerning religion and moral matters, laws concerning the common safety of the state and garrison, laws concerning the duties of captains and soldiers, laws concerning the camp or garrison, laws concerning "sea causes," orders relating to adventures at sea, orders relating to the providers or victuallers of armies and navies, laws relating to ransom and prisoners of war, and finally laws relating to the administration of justice. In each of these categories, Sutcliffe listed all the laws he thought to be useful for an army or navy on campaign and then afterward annotated each law and usually cited some historic example which supposedly proved the law's utility either because commanders used it effectively or because their failure to do so had led to disaster.[31]

To better understand Sutcliffe's work, let us look at his category relating to the safety of the state, garrison, and army.[32] These included treasonable acts committed – either intentionally or through incompetence – against the army. Historical examples proved their necessity.

---

[28] *Sutcliffe*, sig. B4v.

[29] *Ibid.*, 302. By far the most commonly cited classical source was Livy. He also referenced Tacitus, Polybius, Thucydides, Caesar's Civil Wars, and Sallust.

[30] *Ibid.*, 303. Sutcliffe was an avid reader of Francesco Guicciardini's history of Italy, where he would have learned about the Prince of Orange. He also cited actions by Protestants in France in 1568. *Ibid.*, 315. He cited them far less often than Londono. See below.

[31] *Sutcliffe*, 304–42.   [32] *Ibid.*, 310–16.

In regard to articles banning conspiracy, for example, Sutcliffe cited successful generals like Scipio and Cyrus of Persia who executed conspirators for example's sake. In order to justify his article against those who from laziness allowed the enemy to be made aware of the army's presence, Sutcliffe cited how the Protestant armies of France were thwarted in their attempts to take Samur in 1569 because soldiers had set fire to houses on their march and alerted the enemy to their presence. The English in their attempted invasion of Portugal, likewise, were foiled in a plan to trap Spanish horsemen because one of the soldiers shot his firearm too soon. Good law might prevent these mistakes from happening in future campaigns. Sutcliffe was writing an advice manual for the art of ruling a martial polity.

Sutcliffe's legal logic led him to cite Londono's code approvingly on a wide range of disciplinary issues, including drunkenness, market regulations, protections for areas against pillage, camp cleanliness (twice), protections for soldiers against maiming or death by abusive commanders, impeding justice, banning cartels within camps and violence owing to quarrels among soldiers generally, giving false alarm, and skirmishing without leave. In terms of regulating camp hygiene, Sutcliffe observed that the English and Spanish had similar rules, but they "obserue it far better."[33] The method by which he cited Londono was he wrote about a Spanish law or practice, then "footnoted" on the side of the page where he transcribed the particular code from Londono's text that he was discussing.

He even cited the Spanish in matters of religion. Along with being a lawyer trained in Civil Law and a judge marshal, Sutcliffe was the dean of Exeter. A strong supporter of the Church of England, Sutcliffe spent much of the early 1590s attacking both the Catholic Church and Presbyterianism. He was hardly apathetic when it came to the religious debates that raged throughout Europe in the sixteenth century.[34] And yet, in his section on religion, Sutcliffe praised Londono's code on four of the eight laws that he listed, including laws against swearing, unlawful games, banning "common women," and, most surprisingly, laws regulating religious observance. In a law that required the governors of the army to make sure soldiers attended religious service, Sutcliffe claimed that "[t]he Spaniards vnto euery tercio, or Regiment haue diuers Priestes, whom they haue in great estimation, and punish those that doe violate

---

[33] *Ibid.*, 329.
[34] Nicholas W.S. Cranfield, "Sutcliffe, Matthew," in *ODNB*. For his religious views, see Peter Lake, *Anglicans and Puritans? Presbyterianism and English Conformist Thought from Whitgift to Hooker* (London, 1988), 126–7, 129–30.

them either in worde, or deede."[35] For swearers and blasphemers, Sutcliffe noted that "[t]he Spaniards inflict grieuous penalties vpon them that transgresse in this behalf: and all Christians ought to detest and banish all abuses."[36] Sutcliffe also cited Roman devotional practices found in Livy; he claimed that while the Romans were "ignorant of the true God, yet in matters of warre were most deuout, and religious."[37] Their religiosity gave them victory, and they attributed their "evil successe" to lack of piety. For Sutcliffe, the English army needed to incorporate the religious discipline of heathens and heretics in order to become more successful.

Sutcliffe's willingness to look intently at Spanish practices did not mean that subsequent English commanders simply copied the Spanish. Nor does it mean that they simply copied the Romans. Lawmaking, at least when it came to martial law, was never that simple. What people like Matthew Sutcliffe were doing instead was attempting to examine and evaluate any available remedy or tool so that a commander could employ it or adapt it to meet the demands of his particular campaign. The commander and his council often surveyed a variety of past laws, either from English armies or from continental ones, and selected the ones they found most necessary for their upcoming campaign.

This creative impulse was true of the English articles of war of the 1590s, where the Earl of Essex attempted to craft ordinances that would provide the most effective framework for the maintenance of discipline. Essex attempted to redress previous disciplinary problems or anticipate problems due to the unique circumstances of the forthcoming campaign. Let us look at the problem of drunkenness in order to understand this experimentation better. The Earl of Leicester in 1585 ordered drunkards to be banished. Essex in 1590 copied this provision.[38] However, this remedy was apparently not effective (perhaps it diminished his numerical strength too much). So in his 1599 ordinances for his army that was to be sent into Ireland, Essex adopted an escalating clause for those convicted of drunkenness: first, soldiers were to be imprisoned, then fined and imprisoned, and then a "far greater punishment" that went unnamed in the code would fall upon the soldier thrice convicted of drunkenness. In other words, if a law did not work, commanders changed it.[39] Preemptive ordinances included provisions designed to ensure that Essex'

---

[35] *Sutcliffe*, 308.   [36] *Ibid.*, 309.   [37] *Ibid.*, 306.

[38] Cruikshank, *Elizabeth's Army*, 298. "Orders and Articles to be observed by such Captains and Soldiers as are under the Command of the Earl of Essex L. General of her Majesty's Forces in Normandy," BL, Harley Ms. 7018, f. 77.

[39] *Lawes and Orders of Warre established for the Good Conduct of the Service in Ireland* (London, 1599), 9.

Protestant soldiers not be ensnared by the Catholic faith during his 1590 campaign, including an order that no soldier enter a church during mass or matins.[40] Reaction, prediction, adaptation, imitation, and elimination were all strategies that English commanders and their council employed to make the ordinances of war. There was no lack of imagination when it came to martial lawmaking.

Making the Lawes Diuine Morall and Martiall

The adaptability as well as the severity of martial law made it an attractive form of law for new plantations. The ill-fated Roanoke colony had attempted to adapt the ordinances of war in 1585. Ralph Lane, the would-be governor and former sheriff of County Kerry, made out a shortened list of constitutions to govern his men in what is now North Carolina.[41] The Roanoke experiment famously failed, but in 1609, only a decade after the Essex circle was innovating in martial laws for Elizabeth's armies, the recently founded Virginia Company of London decided to adopt a far more complex martial law regime for its floundering, not yet three-year-old Jamestown plantation.[42] It did so after receiving several reports from the planters that detailed the corruption, idleness, and vulnerability of Jamestown. In order to remedy these defects and in order to create a disciplined fighting force capable of expanding the plantation into the interior of the continent, the Company established new leadership that was to govern by martial law. In order to assure its investors who had heard nothing but terrible news about the plantation, the Company published the *Lawes Diuine Morall and Martiall* in 1612 to show that its governors ruled the plantation through laws.[43] The makers

[40] "Orders and Articles to be observed ... 1590," BL, Harley Ms. 7018, f. 77.

[41] The code has been printed in *The Roanoke Voyages* ed. David Beers Quinn 2 vols. (London, 1955), 1: 138–9. For an excellent overview of the Roanoke experiment, see James Horn, *A Kingdom Strange: The Brief and Tragic History of the Lost Colony of Roanoke* (New York, 2010).

[42] The best overviews of the making of the Jamestown plantation are James Horn, *A Land as God Made It: Jamestown and the Birth of America* (New York, 2005). For the history of the Virginia Company, see Wesley Frank Craven, *The Virginia Company of London, 1606–1642* (Williamsburg, 1964), and Craven, *The Dissolution of the Virginia Company: The Failure of a Colonial Experiment* (Gloucester, 1964).

[43] *For the Colony in Virginea Britannia. Lawes Diuine, Morall and Martiall* (London, 1612). The most exhaustive study of the application of these laws in Jamestown is still Sigmund Diamond, "From Organization to Society: Virginia in the Seventeenth Century," *The American Journal of Sociology* 63:5 (March, 1958): 457–75. For the genesis of the code, see Darrett Rutman, "The Virginia Company and its Military Regime," in *The Old Dominion: Essays for Thomas Perkins Abernathy* ed. Darrett Rutman (Charlottesville, 1964), 1–20. The only scholar to attempt to place the *Lawes Diuine Morall and Martiall* in the context of English laws generally is David Thomas Konig,

of this code adapted, combined, imitated as well as generated new laws to govern the plantation.

In order to understand the context of the making of the *Lawes Diuine Morall and Martiall* better, let us examine what the Company's investors in London were learning about the Jamestown plantation circa 1609. The Company had received its charter in April 1606, which had actually authorized two companies: the "Plymouth Company" comprised of West Country merchants had rights to all uninhabited lands between 38 and 45 degrees latitude, while the "Virginia Company" comprised of London merchants had rights to settle in more southerly areas between 34 degrees and 41 degrees latitude. A Virginia Council, made up of Crown officials as well as members of both companies, would supervise the two plantations from London. The plan went into action for the southerly company when three ships of 144 mariners left London bound for the new world in December 1606 and arrived in what is now Virginia in April 1607.[44] After it had landed, the planters formed their government. Unsurprisingly, the form of government the Council of Virginia chose was a presidency council: a multiple jurisdictional tribunal that English monarchs had established in Wales, the north of England, Munster, and Connacht in the sixteenth century to provide English laws to people who lived far away from the central courts of either Dublin or Westminster.[45] The leaders of the plantation were explicitly instructed that all criminal trials were to be decided by twelve honest men.[46] Nothing, including the presidential council, was successful about Jamestown.[47]

The decision to alter Jamestown's governing structure began in the spring of 1608. The Company contacted Sir Thomas Gates, a member of the Company and an experienced soldier who had served on the Cadiz expedition under the Earl of Essex, about possibly becoming a leader of the plantation. Gates, who was at the time serving as a mercenary in the service of the Dutch Republic, was supposed to lead an expedition of around 1,000 settlers and expand the plantation into the interior of the

---

"'Dale's Laws' and the Non-Common Law Origins of Criminal Justice in Virginia," *The American Journal of Legal History* 26:4 (October, 1982): 354–75. None of these works places the code in the context of martial lawmaking.

[44] Horn, *A Land as God Made It*, 33–44. *The Three Charters of the Virginia Company of London* (Williamsburg, 1957), 1–12.

[45] Horn, *A Land as God Made It*, 46–7.

[46] It seems they followed this instruction. *Ibid.*, 57–9; Edward Maria Wingfield, "Discourse," in *The Jamestown Voyages under the First Charter, 1606–1609* ed. Philip Barbour 2 vols. (Cambridge, 1969), 1: 213–33.

[47] Wingfield, "Discourse," in *Jamestown Voyages* 1: 213–33; John Smith, "A True Relation of Such Occurrences and Accidents of Noate as Hath Hapned in Virginia," in *The Complete Works of Captain John Smith (1580–1631)* ed. Philip L. Barbour 3 vols. (Chapel Hill, 1986), 1: 23–97; Horn, *A Land as God Made It*, 132–5.

continent. Gates returned to England in the spring of 1609 after having been granted leave by the Dutch government.[48]

The new form of government was probably decided in January 1609. The Company, under the leadership of Sir Thomas Smith, a notable London merchant and head of the East India Company, held a series of meetings at the house of the Earl of Exeter to discuss its failings.[49] These problems would be resolved through new powers in a re-granted charter the Company was to submit to James I. The new authorization consolidated the two separate but related enterprises into one Company. A new governor, Thomas West, Lord De La Warr, would sit in Jamestown unencumbered by a factional council or a term limit. He would be assisted by his lieutenant governor, Sir Thomas Gates, and eventually his marshal, Sir Thomas Dale, another veteran of the wars in the Low Countries who had served the Earl of Essex in his 1599 campaign in Ireland.[50] The plan was that Gates and later De La Warr take a large number of men with them to Virginia to create interior settlements that would be better protected from Spanish ships. In the process, Gates was to attack the Powhatans, in particular their "priests," who were supposedly responsible for the death and destruction of the "lost colony of Roanoke," the news of whose fate had just arrived in England.[51]

It must have been in these meetings, about which we know almost nothing, that the Virginia Council hatched the idea to rule Jamestown by martial law. The idea could have come from Matthew Sutcliffe – the same Matthew Sutcliffe who had served in the Low Countries with the Earl of Leicester and with the Earl of Essex. Probably through his connections with West Country merchants made during his tenure as Dean of Exeter and through his connections with the Essex circle from the 1590s, Sutcliffe had become a member of the "northerly" company in March 1607.[52] Under the new charter of 1609, Sutcliffe became a member of the Virginia Company and continued to be a member until

[48] For the increased militarism of the colony, see James Horn, "The Conquest of Eden: Possession and Dominion in Early Virginia," in *Envisioning an English Empire: Jamestown and the Making of the North Atlantic World* ed. Robert Appelbaum and James Wood Sweet (Philadelphia, 2005), 44–6.

[49] Horn, *A Land as God Made It*, 131–8; Alexander Brown, *The First Republic in America: An Account of the Origin of this Nation* (New York, 1898), 73. The Company admitted its previous mistakes in *A True and Sincere Declaration of the Purpose and ends of the Plantation begun in Virginia* (London, 1610).

[50] For Dale, see Darrett Rutman, "The Historian and the Marshal: A Note on the Background of Sir Thomas Dale," *Virginia Magazine of History and Biography* 68:3 (July, 1960): 284–94.

[51] Horn, *A Land as God Made It*, 135–50.

[52] *The Three Charters of the Virginia Company of London*, 25.

the Company was dissolved.[53] Unfortunately, we do not know what if any role Sutcliffe played in the meetings of January 1609. But it would be strange if the Company decided to use martial law without at the very least consulting the leading expert on martial law in England who also happened to be a member of the Company.

In the instructions for Gates in June 1609, which were similar to those given to Lord De La Warr in 1610, the Virginia Company outlined a new government of terror. Gates was to rule with the advice of a small council.[54] The instructions authorized Gates "for capitall and Criminal justice in Case of Rebellion and mutiny and in all such cases of [provident] necessity" to "proceede by martiall lawe according to your commission as of most dispatch and terror and fittest for this government."[55]

This government of terror was not authorized in the 1609 charter. However, the Crown had granted the Company a martial law jurisdiction for its overseas enterprises. This had not generally been the case in the sixteenth century.[56] While entrepreneurs like Ralph Lane definitely used martial law, they did not have explicit authorization from their charters.[57] There are probably two reasons why the Crown started inserting martial law powers into commissions and charters for overseas voyages. First, at least by the 1580s, there was a recognition within some charters of the problem of mutiny on board ships, but delegated authorities were still required to hear and determine cases by common law.[58] However, martial law powers were granted to the East India Company to combat mutiny and other wrongs like murder for

---

[53] *Ibid.*, 31. Sutcliffe participated as a member in the 1620s and served as a commissioner for the settling of the government of Virginia. *The Records of the Virginia Company of London* ed. Susan Myra Kingsbury 4 vols. (Washington, DC, 1906–35), 3: 88, 333; 4: 363, 491, 494.

[54] Virginia Council, "Instruccons Orders and Constitucons to Sr Thomas Gates Knight," May 1609 in *The Records of the Virginia Company of London*, 3: 15. De La Warr's instructions were consistent with Gates'. *Ibid.*, 27.

[55] *Ibid.*, 15.

[56] No martial law powers were granted to either the Levant or Muscovy Companies in the sixteenth century or to the East India Company in 1600. They instead used the laws and customs of the sea to maintain order. *PN* 2: 195–205, 304–16, 5: 192–202; 6: 73–92; M. Epstein, *The Early History of the Levant Company* (London, 1908), 153–211.

[57] The great adventurers of North America did not formally receive martial law powers. *New American World: A Documentary History of North America to 1612* ed. D.B. Quinn 5 vols. (London, 1979), 3: 267–70; *The Voyages and Colonising Enterprises of Sir Humphrey Gilbert* with an introduction and notes by David Beers Quinn 2 vols. (London, 1940), 1: 188–94; *Calendar of the Carew Manuscripts, 1515–74* ed. J.S. Brewer, *et al.* (London, 1870), no. 303. The Essex plantation in Ulster in the sixteenth century received summary martial law powers from the Dublin government. *Fiants, Elizabeth*, no. 2326.

[58] *PN* 7: 375–81. Also see the instructions to Edward Fitton for his eastern voyages, *PN* 11: 164–5.

specific voyages.[59] The Muscovy Company received similar powers in its new charter as well.[60] Walter Raleigh appears to have been given similar powers for his second voyage to the Orinoco.[61] Second, given all of the controversies over martial law in Ireland, the Crown perhaps sought to positively define what martial law powers its delegates possessed when they traveled abroad. As we shall see, these attempts in the early years did little to restrain experimentation with martial law.

The Virginia Company, presumably because it was planning a settled society, received different martial law powers than the governors of the East India Company. The governor in Jamestown was supposed to use martial law "in cases of rebellion or mutiny in as large and ample manner as oure lieutenants in oure counties within oure realme of England have."[62] This clause referred to James' lords lieutenants, who only had the circumscribed martial law powers that we have already examined. This same clause was granted in the 1620 New England charter.[63]

The Virginia Company drastically expanded its martial law powers, seemingly with the support of the Crown.[64] Along with powers of using martial law procedure to punish criminals, Gates and De La Warr possessed the power to make, adapt, or add any laws they thought were necessary for the governing of the plantation. This lawmaking power was delimited to their powers outlined in their commissions, which no longer exists. In the spring of 1610, Gates used his lawmaking power to establish the new laws of the plantation, which De La Warr accepted.[65]

---

[59] *The First Letter Book of the East India Company, 1600–1619* ed. G. Birdwood and W. Foster (London, 1893), 4, 229. Miles Ogborn, *Indian Ink: Script and Print in the Making of the English East India Company* (Chicago, 2007), 52–3.

[60] *Proceedings in Parliament 1628* ed. Robert C. Johnson *et al.* 6 vols. (New Haven, 1977–83), 3: 612.

[61] *The Works of Sir Walter Raleigh, knt...volume 1* (London, 1751), lxviii. Raleigh's instructions to his fleet seem to be a combination of the traditional ordinances of the sea with several ordinances of war, all of which were probably determined by a marshal's court. "Orders to be Observed by the Commanders of the Fleet and Land Companies, under the Charge and Conduct of Sir Walter Ralegh Knight ...," in *ibid.*, xcvii–civ.

[62] Virginia Council, "Instruccons, Orders and Constitucons," *The Records of the Virginia Company of London*, 3:15.

[63] "Charter of New England, 1620" Accessed on 25 July 2014 at: http://avalon.law.yale.edu /17th_century/mass01.asp.

[64] Ken MacMillan has posited that the Crown was fully aware of, and supported, the Company's decision to use martial law in lieu of common law. This claim is certainly possible. At the very least, James and his ministers were unconcerned about the policy. MacMillan, *Sovereignty and Possession in the English New World: The Legal Foundations of Empire, 1576–1640* (Cambridge, 2006), 138–40.

[65] Gates dated the making of the laws to 24 May. De La Warr approved of the laws on 12 June. These comprise the first thirty-seven articles of the code. *Lawes Diuine Morall and Martiall*, 1.

Most of these dealt with religious observance, crimes like theft and assault, and regulated commercial dealings with the Native Americans. By the spring of 1611, after De La Warr had returned to England, Sir Thomas Dale, the new marshal of the colony, arrived and added new laws that delineated the responsibilities of the plantation members selected for military duty. He also codified the laws already made and sent them back to the Company in London. In 1612, William Strachey, the Company's secretary who had accompanied Gates on his initial voyage, published the code and labeled it *The Lawes Diuine Morall and Martiall*.[66]

The Company desired these strict laws because it wanted to prevent the colony from descending into lawlessness. It published them to prove that point to investors. In a sermon given before Lord De La Warr immediately before his departure for Virginia, the pastor William Crashaw preached that the governor had to make sure that his charges would not fall into degeneracy and lose the civility of Englishmen.[67] De La Warr, likewise, when he arrived in the summer of 1610 to Jamestown, declared in his first speech that the planters were guilty of idleness and needed to return to work and religious observance lest they degenerate into "savages."[68] The printing of the code was meant to prove that the Company was maintaining civility among its planters. In the preface written by Gates, the lieutenant governor declared that the printing of the code would quiet those who believed they "liued there laweless, without obedience to our Countrey, or obseruance of Religion to God."[69]

The Company also hoped that strict discipline would help the planters defend the plantation and later engage in conquest. After De La Warr landed in Jamestown, he engaged in military activities against the Powhatans and other neighboring Native Americans. Under Gates, the

---

[66] Dale wrote the last section of the code in June 1611, entitled, "The Summarie of the Marshall Laws," *Lawes Diuine Morall and Martiall*, 20–89 (wrongly paginated as 41). Scholars have often claimed that only this section of the code was martial or "military law." See David H. Flaherty, "Introduction," in *For the Colony in Virginia Britannia Lawes Diuine Morall and Martiall* ed. David H. Flaherty (Charlottesville, 1969), xxv–xxvii. This dubious claim allows Flaherty to assert that the *Lawes Diuine Morall and Martiall* were one of the "first written manifestations of the common law." *Ibid.*, ix. However, the laws as outlined by Gates in the first section of the code were clearly based in part on the articles of war of English armies, see below. Further, the governor, lieutenant governor, and marshal heard and determined all cases involving the breach of these articles at a court-martial. Hence, the very first article in the code states that all those who willfully absent themselves from church services will be "punished according to the martial law in that case provided." *Lawes Diuine Morall and Martiall*, 3.

[67] William Crashaw, *A Sermon Preached before the Right Honorable the Lord LaWarre* ... (London, 1610).

[68] Horn, *A Land as God Made It*, 181.

[69] *Lawes Diuine Morall and Martiall*, sig. A2v. This line was probably written by the secretary of the company, William Strachey.

"general" of the plantation, the colonists took the cornfields of Kecoughton (now Elizabeth City County). The next year, under Thomas Dale, the Virginians established Henrico upriver on the James. Through 1616, the Jamestown colonists continued to wage military campaigns against the Powhatans, guarded their holdings against Spanish attacks, and even on one occasion in 1613 attacked a nascent French settlement in what is now Maine on a privateering expedition.[70]

The template for the *Lawes Diuine Morall and Martiall* has caused consternation among scholars. Some have fought over whether in fact it was a martial law code in the tradition of the English articles of war or whether it was based on a Dutch template.[71] However, the lineage is clear. The makers of the *Lawes Diuine Morall and Martiall* initially relied on the Earl of Essex's 1599 articles of war that governed his English army in Ireland.[72] This is not all that surprising considering that Gates, Dale, and De La Warr had all served with Essex in Ireland in 1599.[73] The code thus drew on the disciplining of *English soldiers* in Ireland and not on the summary martial law powers that governed the poor Irish in the sixteenth century.

Let us see how the two were related and where they diverged. After the opening paragraph, which is different in the two codes, they share consistencies through the first four articles. Let us compare the two paragraphs that justify martial law jurisdiction. The justification from Essex's code reads:

Forasmuch as no good seruice can be perfourmed, or warre well managed where Military discipline is not obserued; And Military discipline cannot bee kept where the Rules or chiefe partes thereof bee not certainly set downe and generally knowen: I haue with the aduise of the Counsaile of Warre set downe these Lawes and Orders following, and doe now publish them vnder my hand, that all persons in this Armie or Kingdome within my charge, may take knowledge of the saide Lawes, and the penalties set downe for the breakers of them.[74]

While the *Lawes Diuine Morall and Martiall* reads:

And Forasmuch as no good seruice can be performed, or warre well managed where militarie discipline is not obserued; and militarie discipline cannot be kept

---

[70] Horn, *A Land as God Made It*, 157–92; Horn, "The Conquest of Eden," in *Envisioning an English Empire*, 25–48.

[71] Walter Prince, "The First Criminal Code of Virginia," *American Historical Association, Annual Report*, 1899 I (Washington, 1899), 319–20. Rutman, "Military Regime," 15–6; Flaherty, "Introduction," xxvi–xxvii. All three scholars have either assumed or sought to deny the assumption that the template came from the Dutch wars because Dale and Gates both spent time in the Low Countries. None have looked to the articles that were in operation in Ireland. See below.

[72] *Lawes and Orders of Warre established for the Good Conduct of the Service in Ireland*, 2–3; *Lawes Diuine Morall and Martiall*, 1–3.

[73] Rutman, "The Historian and the Marshal," 290.

[74] *Lawes and Orders of Warre established for the Good Conduct of the Service in Ireland*, 2.

where the rules or chiefe partes thereof bee not certainely set downe and generally knowne, I haue with the aduise and counsel of Sir Thomas Gates Knight, Lieutenant Generall) adhered vnto the lawes diuine, and orders politique, and martiall of his Lordship (the same exemplified) an addition of such others, as I haue found either the necessitie of the present state of the Colonie to require, or the infancie, and weaknesse of the bodie thereof, as yet able to digest, and doe now publish them to all persons in the Colonie, that they may as well take knowledge of the Lawes themselues, as of the penaltie and punishment, which without partialitie shall be inflicted vpon the breakers of the same.[75]

The two paragraphs start out exactly the same. But about halfway through, Gates diverged from Essex when he felt it necessary to address problems specific to Jamestown. The first four articles of the *Lawes Diuine Morall and Martiall* are identical to the first four articles in Essex's articles, which addressed church attendance, speaking "impiously" against God, the Trinity, or the Christian faith, blasphemy, and treason against the monarch of England.[76] After those prescriptions, Gates and then Dale diverged significantly from Essex. Imitation was part of the code's making, but it did not prevent Dale and Gates from innovating and adapting new laws for their plantation.

Just like Essex in the 1590s, Gates and Dale made laws specific to their polity after having initially copied from a template. Some of the laws they came up with were clearly adapted laws that one could find in any code of war. For example, the *Lawes Diuine Morall and Martiall* prohibited anyone without a license from trading with Native Americans or sailors on ships calling on Jamestown.[77] The code also forbade anyone from attacking "any Indian coming to trade." These market regulations were typical of articles of war in this period, which tried to maintain a controlled market. Other laws were clearly innovations. The *Lawes Diuine Morall and Martiall* regulated the cleanliness and work regime of Jamestown at a level of detail not found in other articles of war. These regulations included detailed instructions for the laundresses of Jamestown, the plantation's tradesmen, and the overseers of workmen.[78] Even the end of the code, which listed articles that outlined the military duties of the colonists, was more detailed than most articles of war.[79]

The most notable aspects of the *Lawes Diuine Morall and Martiall* were the punishments Gates and Dale prescribed for those who transgressed

---

[75] *Lawes Diuine Morall and Martiall*, 2.
[76] *Lawes and Ordinances of Warre, established for the good conduct of the service in Ireland*, 2–3; *Lawes Diuine Morall and Martiall*, 1–2.
[77] *Lawes Diuine Morall and Martiall*, 7. For a comparison, see *Lawes and Orders of Warre established for the Good Conduct of the Service in Ireland*, 5.
[78] *Lawes Diuine Morall and Martiall*, 13; Diamond, "From Organization to Society," 459.
[79] *Lawes Diuine Morall and Martiall*, 20–89 (wrongly paginated as 41).

their laws.[80] For example, Dale supposedly punished a man caught stealing by tying him to a tree and allowing him to starve to death.[81] Apparently a pregnant laundress who failed in her duty was whipped so badly that it led to a miscarriage.[82] The code prescribed galley duty for all sorts of indiscretions.[83] These experiments were effective for a time in disciplining the planters. But quickly, those living in Jamestown began to express their displeasure about living under a martial regime to family members and friends back home. While the Virginia Company attempted to justify its governance in its printed apologies, its governors eventually realized that they could not attract new colonists due to Jamestown's poor reputation.[84] In 1618, the Company's leadership in London, now under Sir Edwin Sandys, circumscribed the plantation's martial law jurisdiction.

The creativity of martial lawmaking made it an attractive option for the Virginia Company in 1609 which sought to reform the behavior of its planters in Jamestown. While lawmaking in English dominions abroad would eventually come to be dominated by colonial assemblies, we can see why the Virginia Company turned to the substantive law of martial law to generate laws specific to the needs of their plantation. Unencumbered by common law customs, the commander could make laws to address specific problems on the spot while also relying on a bevy of past laws created by former generals. Combined with the terror inspired by martial law procedure, the *Lawes Diuine Morall and Martiall* was at least initially a viable solution to life in the New World.[85]

Arundel's code

The *Lawes Diuine Morall and Martiall*, while in many ways extraordinary, was part of a larger trend of experimentation with martial laws. This

---

[80] Unfortunately, we have no courts-martial records from Virginia in this period. The only extant records are several warrants for the deposing of witnesses and four pardons granted in 1617. *Records of the Virginia Company of London*, 3: 69–70, 74, 79.

[81] "A Brief Declaration of the Plantation of Virginia during the first twelve years, when Sir Thomas Smith was Governor of the Company," in *Colonial Records of Virginia* (Richmond, 1874), 75.

[82] Diamond, "From Organization to Society," 459.

[83] See, for example, *Lawes Diuine Morall and Martiall*, 6. The Crown experimented with galleys on the Thames in the late sixteenth century in lieu of capital punishment. See J.S. Cockburn, *A History of English Assizes, 1558–1714* (Cambridge, 1972), 129.

[84] Ralph Hamor, *A True Discourse of the Present Estate of Virginia* (London, 1615), 27. Craven, *Dissolution*, 48–9.

[85] The prevailing opinion of most historians of Jamestown was that the martial law code was initially a successful policy. Horn, *A Land as God Made It*, 193–207. Rutman, "The Virginia Company's Military Regime," 19–20.

creative impulse continued into the next decades of the seventeenth century and culminated in the Earl of Arundel's 1639 articles of war made for Charles' campaign against the rebellious Scots.[86] Arundel's code incorporated many of the innovations English commanders and jurists had been making since 1585. Through an examination of this code, we can trace English martial lawmaking's place within a wider European military law tradition on the eve of the English Civil War.

In common with the articles of war of French and Spanish armies, Arundel allowed his courts discretion to impose penalties for non-capital cases. Often, he dubbed this latitude either discretionary or arbitrary punishment. Discretion was also allowed in Roman Civil Law courts for the sentencing of convicts to whatever corporal punishment or imprisonment it desired provided that the punishment did not involve life or limb.[87] This idea had been present since the Middle Ages when it was often used to imprison convicts instead of executing, maiming, or banishing them. By the sixteenth century, jurists in civilian courts began using *poena extraordinaria* more often because a court could punish without first obtaining full proof. A similar transformation happened in some military courts. Articles of war in the Middle Ages prescribed extraordinary punishment in the form of imprisonment.[88] But imprisonment was expensive for an army, and it prevented the immediate return to active duty. Commanders began to prefer corporal punishments for ordinary soldiers or galley slavery, which still obtained labor from the convict. Over the course of the sixteenth century, commanders left precisely how these offenders would be punished to the discretion of the court. The Spanish began experimenting with extraordinary punishments before the English or the French.[89] While the French and English still mandated chivalric degradation, the Spanish were beginning to prescribe galley slavery and

---

[86] *Lawes and Ordinances of Warre, for the Better Government of his Majesties Army Royall* (London, 1639). For the Bishop's Wars, see Mark Charles Fissel, *The Bishops' Wars: Charles I's Campaigns against Scotland, 1638–1640* (Cambridge, 1994).

[87] John Langbein, *Torture and the Law of Proof: Europe and England in the Ancien Régime* (Chicago, 2006), 45–60.

[88] See, for example, the articles of war of the army of Richard II, which only prescribed imprisonment, loss of horse and armor, death, and in one instance, the loss of an ear. Francis Grose, *Military Antiquities Respecting a History of the English Army from the Conquest to the Present Time* 2 vols. (London, 1812), 2: 63–8.

[89] Londono, *Discurso sobre la forma de reducer la disciplina military a mejor y antique estado*. In France, reservations among jurists in granting military courts powers of life and limb led to the de-capitalization of some offenses, including desertion, which was a common capital offense in English ordinances of war. See David Parrott, *Richelieu's Army: War, Government, and Society in France, 1624–1642* (Cambridge, 2001), 528; John A. Lynn, *Giant of the Grand Siècle: The French Army, 1610–1715* (Cambridge, 1997), 405–8.

other "arbitrary punishments" for their soldiers in the sixteenth century.[90] By the time of the English Civil War, articles of war for English armies granted courts-martial discretion, provided the penalty was not capital, for many of its articles. In contrast, the Dutch rarely granted courts discretion over punishment. Thus, the Dutch code of war, published by Prince Maurice in 1590, was even by the standards of military substantive law unbelievably brutal.[91] While French and English codes often prescribed death for violation of less than half of the articles, the Dutch code mandated death for over 65 percent of its offenses.[92] The English did not universally follow the Dutch example.

Arundel's code had many influences, but the greatest by far was Matthew Sutcliffe's work. It is true that Arundel's article against blasphemy was copied from the Dutch code of 1590.[93] Arundel also made new laws for the perceived dangers his soldiers might experience during the Scottish campaign. Because many agreed with the Scots that Charles was in the wrong, Arundel ordered that "[W]hoever in favor of the enemy, or other pretence whatsoever, shall presume to say or secretly insinuate to any, that His Majesties Forces or *Army Royall* is unlawfull or not *necessary*, shall suffer as an enemy and rebell."[94] But these influences should not diminish Sutcliffe's influence. Sixty-five percent of Arundel's articles were consistent with Sutcliffe's articles, with Arundel slightly adapting their language at times to meet his army's needs. Arundel's code also copied Sutcliffe's categories with the exception of two relating to the navy and one relating to the officers of the army and navy. These categories were found in many of the English articles of war for the rest of the century (See Table 3.1).

The juris-generative impulse lessened but did not end by the middle of the seventeenth century. Commanders continued to adapt ordinances

---

[90] Forty-four percent of the offenses in Londono's code granted some kind of discretion to the court with language like "as the court shall see fit" or "upon pain of arbitrary punishment" or "at the court's discretion." Londono, *Discurso sobre la forma de reducer la disciplina military a mejor y antique estado.*

[91] *Lawes and Ordinances Touching Military Discipline. Set down and established the 13 of August 1590 tr. By I.D.* (The Hague, 1631). I.D. is almost certainly Isaac Dorislaus, the Dutch jurist who would become the judge advocate general of parliament's armies in the 1640s and future regicide. The Dutch code was translated into English a second time by Henry Hexham in *The Principles of the Art Militarie* (London, 1637), Appendix: 9–15 (incorrectly dated 13 August 1580). The Swedish code had also been translated. William Watts, *The Swedish Discipline, Religious, Civile, and Military* (London, 1632), 39–69.

[92] Corporal punishments were prescribed for blasphemy, derision of God's word, and for minor embezzlement. *Lawes and Ordinances touching military discipline*, sig., A2, B2v.

[93] Compare *Lawes and Ordinances of Warre*, 3 with the Dutch, *Lawes and Ordinances Touching Military Discipline*, sig. A2.

[94] *Lawes and Ordinances of War*, 7. Arundel's italics.

Table 3.1 *Comparison between Matthew Sutcliffe's articles of war and the Earl of Arundel's articles of war*

Category	Matthew Sutcliffe[95]	The Earl of Arundel	Articles of War Comparison
1	Laws concerning religion and moral Matters	Concerning religion and breach of moral duties	S1–2/A5, S6/A6, S7/A7, S8/A10, S2/A13
2	Tending to the common safety of the state, army, garrison	Concerning the safety of the Army Royal and of the Kingdom	S1/A2, S2/A3, S3/A5, S4/A6, S5/A8, S6/A9, S7/A10, S7/A11
3	Concerning the duties of captains and soldiers yet more particularly	Concerning duties of captain and soldiers in particular	S1/A1, S3/A2, S4/A3, S5/A4, S6/A5, S7/A6, S9/A8, S11/A10, S13/A12, S14/A13, S16/A15, S18/A16, S19/A17, S21/A20, S22/A21, S24/A22, S25/A25
4	Concerning the camp, or towne of garrison are conteined	Concerning the camp or garrison	S1/A1, S2/A2, S3/A3, S4/A4, S5/A5, S6/A6, S7/A7, S8/A8, S9/A9, S9/A10, S10/A11, S12/A12
5	Concerning sea causes...		
6	Certain orders concerning adventures at sea		
7	Concerning the officers of the army or navy, or that have charge to make any provision for either		
8	Comprising orders concerning booties, spoils, and prisoners taken in war	Concerning lawful spoils and prizes	S1/A1, S4/A3
9	Concerning the execution of laws and administration of justice	Concerning the administration of justice	S1/A1, S2/A2, S3/A4, S4/A8, S5/A9, S6/A10, S7/A11, S8/A14

and create new ones. However, there was no similar transformation in the later seventeenth century to the one that took place at the end of the

[95] *Sutcliffe*, 304–42. Arundel, *Lawes and Ordinances of Warre*. This charts the consistencies between Matthew Sutcliffe's articles and those of the Earl of Arundel. For example S7/A7 under category "1" means that Sutcliffe's seventh article in his first category (which banned "suspitious and common women" from camp and garrison) corresponds to Arundel's seventh article in his first category. Sometimes Arundel's code combined two of Sutcliffe's articles or broke one of his articles into two. When it came to articles relating to the administration of justice, Arundel replaced court-martial with "council of war." See below.

sixteenth. By the middle of the seventeenth century, jurists and commanders transformed the articles of war that had focused on ransom and prisoners of war to a code that detailed duties relating to camp, the safety of the garrison, and to superiors. The codes of the Civil War were a product of experimentation in lawmaking. Adaptation, imitation, and innovation were the strategies jurists adopted when they transformed the articles of war.

Transformations in procedure

At the same time that English commanders and jurists were transforming the substance of martial law and its administration, they were also transforming its procedure.[96] Commanders replaced the court of the marshal – where the marshal or judge marshal on his own heard and determined cases – with a council of war, where somewhere between five and twenty officers evaluated charges of wrongdoing. In this transformation, as in the others, commanders and martial jurists were influenced by continental developments. The end product was procedural rules that spread discretion among a wider group of officers, more lawyers to interpret those rules, and in all probability longer trials. While councils of war often meted out brutal punishments to those who had committed wrongs, soldiers and sailors could nevertheless expect that their case would be tried through a legal process.

We can spot this transformation by contrasting the Earl of Arundel's code with the instructions for courts-martial in the work of Matthew Sutcliffe. The Earl of Arundel and his council were influenced by Sutcliffe's prescriptions in this area as well, with one important exception. Here is Sutcliffe's first command relating to the administration of justice:

That the auctours of disorders may be detected and punishment awarded accordingly, it shalbe lawfull *for the iudge marshall, or others that haue commission from the Generall, or lorde Martiall* to do iustice, to enquire of the auctours, and circumstances of offence committed by the othes of such, and so many as they thinke

---

[96] Francis Grose, *Military Antiquities*, 2: 54. Also see a manuscript history of courts-martial which is now in the National Archives. "Descriptions of court-martial proceedings in several European countries and various articles of war" [late eighteenth century] TNA, WO 93/6. Other brief descriptions of this transformation can be found in Captain David A. Schlueter, "The Court-Martial: An Historical Survey," *Military Law Review* 87 (Winter, 1980): 137–42; James Snedeker, *A Brief History of Courts-Martial* (Annapolis, 1954), 11–19; S.C. Pratt, *Military Law, its Procedure and Practice* (19th ed., 1915), 6–7; C.M. Clode, *The Administration of Justice under Military and Martial Law* (London, 1874), 83–90. All of these works tend to ignore the early seventeenth century with the exception of Gustavus Adolphus' disciplinary regime.

conuenient, and shal further vse all meanes for examination, and triall of persons accused, dilated, suspected, or defamed.[97]

Let us remember what this procedure entailed. Usually by information, a suspect would be brought before a court-martial which consisted of one judge: the lord general, the marshal, or the judge marshal, or sometimes a provost marshal general. If the case was not brought before the judge marshal, he would serve as legal counsel to either the general or the marshal. Once the evidence had been gathered and contemplated, the judge of the court would declare the sentence, which would be carried out by the provost marshal or the executioner.

The Earl of Arundel's code prescribed a different procedure which we can glean from the first article set down for the administration of justice:

First, that such as commit disorders, may be detected, and punishment accordingly awarded; it shall be lawful for the *Councell of warre and the Advocate* for the Army to enquire of Actors and circumstances of offences committed by the othes of suche and so many as they thinke convenient: and shall further use all meanes for examination and trial of persons accused, dilated, suspected, or defamed.[98]

The instructions are nearly identical, except in the place of the "judge marshal and others" Arundel's code had the council of war and an advocate. Gone was the court of the marshal and in its stead was the council of war. Gone too was the judge marshal and in his stead was an advocate, who was distinguished in his responsibilities from those who sat on the council of war. By the end of the seventeenth century, each regiment possessed its own council of war, its own provost marshal, and often retained a lawyer to give the council advice.[99] Unfortunately, we know little about these regimental courts-martial. But much more information survives for general courts-martial. Let us briefly further illuminate the changes that we have detected before we examine why they took place.

The key difference between the courts-martial of the sixteenth century and the councils of war of the seventeenth century was that in lieu of the marshal or general hearing and determining cases on his own, a council of usually between five and twenty officers heard and determined cases. The commissioners heard all of the evidence and decided on the charge. At the head of the council was a president, who was supposed to be a person of "integritie of sound iudgement and of ripe knowledge both in ciuil and military lawes before whome all matters ciuil & criminal that

---

[97] *Sutcliffe*, 339. My italics.   [98] *Lawes and Ordinances of Warre*, 21. My italics.
[99] By the 1690s, each regiment possessed a "solicitor." UCLA, William Andrews Clark Library, "Army Account Book, 1692."

haue relation to ye Armye are to be tried."[100] But the president, unlike the lord marshal or general in the sixteenth century, only possessed slightly more power than the other commissioners on the council. He often but not always had the power of a double vote in case the other commissioners were deadlocked.

Conviction at a council of war, unlike a petty jury, only required a plurality. There were rarely deadlocked councils of war. In this difference, councils of war resembled other conciliar jurisdictions both on the European continent and in England. The Court of Star Chamber, for example, similarly decided cases based upon a plurality; so too did the presidential courts in the north of England, the marches of Wales, Munster, and in Connacht.[101] Like these other tribunals, a council of war decided cases and then punishments by having each officer of the court, starting with the lowest in rank, declare their opinion. If it was a non-capital punishment, the process would end with the lord president making the decision on what punishment the convict would receive.[102]

The role of the legal officers of the army became more circumscribed in this conciliar jurisdiction. Where before judge marshals often heard and determined cases on their own, now the law officers only had powers to obtain evidence and deliver it to the court.[103] According to one prescriptive writer, the officer increasingly known as the "advocate" could not "pass sentence; nor to enter into any debate at ye council-table without ye question be put to him & then he ought to answer according to law, conscience & presidents."[104] This "inquisitor of blood" was the chief detective and prosecutor of the court. It was he who would most often provide informations so that the court could prosecute the case. Like his predecessors, he was responsible for keeping track of all the wills and other legal business of the soldiers.[105] But he had no judicial power.

[100] Sir William Throckmorton, "A Brief Treatise of War, containing ye most essential & circumstantial parts thereof . . . " BL, Harley Ms. 6008, f. 21.

[101] Thomas Garden Barnes, "Due Process and Slow Process in the late Elizabethan-Early Stuart Star Chamber," *American Journal of Legal History* 6:3 (October, 1962): 227–31.

[102] For an example of voting, see Worcester College, Oxford, Clarke Ms. 21, fos. 32–3.

[103] The best history of the office of judge advocate, albeit one that focuses almost exclusively on the eighteenth century, can be found in Frederick Bernays Wiener, *Civilians under Military Justice: The British Practice since 1689, especially in North America* (Chicago, 1967), 165–88.

[104] Sir William Throckmorton, "Commentaries of Caesar," BL, Harley Ms. 4602, f. 84v; this statement conforms to the commissions which judge advocates received after 1660; see the commission to John Henry, who was to be judge advocate general in Tangier in 1661, BL, Harley MS 6844, f. 102.

[105] Probate cases were often decided by delegated commissions that included the advocate. See, for example, BL, Sloane, Ms. 1957, fos. 51, 99–106; BL, Sloane, Ms. 1959, fos. 24–5, 61–4, 102–4, 107v, 109v; BL, Sloane Ms. 1960, fos. 13–14, 15v–16, 36–8, 53–6, 58–60.

Eventually, English armies stopped calling this officer the judge marshal. This transformation began in 1639, when the council of war ordered its auditor to change the title of William Lewin's position from judge marshal to "advocate of the army."[106] The confusing terminology continued. In his commission to George Clark, the advocate general of the army, in 1685, James II granted him all the privileges "any other Advocate Generall or judge Martiall Advocates general or any other Judges Martiall by what name soever" had previously possessed.[107] The title of judge marshal, however, was not abandoned but instead combined with "advocate of the army:" hence why we have the title "judge advocate general," even though the office possesses no judicial capacity.

Conciliar courts were known to the army well before they became normative. In the Middle Ages, we shall recall, the lord general of the army at times called a council of war or a tribunal to hear and determine very important cases. It was probably by this procedure that the Black Prince tried Marshal D'Audreham in 1367 for treason in the aftermath of the battle of Najera. In 1586, a similar tribunal was convened to hear and determine a case against the governor of Grave, "M. Hemert." He and several captains had supposedly given up the city to the Spanish illegally. They were put on trial both for treason and for negligence of duty and cowardice. While lesser men might have been tortured and convicted before a sole judge – as we saw with Joise Lews in Chapter 1 – Leicester in this instance commissioned "Count Hollock and Count Newenar, and divers others, colonels and officers of the field" due to the social importance of these men.[108] Suspects were arraigned before the council, who acquitted them of treason, but convicted them of negligence of duty and cowardice. All of them were executed. Thus, we need to understand why and when this special form of tribunal became normative.

At various moments, English commanders opted for a conciliar tribunal as the normative means to try soldiers. It seems that the Earl of Essex experimented with using the council of war as a judicial body during the 1590s. However, it is almost certain that the Virginia

---

[106] TNA, SP 16/442, f. 224v. Lewin is still listed as judge marshal in the declared accounts of the army. TNA, E 351/292.

[107] TNA, C 66/3268, m. 1d.

[108] The trial was recounted in various correspondences between English commanders and the Privy Council. *CSPF*, 21 (pt. 2): 24–8, 32, 48, 73. It was also relayed in Emanuel van Meteran's *Belgische ofte Nederlandsche Historie van onzen Tijden*, and the story was available in English through Edward Grimstone's *A Generall Historie of the Netherlands* (London, 1627), 827–[8] (mistakenly paginated as 824). Both were cited by William Prynne and Clement Walker in the trial of Nathaniel Fiennes for giving up Bristol in 1643. William Prynne, *A True and Full Relation of the Prosecution, Arraingment, Tryall, and Condemnation of Nathaniel Fiennes* (London, 1644), sig. A2v and pages 118–19.

Company used the simple marshal's court. Sir Thomas Gates, as we have seen, in 1609 when he was stranded on Bermuda, tried, convicted, and then pardoned two soldiers for sedition at a traditional court-martial. By the 1620s, Sir Francis Markham believed councils of war to be normative but, as we shall see, it was not exclusively used in the courts-martial that sat in England in the 1620s. The process of transformation was slow, and the two procedural forms were probably used side by side for some time.

Part of the reason why English commanders and jurists probably opted for conciliar procedure was because they wanted to imitate the procedural transformations that were taking place within continental military courts. It seems that from at least the latter part of the sixteenth century the military courts of the Holy Roman Empire mandated a conciliar jurisdiction. Maximilien II, for example, mandated "three captains, three lieutenants, three cornets and three corporals with one field officer of the Cavalry and with them form the Court."[109] By the 1590s, the Dutch under Prince Maurice of Nassau established the *Hoge Krijgsraad*, a centralized court comprised of between ten and twenty officers who supervised martial cases relating to the Republic's soldiers.[110] Spanish monarchs, likewise, formed a council of war that governed all judicial cases within the Iberian Peninsula.[111] The French, undergoing a transition in the same timeframe as the English, used courts of the constable and marshal less and less in the seventeenth century and opted instead for *conseils de guerre*.[112] By the 1630s, the English would have known that the military courts of Gustavus Adolphus also used

---

[109] These ordinances were translated by the anonymous author, "of the Military Judicature and Method of Proceeding both in Criminal and Civil Causes in the Modern Imperial Armies," TNA, WO 93/6. The author translated these ordinances from the monumental work of Petrus Pappus von Tratzberg, *Corpus Iuris Militaris* (Amsterdam, 1674), a work which had multiple printings and which was originally written in Dutch in the early seventeenth century and later translated into German.

[110] For those who can read Dutch, see Jan Willem Wijn, *Het Krijgswezen in den Tijd Van Maurits* (Utrecht, 1934), 81–115. For those who cannot, see the brief summary in English by Jonathan Isreal, *The Dutch Republic: Its Rise, Greatness, and Fall, 1477–1806* (Oxford, 1995), 267–8. Alas! I have relied on the summation. English mercenaries were less than pleased by this court's claims to jurisdiction over them. Trim, "Fighting Jacob's Wars," 191.

[111] They however did not use conciliar procedure in the Low Countries. I.A.A. Thompson, *War and Government in Habsburg Spain, 1560–1620* (London, 1976), 42–8.

[112] "Of the Method of Proceeding against Criminals and other Offenders in the French Armies," TNA, WO 93/6 (unpaginated, no folio numbers); however, the author here has gotten his dates wrong. He assumed that Louis XIV replaced the provost's court with a "conseil de guerre," but the conseil de guerre as a juridical body was present in French armies at least by the 1630s. See Parrott, *Richelieu's Army*, 528–33, and Lynn, *Giant of the Grand Siècle*, 397–414.

conciliar procedure.[113] Due to the fact that many English martial men fought in continental armies in the early seventeenth century, they might have advocated that Arundel permanently transform the court-martial into a council of war.

Structural changes within the army were also very important for the shift from the marshal's court to the council of war. Prior to the 1570s, English armies possessed almost no intermediate officers. However, by the end of the century, English commanders began emulating the Spanish practice of dividing the army into *tercios* – the English would call them regiments – based loosely on the Roman legion. Each *tercio* had its own officer corps, which included *auditors*, commissaries, clerks, quartermasters, and was led by the *maestro de campo*.[114] In emulation, the English adopted the officer of colonel.[115] By the English Civil War, more middling officers made it easier for a council of war to sit and hear offenses rather than relying on the marshal or the general to exclusively decide cases.[116] The general could delegate matters of justice and concentrate his time on larger strategic concerns.

The structural transformation does not alone explain the shift from a court-martial to a council of war. Political reasons within the army were also important.[117] Commanders were supposed to take counsel from their councils of war. Elizabeth, in her commands to the Earl of Essex in 1596 before his attempt to relieve Calais, for example, instructed him not to take any important measure without first taking counsel from his officers.[118] These were no mere empty words. A commander could get charged for malfeasance for not seeking counsel.[119] Having councils of war decide legal cases was a way to preemptively rebut such charges.

---

[113] Watts, *Swedish Discipline*, 66–8. The Swedish court, however, required a unanimous decision.

[114] For an outline of the Spanish army, see Parker, *The Army of Flanders*, 91–108. The Spanish in Flanders did not adopt a council of war. Instead, due to the king's fears of corruption, he appointed a special judge as prosecutor who oversaw military cases in the Low Countries. González de León, *The Road to Rocroi*, 107–20.

[115] Cruikshank, *Elizabeth's Army*, 51–2. The French likewise adopted this structure. James B. Wood, *The King's Army: Warfare, Soldiers, and Society during the Wars of Religion in France, 1562–1576* (Cambridge, 1996), 106–10.

[116] Lee, *Barbarians & Brothers*, 89.

[117] There also may have been legal reasons. Common lawyers also probably, had they the opportunity, advocated for this shift. Indeed, some wanted a jury trial. An anonymous tract on the laws of Ireland in the late sixteenth century declared that all colonels have powers of martial law but the form of martial law "must be by formall tryall by a jury of his fellow soldiers and nott at the will and displeasure of the colonel." NLI, Ms. 3319, f. 23. The writer might have confused *pro tribunali* procedure with that of a jury trial.

[118] "Instructions of the Queen to Essex" TNA, SP 12/257, f. 135.

[119] Nathanial Fiennes was charged by William Prynne and Clement Walker for acting without the consent of his council of war. *Articles of Impeachment and Accusation, exhibited in Parliament, against Colonell Nathaniel Fiennes*, art. 5 on page 7. Sir John

Francis Willoughby claimed such a defense as governor of Berwick-upon-Tweed in 1600.[120] That year a dispute arose between the master of the ordnance, Sir Richard Musgrave, and the marshal of Berwick, Sir William Bowes, over Willoughby's use of eight guns, which Musgrave claimed were for the town but Willoughby had assigned to his own ship.[121] Musgrave claimed that Willoughby ruled the town by "martial law," a jurisdiction he claimed went unused in the town, and that he had dismissed Musgrave's claim by this arbitrary form of law. In response, Willoughby told Sir Robert Cecil that he had referred the case to a council of war comprised of twenty of the town's "worthiest captains and gentlemen" – hardly in his estimation, an arbitrary form of adjudication.[122]

This same strategy was taken up by Thomas Wentworth, the lord deputy of Ireland, after he had convicted Lord Mountnorris of seditious speech against his commander in the winter of 1635, a trial we have already briefly examined in Chapter 2.[123] The trial raised eyebrows well before the Long Parliament impeached him for treason because it ultimately gave Wentworth control over the Irish customs revenue, which Mountnorris had been in charge of, a lucrative responsibility in seventeenth-century Ireland. In his report to the secretary of state, Sir John Coke, Wentworth stated that nearly twenty men sat on the council of war that tried Mountnorris, including the marshal of the army and the lord president of Connacht. Justice had taken place, according to Wentworth, while he had "sat silent all the while."[124] In another letter to Coke only weeks later, Wentworth repeated that he had remained silent during the whole affair and had allowed the council of war instead to carry out the judicial business against Mountnorris.[125] Not judging at the council of war, just as the monarch did not judge at King's Bench, allowed the lord

Hotham made the unfortunate mistake of trying to defend his actions because he had not taken counsel. HHC, U DDHO 1/35.

[120] Willoughby had also demanded a public trial in a court-martial in the Low Countries in 1589. *CSPF*, 23: 55,125, 332.

[121] Richard Musgrave to the Privy Council, October 1600, TNA, SP 59/39, f. 176.

[122] Willoughby to Robert Cecil, 29 October 1600, *The Border Papers: Calendar of letters and papers relating to the affairs of the borders of England and Scotland*. . . 2 vols. (1894–6), 2: no. 1270.

[123] Mountnorris was convicted of violating several articles: "no man shall give any disgraceful words, or commit any act to the Disgrace of any Person in his Army or garrison or any part thereof upon pain of imprisonment . . .: No man shall . . . contemptuously disobey his Commander . . . upon pain of Death." "Minutes of the Council of War," 12 December 1635, in William Knowler, *The Earl of Strafford's Letters and Dispatches* 2 vols. (London, 1740), 1: 501. For the politics of this trial, see Chapter 4.

[124] Wentworth and Council of War to Coke, 15 December 1635, in Knowler, *Strafford Letters*, 1: 498.

[125] Wentworth to Coke, 3 January 1636, in Knowler, *Strafford Letters*, 1: 505.

general to appear – even when that was clearly not the case – to be above the often rancorous legal debates within the army.

Finally, soldiers by the 1640s expected to have their cases heard before a council of war. If this process was not given to them, complaints, even riots, ensued. In the admittedly radical atmosphere of 1647, the soldiers of Colonel John Poyntz's regiment, who were stationed in the north of England as part of parliament's peacekeeping force in the aftermath of their victory over Charles I, mutinied against their commander. Poyntz, a grizzled veteran of the Thirty Years War who was known to be a disciplinarian, was unpopular for many reasons. The soldiers wrote down charges against the colonel, perhaps unrealistically expecting that the lord general of parliament's forces, Sir Thomas Fairfax, would try Poyntz for his wrongs. The sixth article charged that Poyntz had "arbitrarily" committed some officers for speaking on behalf of the army's wishes and for "hanging one soldier without a council of warr."[126] In another case, on board the Torrington in 1655, sailors accused Captain John Clarke of multiple offenses. One of those included ducking sailors without first having them tried before a council of war.[127] Before discipline could be administered, soldiers and sailors believed that they deserved an opportunity to be heard in court before a council. From 1642 until the end of the century, they were granted this privilege.

By the 1640s, the navy adopted a shortened version of the articles of war as well as the procedures of councils of war. This transformation was made permanent in 1648–9. It was one of a series of changes to the navy the Purged Parliament made in those years. It did so because it feared invasions of England by European monarchies that backed royalist resistance. The new Commonwealth government imported some of the administrative and legal concepts from the New Model Army which by 1649 had been enormously successful in battle. The most important of these changes was the crafting of articles of war adapted from the army. The articles, twenty in length in 1649, were slightly expanded in the 1650s. They were incorporated into statute by the Restoration Parliament in 1661.[128] The laws were to be administered

[126] "Articles against General Poyntz," in *The Clarke Papers: Selections from the Papers of Sir William Clarke* ed. C.H. Firth 4 vols. (London, 1891–1901), 1: 169. John Rushworth, *Historical Collections of Private Passages of State* 8 vols. (London, 1721), 6:620–25. Accessed on British History Online February 2013-September 2015, www.british-history.ac.uk.

[127] "Charges against Captain John Clarke, 1655," Bodl. Rawl. A. Ms. 295, f. 2.

[128] Bernard Capp, *Cromwell's Navy: The Fleet and the English Revolution, 1648–1660* (Oxford, 1989), 58–9; Michael Oppenheim, *A History of the Administration of the Royal Navy and of Merchant Shipping in Relation to the Navy* (Hamden, CO, 1961), 311; *CJ*, 6: 156–7, 7: 235–6. *Lawes of War and Ordinances of the Sea* (London, 1652), 13 Car. II. c.9.

by the same procedures that we have already seen in operation within the army. Judge advocates were regular officers of the navy during the Restoration.[129] Martial law was the standard jurisdiction on naval ships from the 1640s onward.

By the English Civil War, the procedures of courts-martial had been transformed. Just like the confusing titles given to the lawyers of the army, the conciliar courts by the 1640s possessed multiple names. Often commanders and advocates still referred to them as courts-martial. Likewise, they were frequently referred to as "councils of war." Sometimes they were called "courts of war." Regardless of title, the procedures of these courts were fairly consistent.

Coming before the court

These rules were put in practice throughout England, Ireland, and in garrisons abroad. Records of their application exist from campaigns in England and the Low Countries, garrisons in Scotland, Ireland, and Tangier, and from ships located in the Caribbean and Mediterranean.[130] It is tempting to collate all of these together and provide a statistical analysis

---

[129] There is a list of those who served as judge advocates since the Restoration in Pepys' papers. Bod. Rawl. A. 181, f. 252. For a naval JAG commission, see the papers of Sir William Trumbull, who was judge advocate for the fleet and for Tangier between 1681–5. BL, Add. Ms. 72,545 [loose papers].

[130] The main courts-martial records from the seventeenth century are listed below. "Dundee Court-Martial Records," ed. Godfrey Davies *Miscellany of the Scottish Historical Society* 2nd Ser. 3 (1919): 9–67. The originals, which are still worth looking at are in Worcester College, Oxford, Clarke Ms. 21. "The Court-Martial Papers of Sir William Waller's Army, 1644," ed. John Adair *JSAHR* 44 (December, 1966): 205–27. "Minutes of Courts-Martial held in Dublin in the years 1651–3," ed. Heather MacLean, Ian Gentles, and Micheál Ó Siochrú *Archivium Hibernicum* 64 (2011): 56–164. Bodl. Rawl Ms. A 295 and A 314; Bodl. Rawl. Ms. C. 972; TNA, WO 71/121; TNA, WO, 26/6, 32–58; TNA, WO 89/1; TNA, ADM 1/5253; BL, Sloane Ms. 1957, 1959, 1960, 1961, 3498, and 3514. There are other papers that occasionally have records of courts-martial. "The diary of William Clarke," BL, Add. Ms. 14,286, fos. 10, 13v, 14, 16. Pepys had several loose records relating to courts-martial in his papers. Bodl. Rawl A. 171, fos. 149, 172v, 174v, 195, 210–11, 214v, 257, 259, 261, 340, 357, 361, 363, 365–8. There are copies of courts-martial records from Ireland in the Restoration in Bodl. Carte Ms. 48, f. 36; Bodl. Carte Ms 34, fos. 444–6v, 451–2v. The Lords Main Papers contain copies of several courts-martial: PA, HL/PO/JO/10/1/177–8, 209, 243. The courts-martial of the Bristol conspirators are in Bodl. Nelson Ms. 13, fos. 336–76, 399–400. The court-martial of Edward Sexby can be found in *The Clarke Papers V* ed. Frances Henderson (Cambridge, 2006), 26–34. While Lord Mountnorris' court-martial record can be found in HRO, Verulam Ms. XII.B.34a. Families of officers sometimes kept their records of the trial. See the papers of Thomas Sanders in DRO, 1232M/027–033 and of Sir John Hotham in HHC, U DDHO 1/31–46, 48, 57, 61–2. Courts-martial records become slightly more common in the eighteenth century. See, for example, The Churchill Archives Centre, Erle Ms. 4/8/1–2, the "Blenheim Court-Martial Records," BL, Add. Ms. 61,336, and TNA, WO 71/122.

of the types of wrong punished, the conviction rate, and the rate of capital punishment.[131] In doing so, we could make a series of generalizations about rates of conviction, capital punishment, and types of wrong punished. But in making these generalizations we would have to ignore the wide variation that exists among the surviving records. This inconsistency is a product of differences between courts-martial in geography and time. Even the cognizance of the courts varied depending on time and place. In Dublin in the 1650s, and in London at various points in the 1640s, certain civilian offenses were heard before the courts. This was not true of the naval courts-martial of later periods, and it was only rarely true of the garrison courts-martial at Tangier. Certain records, like that of William Waller, were taken in the field when the army was on active campaign. Others were recorded when the army was in garrison. As Barbara Donagan has rightly noted, armies in the field were more severe in their punishments than those in garrison.[132] But even garrison courts-martial varied. The Tangier courts-martial, in all likelihood because it was consistently threatened by Moroccan forces, generally punished desertion with death, while in Dublin, the court rarely punished with death for the same offense.

The personality of the commanding officer played a role in these differences. Their understanding of the mood and training of their soldiery was also taken into account. Would they mutiny in response to harsh discipline, perhaps because they had not been paid recently? Did they need to learn to be more disciplined through the terror of watching a former colleague die or were they disciplined veterans? Officers of the court took their highly specific environment into account when they deliberated any given case.

Nevertheless, there are consistencies that run through the records. Procedures began either by written information or by a formal accusation. The judge advocate facilitated the investigation and organized the deputation of witnesses. A council heard and determined the case and voted on guilt or innocence based on majority. The lord general reserved the right to pardon. Officers and soldiers were treated differently both procedurally and in terms of punishment. Further, the types of wrongs that courts-martial were concerned with were similar across the century even if their

---

[131] Analysis of courts-martial in the Civil War can be found in Donagan, *War in England*, 134–96. Also see C.H. Firth, *Cromwell's Army* (3rd ed., London, 1961), 276–310. For the Restoration, see John Childs, *The Army of Charles II* (London, 1976), 75–89. For Tangier, see E.M.G. Routh, *Tangier: England's Lost Atlantic Outpost, 1661–1684* (London, 1912), 308–42. For naval courts-martial, see Robert E. Glass, "Naval courts-Martial in Seventeenth-Century England," *in New Interpretations in Naval History: Selected Papers from the Twelfth Naval History Symposium held at the United States Naval Academy, 26–27 October 1995* ed. William B. Cogar (Annapolis, 1997), 53–64.
[132] Donagan, *War in England*, 178–9.

decisions to punish them often dramatically differed. While officers were always treated with more respect, councils of war also protected soldiers and sailors from tyrannical superiors, both in allowing them to accuse their officer of abuses and also by supervising the punishments of wrongs. Through martial law process, the court supervised their officers, their soldiers, and the relationships between them.

Martial law began for a soldier when he took the oath that gained him entrance into the martial political body. Some compared the army to an urban corporation or to a state, and just as a state needed law for the maintenance of order, so too did an army. Before one could enter into the martial polity, a soldier had to swear an oath. The 1586 oath mandated that the soldier "sweare and promise to doe all loyal true and faythefull service unto the Queen of Englande her most Excell. Majesty."[133] Before making this oath, the soldier's military officer had to make him aware of the articles of war, and the soldier had to agree to live under those rules.[134] By the seventeenth century, the new recruits had to declare that "All these lawes and Ordinances which have publikely here beene read unto us, we do hold and allow of as sacred and good."[135] Commanders and their council were concerned that all new recruits be read the ordinances of war within three days of entering into their camp.[136] The substance of martial law was in general the word of the commander, as Sir Thomas Smith in his widely read work *De Republica Anglorum* suggested. However, the word of the commander needed to be known by all parties before it counted as law.[137]

Courts-martial took this initiation very seriously. Joseph Barrett and Sadler Stonehouse were lucky that they did. On 1 September 1663, the two along with two others left their camp in Tangier without license. The advocate brought an information against them on 8 September and claimed they had never planned on coming back. Potentially, the two could have been tried by Article 16 under the heading "duties in camp and garrison" which demanded no one depart without license.[138] This article prescribed death for its violators. However, the two claimed that they had never "heard the articles of warr read."[139] Their commander affirmed the story. Stonehouse and Barrett, however, did not get off.

---

[133] This oath is printed in Charles Cruikshank, *Elizabeth's Army* (Oxford, 1966), 293. Also see LPL, Ms. 247, fos. 71v–72.

[134] Thomas Audley, "Art of Warre," BL, Add. Ms. 23,971, f. 3v.

[135] *Lawes and Ordinances of Warre*, 27.

[136] C.G. Cruikshank, *Elizabeth's Army*, 303. At least in the French case, the soldier had the ability to leave if he did not like the codes, or if he felt mistreated by his captain. Digges, *Stratioticos*, 298.

[137] Sir Thomas Smith, *De Republica Anglorum* ed. Mary DeWar (Cambridge, 1982), 85.

[138] TNA, CO 279/1, 10.   [139] BL, Sloane Ms. 1957, f. 31.

Apparently, there had been a subsequent proclamation against soldiers leaving camp. Failure to meet this requirement, however, was not life-threatening. They both had to pay a fine out of their wages.[140] The court forced the other two to roll dice on a drumhead for their lives. Through the articles of war, the council of war attempted to make examples of these deserters. Through legal process, these two, barely, survived with their lives.

Cases like this usually began through accusation or an information brought by the judge advocate. For Thomas Minion, for example, it began when he let the wrong man into his conspiracy. Serving in the English army in the Low Countries that was fighting France in 1697, Minion hatched a plan to escape from service. He and several co-conspirators would flee to Brussels, where they would find work until the army departed the area. Then they would make their way back to England. Unfortunately for Thomas, one of his companions "discoursed" the plan with a sergeant, and his superiors caught Minion before he had a chance to escape.[141] Others were often captured after a slip of the tongue or a slip of the fist toward an unbearable superior.[142] Provost marshals arrested others after an informant complained to the judge advocate general that they had committed a wrong.[143] For officers, process began when they had been formally accused. After they had been caught, the provost marshal supervised the accused in the jail that the army had constructed.[144]

Prosecution often began in the office of the judge advocate general. It was he who formalized and registered the complaint. It was to this office that Elizabeth Michelson and Margaret Patterson came to in Dundee in 1651 in the aftermath of one of the most traumatic nights of their life.[145] At midnight, the soldier James Grahame came to their door. He decided to take off all his clothes, and then threw himself at Michelson, who he beat after she attempted to resist him. He then tried with Patterson, who also resisted him. He threatened to burn their house down, but settled for more physical attacks. In response, the two women sought out the judge advocate general. He deposed them, which helped them gain a conviction. Just as often, the judge advocate wrote up the charge based on his own information he had obtained as an investigator. It was by this method that Dudley Loftus, the judge advocate for the

---

[140] *Ibid.*, f. 32.
[141] "At a Court-Martial held at the Camp ... the 7th of September 1697," TNA, WO 71/121.
[142] TNA, WO 89/1, 69–70.   [143] TNA, ADM 1/5253, f. 27.
[144] The army constructed makeshift jails. See, for example, TNA, AO 1/299/1137.
[145] Worcester College, Oxford, Clarke Ms. 21, fos. 32–3. Donagan, *War in England*, 185–6.

Dublin garrison, in 1651 brought Gerrald and Henry Beagtagh before a court-martial for spying.[146] The advocate, as detective and lawyer, was essential to martial law process.

Information had to be provided to the judge advocate quickly after a suspect was detained. By the English Civil War, the army stipulated that those incarcerating soldiers needed to provide the marshal with a cause. He in turn needed to notify the advocate forty-eight hours after incarceration, otherwise they would be released, and the jailer subject to punishment by the court.[147] In the 1650s, this timeframe was reduced to 24 hours. In the armies of the Low Countries, William III likewise lowered the temporal requirement to 24 hours.[148] In Dundee, the court-martial chastised the commanding officer of Phillip Powell for not providing it with an information for why he was imprisoned. The officer eventually submitted a plaint against Powell for swearing, and Powell was sentenced to the ten days imprisonment he had already served.[149] The Tangier court released prisoners who had sat in jail for over 48 hours without charge.[150] We often now think of martial law as being a site where prisoners could languish seemingly forever before they were charged or came to trial.[151] This perpetual detainment was hardly the case in the seventeenth century.

In cases involving officers, a formal accusation by another was more common.[152] The accuser in these cases often had to put his reputation on the line in prosecuting the officer. If accusations proved malicious or unnecessary, the accuser could face punishment.[153] In 1680, a court-martial on board the ship Bristol handed down this penalty to Thomas Woodgreen for making false accusations against his commander, captain Richard Dickinson, in two "very abusiue letters."[154] For his wrong, to which he confessed, the court ordered Woodgreen whipped five times on

---

[146] "Dublin Court-Martial Records," 98.

[147] *Lawes and Ordinances of Warre* (London, 1646), sig. D3.

[148] "Order of the Court, 1697," TNA WO 71/121.

[149] "Dundee Court-Martial Records," 21.

[150] BL, Sloane Ms. 1960, f. 36. This being said, once charged, a court could remit a prisoner back into jail until more evidence was found against him. *Ibid.*, f. 30.

[151] For other examples of soldiers being released, see BL, Sloane Ms. 1957, f. 60.

[152] There are exceptions to this rule. For example George Walsh, a former captain, had abandoned the Commonwealth's armies in Ireland in 1652 for those of the royalists forces. He was arraigned upon an information by the advocate, convicted, and executed. "Dublin Court-Martial Records," 103.

[153] For the *poena talionis*, see R.H. Helmholz, *The Oxford History of the Laws of England: Volume I The Canon and Ecclesiastical Jurisdiction from 597 to the 1640s* (Oxford, 2004), 605–8.

[154] TNA, ADM 1/5253, f. 3. Also see *Concilium apud Fernham* (London, 1644). The Tangier court-martial thought about giving a similar punishment to John Pickering but decided against it. BL, Sloane Ms. 1957, f. 53.

the side of each ship in the fleet with his wrong written on a placard hanging around his neck.

In order to avoid this fate, accusers needed to provide detailed charges against officers.[155] This was true even of superior officers desirous to take their inferior officers to court for some perceived wrong. These charges, which often stretched to over ten in number, did not directly reflect the prescriptive ordinances in the articles of war. Instead the charges pointed to highly specific abuses of power or neglect of duty that might prove through accumulation the defendant's guilt of transgressing one of the ordinances of war. Let us examine one such charge, made by Major John Miller against Lieutenant George Lascelles and Ensign Roger Kirkby on 20 November 1672 about wrongs supposedly committed by the two men stationed in England on 14 and 15 November.[156]

The process against Kirkby and Lascelles was continued with a command to commence a court-martial. On 15 November Charles II issued a warrant to the commander, the Earl of Craven, to convene a court-martial of twelve captains with the colonel of the Coldstream guards to act as president.[157] The court-martial was to abide by the rules set forth by Charles, and to decide the case according to the rules of military discipline. This particular court-martial was to meet in the Officer's Room of the guard house at Whitehall.[158] On the same day after the warrant was issued, the Earl of Craven ordered the two men committed to the custody of the marshal. In other courts-martial the command to convene a court-martial became *pro forma*; commanders issued them on an assigned day for the court-martial to convene. At least in Tangier, these forms emulated the spirit of the "gaol delivery" writs at common law, where the commander ordered the court-martial to hear and determine all of the cases of those currently incarcerated.[159]

Major Miller, presumably the commander of both Kirkby and Lascelles, made ten accusations in writing against the two men for the court which convened on 20 November.[160] The charges detailed the various ways in which both men violated their duties as officers. Apparently after a bout of wine drinking, Lascelles had won a contest of strength "of their armes by straining hands," the loss of which apparently

---

[155] "Charges against Captain John Clarke, 1655," Bodl. Rawl. A. Ms. 295, f. 2. "Articles against General Poyntz," in *The Clarke Papers* 1: 169.

[156] TNA, WO 71/121. The charge was dated 20 November 1672.

[157] TNA, WO 26/1, f. 446. For other warrants, see *Ibid.*, 23, 356 and "Order for a court-martiall to examine a complaint of misdemeanor against Lieut. Saddlington, February 1674," TNA, WO 71/121.

[158] "Judgement of the Court-Martiall agt Ensigne Kirkeby," TNA, WO 71/121.

[159] See, for example, BL, Sloane Ms. 3514, f. 8.

[160] Major Miller's charge against Lascelles and Kirkby, TNA, WO 71/121.

infuriated Kirkby.[161] The two fought one another, and afterward Lascelles threatened several others and brandished his sword. He followed this act by making a variety of indiscreet statements such as he "cared nott a Turd" for his commission as a lieutenant.[162] The tenth charge alleged that while Kirkby submitted to being detained the following morning, Lascelles refused to leave his quarters. Mysteriously, he was too ill to leave his bed.

After Miller submitted the complaint, the court obtained more detailed information concerning every charge. Both Lascelles and Kirkby had the opportunity to respond. Lascelles' answers provided the court with an alternate narrative of the night and following morning in question.[163] Lascelles claimed that he was "highly provoked by Kirkby," because the ensign had called him a coward, and therefore had not instigated the fight. Lascelles vigorously defended himself against the other charges as well, often claiming his statements had been misinterpreted and that he was not responsible for the subsequent assaults after his affray with Kirkby. In a much different strategy, Kirkby responded that he, "as a louer of truth," confessed to his guilt in the first and ninth articles and submitted to the judgment of the court.[164]

After the answers were provided, the court then sought more information. Captain Miller responded to Lascelles' narrative in a written rejoinder.[165] Miller argued that Lascelles had in fact through his answer confessed to many of the charges and that his excuses were ludicrous. Along with this response, the advocate, John Barron, obtained depositions from five of the officers in the regiment. Much of the information taken was consistent with the charge made by Miller. The court had informations from five officers who had witnessed the altercation as well as two statements from the accuser and responses from the defendants.

The court then interrogated the witnesses. In this case, it did so in a manner where depositions were taken in advance, but the witnesses were still required to confirm their testimony *viva voce* upon oath.[166] The courts commenced by having the officers swear upon a bible that

---

[161] We find this out later during the examination of the witnesses. "Examination Taken in Court 20 & 22 November 1672," TNA, WO 71/121.

[162] Miller's charge against Lascelles and Kirkby, TNA, WO 71/121.

[163] "An Answer to the Articles exhibited against Lieutenant George Lascelles," TNA, WO 71/121.

[164] "The Answer of Roger Kirkeby Ensigne to the Articles exhibited at the Court-Martiall," TNA, WO 71/121.

[165] "The Reply of Maj. John Miller to lieut. George Lascelles," TNA, WO 71/121.

[166] John Langbein, *Prosecuting Crime in the Renaissance: England, Germany, France* (Cambridge, MA, 1974), 231–9.

they would hear and determine the matter truly.[167] It then deposed witnesses who had already provided written depositions so that the court could interrogate the witnesses about the defendants' counter-claims.[168] Sometimes, the witnesses did not appear *viva voce*. Instead, the judge advocate or sometimes the provost deposed the witnesses upon oath and brought the evidence before the court.[169] Commissioned military officers also at times received the initial depositions. It was by this same process that Isaac Dorislaus, the judge advocate general of the parliamentary army of the Earl of Essex, probably facilitated the deposition of witnesses for the 1644–5 case between Thomas Sanders and Sir John Gell, his commanding colonel.[170] Gell had accused Sanders of disobedience. In order to better make sense of the charges laid by Gell and the responses made by Sanders, Dorislaus commissioned several officers to examine witnesses that were provided from both sides.[171] Along with the commission, Dorislaus issued instructions to his interrogators which included specific questions they needed to ask each witness in order to prove or disprove the charges and responses.[172] These questions were made by both the plaintiff and defendant who submitted them to the advocate.[173] Once the depositions had been taken, the court would have examined them in order to better evaluate the charges and answers.

After evaluation and meeting in private, the president put questions to the court for each article. These questions included guilt, intent, and if the charge was valid or redundant. Each commissioner would vote on the question given, and the answers would ascend from the lowest ranking officer on the court-martial to the president. A simple majority was necessary for affirmation of guilt. The commissioners in the Lascelles and Kirby case decided that Kirkby was the aggressor and that Lascelles was justified in drawing his sword. Lascelles' responses worked to a degree, as he was acquitted of several charges based on the arguments he had made.

The judgments came to the officers on 22 November. The court declared that Kirkby was the instigator of all the trouble and that he was

---

[167] For an example of the oath that court-martial officers took, see TNA, CO 140/3, 648.

[168] "Examination Taken in Court 20 & 22 November 1672," TNA, WO 71/121.

[169] Witnesses could be brought *viva voce* or could be deposed, provided it was on oath. Sir Richard Raines to Samuel Pepys, 23 July 1688, Bodl. Rawl. A 171, f. 48.

[170] The preliminaries of the case survive in Sanders' archive. DRO, 1232M/027–033.

[171] The commission does not survive. But two survive from the period, including one from Dorislaus. See LPL, Ms. 709 (Shrewsbury MS), f. 80, and BL, Add. Ms. 29,974, f. 371.

[172] "Interrogations to be ministered or whatsoever witnesses that are to be p[ro]duced sworne and examined vpon additional articles ... " DRO, Ms. D1232M/033.

[173] Sir John Hotham went through several drafts when making his questions. See HHC, U DDHO 1/40–41.

to be suspended from duty and confined until his majesty's pleasure be further known.[174] Lascelles was convicted of continuing the fight, of neglect of duty, and of "mutinous misdemeanors."[175] He, like Kirkby, was suspended and confined indefinitely until Charles decided that his pleasure in the matter be known. The time from the fight to the sentence totaled eight days. Courts-martial in general moved quickly but also took their time when necessary.[176] These officers would have had a different experience had they been common soldiers. In all likelihood, they would have been corporally punished for their misdeeds. If only one of them had been a private soldier, had he been outside England, he would have faced the death penalty for fighting his superior.[177]

Let us better understand this distinction through a case that took place on the ship Harwich in June 1676.[178] The court heard a case involving four men who had conspired together to steal the goods of a merchant traveling on the ship. They confessed and were found guilty according to Article 29 of the Naval ordinances of war, which mandated that all robbery and theft be punished with death or otherwise as the court-martial shall think fit.[179] The two chief conspirators were officers. The court fined them and demoted them. Further, they had to wear ropes around their necks on a boat that would travel between all the ships in the fleet. However, they were spared corporal punishment. That was only given to their two helpers, who were not officers. These men were not fined but they were whipped with a cat of nine tails during their voyage around the fleet. The brutality of martial law was mostly reserved for the lowly.

Nevertheless, common soldiers, just like their commanders, had their day in court. And army and navy lawyers cared about obtaining proof of the wrong they committed. Granted, if a soldier was brought up on charges of insubordination or blasphemy, his trial was not nearly as complicated or as long as that of an officer. The chances of a soldier being acquitted of a non-capital offense were low.[180] Nevertheless, judge advocates insisted on deposing witnesses and obtaining informations. John Bayly, who was charged with blasphemy on board the Torrington, for example, was ultimately convicted based on the testimony of multiple witnesses.[181] The same can be said for William Godfrey, who was

---

[174] "Judgement against Kirkeby," TNA, WO 71/121.

[175] The sentence was recorded on the judge advocate's calendar. TNA, WO 92/1.

[176] An even longer case took place in Ireland in 1652 between Captain St. George and Lieutenant Scott over the sale of a gelding. "Dublin Court-Martial Records," 106, 108, 110.

[177] For the restrictions on the death penalty in the Restoration, see Chapter 7.

[178] Bodl., Rawl Ms. C. 972, fos. 20v–26v.   [179] 13 Car. II. c.9.

[180] I have found only a handful. See BL, Sloane Ms. 1957, fos. 6, 55.

[181] Bodl., Rawl. Ms. A 295, f. 12.

convicted of multiple misdemeanors based on eyewitness testimony.[182] Evidence mattered.

By the middle of the seventeenth century, martial jurists and commanders had invented a variety of creative, painful, and intensely humiliating punishments for soldiers who in one way or another neglected their military duties. These punishments were always carried out by the provost marshal and his assistants on "parade day" or muster day, where the regiment gathered together in an open space to learn the gruesome lesson. Public whipping was a common punishment.[183] "Loping the gantlope" was another.[184] The culprit had to run through a narrow opening with his company members on either side, who whipped him with sharpened reeds. The gantlope, or eventually, gauntlet, would become a staple punishment within English armies from the 1640s onward. So too would "riding the horse." The convict would have to sit on a wooden horse, with his hands tied behind his back and often with weights attached to his feet.[185] "Picketing," lying "neck and heels tied together," or being tied until one had to stand on tip-toes for hours were other punishments. In Tangier, forced unpaid labor was common.[186] Some faced short periods of imprisonment chained in irons with only bread and water for sustenance.[187]

Those who were punished were supposed to teach a lesson to their colleagues.[188] As many scholars have noted, however, those watching the punishments did not always receive the message. Perhaps, some simply found the punishments of their peers amusing. Richard Long, for example, could not contain his laughter upon the sentencing of his former comrade James Turner to death for arson.[189] Meanwhile, soldiers who disapproved of their comrade being tied neck and heels together in Tangier continuously shouted "tye one tye all" during the parade in

---

[182] *Ibid.*, f. 16.

[183] See, for example, "Dublin Court-Martial Records," 73; TNA, ADM 1/5253, fos. 27v. "Dundee Court-Martial Records," 14.

[184] William Watts, *The Swedish Discipline, Religious, Civile, and Military*, 59; Firth, *Cromwell's Army*, 287–8; James Turner, *Pallas Armata, Military Essayes of the ancient Grecian, Roman, and Modern Art of War* (London, 1683), 348–9.

[185] Firth, *Cromwell's Army*, 288.

[186] BL, Sloane Ms. 1957, fos. 6–7, 9–10, 21, 24–5, 26–9; BL, Sloane Ms. 1959, fos. 48, 74, 107; BL, Sloane Ms. 1960, fos. 25–8, 20, 35.

[187] Grose, *Military Antiquities*, 2: 101–9.

[188] On the spectacle of punishments, see Petrus Cornelius Spierenburg *The Spectacle of Suffering: Executions and the Evolution of Repression: from a Preindustrial Metropolis to the European Experience* (Cambridge, 1984). For the ways in which public punishments simultaneously undercut and transmitted Crown authority, see P. Lake and M. Questier, "Agency, Appropriation and Rhetoric under the Gallows: Puritans, Romanists and the State in Early Modern England," *Past and Present* 153 (November, 1996): 64–107.

[189] Bodl. Rawl. C. 972, f. 19v. For Turner's sentence, see *ibid.*, f. 15.

protest.[190] For others, the punishment of soldiers had more to do with the execution of justice on those who had wronged them. Or to put it more basely, accusers got to look on with glee as the violence of the law was applied to their opponents. Eliza Swinford, a widow and shopkeeper in Tangier, knew how to co-opt the violence of martial law to humiliate her enemies better than most.

Swinford's use of martial law began in October 1670, when she brought a petition to John Luke, the advocate general of the garrison, about the actions of the soldier John Matthews, who had come into Swinford's shop and loitered around the entrance.[191] As most shop-keepers would be, Swinford was annoyed by Matthew's behavior and told him to stop pestering her customers. Outraged, Matthews called Swinford a "bitch" and a "whore" and swore that he would ransack both her shop and her home. He began throwing Swinford's goods on the ground and then he pulled her hair and tried to choke her before the distressed woman's customers came to her rescue. In her petition, Swinford stated that she "hath beene often times fformerly abused by soldiers wch on the request of their officers or friends willingly putt up with" in the hope that such abuses would stop.[192] They had not stopped, and the widow Swinford decided to take action.

In her petition, Swinford wove a narrative of disorder within the city that might in the end force her to abandon her business and depart.[193] This was a savvy veiled threat. Tangier's leadership, parti-cularly after 1667, was aware that many were fleeing the port due to its unruliness and actively sought to de-militarize the colony by providing the city with its own charter and by creating a merchant court to preside over contract disputes.[194] Both John Luke and the governor were sensitive to the depredations of soldiers upon the civilian populace and were thus receptive to Swinford's plight. Luke had John Matthews arrested and imprisoned to await trial. Swinford was ready with two eyewitnesses. Later in the month, a court-martial convicted Matthews and sentenced him to be whipped publicly in the parade. Matthews' violence against Swinford had been in words

---

[190] BL, Sloane Ms. 1959, fos. 109–10.
[191] BL, Sloane Ms. 3514, f. 45. Swinford had been a deponent as an eyewitness to a homicide in 1666. It happened outside of her still-alive husband's home. BL, Sloane Ms. 1959, fos. 57–8. For other cases involving violence against women, see BL, Sloane Ms. 1959, fos. 10, 21, 40, 60, 66, 65–8 (all on verso), 81–2, 85v; BL, Sloane, Ms. 1960, fos. 10v–11; BL, Sloane, 3514, f. 172.
[192] BL, Sloane Ms. 3514, f. 45.   [193] *Ibid.*
[194] Routh, *Tangier, England's Lost Atlantic Outpost*, 113–32.

and with his hands. The widow responded with the violence of the law.[195]

Widow Swinford's problems with soldiers did not end with Matthews. Early in November, Swinford complained to Advocate Luke about abusive actions by two soldiers. In the first case, Swinford charged that the soldier Laurence Ross had attacked her after she tried to get the Mayor's Court to force him to pay his debts to her.[196] Then, on three separate days in early November, a soldier named Robert Moody had come into her shop and had shouted expletives at the widow.[197] On the last day, Moody accused her of being a whore and threatened to rape her young daughter. Swinford told Moody that she would see him hanged in front of her door, and Moody responded that if she tried to have him whipped like his friend Matthews, he would kill her. Swinford was not deterred.

With the help of eight depositions either she or Luke had taken from witnesses, Swinford convinced Luke to imprison and charge both Moody and Ross. On 10 March 1671, a court-martial heard both cases. The court sentenced Ross to ride the horse with his mouth gagged and to be whipped for three parade days. It sentenced Moody to ride the horse during the parade for three consecutive days, with his hands tied and his mouth gagged.[198] On the third day he was to apologize to Swinford. When the court read the sentence, Moody protested and declared that he would never apologize to her. The court then ordered a second trial for Moody's insolent behavior where it was ordered that he be whipped. If he refused to apologize to Swinford on the appointed day, he was to be whipped again; this time he would receive thirty-nine lashes per day until he apologized. Chances are Moody complied with the court's wishes and, after his physical humiliation, made an apology. No diarist recorded these events, but it is almost certain that upon receiving his public submission, a broad and satisfied smile graced widow Swinford's face.

The court spent more time in cases involving blood sanction. Courts desired either eyewitnesses or a confession before they sent down a capital conviction, but they still had discretion about what in the end was sufficient.[199] In the murder case against Corporal Joshua Waddington in 1688 onboard the Ship Mary, for example, the court deposed multiple

---

[195] My language has been influenced by Robert Cover, "Violence and the Word," *Yale Law Journal* 95 (1985–86): 1601–29.

[196] BL, Sloane Ms. 3514, f. 54.

[197] BL, Sloane Ms. 3514, f. 52. Ross had already been convicted for beating his wife. See BL, Sloane Ms. 1959, f. 85v. Moody had been convicted of beating the wife of another. *Ibid.*, fos. 60, 66.

[198] *Tangier at High Tide: The Journal of John Luke, 1670–1673* ed. Helen Andrews Kaufman (Geneva and Paris, 1958), 73–4.

[199] Raines to Pepys, 23 July 1688, Bodl. Rawl. A 171, f. 48.

witnesses and obtained a confession from the defendant before it sentenced him to death.[200] Courts-martial also acquitted defendants based upon declarations of insufficient evidence. John Fryer, a soldier in William III's army, got off for this reason in 1697. At his court-martial in Bruges, Fryer stood accused of kicking one of the burghers of the town and of taking his sword.[201] The court declared Fryer to be not guilty because the evidence provided was insufficient. The soldiers John Still and John Ware in 1697 likewise were acquitted on a desertion charge due to the insufficiency of the evidence brought against them.[202]

The court's concern over evidence extended even to supposed "Irish spies" in the 1650s. Let us examine the case of Rowland Eustace heard before the Dublin Court-Martial in 1651. In that year, the judge advocate submitted an information against Eustace, an inhabitant of County Kildare, which accused him of spying and of aiding the enemy against the Commonwealth's forces. We do not know what the information contained. But a short record of the Court's decision to not punish Eustace with death reveals its concerns about evidence. The court declared that after hearing the evidence against Eustace, there were "strong and pregnant presumpcions" that he was guilty.[203] But a presumption was not enough to convict capitally for this court-martial. The court voted against conviction based on insufficiency of evidence.

An even clearer example of the court's concern over evidence comes from a court-martial that took place on the ship Harwich, which was stationed in Malta Harbor at the end of 1675.[204] On 24 December, the acting judge advocate William Franklin began taking depositions in an investigation into a fire that had broken out on the Europa, another ship in the fleet. He received three depositions that claimed one John Wright threatened to burn the ship only days before. Another claimed that the fire was started during his watch and "at his leaving the watch it brake forth into a flame."[205] Two more testified to the time of the fire. But the court was uneasy about the evidence given. According to the court, there were "many circumstances" which suggested Wright's guilt. But that was not enough to convict him of a capital offense. It was a good thing the court processed evidence in such a manner; for one of the deponents against Wright, John Wade, was the actual arsonist. Several months later, he started a much more serious fire that killed an English consul on board the Europa. He eventually confessed to both fires and was hanged for his wrongs.[206]

---

[200] TNA, ADM 1/5253, fos. 67–8.   [201] TNA, WO 71/121.   [202] Ibid.
[203] "Dublin Court-Martial Records," 139.   [204] Bodl. Rawl. C. 972, fos. 6v–8.
[205] Ibid., f. 6v.   [206] Ibid., fos. 9–16.

But the court did not acquit poor John Wright. Nor did the Dublin court-martial acquit Eustace. Wright was whipped for example's sake. Eustace was banished to Connacht. Their fates were not uncommon. The court-martial convicted Wright by what is commonly referred to as "the devil's article."[207] This was the last article of the "Administration of Iustice," which stipulated that all "other Faults, Disorders, and Offenses not mentioned in these articles, shall be punished according to the general Customs and Laws of War."[208] The naval articles of war possessed a similar ordinance.[209] From the example of Wright we can see that the court used this article to convict those who it did not want to convict of capital offenses of misdemeanor offenses instead. The devil's article, it would seem, was enormously unfair to defendants.

But in many cases, courts used the devil's article to give equitable judgments. For example, in 1652, John Bayly appeared before a Dublin court-martial for "running away from his colours at Killencarick," an offense punishable "upon paine of death."[210] Yet Bayly was not convicted on this article. Instead, the court tried and convicted him upon "the last article of the administracion of justice."[211] The court ordered Bayly to "lope the gantlope" through his entire regiment, a humiliating and painful punishment, but a non-capital one. The Dublin court convicted eighteen people on the last article of the administration of justice. The Dundee court convicted thirteen offenders by the same article, which it labeled the article of misdemeanor. In Tangier, the practice was very common, as it allowed courts-martial to save soldiers' lives and also obtain forced labor for their fortifications and other projects.[212] The soldier John Hawkins, for example, was guilty of desertion in 1664, but because he was sorry the court mitigated his punishment: he was to be a slave in irons in the king's works instead.[213] The navy conducted a similar practice. During 1689–90, naval courts-martial convicted four men by the devil's article.[214]

---

[207] Donagan, *War in England*, 146–7, 150; G.A. Steppler, "British Military Law, Discipline, and the Conduct of Regimental Courts-Martial in the Later Eighteenth Century," *EHR* 102:405 (October, 1987): 863.

[208] Firth, *Cromwell's Army*, 412.   [209] 13 Car. II. c.9.

[210] "Dublin Court-Martial Records," 78.   [211] Firth, *Cromwell's Army*, 412.

[212] In Tangier, it was referred to as the 12th article in the category of administration of justice. BL, Sloane Ms. 1957, fos. 8, 13–14, 35, 52, 57–62; BL, Sloane Ms. 1959, 12v–19v, 29–32, 55, 66, 69, 71v, 75–6 and 75v–76v, 78–v, 81–2, 85v, 93, 96, 105v–6v, 109–10, 113v–15v, 117–19; BL, Sloane Ms. 1960, fos. 6–7, 10v–12, 30, 52–3.

[213] BL, Sloane Ms. 1960, fos. 25–6.

[214] TNA, ADM 1/5253, fos. 93, 101. The Navy's devil's article was the last of 33 in 13 Car. II. c.9. Apparently, it was through this article that naval officers continued to enforce the laws and customs of the sea even though they were not written into the navy's official ordinances. See Sir Richard Raines to Samuel Pepys, 23 July 1688, Bodl. Rawl. A 171, f. 48.

As well as being the article of "misdemeanor" the devil's article was also the article of manslaughter. Both the Tangier and Dundee courts used it to make such a distinction even though the formal articles of war did not. In Dundee, for example, the court heard a case against John Dodd, a soldier who had killed another soldier, Henry Thompson.[215] When examined before the court, Dodd claimed that he had struck Thompson because the two had gotten into a fight, but he had not intended to kill him. Therefore, he should not be convicted of capital or willful murder, but instead of manslaughter. The court, in particular the president, General Cobbett, believed Dodd. Instead of looking to the rules embedded in the articles of war, the court instead looked to the bible. Cobbett had the clerk of the court read Numbers 35.22:

But if hee thrust him suddenly without enmity, or have cast upon him any thinge without laying of any waite, or with any stone wherewith a man may die, see him nott and cast itt uppon him that hee may die, and was nott his enemy neither sought his harme, then the congregation shall judge between the slayer and the revenger of bloud according to these judgments.[216]

If the congregation found that it was not a purposeful murder, they "shall deliver the slayer out of the hand of the revenger of bloud."[217] Through the devil's article, the court delivered Dodd. Instead of killing him, it voted him to be imprisoned for two months and to pay Thompson's widow twenty pounds. Likewise, in Tangier, the courts branded or imprisoned convicts of manslaughter through the devil's article.[218] Mitigation of punishment was granted through the last article of the administration of justice.

Commanders had the power to grant mercy for certain wrongs. However, this formal power was used less often than at common law. At common law, a pardon from the monarch was always a possibility. More importantly, particularly for the unimportant and un-influential men and women of the world, common law in the seventeenth century had two forms of structured mercy: benefit of the belly and benefit of clergy. Benefit of the belly meant that a pregnant woman could obtain a respite from execution, at least until she gave birth. Benefit of clergy allowed a convict who had the ability to read to obtain a pardon for some felony offenses, if it was his first offense, by claiming the fiction that he was a member of the clergy. While there is one instance of benefit of the belly at courts-martial, there is no evidence that the court allowed benefit of clergy.[219]

---

[215] "Dundee Court-Martial Records," 65.   [216] *Ibid.*   [217] *Ibid.*
[218] BL, Sloane Ms. 1959, fos. 5–6, 12v–13, 16–18, 31–2; BL, Sloane Ms. 1960, fos. 6–7.
[219] "Dublin Court-Martial Records," 115. For pardon at common law, see Herrup, *The Common Peace: Participation and the Criminal Law in Seventeenth-Century England*

Instead, those who desired mercy depended on the recommendation of the court to the commander. In one instance in 1697, the court-martial sitting in Bruges managed to convince the general that Thomas Pew, a soldier in the army, was worth saving.[220] Convicted of murder, Thomas had confessed that he was so drunk he could not even remember that he had taken another's life. Inebriation was no excuse for committing wrongs at an English court-martial.[221] However, the court learned that Thomas' father, a sergeant in the regiment, had just been killed on the campaign. It decided to petition the general to grant him his life; the commander agreed that he should be spared. Others drew lots for their lives. William III charged one of his companies with mutiny in 1694, and the court-martial capitally convicted them. The king ordered that all but four and the ringleader be pardoned: which four depended on luck.[222] Very few were formally pardoned at courts-martial.

Between sentence and execution, specialists administered to the needs of the condemned. The provost earned rates for giving the bad news to the defendant. Later, the condemned was supposed to receive several forms of solace: first came an "extraordinary treat," which included several pots of beer and a couple of pounds of meat. In those lonely hours, paid servants "did sit up with and wait upon the patients after ther condemnation to death" and provided them with comfort and company.[223] They earned rates per day for their efforts. The machinery of death – the rope, the ladder, and the bolts required for execution by hanging – put the army back three shillings. The executioner earned rates for raising the condemned and for taking down the corpse. The provost received rates for assistance in the execution, as did his assistants. The two servants assigned to bury the deceased each were paid.[224] The legal machinery of courts-martial by the end of the seventeenth century was complex and included many participants who had specialized duties.[225]

Seventeenth-century councils of war possessed discretion as the translators of wrongs and evaluators of evidence. Through this power it supervised the disciplinary regime of the army and navy. This equitable power,

---

(Cambridge, 1987), 48–50, 143; Krista Kesselring, *Mercy and Authority in the Tudor State* (Cambridge, 2003).

[220] Case of Thomas Pew, 1697, TNA, WO 71/121.

[221] This excuse was used unsuccessfully in Tangier. See, for example, BL, Sloane Ms. 1957, f. 10; BL, Sloane Ms. 1959, f. 75.

[222] TNA, WO, 71/121.

[223] "Account of the Charges and disbursements done by ye provost marshal general Velthoven, 1690," BL, Harley Ms. 6844, f. 275. Velthoven was accused of not actually providing these comforts. *Ibid.*

[224] *Ibid.*

[225] In another account, the army paid out for the setting up of a gibbet, and for the burial of two men, who presumably had been hanged. TNA, AO 1/300/1140.

however, was fairly normal. Judges throughout English law courts possessed similar powers.[226] And the discretion of the courts should not blind us to the fairly extensive set of rules which organized martial justice at the end of the seventeenth century. Through this combination of equity and law, martial law commissioners regulated the relationships between members of their political body.

Conclusion

With their minds fixated on the practices and proceedings of the armed forces of European monarchs and the ancient practices of the Romans, the Crown and its council transformed martial law. They expanded and experimented with the articles of war. They transformed martial law procedure. And they redistributed discretion to a council of war. These experimentations were applied to colonial ventures, where officials of the Virginia Company believed that better discipline might in the end save its fledgling plantation. By the end of the seventeenth century, courts still desired to make examples of offenders for the terror of others in order to improve discipline. But the manner in which they did so was quite different from their sixteenth-century predecessors. With more lawyers, more judges, more rules relating to procedure, and more articles of war to consider, martial law process slowed down.

---

[226] For the use of equity in making judgments, see Paul D. Halliday, *Habeas Corpus: From England to Empire* (Cambridge, MA, 2010), 99–136.

Part II

Martial law and English parliaments

In the spring of 1628, Charles I consented to parliament's "Petition of Right," which concerned "divers Rights and Liberties of the Subjects." Almost immediately after the petition was granted, it joined the canon of English legal documents – Magna Carta, 25 Edward III, and, later, the Bill of Rights – that have been thought to protect the rights and liberties of English men and women.[1] But like Magna Carta, the Petition of Right dealt not in abstract universals but in highly specific grievances parliament desired redressed. One of these were commissions of martial law Charles had given to local officers so that they might hear and determine cases against soldiers stationed throughout the south of England. Complaining that these commissions authorized trial by life and limb by procedures other than those of common law, parliament asked that those commissions

> may be revoked and annulled; and that hereafter no commissions of like nature may issue forth to any person or persons whatsoever to be executed as aforesaid, lest by color of them any of your Majesty's subjects be destroyed or put to death contrary to the laws and franchise of the land.[2]

In trying to make sense of this clause, jurists looked to the law of martial law crafted by those directly involved in the making of the Petition of Right. All of these argued that Charles had erred because he had violated the temporal restrictions on martial law jurisdiction. Martial law for these jurists was only legal in times of war. But what defined a time of war was contested among these writers. These various interpretations would be used, adapted, and debated across the English-speaking world in the seventeenth century. In England, at various moments in the seventeenth century and in its overseas dominions, English subjects, MPs, governors, and members of the Privy Council debated when and if martial law could be used through various interpretations of the Petition of Right. While in

[1] Paul Halliday, *Habeas Corpus: From England to Empire* (Cambridge, MA, 2010), 15.
[2] *The Constitutional Documents of the Puritan Revolution, 1625–1660* ed. S.R. Gardiner (Oxford, 1906), 69.

many cases the wartime boundary restrained martial law, in other cases it empowered its expansion.

The Petition of Right had such a strong hold on the imagination of English men and women. It was such a weak barrier against parliamentary authorizations of martial law. In the end, various parliaments authorized martial law in experimental jurisdictions in the same way that the Privy Council had done in the sixteenth century. However, because of the Petition of Right and parliamentary process, restraints were always placed upon martial law powers even as they were being authorized. Through parliament, martial law in adapted form remained one of England's many laws.

4   Bound by wartime
Martial law and the Petition of Right

In a speech given in the 1628 Parliament about the Crown's recent delegation of martial law powers to local officers in order to discipline unruly soldiers, the lawyer and MP Robert Mason argued that while few in fact had been executed by martial law, "[a]ll innovation comes in gently at first, and it grows strong by degrees."[1] Due to fears by jurists like Mason that martial law process might replace common law process, an elaborate, divisive, and enormously consequential debate erupted in 1628 over martial law and its jurisdiction in England. Because MPs like Mason were worried about Crown innovations in martial law, they creatively re-shaped medieval ideas in order to restrict martial law to a wartime that was beyond the king's power to invoke.

This suspicion that martial law might become normative for the super-vision of soldiers and possibly others was heightened by a variety of other controversial practices, including billeting, a forced loan, and arbitrary imprisonment that the Jacobean and then Caroline governments had employed to prosecute its wars beginning in 1624.[2] It was also heightened in all probability by knowledge that the Privy Council might attempt to use martial law in order to solve other legal problems.[3] The fear for Mason and others was that what they considered to be due process might be unraveled. Subjects in England – including soldiers in pay – for these jurists should only be tried by common law process in cases that involved potential blood sanctions.

---

[1] *Proceedings in Parliament 1628* ed. Robert C. Johnson *et al.* 6 vols. (New Haven, 1977–83), 2: 461.

[2] For general histories of the period, see S.R. Gardiner, *History of England from the Accession of James I to the Outbreak of the Civil War, 1603–1642* 10 vols. (new ed., London, 1896), vols. 5 and 6; Conrad Russell, *Parliaments and English Politics, 1621–1629* (Oxford, 1979); for the policies that provoked debate in the 1628 Parliament, see Richard Cust, *The Forced Loan and English Politics, 1626–1628* (Oxford, 1987); Mark Kishlansky, "Tyranny Denied: Charles I, Attorney General Heath, and the Five Knights Case," *HJ* 42:1 (March, 1999): 53–83; Lindsay Boynton, "Billeting: the Example of the Isle of Wight," *EHR* 74:290 (January, 1959): 23–40. For an overview of the legal politics of the period, see Christopher Brooks, *Law, Politics and Society in Early Modern England* (Cambridge, 2008), 162–89.

[3] Cust, *The Forced Loan*, 57–8.

The debates over martial law have caused confusion among scholars for several reasons.[4] First, there was much disagreement, even among those who agreed that the Caroline commissions of martial law were illegal. This divisiveness produced three important arguments on martial law by Sir Edward Coke, John Selden, and by William Noy. Second, Selden relied on the little-known medieval Court of the Verge to craft his argument, and Noy likewise developed a geographical restriction to martial law based on the location of the enemy's raised banner. Third, both Selden and Noy were deeply concerned with the relationship between martial law and soldiers in armed camps. They did not make a military law/martial law distinction. This perhaps has proved most confusing to modern scholars who have attempted to put this distinction back into the seventeenth century. Finally, none of them wanted to eliminate martial law. Instead, they wanted to restrict it to wartime.

The Privy Council made the commissions of martial law in the first place to appease local officers.[5] In so doing, it reversed a trend that had been taking place since the 1590s, when Elizabeth's Privy Council had decided to assert more control over the delegation of martial law powers. While the Privy Council was initially apprehensive about delegating martial law, it decided to accommodate its local officers by granting them commissions of martial law to govern soldiers. Funnily enough, once received, these martial law commissioners almost never used their powers. No civilians were executed by martial law; the commissioners only executed a handful of soldiers. These martial law commissioners were still highly controversial, but more because they sometimes blocked legal proceedings through the "petitioning system," a practice that allowed commanders to intervene in misdemeanor cases involving their soldiers in order to prevent them from being jailed. Only the jurists in parliament were concerned about the abstract rules relating to martial law jurisdiction.

Let us first examine the mechanisms by which the Jacobean and Caroline governments managed the war effort, why they decided upon granting martial law jurisdictions to county officials, and how those commissions were ultimately executed. Context in hand, we can then examine the debates over martial law and their consequences for Caroline England.

---

[4] Paul Christianson, for example, has neglected William Noy's argument. Christianson, "Arguments on Billeting and Martial Law in the Parliament of 1628," *HJ* 37:3 (September, 1994): 539–67; Lindsay Boynton's work stands the test of time for how martial law was practiced in the countryside, but his discussion of the debates in 1628 is sketchy at best. "Martial Law and the Petition of Right," *EHR* 79:311 (April, 1964): 255–84. Stephen Stearns incorrectly believes that Selden and Coke made a distinction between military and martial law. Stearns, "Military Disorder and Martial law in Early Stuart England, in Law and Authority in Early Modern England: Essays presented to Thomas Garden Barnes ed. Mark Charles Fissel (Newark, 2007), 125.

[5] This point was well made by Lindsay Boynton, "Martial Law and the Petition of Right."

The council of war, the army, and war c. 1624

In 1624, war was raging on the European continent. Many, including the Crown prince and the Crown favorite, the Duke of Buckingham, wanted their king to join in the war effort on the side of the Protestant princes of Germany and recover the Palatinate for Frederick, the king's son-in-law, from the control of the Austrian Hapsburgs. James, likewise, wanted Frederick restored, but he was still cautious and wanted to avoid war with the king of Spain. This caution proved problematic because the Crown had over the course of the year engaged in negotiations for a military alliance with the king of France, who desired English aid in his war against the king of Spain. By November, James had come to tentative agreements with the king of France and had agreed to allow Charles to marry the king's daughter Henrietta Maria. That same month, the king of France entered into an alliance with the Dutch Republic against Spain. However, this new pact formed problems for James, because the two kings had tentatively been planning a joint military enterprise, to be commanded by the German mercenary Ernst Von Mansfeld. The plans had accelerated in England to the extent that by the end of November, Mansfeld had recruited troops in England for the expedition.[6]

At this point, England had formed a sitting Council of War to oversee military operations. Councils of War, which had been used from time to time in the sixteenth century, became more regular in the 1620s.[7] The 1624 Council of War initially existed to make sure that the subsidy parliament promised to James I would only be used for the preparation and execution of James' proposed intervention into the Thirty Years War and not to pay off his substantial debts or to reward his favorites.[8] For the next two years, the Council of War – re-commissioned upon James' death in 1625 by his son Charles I – supervised the disbursal of parliamentary subsidies for the war effort and advised the Crown on military strategy.[9]

---

[6] Gardiner, *History of England*, 5: 249–86. Between 8 and 9,000 ended up near Dover. Boynton, "Martial Law and the Petition of Right," 256–8.

[7] Stephen A. Stearns, "The Caroline Military System, 1625–1627: The Expeditions to Cadiz and Ré" (unpublished PhD dissertation, University of California, Berkeley, 1967), 129–52. Stearns' account of the Council of War in general is excellent. He relied on TNA, SP 16/28: the minute book for the Council of War starting in 1626. However, he was not aware of, or did not use, the notes made by one of its clerks, William Trumbull. These can be found in BL, Add. Ms. 72,422. I will supplement Stearns' account with these.

[8] Stearns, "The Caroline Military System," 132–4; M.B. Young, "Revisionism and the Council of War," *Parliamentary History* 8 pt. 1 (1989): 1–27. For the politics of the parliaments of 1621–4, see Thomas Cogswell, *The Blessed Revolution: English Politics and the Coming of War, 1621–24* (Cambridge, 1989).

[9] Stearns, "The Caroline Military System," 139–42.

In 1626, after two disastrous expeditions, Charles re-authorized the Council of War to sit but this time gave the body more administrative duties. This Council of War, comprised of veteran military officers and important members of the Privy Council, had responsibilities over the security of the realm, the furnishing of naval ships, assisting the king's allies, rewarding good military service, and offering other relevant advice to the king.[10] The Council of War also took on the responsibilities the Privy Council gave to it, including the hearing of petitions from aggrieved hosts of billeted soldiers. It did not have martial law jurisdiction, but it did make ordinances of war. Occasionally, it supervised the "martial law commissioners" in the counties who were responsible for the discipline of the soldiers.[11] Nevertheless, neither the soldiers collected for Mansfeld's operations nor those billeted in later periods had to worry about the Council of War punishing them by martial law.

Instead, the immediate supervision of soldiers was left to overwhelmed local officers who initially in 1624 had to use common law. This was in keeping with precedent. For both Elizabethan and Jacobean regimes, a "conductor" led the impressed men through the countryside until they reached their destination, which in the Elizabethan period often meant western port towns.[12] The most commonly used port for the Irish wars was Chester, but Bristol and Barnstaple were also used. Once they reached the port, the troops were often under the command of the mayor of the town, and sometimes a Crown muster master, who aided the mayor in securing ships and munitions for the journey across the sea.[13] One of the most common wrongs local officials had to prosecute was desertion. Mayors often had a difficult time catching deserters who could run away to different parts of the country. Once soldiers escaped the town limits, the mayor and his officials had little ability to search for them.[14]

---

[10] For the business that it considered, see TNA, SP 16/525, fos.104–5; TNA 16/35, f. 84; TNA, SP 16/31, f. 24; TNA, SP 16/540/1, f. 1; TNA SP 16/522, f. 163; TNA, SP 63/244, fos. 44, 296.

[11] The responsibilities are outlined in the privy seal commission. TNA, C 82/2006, no. 219. A draft of this commission can be found in TNA, SP 16/26 no. 33. A commission under the great seal was apparently dated 14 April 1626. The responsibilities are also outlined in Trumbull's notebook, BL Add. Ms. 72,422, fos. 3–4. Minutes of the meetings show that the Council was primarily concerned with financing and provisioning the ships for the upcoming expedition to the Isle of Rhé. See TNA, SP 16/28, fos. 1ff. The council of war debated a proclamation eventually made by Charles I that demanded those mariners who had on furlough entered London or other towns return to their ships on pain of martial law. BL, Add. Ms. 72, 422, f. 17. *SRP*, 2: no. 81. *APC*, 43: 243. For the draft ordinances, see TNA, SP 16/13, fos. 75–6v; TNA, SP 9/208/37.

[12] This account is heavily indebted to the work of John McGurk, *The Elizabethan Conquest of Ireland: The Burdens of the 1590s Crisis* (Manchester, 1997), 29–47.

[13] *Ibid.*, 137.   [14] *Ibid.*, 146–51, 168; *HMC*, Salisbury, 10: 268.

In certain instances, mayors issued special proclamations for the regulation of soldiers. But they still had to prosecute by common law process.[15]

Twice, mayors in the Elizabethan period requested martial law jurisdiction. The first instance came in 1581 in Chester, when a contingent of 300 men from North Wales and Derbyshire became mutinous and demanded a pay increase.[16] Over forty of the men deserted. Others refused to obey commands and "drewe theire wepons againste our officers."[17] In order to calm the situation, the mayor asked the Privy Council to have the "cheefe doers" executed by martial law. The mayor of Bristol had a similar sense of exasperation in 1602. Soldiers waiting to embark for Ireland had mutinied on several occasions. The commissioners attempted to arrest and imprison the ringleaders, but they had to continually fight back the recruits who on a nightly basis attacked the jails where their colleagues were held. In one attempt to break up a fight, the mayor was stoned by a group of soldiers. The commissioners then decided to engage in make-believe: "hauing no marshall lawe wee thowght good to mack them beleue we hadd."[18] The commissioners constructed a gibbet in the town and had guards inform the prisoners to prepare for death the next day. The following morning, they called all the soldiers to the town square, where the jailed had halters on their necks, and were about to climb the gibbet in preparation for execution. Right before they were to be "executed," the commissioners pardoned the men. The Privy Council, however, never granted martial law jurisdiction to these mayors. Perhaps because it did not want to delegate this jurisdiction to too many officers, or perhaps because it believed such a delegation might be an affront to the honor of the commanding general, no martial law jurisdictions were granted to mayors in the Elizabethan period.

The mayor of Dover in 1624 would have had sympathy for the sixteenth-century mayors of Bristol and Chester had he heard their stories because in December of that year he had to cope with more than 8,000 disgruntled soldiers organized under Mansfeld.[19] This army was now caught between the varying goals of James and Louis XIII, who wanted it to aid the Dutch in the fight against Spain. Louis refused to allow the army to pass through France in order to pressure James into sending them

---

[15] "Divers Proclamations emitted by Maiors of Chester, temp Eliz.," BL, Harley MS 2057, f. 59. Many thanks to Professor Robert Tittler for this reference. Privy Council to Sir Henry Docwray, *APC*, 30: 163–5.

[16] CALS, M/MP/3/49.   [17] *Ibid.*

[18] Commissioners of Bristol to the Privy Council, 29 May 1602, HH, CP 184/30. The mayors of Chester tried a similar tactic. McGurk, *Conquest of Ireland*, 150.

[19] Boynton, "Martial Law and the Petition of Right," 256–8.

to the Low Countries. James, who did not want to provoke war with Spain, initially balked at Louis' demands.[20] By the middle of December, the funds that the Council of War authorized for disbursement in November had run out. The soldiers, already unhappy, were now destitute. It appears that Mansfeld cared little about supervising his men, as according to one source there were no "officers of martiall discipline attending to restreyne the rascall fury."[21] Reports began to come in to the secretary of state, Sir Edward Conway, and to Buckingham about the chaos the soldiers were creating in Dover. Sir John Hippisley, the deputy warden of the Cinque Ports, reported on 24 December that victuals in Dover were running out and requested that the soldiers be moved. Two days later, Hippisley reported that the soldiers were engaged in the "pulling downe of houses & takeing away mens cattaile & other goods."[22] After trying to imprison some of them, their colleagues promptly broke them out. Soldiers appropriated any victual that came into the town. Due to these outrages, both the mayor and Hippisley prayed for victuals and for a "spetiall order from the lords for marshall lawe."[23] The dislocation of soldiers from the high command of the army posed challenges for civilian authorities.

The Privy Council in late December 1624 attempted to alleviate this burden they had imposed on their civilian authorities in and around Dover. They were, however, still hesitant to grant powers of life and limb by martial law. The Council of War drafted ordinances of war which the local officers could use to govern the soldiers. The Council decided that three or more "commissioners," who would be the deputy lieutenants, mayors, and other prominent county officers in charge of the area around the billeted troops, could convene a court-martial and punish the soldiers by the articles of war. However, they only had powers over life and limb upon the approval of the commander who would decide whether or not the soldier deserved death after evaluating the evidence.[24]

On 30 December, the Privy Council finally consented to delegate martial law jurisdiction through a commission under the Great Seal.[25] It did so because of the continued complaints by the officers in and around Dover and due to the fact that no resolution had yet been reached on when the soldiers were to depart. Within the commission, the Crown

[20] Gardiner, *History of England*, 5: 249–86.
[21] William Jones to Nicholas, 27 December 1624, TNA, SP 14/177, f. 41.
[22] The Mayor of Dover and others to the Privy Council, 26 December 1624, TNA, SP 14/177, f. 23. Hippisley to the Privy Council, 24 December 1624, TNA, SP 14/177, f. 21.
[23] Hippisley to the Privy Council, 26 December 1624, TNA, SP 14/177, f. 24.
[24] TNA, SP 9/208/37; TNA, SP 16/13, fos. 75v–6.
[25] TNA, C 66/2327, 7d. The commission was received in Dover on 1 January 1625. Hippisley to Nicholas 2 January 1625, TNA, SP 14/181, f. 14.

referenced the breaking of houses and the robberies that Hippisley and the mayor of Dover had reported to it earlier in the month. In order to stop these outrages from continuing, the mayor of Dover and Sandwich, the deputy warden of the Cinque Ports, several commissioned colonels, and the deputy lieutenants of county Kent were to have martial law jurisdiction over all of the soldiers stationed in and around Dover. With three making a quorum, these martial law commissioners could convene a court-martial and try by life and limb any soldier accused of any "robberies felonyes mutinies or other outrages" cognizable at martial law. In a clause that would come back to haunt the Crown in 1628, the commission also authorized the commissioners to try any other "dissolute p[er]sons" who joined with the soldiers in committing outrages.[26] It is unclear why the Crown thought this clause was necessary; there is no evidence it was used to try civilians by martial law. Perhaps other non-soldiers had joined in the riots and outrages in Dover throughout the month of December. In any case, the commission was meant to give local officers the power to discipline soldiers. Yet another variation of martial law had been made.[27]

Along with attempting to appease local officers, the government believed that immediate punishment of wrongs was necessary for the reformation of discipline. The Privy Council in the commission ordered that a gallows or a gibbet be constructed in a place the commissioners thought fit. There, they were to execute offenders in open view in front of their peers, "for an example of terror to others and to keepe the rest in due awe and obedience."[28] When the officers began to implement the commission, they started only with terror. On 3 January, Hippisley reported that the commissioners convicted a soldier of a capital offense, but after bringing him before the gallows, the soldier was pardoned because it was the first case.[29] Hippisley reported that the spectacle had inspired the

---

[26] Boynton, not examining the original commissions on the patent rolls, believed that this clause was only issued in the spring of 1625 after Charles I had assumed the throne. Boynton, "Martial Law and the Petition of Right," 260. This interpretation, however, is inaccurate.

[27] J.V. Capua has stated that the paradigm for this commission was made in 1617. This is incorrect. The 1617 commission allowed the President of the Council of the Marches of Wales to execute traitors and invaders by martial law. Thomas Rymer, *Foedera* (2nd ed., 1727), 17: 43–4. Other martial law commissions granted in the 1620s were for overseas voyages. *Ibid.*, 57, 246, 255, 408, 450–1. These were not consistent with the powers granted in the 1624 commission. "The Early History of Martial Law in England from the Fourteenth Century to the Petition of Right," *The Cambridge Law Journal* 36:1 (April, 1977): 171.

[28] TNA, C 66/2327, m. 7d.

[29] Hippisley to Nicholas, 3 January 1625, TNA, SP 14/181, f. 15. The gallows were set up in the market place, Anthony Hall to Nicholas, 10 January 1625, TNA, SP 14/181, f. 52v.

soldiers to act more obediently to their officers. Future offenders were less fortunate. Several days later, Hippisley reported that they had hanged a soldier and had caught two others for stealing. One was hanged; the other's life was respited and the offender was sentenced to jail instead. The disorders did not stop in January, but apparently they lessened. One report early in January declared that the martial law commissions had ended the storm that had gone on in December. Another claimed that the martial law commissions had brought order to the town.[30] It was maintained through the end of the month. Finally, on 31 January, James allowed Mansfeld to set sail for Flushing but refused to allow him to relieve the Dutch city of Breda, which the king of France had desired. Instead of wasting away in Dover, the army wasted away in Flushing. The expedition was a disaster.[31]

The newly crowned Charles I was determined to continue the fight. Further, unlike his late father, he was willing to go to war with Spain. By May 1625, commissions of impressment were dispatched to local officers, with the goal that 10,000 men arrive in Plymouth.[32] On 23 May, Charles sent a commission of martial law to the mayor and deputy lieutenants of Plymouth. The same day, he issued a commission of martial law for the magistrates of Kingston-upon-Hull.[33] The two commissions were nearly identical to that created for Dover back in December. Once again, local officers were authorized to use martial law upon the soldiers and any other "dissolute persons" that joined with them for any felony or other wrong according to martial law. Eventually, the soldiers convened near Plymouth as Buckingham and Charles decided that they would attempt a strike on the Spanish silver fleet as it returned to Cadiz. But preparations for the expedition went slowly. And throughout the summer, the mayor of Plymouth and the deputy lieutenants in Cornwall had to supervise the soldiers. The soldiers were better behaved than those stationed in Dover, but by mid-August some from London engaged in a mutiny. A court-martial convicted the ringleaders and forced them to draw lots for their lives.[34] Finally, on 8 October, the long-awaited expedition to Cadiz finally left from Plymouth. Like

---

[30] Sir Thomas Dutton to Lord Chamberlain Pembroke, 7 January 1625, *CSPD*, 1623–5, 457. Sir John Ogle to Dudley Carleton, 2 January 1625, TNA, SP 14/181, f. 12v. The disorders subsided until the men were put on ships on 23 January. William St. Leger and Ogle to Conway 23 January 1625, TNA, SP 14/182, f. 65v. The mayor of Sandwich apparently did not participate in the commission, and received a rebuke by the Privy Council. *APC*, 39: 481.

[31] Gardiner, *History of England*, 5: 286–90.   [32] *Ibid.*, 317–36.

[33] TNA, C 66/2351, m. 16d–17d.

[34] "A Letter from the Mayor and Commissioners at Plymouth to the Privy Council," 15 August 1625, TNA, SP 16/5, f. 77.

Mansfeld's expedition, the Cadiz voyage was a disaster.[35] The remnants of the expedition returned to Ireland and England in mid-December. Charles and Buckingham in the winter of 1625 were concerned that the king of Spain might retaliate through an invasion of either the southern English or Irish coast. Therefore, in the coastal towns of Ireland and in the southern counties of England, they billeted the troops upon the countryside.[36]

The Privy Council in England once again resolved upon granting martial law commissions to its county officers. On 12 December, the Privy Council made the deputy lieutenants and relevant mayors aware that they would once again have powers of martial law over the returned soldiers.[37] The commissioners in the counties likewise desired martial law commissions and requested the jurisdiction so that they might discipline the soldiers who were so poor and deprived, that without strict discipline, might resort to stealing.[38] The resulting commission, which passed through the Great Seal on 28 December, was meant to give the mayor of Plymouth and the deputy lieutenants of Devon powers to participate in the disciplining process. The Privy Council likewise gave deputy lieutenants and mayors in the county of Hampshire powers of martial law over soldiers stationed there.[39] Three months later in March, the Privy Council gave commissioners of Middlesex powers of martial law because so many soldiers and sailors were leaving their posts and coming to London in attempts to find sustenance.[40] In the late summer of 1626, when the Crown was trying to organize yet another raid on the Spanish silver fleet, this time to be led by Lord Willoughby, it granted martial law commissions to its county officers in Surrey, Hampshire, Sussex, and Kent, where mariners and soldiers were awaiting departure.[41] The county of Hampshire received another commission that December, when

---

[35] Gardiner, *A History of England*, 6: 10–23.
[36] Boynton, "Martial Law and the Petition of Right," 261–2; Aidan Clarke, "The Army and Politics in Ireland, 1625–1630," *Studia Hibernica* 4 (1964): 28–53.
[37] *APC*, 40: 266–7, 271.
[38] Commissioners at Plymouth to the Privy Council 15 December 1625, TNA, SP 16/11, fos. 145–6.
[39] TNA, C 66/2352, m. 2d, 7d.
[40] TNA, C 66/2356, m.10d (21 March); TNA, C 66/2384, m. 3d.
[41] TNA, C 66/2384, m. 3d. TNA, C 66/2385, m. 6d, 12d–14d. The Kent commissioners received two commissions. *APC*, 41: 101, 221, 223–5. It is unclear if Dorset received a commission of martial law in 1626. See *A Calendar of the Docquets of Lord Keeper Coventry* ed. Jan Broadway, Richard Cust, and Stephen K. Roberts, *List and Index Society* 34 (2004): 32. Likewise, in November 1626, the Privy Council ordered a commission for martial law for county Berkshire. *Ibid.*, 365. The Berkshire billeting commissioners clearly expected to have powers of martial law, see BL, Add. Ms. 21,922, f. 86. However, it had still not been made in December. *APC*, 41: 428. The commission was not enrolled, if it was ever actually made.

Willoughby's fleet returned (unsuccessful in its mission to capture the fleet), to discipline the sailors stationed in and around Portsmouth.[42]

During this same period, the Privy Council began to demand that counties hire a provost marshal to catch deserters and "vagrant soldiers." However, they did not grant these provosts powers of martial law.[43] The policy began in the summer of 1626 when the Privy Council wanted to appoint a provost in Hampshire to use martial law, but only in case the Spanish landed in Portsmouth. The policy was expanded when the commander of the Cadiz expedition, the Viscount Wimbledon, wrote to Sir John Coke in March 1627 that provost marshals should be appointed in every county because the constables had failed in their duty to round up deserting soldiers and vagrant and masterless men.[44] Coke agreed and the Privy Council sent out letters to every lord lieutenant that they should appoint a provost marshal for that purpose. However, the Privy Council only empowered these officers to imprison deserters and vagrants so that they might be tried by common law.[45] In any event, many counties, including Hampshire, refused to appoint the provost because they did not want to pay for his entertainment.[46] Martial law was reserved for those named in the commissions made by the Privy Council.

By 1627, Charles and Buckingham had become frustrated with the king of France to the point where they began considering ending the alliance and declaring war.[47] They eventually decided that they would send an expeditionary force to the Isle of Rhé, which would aid the Huguenot rebels at La Rochelle. The expedition set sail in late June 1627.[48] Like the others, the Isle of Rhé expedition was a disaster. And as in the aftermath of the others, the 3,000 or so soldiers who straggled home in November 1627 were kept in active service. Both Charles and Buckingham were determined in the next year to continue their war against the king of France. But this time, the Privy Council,

[42] TNA, C 66/2385, m. 21d.

[43] Boynton seemed confused about the powers of martial law that the provost actually possessed, which were only during times of rebellion and invasion. "Martial Law and the Petition of Right," 266. The council of war only intended that they use martial law should the Spanish, or later, the French land in England. See "A Discourse of Captain Brett concerning the preparations in Spain, 1626," BL, Harley, Ms. 3638, f. 133v.

[44] Wimbledon to Coke, 5 March 1627, BL, Add. Ms. 64,890, fos. 91v-2.

[45] They were meant to assist the sheriff and constable, not the martial law commissioners. *Ibid.*

[46] Deputy Lieutenants of Hampshire to the Privy Council, 17 September 1626, BL, Add. Ms. 21,922, f. 77v.

[47] Gardiner, *History of England*, 6: 147-99.

[48] As in 1625, it appears the Mayor of Hull received powers of martial law over soldiers. TNA, SP 16/540/1, f. 1. Local officers in Kent also received martial law powers. TNA, C 66/2409, m. 10d.

recognizing the discontent stationed soldiers had caused in Hampshire, Devon, and in Kent, decided to fan them out throughout the south of England.

Once again, the Privy Council accommodated local officials by granting them martial law commissions. By the end of December 1627, the Privy Council ordered the making of commissions of martial law to county officers in Hampshire, Kent, Berkshire, Sussex, and Dorset. Along with these county commissions, the Privy Council ordered martial law commissions to be made for officers in the Cinque Ports, the city of Exeter, the city of Plymouth, and on the Isle of Wight.[49] The City of Exeter's commission, it seems, arrived after a soldier did "sweare that he would cutt ye said maior in peecs and carry his head wth him and would make garters of his guts."[50] By April 1628, the Privy Council had ordered martial law commissions to county officers in Essex – where soldiers were garrisoned in preparation for an expedition to Denmark where they would fight for that king in northern Germany – Gloucester City and the county of Gloucester, Kent, and Northampton.[51] The deputy lieutenants of Essex had complained about the abuses of the soldiery and had asked for martial law commissions.[52] The deputy lieutenants in Gloucester likewise had asked for a commission of martial law to discipline soldiers in February 1628.[53] The commissioners of Dorset thanked the Privy Council for sending them a commission of martial law at the end of December 1627.[54] Martial law was desired in the countryside.

Let us take a closer look at how local officers tried soldiers by life and limb in this period.[55] First, while many requested martial law commissions, few of the mayors, deputy lieutenants, or other civilian officials knew anything about martial law. Sir William St. Leger, one of the colonels retained from the Cadiz expedition to oversee the soldiers,

---

[49] TNA, C 66/2409, m. 6d, 7d, 12d–15d, 17d. TNA, C 66/2422, m. 4d, 6–7d, 10d, 14d–15d, 17d.

[50] "Information against Walter Little, John Hill, and others ... for riotous conduct in Exeter," 12 November 1627, TNA, SP 16/84, f. 84.

[51] TNA, C 66/2422, m 3d, 8d, 11d–13d.

[52] Sir John Maynard and Others to the Privy Council 19 January 1628, TNA, SP 16/91, f. 10. The deputy lieutenants crafted a smaller code of war to govern the soldiers in Essex. Bodl. Firth C.4, fos. 439–40.

[53] Deputy Lts. Of Gloucestershire to the Privy Council, 16 February 1628, GA, GBR H 2/ 2, 136.

[54] The Commissioners of Dorset to the Privy Council, 31 December 1627, TNA, SP 16/ 87, f. 99.

[55] Unfortunately, for one of the most important regions, Devon, we only know about martial law practice from State Paper correspondence and from a reference to a captain in Exeter holding a martial court in 1627. DROE, "Auncient Letters," no. L290. A copy of the mayor of Exeter's commission of martial law from 1627 is still extant. DROE, Misc. rolls. no. 35.

complained that he only had as much power of governance as the town authorities of Plymouth: "without whome I can doe nothing and without mee they know nothing."[56] The Crown and Privy Council did not help alleviate this confusion. Therefore, county officials often opted for common law process instead. For example, the mayor of Southampton in the summer of 1626 requested that one John Scott, a soldier accused of killing another soldier, be tried at common law. The Privy Council allowed the mayor to remove this case into common law because they thought it was not pressing.[57] Scott was acquitted by a jury in September. Thus, while there are scattered accounts of soldiers being disciplined by martial law from 1626–8, it was much more likely that the martial law commissioners would simply refer soldiers to common law process.

The Privy Council, in general, not only accepted this choice but tried to give their county officials powers to hold common law sessions immediately. In the winter of 1626, the Privy Council stated that martial law commissioners "forbeare to make use of the power given for marshall lawe but in cases of great necessitie and extremitie."[58] As a consequence, they began issuing special commissions of *oyer* and *terminer* with the commissions of martial law so that soldiers could be immediately tried at common law for any wrong they had committed.[59] In Dorset, for example, the Privy Council sent out Sir Francis Ashley with a special commission of *oyer* and *terminer* to try seven soldiers for burglary in January 1627. All were convicted, although only one was executed.[60] The strategy of removing these cases into common law was alarming to some. In 1627, Mary Holland, the mother of Michael Holland, a soldier accused of murdering a town bailiff in Andover, petitioned Edward Conway, one of the deputy lieutenants of Hampshire, to remove the case to a court of war. Presumably, she believed that her son would receive more favorable treatment before a council of war.[61] Common law and martial law were both used to try soldiers.

On several occasions, the Privy Council pushed for trial by martial law. By 1627, it believed that a harsher disciplinary regime was necessary as it issued new ordinances of war which mandated the death sentence more

---

[56] Sir William St. Leger to Buckingham 7 January 1626, TNA, SP 16/18, fos. 33–4. Sir John Hippisley asked for the opinion of "all the coronells and captens" before deciding on how to act in one of his first cases after he had received the commission. TNA, SP 14/181, f. 34.

[57] *APC*, 41: 239.   [58] *APC*, 41: 425.   [59] *APC*, 43: 237, 288–9, 372, 375.

[60] "Whiteway's Diary" BL, Egerton 784, f. 62v. Indictments for desertion can be found in the Middlesex county records from this period. *Middlesex County Records: Volume 3, 1625–67* ed. John Cordy Jefferson (London, 1888), 15, 17.

[61] "The Petition of Mary Holland," HRO, Jervoise Ms. 44M69/G5/37/5.

often than the instructions issued in 1625.[62] In the spring of 1627, the provost marshal of Middlesex caught four soldiers in London who had deserted their regiments. Seeing an opportunity to terrify the many others who had fled their regiments, the Privy Council ordered the marshal to turn the men over to the martial law commissioners of Middlesex who were to try them by martial law. All four were convicted and had to roll dice for their lives.[63] In December 1627, the Privy Council wrote a letter to the commissioners in Hampshire and commanded them to try a surgeon named William Lawson by martial law. Lawson, according to the Privy Council, had drawn his sword on his captain and had rushed at him. His attack was prevented by other sailors who intervened in the affair.[64] The commissioners removed Lawson into the county jail, but they wrote back to the Council that Lawson should be tried at the assizes, not by martial law. They worried that the wrong was committed before their commission had been issued. They were also concerned, given that Lawson faced the death penalty at martial law, that they did not have the power to depose witnesses. Perhaps, the commissioners were simply uncomfortable with martial law. The assault by Lawson was capital in that jurisdiction; it was not capital at common law.[65] They removed the case from martial law to the assizes. The Privy Council, in spite of being openly challenged, apparently assented to the commissioners' jurisdictional switch.[66] Trials by life and limb at martial law were hardly threatening the supremacy of common law process.

The petitioning system and trial for misdemeanor

The martial law commissions were not a source of complaint among the county gentry in the south of England. Instead, certain JPs expressed frustration over their inability to prosecute soldiers. It was their informal exclusion – which was probably not systematic – from the criminal process that infuriated them. Let us examine the background to the ways in which the Crown managed civilian misdemeanor prosecutions of soldiers

---

[62] The commissioners of Hampshire had copies of these articles of war. "Southhampton Marshal Business," HRO, 5M50, fos. 109–16v.

[63] *APC*, 42: 257. Another example comes from Devon in 1628, when the Privy Council wanted mutinous mariners tried by martial law. *APC*, 43: 360.

[64] "Southampton Marshal Business," HRO, 55/M50, f. 117.

[65] Commissioners of Hampshire to the Privy Council, 10 January 1628 BL, Add. Ms. 21,922, f. 128. The commissioners had sought out evidence earlier in December by warrant. Perhaps they were unsuccessful in securing it. *Ibid.*, f. 127. Lawson was tried at the assizes in Hampshire. "Southhampton Marshal Business," HRO, 55/M50, f. 118.

[66] For the Privy Council's failures to enforce its policies in general, see Derek Hirst, "The Privy Council and Problems of Enforcement in the 1620s," *JBS* 18:1 (1978): 46–66.

prior to the 1620s: a process that required the civilian to petition the commander before formal prosecution could commence. Then, through admittedly scanty evidence, we explore how and if martial law commissioners applied this petitioning system from 1624–8 and how the Privy Council employed a variety of legal strategies to keep soldiers disciplined. It is likely that at times JPs were prevented from prosecuting soldiers.

In Roman Civil Law, jurists crafted a strict boundary by status of person between soldiers and civilians. Fellow soldiers convened tribunals that would try those who had failed to uphold the laws put down in *de re militari*.[67] Civilian courts had no jurisdiction over soldiers. By the early modern period, some European monarchs adopted this strict jurisdictional division. The clearest example comes from the king of Spain, who granted his soldiers the *fuero militar*, which exempted them from civilian jurisdiction. As Balthazar D'Ayala, the famous Spanish advocate general, put it, "[s]oldiers cannot be summoned before any but their own judge, or be punished by any other if in fault; and so, if arrested by a civil official, they ought to be remitted to their own judge."[68] Soldiers if brought before a civilian tribunal could make a *praescriptio fori*, or a claim to jurisdiction, and gain exemption from the proceedings.[69]

This division was never so simple for English armies. English commanders often sought to accommodate civilian officials whenever they were able to do so and allowed them to hear and determine cases against soldiers.[70] However, by the sixteenth century, the English Crown began to develop a legal system in garrison towns that sought to prevent magistrates from jailing soldiers over misdemeanors like debt. It decided upon a rule that civilian magistrates could hear and determine felony cases against soldiers, but they could not prosecute soldiers for misdemeanors unless they had received permission from the suspect's commanding officer. In Berwick, for example, civilians were forced to petition the marshal of the town to hear cases involving the debts of soldiers to civilians.[71] Only in Ireland in the sixteenth century were soldiers completely exempt from common law. However, if the commander refused to

---

[67] *The Digest of Justinian* ed. Theodor Mommsen with the aid of Paul Kreuger trans. Alan Watson 4 vols. (Philadelphia, 1985), 4: bk. 49, ch. 16.

[68] Balthasar Ayala, *De Jure et Officis bellicis et disciplina militari libri III* ed. John Westlake 2 vols. (Washington, 1912), 2: 205.

[69] Fernando González de León, *The Road to Rocroi: Class, Culture, and Command in the Spanish Army of Flanders, 1567–1659* (Leiden, 2009), 108.

[70] See B.J.H. Rowe, "Discipline in the Norman Garrisons under Bedford 1422–35," *EHR* 46:182 (April, 1931): 194–208.

[71] See TNA, WO 55/1939, fos. 7–14. Krista Kesselring, "'Berwick is our England:' Local and National Identities in an Elizabethan Border Town," in *Local Identities in Late Medieval and Early Modern England* ed. Daniel Woolf and Norman Jones (Palgrave, 2007), 92–112.

act on a complaint in three months, the complainant could take the case to a common law court.[72]

The point of the petitioning system was not to exempt soldiers from law, although that may have happened at times through corruption. Instead, commanders were given an opportunity to act as an arbitrator, where the dispute could be resolved without the soldier having to be jailed. This system of courtesy makes an examination of exemption difficult because, in all likelihood, if soldiers were exempted from common law, it was decided on a case-by-case basis. There was no systematic attempt to exempt soldiers from common law.

In 1625, the Council of War in its instructions included a provision authorizing the martial law commissioners to utilize the petitioning system. It stated that "if anie soldier or officer doe abuse anie man or woman the partie grieued shall goe to the officers commanders therein" and if not to them then to an officer of the peace. The officer of the peace then needed to send in writing a request for the commanding officer to call a council of war to hear and determine the case. If it found the defendant guilty, the council could punish the soldier "w[i]th imprisonment or the strappadoe, or with more or lesse as the fault requireth."[73] Civilians had to go through the martial law commissioners.

This system seemed to be in place through the spring of 1628 in all likelihood for cases involving indebted soldiers. For example, in the remnants of Sir John Hippisley's papers from the autumn of 1626, there is a plan for how civilians could complain about wrongs committed by soldiers while being billeted.[74] The complainant had to submit in writing the name of the soldier and his supposed offense to the commissioners; otherwise the martial law commissioners would not investigate the offense any further. The potential offenses were included in articles that supervised the relationship between host and soldier. For example, if a soldier struck the child or servant of his host family, a council of war would punish him severely.[75] Hosts, meanwhile, were required to provide a certain amount of food and drink per week. Similar instructions were given to Lord Conway for the billeting of soldiers on the Isle of Wight in February 1628. The soldiery had complained that they had been put up in indigent houses while the inhabitants of the island complained that the soldiers took more than their daily allotment. The Privy Council

---

[72] "Instructions to Sir Anthony St. Leger, 1550," HEHL, EL Ms. 1700, f. 5v. *CPR*, 1549–51, 346.

[73] TNA, SP 16/13, f. 75.

[74] BL, Egerton Ms. 2087, f. 30. The Hampshire commissioners made a meeting schedule so that petitioners "may know where to complaine." HRO, 44M69/G5/37/115.

[75] BL, Egerton Ms. 2087, f. 24

informed Conway to place the soldiers in the houses of the better-off. If the soldiers took more than their daily allotment, the civilians could complain to the offending soldier's captain. If the captain did nothing, the civilian could complain to the deputy lieutenants who were required to inform Buckingham of the captain's malfeasance in not prosecuting the case.[76] No civilian option was provided.

There is some evidence of this system in action. The commissioners of Hampshire, for example, heard plaints from civilians, officers, and soldiers and attempted to act upon their acquired knowledge. In 1626, the commissioners instructed the regimental commanders that they would be meeting in October to address the complaints they had received from officers, soldiers, and those billeting soldiers about wrongs committed.[77] The commissioners, for example, received information that Captain Ogle's regiment had committed diverse misdemeanors while stationed in Winchester. They commanded his appearance before them at a meeting to be held in Alreford. A copy of the warrant was sent to the mayor of Winchester to show him that justice was being performed.[78] Perhaps, given what we know about the petitioning system, the mayor had made a formal complaint to the martial law commissioners.

Civilians along with soldiers could be brought before the martial commissioners for failure to perform the services assigned to them. Hippisley, for example, commanded the body of Edward Ryden of Awcombe to appear before the commissioners on 15 December 1626.[79] Although we know nothing more about the case, it appears Ryden was a civilian. The commissioners in Hampshire likewise commanded Thomas Phillips of Romsey, John Ivey, and Thomas Rolfe to appear before the commissioners at Winchester because they refused to allow their horses to go with the soldiers as commanded by the constable. Upon information from the constable, the commissioners decided to hear the case.[80] In effect, the commissioners had powers to punish civilians who committed contempt of the Privy Council by not obeying its orders.[81] It was not strictly speaking martial law. However, they were interventions by martial law commissioners over offenses relating to billeting and other affairs of war. Local officials not included

---

[76] Copy of a Letter from the Privy Council to Lord Conway, 13 February 1628, IWRO, OG/BB/153.

[77] BL, Add. Ms. 21,922, f. 82v. Mostly, the records that survive for our understanding of these proceedings are warrants in collected papers of deputy lieutenants. One such warrant can be found in HRO, Jervoise Ms. 44M69/G5/48/125.

[78] BL, Add. Ms. 21,922, f. 88.   [79] BL, Egerton 2087, f. 37.

[80] BL, Add. Ms. 21,922, fos. 88v–9; HRO, Jervoise Ms. 44M69/G5/38/4.

[81] The Privy Council also commanded the deputy lieutenants of Essex to imprison those who refused to billet soldiers in 1628. Bodl. Firth C.4, f. 446.

in commissions of billeting or martial law were probably irritated by these intrusions.

The commissioners of martial law heard cases involving the misdemeanors of soldiers and, even in certain instances, civilians. But could civilians prosecute soldiers through other means than the court-martial? It seems clear that in general civilians could pursue other legal avenues. The sessions of the peace for the city of Exeter, for example, contain several court cases involving wrongs supposedly committed by soldiers.[82] The city's sessions of the peace in November 1627, for example, heard a case involving eight soldiers who had been accused of killing some sheep. From these records, it does not appear that the high command in any way tried to prevent the case from going forward.

On certain occasions, however, the Privy Council acted as a gatekeeper when complaints were made to it about wrongs committed by soldiers. For example, Conway wrote to the martial law commissioners in Hampshire about three soldiers who had supposedly stolen a horse from someone while marching through Wiltshire. The Council ordered that they repay that person for the horse, but in doing so also gave him the opportunity to be removed from the ambit of prosecution.[83] The Privy Council also authorized martial law commissioners to remove soldiers who had been jailed for misdemeanors so that they might continue to serve the Crown. However, it warned the commissioners not to release those who had committed egregious or violent offenses.[84] Nevertheless, at least once, a soldier charged with felony was seized from a jail. In the fall of 1627, the jailor in Southampton Richard Overy was deposed for allowing a soldier named John Landen to go free. Overy claimed that "the said prisoner was let forth by the marshall of the souldiers lying then in Southampton and carried pinnacled by him to be tried for theire offenses before the duke by martiall lawe."[85] If true, this and similar types of actions must have infuriated local law officers.

In the end, these policies along with the failure to properly discipline soldiers irritated those excluded from the commissions of martial law and of billeting as well as ordinary subjects. Riots erupted among and against the soldiery in Essex, both in Harwich in 1627 and in Witham in 1628,

---

[82] DROE, ECP BK, 62, f. 328vff; *The Book of Examinations and Depositions, 1622–1644* ed. R.C. Anderson 4 vols. (Southampton, 1929–36), 1: 83–4, 91, 101; *Ibid.*, 2: 17–9.

[83] Conway to the Martial Law Commissioners, 9 January 1628 HRO, Jervoise Ms. 44M69/G5/39/2.

[84] Privy Council to the Commissioners of Martial Law, HRO, Jervoise Ms. 44M69/G5/48/16.

[85] *Book of Examinations and Depositions*, 1: 103.

and in Cork in 1626.[86] Further, the inhabitants of the Isle of Wight, whose army officers had no money to compensate them for billeting, complained that they were falling into debt.[87] The Privy Council was aware of these problems, and in the spring of 1628 perhaps unfairly laid the blame on its martial law commissioners. It scolded the Hampshire commissioners for meeting too infrequently and for not adjudicating complaints made by civilians on various depredations of soldiers.[88] MPs when they convened in March likewise had few kind things to say about the deputy lieutenants and their supervision of soldiers.

Wartime and the 1628 Parliament

Charles convened parliament to meet in 1628 because he desperately needed supply. The MPs wanted to redress perceived injustices committed by Charles' ministers. Due to the weakness of the Crown, the 1628 Parliament possessed the political capital necessary to effect changes. Several leading legal minds who sat in this parliament like Sir Edward Coke, John Selden, William Noy, and Sir John Bankes all opposed James' and Charles' martial law commissions. These men crafted interpretations of martial law that were dependent upon wartime in order to restrain it. There was little agreement between them about what constituted such a state.

The debates in the Commons over the Crown's martial law policies began with protests over the office of deputy lieutenant. On 24 March, MPs, including ones from Devon, complained that soldiers had been abandoned in their counties with no instruction from the Privy Council.[89] Sir Edward Coke worried that there were few known boundaries for the office of deputy lieutenant because it was new.[90] He called for a committee of lawyers and soldiers to examine the deputy lieutenants, so that it could make new laws to govern their activities. Over a week later, in another discussion on the billeting of soldiers by deputy lieutenants, John Selden declared that both were illegal. Deputy lieutenants only had

---

[86] G.E. Aylmer, "St. Patrick's Day 1628 in Witham, Essex," *P&P* 61 (November, 1973): 139–48; Boynton, "Martial Law and the Petition of Right," 262–3; TNA, SP 63/242, fos. 235–40v.

[87] "The Humble Petition of your most loyall Subiectes the inhabitants of the Isle of Wight," IWRO, OG/BB/158, 160. According to contemporary sources, soldiers were not even prosecuted for felonies on the island. Boynton, "Isle of Wight," 28–9.

[88] Privy Council to the Commissioners in Hampshire, 13 February 1628, BL, Add. Ms. 21,922, f. 132v. For the lieutenancy's failures in general, see Thomas Garden Barnes, "Deputies not Principals, Lieutenants not Captains: the Institutional Failure of Lieutenancy in the 1620s," in *War and Government in Britain, 1598–1641* ed. Mark Charles Fissel (Manchester, 1991), 58–86.

[89] *Proceedings in Parliament 1628*, 2: 79–80.   [90] *Ibid.*

powers in certain states of time: "deputy lieutenants ... are appointed by a writ under the Great Seal, to kill, slay, and depress [sic] all rebels, in times of rebellion, or any open violence of the King's peace."[91] For Selden, deputy lieutenants should only hold appointments during wartime.

This same pattern continued on 8 April. Sir Walter Erle, an MP from Dorset, opened the subject by complaining once again about billeting.[92] Others complained about the numerous depredations soldiers had committed in their localities. Some argued that the officers in the army actively prevented them from prosecuting soldiers for these wrongs. Once again Sir Edward Coke intervened in the debate. He was concerned about restraining the lieutenancy to wartime. "Here is a secret of the law" he opened, "Before the 27th of Queen Eliz. no man [i.e. deputy lieutenant] was to have a continual commission; it was only for a time."[93] According to Coke, in times of peace, the deputy lieutenant could do nothing but according to law. His powers of martial law were restricted to wartime. It was in this context that the commissions of martial law were first debated: from a discussion of the depredations of soldiers, to one of billeting, to one of the temporal constraints of powers of lieutenants who supervised billeting, and finally to a discussion of martial law as an example of the powers that deputy lieutenants should only possess during times of war.

In the first discussion of martial law, Coke provided it a negative definition. It was a trial that did not use indictment or presentment but that nevertheless punished by taking a convict's life or limb. Through this broad definition, Coke invoked debates about due process that had taken place in the fourteenth century. He looked to the overturning of the conviction of Thomas of Lancaster by the first parliament under Edward III in 1327: "Thomas Lancaster in E.2 made an insurrection and was taken *flagrante crimine*, and they gave judgment without indictment, and he was beheaded."[94] According to Coke, in its reversal, parliament declared: "[i]f the courts of justice be open, none ought to be executed." In this reading, Coke understood martial law and conviction by record as committing the same error.[95] Surprisingly, he also lumped the reversal of the 1330 conviction of Roger Mortimer, the Earl of March. Mortimer, like Lancaster was convicted by manifest proofs, although his conviction was before parliament. For Coke, these types of tribunal could not be used while the Courts of Westminster were open.

---

[91] *Ibid.*, 268. I am guessing the word should actually be suppress.   [92] *Ibid.*, 360–8.
[93] *Ibid.*, 367.   [94] *Ibid.*, 363. Also see, *ibid.*, 367–8, 370.   [95] *Ibid.*, 363.

Let us examine more closely what the reversal of the conviction of Thomas of Lancaster actually said. As we shall recall, Edward II had convicted Lancaster of treason upon his record due to the notoriety of his offense in 1322 at Pontefract Castle. Parliament, concerned about this practice, reversed the decision in 1327 which restored the real property of the descendants of Thomas. In the reversal, parliament asserted that conviction upon record could only be used in times of war, defined *either* as when the Chancery was closed *or* when the king had raised his banner. Anyone within the verge of the banner could be subject to conviction upon record.[96] It is unlikely that it was a coincidence that Coke ignored the banner as it would have allowed the king to use martial law upon his discretion. At least initially, Robert Mason and John Bankes sided with Coke's views.[97] Jurisdictional politics played an important role in the 1628 debates on martial law.

Edward Coke's intervention provoked further debate on the legality of martial law in England. Once again, the focus of the debate swayed from the real problems that soldiers presented to county officers and the jurisdictional politics the jurists wanted to pursue. On 11 April, MPs examined a sample commission of martial law and the accompanying ordinances of war – glossed by the MPs as "instructions."[98] The prevalence of the death penalty within the instructions was shocking to men like Coke, who once again declared that martial law could not be used while Chancery was open. Those who had served as JPs focused more on their own inability to punish soldiers than on martial law. John Eliot reported that in the West Country he was prevented from punishing soldiers by their commanders who claimed that if a justice of the peace "meddled with any offense of the soldiers, he was threatened to be punished."[99] Eliot and others were not that opposed to the martial law commissions either.

John Selden then entered the debate. For Selden, the question of the legality of the commissions was pressing. Commissioners were hanging soldiers and perhaps preventing JPs from performing their judicial duties. He was concerned about the language within the commission: "it is not only to execute soldiers but any dissolute man that joins with them."[100] What constituted a "dissolute man" concerned Selden. The legality of martial law was essential for Selden because "[t]his concerns our lives."[101] A tribunal that did not follow common law procedure nevertheless had powers to take the lives of convicts. He thus moved for further

---

[96] For more details on the reversal, see the prologue.
[97] *Proceedings in Parliament 1628*, 2: 364.   [98] *Ibid.*, 412–3, 416, 420, 423–6.
[99] *Ibid.*, 413.   [100] *Ibid.*, 417.   [101] *Ibid.*, 413.

debate on the rights of martial law commissioners to punish with a blood sanction.

It was this key point – when could the Crown punish by life and limb without using indictments or presentments – that structured the ensuing debates. On 15 April, this debate became more divisive, even among the MPs who agreed that the current martial law commissions were illegal. Robert Mason was the first to elaborate on Coke's initial proposition. Although Mason agreed that the current commissions were illegal, and that martial law was legal if the courts were closed, he also argued that an army royal in the field could employ martial law: "the Marshal is judge and he is to judge according to the law martial."[102] The soldiers as currently billeted did not constitute a force in the field.[103] Selden was motivated to respond to these claims to martial law jurisdiction. The first great attempt at restricting martial law had been challenged. In his response, Selden made the second great attempt at restricting it.

Selden argued, contrary to Mason, that the Court of the Verge governed the host.[104] Let us recall that the Court of the Verge was the king's ambulatory court which had cognizance over the twelve-mile circumference around the king's body. We shall also recall that the king's host in the Middle Ages often fell under the jurisdiction of the Court of the Verge. The army plea roll from the time of Edward I, the *placita exercitus*, revealed this heritage. Selectively using the *placita exercitus*, Selden argued that common law as constituted in the Court of the Verge governed the king's hosts in the medieval period. In future periods, commissions of *oyer and terminer* should be used to prosecute wrongs in the army in England. Martial law thus played no role in the disciplining of troops.[105]

More importantly, Selden argued that martial law powers of lieutenants were merely those of execution upon wrongdoers while they were committing a wrong. Thus, the constable and the marshal for Selden only had powers of execution when they encountered rebels in the act of rebellion or invaders in the act of invasion. This power, to execute those *in flagrante crimine*, "is the legal power of the lieutenants now."[106] Basing

---

[102] *Ibid.*, 462.   [103] *Ibid.*, 461–2, 466–7, 469–70.   [104] *Ibid.*, 462–5, 467–9, 470–6.

[105] The Placita Exercitus roll can now be found in TNA, E 39/93/15. Selden's notes on the roll are still extant. LPL, Ms. 3474, f. 7v. In *ibid.*, fos. 9–10v, there are notes taken by Joseph Bradshaw, who was a member of the sub-committee to examine legal precedents, on 14 April 1628 – one day before Selden's speech – on a *coram rege* roll from the same reign (33 Edw. 1). It seems as though Selden, apparently with the help of Bradshaw, was comparing the *placita exercitus* with a "common" plea roll. These records are now located in the manuscript collection of Sir Matthew Hale, Selden's executor. For the list of the members of the sub-committee to examine legal precedents, see *Proceedings in Parliament 1628*, 6: 105.

[106] *Proceedings in Parliament 1628*, 2: 463.

his reading on the lieutenancy commissions, and combining it with his claims about the Court of the Verge, Selden attempted to eliminate sitting courts-martial that could punish wrongs committed by subjects in England by life and limb.

Lieutenants possessed this power of execution even when the Courts of Westminster were open. This was true because for Selden, a time of war, while it could mean when the courts were closed, also meant "a time of wrong." He made this claim through a reading of the medieval jurist Bracton, who, as we shall recall, believed that wartime constituted specific acts of illegality as well as a more general time of war. He provided a detailed discussion of this point in his reflections on the assize of Darrein Presentment, a body that enquired into who had been the last person to present a benefice to a vacant church. Bracton claimed that a person who had taken the benefice "in war" could not claim a right to it.[107] In other words, if that person had taken it through extortion or force and not by lawful action or agreement, he could not claim a right to the advowson. These acts did not need to take place in a state of general warfare – some kind of rebellion or invasion – but instead could be done individually. Thus, for Bracton, "it may be at any time a time of war and a time of peace, not absolutely but with respect to some."[108] While war was raging all around them, two free men could make an arrangement in peace that could be upheld in general times of peace. Meanwhile, while peace reigned all around them, someone could lose their legal rights due to wrongful force. Wartime and peacetime could co-exist within the realm.

What were the limits to this "time of wrong?" Selden, of course, did not care about advowson claims. He was focused on explaining the powers of the lieutenancy. Martial law was allowable on those committing an act of invasion or rebellion because while others were in a time of peace, their wrong placed them in a time of war. However, if they were taken prisoner, they once again entered into a time of peace. But what about other offenses that violated the peace? Could one punish rioters while in the act of rioting? What about vagrants? What about those who resisted arrest? Selden provided no answers to these questions.

Selden also used the medieval Court of Chivalry to further his argument that martial law had no jurisdiction in England in peace time. We shall recall that the Court of Chivalry was established as a permanent court in the fourteenth century to handle the legal business of the wars taking place in France. We shall further recall that in the

---

[107] *De Legibus et Consuetudinibus Angliae* ed. George E. Woodbine, trans. Samuel E. Thorne 4 vols. (Cambridge, MA, 1968), 3: 57, 213; 4: 171.
[108] *Ibid.*, 3: 213.

thirteenth year of the reign of Richard II and then in the first year of Henry IV's reign, parliament passed statutes that restricted the court's jurisdiction to treason and all matters relating to war overseas, and to all matters of war not cognizable at common law within the realm.[109] While this tribunal had gone into abeyance in the sixteenth century, James I had revived it to handle cases relating to honor and heraldry.[110] Selden claimed that martial law and this newly reconstituted Court of Chivalry were one and the same. And because it used Roman Civil Law procedures, the Court of Chivalry could not deprive subjects of life or limb in England. But outside the realm, the court could deprive those of life and limb. Coke agreed that martial law and the Court of Chivalry were one and the same.[111] The jurisdictional politics of both were clear: by turning martial law into the Court of Chivalry, they could bind martial law in England through 13 Richard II. On the one hand, martial law as constituted in the lieutenancy commissions possessed no substantive law that differentiated from common law; on the other, martial law as constituted overseas was that practiced by the Court of Chivalry. This claim was accepted in spite of the fact that no one believed the sitting Court of Chivalry in England bore much resemblance to the courts-martial that sat in the counties from 1624–8.

Martial law could also be applied to enemies within the realm. Here Selden and all the other jurists came to an agreement.[112] They understood this point from the trial of Perkin Warbeck, the pretender who claimed to be a Yorkist heir who in 1497 invaded England. Henry VII caught him after his rebel army had dissipated in October. Eventually, the king tried Warbeck before a court of the constable and marshal where he was convicted of treason and executed. The reports of the case in the sixteenth and seventeenth centuries claimed that Warbeck was tried before the Court of the Constable and Marshal because he was not an English subject; he had been born in Tournai, which was held by the king of France.[113] Using this case, Selden and all the other jurists agreed that courts-martial had jurisdiction over enemies of the realm.

---

[109] *Proceedings in Parliament 1628*, 2:464.
[110] G.D. Squibb, *The High Court of Chivalry: A Study in the Civil Law in England* (Oxford, 1959), 47–67; for an analysis of the High Court of Chivalry during Charles' reign, see Richard Cust, *Charles I and the Aristocracy, 1625–42* (Cambridge, 2013), 140–71.
[111] *Proceedings in Parliament 1628*, 2: 466.   [112] *Ibid.*, 463.
[113] For the Warbeck case see, *Reports from the Lost Notebooks of Sir James Dyer* ed. J.H. Baker 2 vols. (London, Selden Society, no. 109, 1994), 1: 206; *Reports of Cases by John Caryll part one 1485–1499* ed. J.H. Baker (London, Selden Society, no. 115, 1999), 383; *The Notebook of Sir John Port* ed. J.H. Baker 2 vols. (London, Selden Society, no. 102, 1986), 2: 125.

Thus, there was a duality to Selden's thinking on martial law. Martial law could be by *viam executionis*, where a lieutenant or commander had the power – even in England – to execute "in sight" rebels or enemies during a chase or a battle.[114] Lords lieutenants in other words possessed a limited power of summary martial law. Or martial law could be by *viam judicii*. This power lay exclusively with the marshal's court, or the Court of Chivalry, which only had powers to deprive subjects of life and limb on acts committed beyond the seas. The substantive laws of martial law were not particularly important for Selden in either of these two variants in no small measure because he argued that soldiers had been disciplined by the Court of the Verge within the realm.

When it came to Selden's definition of martial law, his colleagues remained unconvinced. Sir Francis Ashley, a sergeant of the king and an expert on Habeas Corpus, was one of the skeptics.[115] Ashley agreed that martial law "could not be exercised in times of peace." He nevertheless continued that "in time of invasion or other times of hostility when an army royal is in the field and offences are committed ... then such imprisonment, execution, or other justice done by the law martial is warrantable."[116] By 18 April, MPs trained in Roman Civil Law began to assert more aggressively the scope of martial law jurisdiction. Their responses were aimed at Selden. Thomas Eden, a master in Chancery, argued that soldiers must be tried not only by laws unique to the army but also by military men. Speaking next, Sir Henry Marten, who had served James I as his advocate, made a more extended defense of martial law. Marten was incredulous over Selden's argument that martial law was simply the execution of common law substance without common law process: "Is this not a law? Have we not military men? Have we lived so long lawless?"[117] Marten then defended martial law process. Drawing up an indictment for a soldier who committed a wrong and then trying him at the next assizes missed a critical teaching opportunity for the rest of the soldiers. For Marten, "present death is present terror."[118] Along with these justifications, Marten dismissed the temporal constraints that Coke, Selden, and others offered for martial law: "Execution of martial law is necessary where the sovereign and state think it necessary."[119]

In this context of divisiveness, William Noy offered the third important interpretation of martial law and its jurisdiction. Noy, like Selden, was by 1628 a highly respected but controversial jurist. He had with Selden sided with the five knights in their Habeas Corpus case in 1627.[120] However,

---

[114] *Proceedings in Parliament 1628*, 3: 72.   [115] Halliday, *Habeas Corpus*, 145–6.
[116] *Proceedings in Parliament 1628*, 4: 282.   [117] *Proceedings in Parliament 1628*, 2: 548.
[118] *Ibid.*, 549.   [119] *Ibid.*   [120] James S. Hart, Jr. "Noy, William," in *ODNB*.

Noy did not agree with Selden on what constituted wartime. Noy began instead by asserting that martial law was a valid jurisdiction in England, but *only* for soldiers and only in a time of war. A time of war, further, was not solely signified by the Courts of Westminster being closed. Looking back to the Battle of Lewes and Evesham, Noy noted that "war is entered into the *Red Book of the Exchequer* ... and yet the courts of justice were open."[121] For Noy, the law of the camp could operate even when the courts of Westminster were open. What then signified a time of war? For Noy, martial law was "not to be executed but when there is a banner displayed."[122] He had re-discovered the banner as a badge of wartime. But for Noy, it was the enemy's banner: "[t]he law intends that the enemy's banner should be first displayed in the field."[123] It was only when the army royal was near the enemy in expectation of battle that martial law could be deployed. The enemy, and its banner, now controlled time.

Like Selden and Coke, Noy was selectively deploying medieval examples to reshape the law of martial law. His claim about what constituted wartime was not wrong, but it ignored all of the examples that were inconvenient to his legal project. What was his project? In all likelihood, Noy wanted Crown commanders to use martial law to discipline the hosts, but he also wanted to remove discretion from Charles so that the king could not assert wartime and use martial law whenever he so desired. Thus Noy gave the jurisdictional power to the enemy.

While Coke continued to speak about the Courts being closed, Noy's interpretation became more influential during the remainder of the proceedings. Selden on 22 April slightly changed his argument. He now admitted "[i]f an army were gathered together against an enemy, martial law may be used."[124] All of the men of the army, and any of those rebels or disobedient near the verge of the army, were bound to obey. Selden had been influenced by Noy. He could not, however, bring himself to grant martial law commissioners powers of life and limb. Commanders for Selden could only punish through imprisonment. Others also came around to Noy's point of view as well. Sir Dudley Digges on 22 April argued that armies were governed by commissions of *oyer* and *terminer*

---

[121] *Proceedings in Parliament 1628*, 2: 544.   [122] *Ibid.*, 558.

[123] *Ibid.*, 549. Other versions of the speech state that the army needed to be "expecting an approach of an enemy." *Ibid.*, 545. According to the diarist Henry Sherfield, Noy stated that "martial law may be executed: not when an army is preparing, or billeted, or in conduct, unless the enemy be near approaching, or under a banner marching or intrenched – then martial law will be executed, but not at any other time. *Proceedings in Parliament 1628*, 6: 73.

[124] *Ibid.*, 3: 25.

until "there's an enemy near."[125] In peace, the army was governed by common law. In war, now signified by the enemy's banner, commanders could discipline by martial law.

The Crown's position that its delegation of martial law had been legal was lost by 22 April. That day, Sir John Coke, the king's principal secretary of state, gave a speech to the commons where he pleaded with them that the king's power to create martial law jurisdiction was part of his prerogative.[126] Sir John Coke believed that martial law was necessary to keep soldiers in awe and obedience, whether or not England was in a state of internal war because the common law had no cognizance over matters pertaining to war. And lest anyone should forget, Coke asked the Commons: "[d]id not the commissions go out at the request of the gentlemen of the country?"[127] This was true. Like Selden's, Coke's, and Noy's arguments, John Coke's were selective but not wrong. Upset over all the innovations made to sustain the war for the past three years, the Commons dismissed the secretary of state's arguments. It ordered the sub-committee for martial law to examine its history before it made a final determination on the legality of the martial law commissions.

The ensuing reports were on the history of the disciplining of hosts. Unlike Edward Coke, both Selden and Noy wanted to examine sufficiently similar past practices. After they had been officially assigned the task, Selden investigated the history of martial law from between the reign of Edward I and Henry VII, while Noy focused on the Tudor era. They gave their reports on 25 April and on 7 May.[128] Their interpretations did not change as a basis of their examinations. Some of the commissions they found certainly proved their points. Other examples that disputed their interpretation were omitted or rationalized. The several commissions that authorized generals to deprive convicts of life and limb by simple information process made sense to Noy and Selden only because they were for armies outside of the realm. The several known examples from the sixteenth century of commanders executing soldiers in England – the most prominent being the Earl of Essex executing soldiers in 1596 prior to his Cadiz expedition – were explained away by the claim that he had required a pardon (he had not). A comprehensive history of martial law was not that useful for those who desired to restrain it.

Sir Henry Marten was not convinced. He was deeply troubled by the attempts of the common lawyers to bind the king's ability to alter time: "[t]he King has power to proclaim war or to make peace; and by consequence they are to judge when it is time of peace or time of war."[129]

---

[125] *Ibid.*   [126] *Ibid.*, 23–4, 27–8, 31–2, 34–5, 38.   [127] *Ibid.*, 24.
[128] *Ibid.*, 72–4, 79–80, 83–9, 302–7, 312–5, 318.   [129] *Ibid.*

Marten was right that the king previously had discretion over wartime. But when it came to trials by life and limb, his was no longer the sole legal understanding in England.

The law of martial law, 1628–40

While the Petition of Right forced Charles' government to restrain martial law commissions in the immediate aftermath of 1628, the juristic arguments made by the leading lawyers of the realm mattered far more for the future history of martial law. As in the aftermath of the 1580s, when the first major arguments were made to restrict martial law practice, the arguments made were only partially successful in restraining martial law jurisdiction throughout the 1630s.

Let us begin with the reception of the arguments made in the 1628 Parliament. Diarists realized the arguments were important; they also realized they were confusing. Some, like the manuscript interpretation of the Petition of Right, found in the judge Sir George Croke's papers, stated only that "Martiall Law to be nulled in pece."[130] Others tried to untangle the complex arguments made in 1628. The diarist and lawyer Henry Sherfield, for example, wrote down the various arguments and then the ground rules in order to try and teach himself martial law jurisdiction.[131] He was taken with the arguments of both Selden and Henry Marten. Dividing one page into half, Sherfield listed all of the arguments Selden made on the top, including Selden's employment of the *placita exercitus*, and all those Marten made on the bottom.[132] Then he wrote a hypothetical scenario. Martial law could not, according to Sherfield, be used "in this nacon" in a time of peace which was signified when "noe enemy or Rebell [is] in the field w[i]th banner displayed." Here he was informed by Noy's later argument. But what was less clear to Sherfield was the legality of execution by martial law if the army was near an enemy. This confusion was understandable as Noy and Selden disagreed on this point. In trying to figure it out, Sherfield played out a hypothetical: "a capten kills a souldier of his owne in the battayle or nearby the battayle ... what law doth he kill him by ... shall not the common lawe judge of it after[wards?]"[133] An execution by martial law was "p[er]haps justifiable" Sherfield mused, but "p[er]haps not." The common law might have cognizance over the case, but it also might

---

[130] HRO, Verulam Ms. XII.A.31.
[131] HRO, Jervoise 44M69/52/34. Sherfield's diary can be found in the same archive. It has been printed in *Proceedings in Parliament 1628*, 6: 58–93.
[132] *Ibid.*
[133] There is an ink blot that mars the last word, but it seems like it reads as "afterwards."

come before the marshal who had jurisdiction in the field. The debate over whether or not soldiers could be punished by martial law confused even the most active participants in the 1628 Parliament.

Others who took notes also stressed the importance of the enemy's role in authorizing martial jurisdiction. A notebook of legal precedents, for example, from Charles' reign kept track of the debates on martial law since Sir Edward Coke began it on 7 April through 1637 when Oliver St. John made speeches on Ship Money.[134] In it the diarist began with Coke's arguments that unless the "courts be hindered" martial law was not legal in England. He understood that "abroad it hath power indefinite." It had power over enemies even in states of peace. But the notes eventually moved on from Coke and ended with Noy's claims. In times of war, martial law could not be used "vnless another army were against them." The key point for this note-taker was that in times of peace in England, subjects could only be tried by life and limb "by due process of law."[135] These same arguments were developed in manuscript notes on martial law in later periods.[136] Jurists paid attention to Noy, Selden, and Coke, even if they were not always clear on who they believed won the debate.

In practice, the 1628 jurists were largely successful in immediately restraining martial law. On 7 May, the Commons voted to state that the commissions were illegal, and eventually they included a clause that asked for the revoking of the current commissions of martial law into the Petition of Right. Charles and his council, after thinking about responding by stating they would make commissions of martial law that only had cognizance over soldiers in pay, consented to the request.[137] The JPs' desire that no man should be exempt from common law was included in the Petition as well. The Crown only issued commissions of martial law to officers on Guernsey in the summer of 1628 for the discipline of 200 garrisoned soldiers.[138] The Petition of Right was immediately successful.

Thus, when the Council of War was reformed in 1629 in order to provide a more effective bureaucracy for the Crown's martial affairs, it did not possess powers to deprive convicts of life and limb. The newly reformed council nevertheless had expanded powers in other areas.[139]

---

[134] "The Inconveniencies of billeting Soldiers: From the Petition in Parliament, A.D. 1627," BL, Harley Ms. 980, f. 164v.

[135] *Ibid.*   [136] BL, Add. Ms. 4159, f. 179.

[137] For the drafts of the responses to the Petition the Crown made, see *Proceedings in Parliament 1628*, 6: 47–50.

[138] TNA, C 66/2481, m. 5d, 7d; *APC*, 43: 204. The commissions were recalled, at the request of the inhabitants of Guernsey, in 1629. *APC*, 44: 546.

[139] Trumbull's notes contain an examination of the Spanish Council of War. BL, Add. Ms. 72,422, f. 88.

Eventually, the new commission gave the Council powers to gather intelligence about the king's enemies, to price victuals, and to have authority over promotions and retentions within the army.[140] The commission also declared that the Council of War, with a quorum of seven, had the ability to "take due examinacon vppon oath or otherwise as needs and occasion shall require of all such misdemeanors abuses and offences touching martiall affaires or prisoners of warr, as shall come to yor knowledge by information or otherwise."[141] Over the next four years, it engaged in a variety of judicial adjudication over matters relating to war.[142]

The legal business the Council heard related to supposed wrongs committed upon or by soldiers during the wars of the 1620s.[143] The Council heard petitions for beds in hospitals for wounded soldiers.[144] It disciplined officers for poor performance.[145] It also heard petitions from widows for the pay of their late husbands. Magarett Le Home, for example, successfully petitioned to receive the pay owed to her husband, who had died while participating in the La Rochelle expedition.[146] Others petitioned the Council of War for the salary they would have received serving in the armies of the Dutch Republic, which they had abandoned to serve the king.[147] Others petitioned for arrears.[148] Some former military officers petitioned for pensions.[149] Others complained of fraud or neglect by their superiors which prevented them from being paid their full salary.[150] Often, these requests were made in combination with some claim of financial trouble.[151] The Council of War spent

---

[140] A copy of the commission can be found in TNA, SP 16/28, f. 59v.

[141] TNA, SP 16/28, f. 56v. The Council's power to displace office-holders meant that its recommendations could sometimes be supervised at the Court of Star Chamber. See TNA, SP 16/218, f. 178. The attorney general, on the advice of the Council would write out a grant for a new officeholder. TNA, SP 16/214, f. 165. For an order to remove an officer see TNA, SP 16/214, f. 125.

[142] These can be found scattered throughout the State Papers Domestic general series. For minutes of council meetings see, TNA, SP 16/176, fos. 37–9. TNA, SP 16/193, f. 96; TNA, SP 16/188, fos. 173ff; TNA, SP 16/186, f. 57; TNA, 16/185, fos. 93ff. TNA, SP 16/184, f. 93ff. TNA, SP 16/184, f. 66ff. TNA, SP 16/166, f.7ff.

[143] TNA, SP 16/146, f. 25.

[144] There are over sixty five such petitions. TNA, SP 16/28, fos. 65v–70v.

[145] See for example, TNA, SP 16/28, f. 55v. TNA, SP 16/144 f. 1.

[146] TNA, SP 16/28, f. 65v and 16/226, f. 15.

[147] TNA, SP 16/136, f. 99. For a similar case, see TNA, SP 16/220, f. 109.

[148] For example, see TNA, SP 16/136, f. 89, 91–5; TNA, SP 16/138, f. 61; TNA, SP 16/138, f. 65.

[149] TNA, SP 16/218, f. 162; TNA, SP 16/195, f. 102. TNA, SP 16/183, f. 68. TNA, SP 16/139, f. 94.

[150] This was a particular problem on the Denmark expedition. TNA, SP 16/145, f. 61. TNA, SP 16/187, f. 148.

[151] TNA, SP 16/139, f. 151.

most of its time from 1629 to 1633 adjudicating cases such as these. The Council, after hearing the petition, often sought official approval to act from upwards in the chain of command – either from Charles, the Privy Council, or from one of his secretaries of state. If the petitions were not all that important, the Council delegated them to others – usually officers of the army.[152] The Council possessed a specialized and distinctively martial jurisdiction. But the business it conducted was not martial law according to the jurists who had debated the jurisdiction in 1628 because it did not involve trials by life and limb.

The restrictions on martial law only became tested when Charles sent royal armies in 1639 and in 1640 to Scotland to quell a rising in that kingdom over his attempts to mandate an episcopal government for the Scottish church. In both campaigns, Charles issued fairly standard orders to his commanders, who in turn issued ordinances of war to discipline their soldiers – one of these was Arundel's code which we examined in the last chapter.[153] But in spite of these commissions, there was considerable debate over when martial law could be used. This uncertainty became pressing in the spring and summer of 1640, during the Second Bishops' War. In May 1640, Edward Conway, a commander in the north, had put a soldier to death by firing squad for mutiny. Many around the army were shocked at the execution, and lawyers told Conway he had no authority to take life or limb without a common law trial.[154] The disorders did not stop over the summer, and Conway wrote to William Laud in July about his problems with maintaining discipline. He informed Laud that the commander of the army, the Earl of Northumberland, had told him that he could not execute his commission of martial law in Newcastle, except "when an enemy is really neare to an Army of the Kings."[155] Here was Noy's understanding of wartime. Conway was furious: trial by a jury instead of a court of war "will take away the respect of the souldier to the officer and therewith presently be noe obedience or care in either soldier or officer."[156] Conway's solution was to hang the lawyers. But finally Northumberland in the summer delivered a warrant to Conway which allowed him to try soldiers by martial law along with a pardon. In order to

---

[152] "Minutes by Nicholas of answers directed by Sec. Coke to be given to various petitions, etc." 25 June 1630 TNA, SP 16/153, f. 29; TNA. SP 16/169, f. 71; TNA, SP 16/169, f. 55. TNA, SP 16/168, f. 31. The Council often commissioned others to examine evidence in relation to petitions. See TNA SP 16/193, f. 85, and TNA SP 16/185, f. 38. Sometimes it delegated its powers. TNA, SP 16/184, f. 68; TNA, SP 16/531, f. 138.

[153] The Council of War was revived in 1637. Its minute book is TNA SP 16/396. It handled little judicial business. Mark Charles Fissel, *The Bishops' Wars: Charles I's Campaigns against Scotland, 1638–1640* (Cambridge, 1994), 62–77.

[154] *CSPD*, 1640, 189.   [155] Conway to Laud, 6 July 1640, LPL, Ms. 943, fol. 695v.
[156] *Ibid.*

get around the new boundaries on martial law, the Crown needed to grant mercy to its commissioners.

The claims made by the 1628 MPs were also validated in the treason trial of the Earl of Strafford. As we have seen, while he had been lord deputy of Ireland, the Lord Mountnorris had been convicted of a capital offense by martial law.[157] Strafford had also executed a soldier by martial law in 1638 for desertion and theft. The prosecutors, who were trying to prove that Strafford systematically attempted to subvert the king's laws, claimed that he had violated the Petition of Right. Wentworth, after he conceded that the Petition of Right was law in Ireland, claimed that he could be tried for murder but not treason, and that he would receive a pardon for his execution of the soldier in the same way that Conway had received one. This plan, as he would later discover, was not foolproof.[158]

Conclusion

While Strafford's trial is sufficiently famous for us not to dwell at length on it, we should nevertheless pause to weigh the implications of his prosecution. In 1641, it was at the very least murder and perhaps treason for the lord general of an army in a time of peace to execute by martial law one of his soldiers. This was true because soldiers were subjects. And subjects in England and Ireland – unless they were poor and Irish – were entitled, according to those who agreed with Coke and Selden, to common law process should their life be at stake.

Nevertheless, soldiers in hosts proved a thorny problem. This is why Selden and Noy investigated the history of how English kings had disciplined their hosts. It is also why Selden and Noy disagreed about what constituted wartime, as Noy believed that hosts before an enemy needed to be supervised by a harsher legal regime than common law could provide. When did necessity mandate sharper measures for the disciplining of soldiers? The answers to this perplexing question led to divisions among jurists who otherwise shared very similar worldviews. It is no wonder that one of the most perceptive listeners to these debates – Henry Sherfield – was so confused about this issue. The problem of

---

[157] "Copy of the Sentence of the Councell of Warre pnounced agt Lord Mountnorris the xiith daye of December 1635," HRO, Verulam Ms. XII.B.34a.

[158] John Rushworth, *Historical Collections of Private Passages of State* 8 vols. (London, 1721), 8: 186–205. Accessed on British History Online February 2013–September 2015, www .british-history.ac.uk. The Long Parliament also investigated Sir Thomas Danby for executing soldiers before a council of war in the north of England in 1640, although nothing seems to have happened from it. *Proceedings in the Opening Session of the Long Parliament: House of Commons* ed. Maija Jansson 7 vols. (Rochester, 2000–07), 2: 362, 366, 374.

supervising soldiers would in the end lead to the partial unraveling of the Petition of Right's ban on martial law.

The jurists sitting in the 1628 Parliament forever transformed martial law jurisdiction, but, as we shall see, not in ways that they had necessarily intended. The Crown and its delegated authorities had experimented with martial law to punish soldiers, mariners, pirates, rebels, vagrants, rioters, and Virginians. In its latest experiment, the Privy Council under James and Charles sought to grant martial law jurisdiction to mayors and deputy lieutenants so that they might terrify soldiers into obedience through exemplary punishment. In response, jurists sitting in the 1628 Parliament selected historical examples to re-imagine the law of martial law. Soldiers were central to their arguments because Coke, Selden, and Noy disagreed over when and if they could ever be punished by life and limb in England by martial law when the courts of Westminster were open.

Martial law – in the various definitions granted it – was confined to wartime. Only in that tract of time could common law process be suspended. Most claims to martial law jurisdiction by the Crown or its delegated authorities now often included a claim to wartime, either signified by the king's or the enemy's banner or by the closing of the courts. The jurists of the 1628 Parliament, however, did not bring an end to martial law. Further, they did not fully address – outside of one brief affirmative statement by Selden – whether parliament could make martial law legal in a time of peace. Nor, as we shall see, did those debating martial law jurisdiction in 1628 ever stop to consider what would happen if a magistrate decided to close the courts down.

5   Unbound by parliament
Martial law and the wars of the three kingdoms

The controversialist William Prynne had become a strong opponent to the Cromwellian government. Citing the tyranny of the "swordsmen" that ruled England, by 1656, Prynne argued that the English body politic had become grievously ill: "Is there no balm in Gilead? Is there no physician there? Why then is not the health of the Daughter of my people recovered?"[1] The balm came from the 1628 Parliament, which for Prynne had declared the ancient liberties of the English people. One of them was the declaration that martial law should not be used "when the King's Courts of Law were open, and other Legal trials might be had by Juries in Courts of Justice."[2] Over the course of the Civil Wars and Interregnum, this boundary that had restricted martial law had been transgressed on multiple occasions. Courts-martial had been authorized to punish soldiers, sailors, conspirators, and spies. Most importantly, new hybrid tribunals, styled as "high courts of justice," had powers to take life and limb even though their procedures were consistent with courts-martial and not with common law courts. For Prynne, in order for England to heal, the Petition of Right needed to be applied.

Yet Prynne himself had participated in the flouting of the Petition of Right when he had accepted parliament's powers to try spies and conspirators by martial law in 1643. Royalists likewise applied martial law upon soldiers, without making justifications based on Noy's, Coke's, or Selden's understandings of martial law jurisdiction. Further, parliamentary garrison courts-martial, which sat periodically throughout the war, tried civilians and soldiers for treason by martial law. They also seized the real property of those they convicted of treason, a power that courts of war had not possessed since the middle of the fourteenth century.

---

[1] William Prynne, *A Summary Collection of the Principal Fundamental Rights, Liberties, Proprieties of all English freemen* (London, 1656), [1]. Part of this chapter can be found in John M. Collins, "Hidden in Plain Sight: Martial Law and the Making of the High Courts of Justice, 1642–1660," *JBS* 53:4 (October, 2014): 859–85.

[2] Prynne, *A Summary Collection of the Principal Fundamental Rights . . . of all English freemen*, 3.

The boundaries that had been made in the parliament of 1628 became undone during the tempestuous 1640s.

Martial law practice did not end when the First Civil War ended. Nor did it end when the Second Civil War ended. By 1647, soldiers had successfully petitioned for indemnity for their acts during the war – a practice explicitly banned by the Petition of Right. By November 1648, MPs looked to all of those past procedures which had been banned by strict readings of Clause 29 of Magna Carta and combined and reformatted them to make new procedures and laws to meet their legal problems. The first was the trial of Charles in January 1649. Legal innovations continued into the 1650s, when the Commonwealth and Protectorate adapted court-martial procedures and ordinances of war to create the High Courts of Justice to sit in Westminster and try traitors. At times, MPs citing the Petition of Right stopped the authorization of martial law. Often, even if they failed to stop the authorization of martial law, they managed to include sunset clauses, mandatory quorums, and other devices that the Privy Council had used in earlier periods to restrict and monitor the powers of martial law commissioners. Nonetheless, those protesting from the outside, who like Prynne frequently resorted to Edward Coke's arguments for martial law jurisdiction, had no ability to stop a determined parliament from authorizing martial law.

Prosecuting soldiers

Experimentation with martial law began with the governance of soldiers. The Long Parliament, when it became in charge of armies, eventually resorted to granting martial law commissions even though the Petition of Right had banned them and even though the Long Parliament itself had tried the Earl of Strafford for treason in part because he had used martial law to take a soldier's life when the realm of Ireland was in peace.

Initially it refused martial law powers and instead only granted its lord general supervising the remainder of the army that had recently fought the Scots a commission of *oyer* and *terminer*. Attempts to grant generals martial law jurisdiction over soldiers had been cried down. On the last day of December 1640, for example, Sir Simonds D'Ewes opposed a bill that would have authorized the commanders in the north of England to discipline the army by martial law because "without exception that where the courts were open martial law ought not to be exercised."[3] For

---

[3] *Proceedings in the Opening Session of the Long Parliament: House of Commons*, ed. Maija Jansson 7 vols. (Rochester, 2000–07), 2: 78–9. D'Ewes here viewed Parliament itself to be one of the Courts of Westminster.

many, allowing martial law would have been seen as radical and as a betrayal of the efforts of those who had made the Petition of Right.

Nevertheless, parliament began to change its policies. Its first authorization for martial law came in July 1642 to discipline the soldiers under the command of the third Earl of Essex. While the fighting had not yet started, most realized that the disputes between Charles and his parliament would now be decided by military force.[4] Parliament passed an ordinance that authorized Essex to use either common law or laws relating to the customs of war to discipline his troops.[5] The makers of the ordinance could not bring themselves to write the phrase "martial law." This unclear phrasing seems to have caused problems, as by November of that year parliament felt the need to explicitly authorize Essex to take life and limb for wrongs committed against the customs of war.[6] Parliament likewise granted its generals at sea powers of martial law. Initially, in its ordinance to the Earl of Warwick in July 1642, parliament did not explicitly allow martial law jurisdiction. But it did provide a covering indemnity for all actions undertaken for the public good. In February 1643, parliament granted Warwick a "martial power, as the General now hath at Land."[7] Slowly, those sitting in the Long Parliament became more comfortable with granting powers of martial law. No reference was made in these authorizations to a standing enemy army in the field or to the status of the courts.

Over the years, the writers of the parliamentary ordinances became more confident in granting martial law jurisdiction. By 1645, in its ordinance granting Sir Thomas Fairfax powers of commander in chief of the "New Model Army," parliament ordered him to "execute Martial Law, for the Punishment of all Tumults, Rapines, Murders, and other Crimes and Misdemeanors, of any Person whatsoever in the said Army."[8] The wording of the commission to Fairfax was almost exactly the same as that of Essex. And the intention was almost certainly the same. But by 1645, parliament had overcome its embarrassment over the phrase "martial law." In ensuing ordinances, MPs granted powers of martial law to its top commanders to discipline soldiers under their command. It was legal because parliament willed it to be legal.

Although we know less about their practices, royalists likewise used martial law for their soldiers. Charles I raised his standard at Nottingham signifying war. In what were probably the first written articles of war, Charles justified the raising of arms to defend himself against the

---

[4] For the causes of the Civil War, see Conrad Russell, *The Causes of the English Civil War: The Ford Lectures delivered in the University of Oxford, 1987–88* (Oxford, 1990). J.S. Morrill, "The Religious Context of the English Civil War," *Transactions of the Royal Historical Society* 5th Ser., 34 (1984): 155–78.
[5] *A&O*, 1: 14–16.   [6] *Ibid.*, 39.   [7] *Ibid.*, 76–7.   [8] *Ibid.*, 660–2.

rebellious acts of parliament.[9] But he made no mention of delimiting martial law to the verge around his or the enemy's banner. Nor did he invoke the status of the courts. It is likely that royalist soldiers were always governed by martial law. The Council of War that sat in Oxford supervised this martial jurisdiction.[10] Its most important duty was to draft the proclamations relating to discipline that Charles would eventually publish for his armies. It also punished officers for neglect of duty.[11] For example, it commanded one of Charles' provosts to execute a detained man declared to be a rebel.[12] It also investigated a case against one of its colonels, William Hide, who apparently had conducted himself terribly.[13] Finally, it operated as a court of war for very important cases, where the life and reputation of Charles' officers was at stake. This included the court-martial of Prince Rupert.[14] Unfortunately, no other royalist court-martial record seems to have survived.

Little changed after the end of the war. Due to mutinies, parliament extended powers of martial law to its commanders. By 1645, parliament had no capability of paying its soldiers, who were now owed considerable sums in arrears. The consequence of this financial failure was that many soldiers either decided to take their pay informally through pillage, or that they engaged in increasingly sophisticated mutinies to protest their situation.[15] Further, parliament could not disband the troops because it still needed the army to enforce its victory. In response to these problems of possessing a standing but unpaid and unhappy army, parliament granted powers of martial law to its inferior commanders. William Brereton, the commander of parliament's forces in Cheshire, for example, received powers of martial law in the aftermath of a mutiny by the troops there. Parliament granted the same powers to Colonel Poyntz in the north in the winter of 1646 so that he could quell a mutiny.[16] Other

---

[9] *Military Orders, and Articles, Established by His Maiestie, For the better Ordering and Government of his Maiesties Armie. With the Oath which every souldier is to take* (Oxford, 1643). As Barbara Donagan has noted, this is a reprint from articles first issued under the Earl of Lindsey, who died in October 1642. Barbara Donagan, *War in England, 1642–49* (Oxford, 2006), 407.

[10] Ian Roy, "The Royalist Council of War, 1642–6," *Bulletin of the Institute of Historical Research* 25 (1962): 150–68. The main manuscripts that illustrate the Council of War's administration during the Civil War are the surviving minutes recorded by its secretary, Sir Edward Walker. BL, Harley Ms. 6802, 6851–2.

[11] It examined the mayor of Oxford and others over their failure to fortify the city in 1643. BL, Harley Ms. 6851, f. 140.

[12] *Ibid.*, f. 167. The Council of War sometimes ordered its generals to execute mutineers and rebels by martial law. *Ibid.*

[13] BL, Harley Ms. 6851, fos. 72, 79, 81–91.

[14] BL, Harley Ms. 6802, fos. 129–31. Roy, "Royalist Council of War," 158.

[15] J.S. Morrill, "Mutiny and Discontent in English Provincial Armies, 1645–7," *P&P* 56 (August, 1972): 49–74.

[16] *Ibid.*, 69–70; *CJ*, 4: 723–4.

garrison commanders, like those of Kingston-upon-Hull, continued to have martial law jurisdiction. The Isle of Wight garrison commander was granted martial law jurisdiction in January 1648 after parliament was made aware of a mutiny that had taken place in late December.[17] The commanders of the troops to be sent to Ireland possessed similar powers.[18] Martial law jurisdiction continued in England even after the state of war had passed. The period 1645–7 would not be the last time MPs authorized martial law in response to the mutinies of soldiers.

Martial law jurisdiction, especially after 1646, generated protests. The key text for these was Edward Coke's *Third Part of the Institutes of England*, which had been published in 1644. In it Coke tellingly discussed martial law in his section on murder. There he claimed that those with "commission of martial authority, in time of peace hang or otherwise execute any man by colour of marshall law, this is murder, for this is against Magna Carta cap. 29."[19] His chief example was the execution of Thomas of Lancaster, which he incorrectly dated as 14 Ed. 4. Later versions included the reversal of the conviction of the Earl of March. Both had been convicted of treason by the manifest proof of notoriety. Parliament had ordered the publishing of the very text that its critics would use to protest its authorizations of martial law.

John Lilburne, the oft-imprisoned leader of the "leveller movement" of the late 1640s, was one of the most vocal critics against martial law.[20] After a mutinous assembly had been quelled in March 1649, a court-martial had sentenced the ringleaders to draw lots for their lives. Lilburne and other agitators argued that the recourses the parliamentary commanders took were illegal: "we do protest your exercise of Martial law against any whomsoever, in times of peace, where all courts of Justice are open, as the greatest encroachment upon our Laws and Liberties that can be acted against us."[21] As Lilburne suggested, the courts of Westminster had never closed, and according to him, the use of martial law in England was therefore illegal.

While many MPs were probably sensitive to these arguments, they also had to accommodate citizens that wanted soldiers disciplined. At times, the Commonwealth and later the Protectorate published the sentences of

---

[17] *CJ*, 5: 413–15. [18] *LJ*, 9: 98–102.
[19] Sir Edward Coke, *The Third Part of the Institutes of the Laws of England* (London, 1644), 52.
[20] For Lilburne, see Pauline Gregg, *Free-Born John: A Biography of John Lilburne* (London, Harrap, 1961). For his legal thought, see Diane Parkin-Speer, "John Lilburne: A Revolutionary Interprets Statute and Common Law Due Process," *Law and History Review* 1 (1983): 276–96. Paul D. Halliday, *Habeas Corpus: From England to Empire* (Cambridge, MA, 2010), 193–7.
[21] John Lilburne, *Copie of a Letter, written to the General* (London, 1649), [1].

courts-martial to show that this was indeed taking place. In the winter of 1648, for example, after the London government had complained in the previous year about how soldiers garrisoned in the city were causing havoc on its citizens, news-books sympathetic to the new regime published accounts of soldiers being disciplined.[22] *A Perfect Diurnall* in 1649 reported the hanging of a soldier at Smithfield for beating a London constable and shouting abuses at his wife. In 1655, news-books informed the reading populace of the disciplining of soldiers for various moral outrages.[23] When it came to punishing soldiers, the various regimes of the 1650s at times publicized their actions.

They did so in all probability because there was among some skepticism that soldiers had to face justice. This belief in their exempt status arose in response to the establishment of the Committee of Indemnity in the summer of 1647. The problem for the soldiers fighting for parliament was the dubious legality of their actions during the war. From 1642–6, soldiers had plundered homes, taken horses for the war effort, and imprisoned royalists. Further, commanders on both sides had protected them from misdemeanor prosecutions through the petitioning system.[24] Due to the continued fear that once they left the army soldiers might be prosecuted for their acts during the war, parliament eventually consented to the creation of a Committee of Indemnity in the spring of 1647.[25] Some of the most radical members of the Commons comprised the Indemnity Committee which had the power to protect any current or former servant of the parliamentary cause against prosecution for executing orders during the war. Under its provisions, a defendant being prosecuted for acts committed during the war could petition the committee for a suspension of proceedings. The committee, with five making a quorum, heard the petition and usually commanded JPs in the country to depose witnesses. If the Committee believed that the petitioner's case had merit, it had the powers to intercede. Should the plaintiff continue his or her suit, the Committee had powers of imprisonment for contempt, and could fine the plaintiff three times

---

[22] For the city's complaints, see LMA, Rep. 59, fos. 322v, 339v. Two soldiers were punished at a court-martial for attacking city grocers. *Kingdomes Weekly Intelligencer*, 19–26 December 1648, 1197–8.

[23] H.M. Reece, "The Military Presence in England, 1649–1660," (unpublished D.Phil Dissertation, University of Oxford, 1981), 120; *Perfect Proceedings of State Affairs* 24–31 May, 1655, 4694.

[24] Essex's 1643 *Ordinances of Warre*, articles iv and v in "of administration of Iustice." For the royalists, see *Militarie Orders and Articles established by his Majesty*, sig. B3.

[25] *A&O*, 1: 936.

the amount they had asked for in their original suit against the defendant.[26]

From 1647–1655, the Committee of Indemnity heard petitions from parliamentary soldiers, parliamentary civil servants, and even supporters of parliament who were being sued by royalists.[27] Many of the cases involved the taking of horses or of supposed plunder done by soldiers. These quite substantial powers generated outcries by the judiciary. Its purpose and its legality have been hotly debated ever since.[28] Whether or not it was a form of "parliamentary tyranny," the creation of the indemnity committee was certainly novel. Through its lawmaking powers, parliament in the aftermath of the First Civil War altered what had been the law of the land.

Spies, traitors, and prisoners

Whether or not the fighting in the three kingdoms would be treated as a war or as a rebellion depended on the relative fighting strengths of the two sides. In Ireland, after rebellion broke out in 1641, Charles quickly sent martial law commissions for the summary execution of rebels.[29] While the Earl of Strafford had been convicted of treason in part because he had tried Lord Mountnorris and English soldiers by courts-martial in times of peace, MPs had also revealed how little they cared about executions of Irish "rebels and traitors" by martial law throughout Strafford's trial. Thus, there was little resistance to using martial law on Irish rebels throughout the 1640s. Sir Anthony St. Leger and Sir Charles Coote carried out brutal reprisals throughout 1642. As Micheál Ó Siochrú has

---

[26] The best work on the Committee is John Shedd, "Friends of the Revolution: The English Parliamentary Committee for Indemnity, 1647–1655," (unpublished PhD dissertation, University of Tennessee-Knoxville, 1990). He has summarized his work in Shedd, "Thwarted Victors: Criminal and Civil Prosecution of Parliamentary Officials during the English Civil War and Commonwealth," *JBS* 41:2 (April, 2002): 139–69: and in Shedd, "Legalism over Revolution: The English Parliamentary Committee for Indemnity and Property Confiscation Disputes, 1647–55," *HJ* 43:4 (December, 2000): 1093–1107.

[27] Shedd, "Friends of the Revolution."

[28] John Morrill, *Revolt in the Provinces: The People of England and the Tragedies of War, 1630–1648* (2nd ed., London, 1999), 106, 108; Robert Ashton, "The Problem of Indemnity, 1647–1648," in *Politics and People in Revolutionary England: Essays in Honour of Ivan Roots* ed. Colin Jones, Malyn Newitt, and Stephen Roberts (New York, 1986), 117–40. Anne Hughes, "Parliamentary Tyranny? Indemnity Proceedings and the Impact of the Civil War: A Case Study from Warwickshire," *Midland History* 11 (1986): 49–78. Ronan Bennett, "War and Disorder: Policing the Soldiery in Civil War Yorkshire," in *War and Government in Britain, 1598–1650* ed. Mark Charles Fissel (Manchester, 1991), 248–67.

[29] For the origins and course of the Irish rebellion, see Nicholas Canny, *Making Ireland British, 1580–1650* (Oxford, 2001), 461–550.

shown, it was not until ex-patriots with continental military experience arrived from Europe that both sides began to treat prisoners as enemy combatants.[30] Once both sides recognized equality of strength, the war began to be fought according to internationally recognized laws of war.

For English, Welsh, Scottish, and Protestant prisoners, it was decided early on in the Civil War that the opposing sides would treat the captured not as rebels – either against parliament or against the king – but as enemies who should be treated as prisoners of war.[31] This classificatory scheme was meant to save lives.[32] But it also meant that civilians who committed wrongs according to either the articles of war of the army or the unwritten laws of war were subject to martial law because they were now construed as "enemies" or, from the perspective of parliament, "malignants" – those who actively stood against the MPs at Westminster.

Parliament began experimenting with using martial law on civilians in the spring of 1643. One of the first instances took place in Bristol, when Nathaniel Fiennes, through his soldiers on guard, discovered a plot made by prominent citizens to overthrow the town and hand it over to the king on 7 March.[33] His advocate, Clement Walker, took a deposition from George Boucher about it on 10 March.[34] Over the course of April, a full council of war heard examinations upon oath from all those involved in the plot who were willing to speak. It also took informations from the soldiers who foiled the plot.[35] They discovered that the plotters were going to take the guns of the city, disarm the guards, and allow Prince Rupert and his forces to take it without bloodshed for Charles. After taking over thirty examinations, the court impeached the chief conspirators, Robert Yeomans and others, of treason on 8 May. The impeachment accused them of committing traitorous intelligence with the enemy as well as plotting for the overthrow of the garrison established by the Long Parliament. The impeachment focused on their treachery "agt this citty of Bristol being possessed by a Garrison under ye command of ye . . . Earle of Essex."[36] This was in keeping with the martial law of treason, which focused on acts that might endanger fortified places

---

[30] Micheál Ó Siochrú, "Atrocity, Codes of Conduct and the Irish in the British Civil Wars, 1641–1643," *P&P* 195 (May, 2007): 55–86.

[31] This was not true for Irish soldiers attempting to enter the English theater. See Elaine Murphy, "Atrocities at Sea and the Treatment of Prisoners of War by the Parliamentary Navy in Ireland, 1641–1649," *HJ* 53 (March, 2010): 21–37.

[32] Barbara Donagan, "Atrocity, War Crime, and Treason in the English Civil War," *American Historical Review* 99:4 (October, 1994): 1140–1.

[33] *A Brief Relation, Abstracted out of Severall Letters, of a most Hellish, Cruel, and Bloudy Plot against the City of Bristoll* (London, 1643); *CJ*, 3: 97.

[34] The depositions taken explicitly by Walker are in Bodl. Nalson Ms. 13, f. 399.

[35] *Ibid.*, fos. 334–69.   [36] *Ibid.*, f. 370.

through conspiracy. Because of their treachery to the garrison, the conspirators by trying to help Charles I had committed treason "agt his matys p[er]son Crowne & dignity."[37] These were strange times, indeed.

A council of war, sitting upon a commission from the Earl of Essex, convicted Yeomans and multiple others of treason that month in what became very controversial hearings. Yeomans seemed to submit to the court. But the other conspirators did not submit and refused to answer or acknowledge the court's authority. Furious, the court of war convicted them anyway.[38] Fiennes appealed to parliament, which was not dissuaded from action. On 22 May, it allowed the council of war to execute the ringleaders, and three days later, it published an explanation for doing so.[39] In the Bristol case, parliament justified its executions by stating that although the king's soldiers and those who had actively declared for the king could not be executed for treason, "the Law of Armes amongst all souldiers, maketh a difference betweene open enemies and secret Foes, and Conspirators."[40] Civilians were now subject to martial law in certain cases of treason.

A similar case arose less than a month later in London – the so-called Waller Plot. On the last day of May, John Pym had made public a plot by the MP Edmund Waller and several prominent London citizens to take the city for the king.[41] Pym wanted the conspirators tried by martial law. Sir Simonds D'Ewes opposed Pym and argued that "martial law which was in former ages vtterly vnknowne to the subjects of England."[42] Others were unsure as to martial law's legality. In order to appease the doubters, the supporters of martial law brought in Isaac Dorislaus, a learned Dutch lawyer trained in the Civil Law and the judge advocate general of Essex's army, who reassured the Commons that trying conspirators at martial law was common among all armies during times of war. Others within parliament were appeased. Six men ultimately came before a court-martial on 30 June; the council of war executed two of them.[43] Because London was considered a garrison of Essex's army, the Commons asked for a commission for a sitting court-martial from its lord general.[44]

---

[37] *Ibid.*

[38] *Ibid.*, fos. 374, 376. The date of the sitting of the court of war was not given in the record but *Mercurius Civicus* reported it as 20 May. *Mercurius Civicus* 18–25 May 1643, 20–1.

[39] *The Several Examinations and Confessions of the Treacherous Conspirators against the Cittie of Bristoll* (London, 1643); *Mercurius Civicus* 18 May to 25 May 1643, 20–2.

[40] *Mercurius Civicus* 18 May to 25 May 1643, 22.

[41] The best account of Waller's plot is still S.R. Gardiner, *History of the Great Civil War* 4 vols. (Gloucestershire, 1987 ed.), 1: 146–9, 156–8.

[42] Journal of Sir Simonds D'Ewes, BL, Harley Ms. 165, f. 102v.

[43] Laurence Whitaker's Diary, BL, Add. Ms. 31,116, fos. 59v–60v; *ST*, 4: cols. 626–54; *A Brief Narrative of the Late Treacherous Plot and Horrid Designe* (London, 1643).

[44] Laurence Whitaker's diary, BL, Add. Ms. 31,116, f. 56.

Over the course of 1643, parliament expanded the cognizance of martial law so it could punish other betrayals against the war effort.[45] These expansions often came at the behest of the faction that ruled the City of London. It had only gained the office of mayor late in the summer of 1642 and still faced strong opposition from those who either supported the king or who wanted to make peace on more generous terms with him than the hardliners desired.[46] In early August 1643, after the fall of Bristol to royalist forces, peace petitions became more common. A group of women on 9 August presented a peace petition at Westminster. The House of Lords likewise devised peace propositions on favorable grounds to the king.[47] The mayor and common council wrote several petitions to the Commons in protest of these petitioners. Among their demands, they wanted to make sure "traytors and delinquents" were speedily punished.[48] In response, a protest from the peace faction erupted within London.[49]

Due to this disturbance, on 17 August, parliament passed an ordinance that gave the committee of the militia within London the power to punish by life and limb by martial law "all such as shall weare any Markes Signes or Colours to distinguish themselves as a party against that of Parliament."[50] The militia also had powers to punish their soldiers and officers according to the ordinances of war issued by the Earl of Essex. This new court-martial also had cognizance over any insurrection, tumult, or unlawful meeting within the City. Further, if any refused to swear an oath of loyalty to parliament and the City, the militia could seize that person's arms and horses. It could also order any shop to be closed. The militia possessed frightening powers in a city that began to resemble 1590s London.

Throughout the autumn, parliament continued to expand the cognizance of martial law to supervise punishment over a variety of acts that it considered betrayal. In September, parliament ordered that any who tried to take war provisions out of London was to suffer death by martial law.[51] In November, the Commons wanted to try a king's messenger as a "spy" for bringing in a commission of array and royal proclamations to London.

---

[45] It considered granting martial law powers to its commissioners in Kent in 1643 to punish rebels, but probably did not end up doing so. *CJ*, 3: 178.

[46] Valerie Pearl, *London and the Outbreak of the Puritan Revolution: City Government and National Politics, 1625–43* (Oxford, 1961), 160–276; Keith Lindley, *Popular Politics and Religion in Civil War London* (Aldershot, 1997), 201–15, 337–45.

[47] Gardiner, *History of the Great Civil War*, 1: 181–8; Lindley, *Popular Politics in London*, 351–3.

[48] *Mercurius Civicus* 3–11 August 1643, 86–7. LMA, Letter Book QQ, f. 83; LMA, Journ. 40, fos. 69v–70; *LJ*, 6: 172; *Kingdomes' Weekly Intelligencer* 8–15 August 1643, 227–8.

[49] Whitaker's Diary, BL Add. Ms. 31,116, f. 138v.   [50] *A&O*, 1: 249–51.

[51] *CJ*, 3: 254.

The rationale in this case was similar to that in the earlier cases: the messenger was attempting to create a faction within London that would take the city for the king. That same month, the Commons imprisoned three printers to await a court-martial for producing royalist propaganda.[52] By January 1644, it declared that any who challenged the authority of its great seal in court or that brought legal documents into London that contained the king's great seal would be tried as a spy at a court-martial.[53]

Parliament had expanded the boundaries of martial law's cognizance to include treasonable acts made against its war effort. But with the very important exception of the London court-martial, parliament had not delegated jurisdiction outside of the army. This began to change in the fall of 1643, when those in support of the war effort wanted to punish commanders who they believed had surrendered garrisons too easily. This desire led to the imprisonment of Sir John Hotham and his son for keeping traitorous intelligence with royalists, Sir Nathaniel Fiennes, for surrendering Bristol too quickly, as well as others. Through the persistent and public efforts of Clement Walker and William Prynne, Fiennes was tried before a court of war that December. He was found guilty, after a lengthy trial that included multiple witnesses, but his father, the powerful Lord Saye and Sele, ensured that he would be pardoned.[54] At this stage, many within the City and within the Long Parliament wanted a tribunal in London so that these cases might be tried more swiftly.

It was not easy to get the court established. The Commons sent Henry Mildmay and another in the autumn of 1643 to request that Essex issue a standing commission for a court-martial in London and to name a president so that delinquents guilty of crimes against the laws of arms could be punished.[55] After not receiving a reply, messengers went again on 12 October to ask the general to grant the commission in order to fulfill "the great Expectation and desire of the City and Kingdom that Justice should be done."[56] Essex refused to allow a court-martial to try men under his charge. Instead, he delivered a commission that left the position of the presidency vacant and declared that any who served under the general was exempt from the court's jurisdiction. Essex was extremely

---

[52] *Ibid.*, 296–7, 307. The Commons, after receiving a commission from Essex, ordered the Oxford spies to be tried on 22 November. *CJ*, 3: 318. One of the spies, a man named Kneiveton, was hanged on 27 November. *Kingdomes Weekly Intelligencer* 21–28 November 1643, 257.

[53] *CJ*, 3: 374.

[54] *Articles of Impeachment and Accusation, exhibited in Parliament, against Colonell Nathaniel Fiennes* (London, 1643); William Prynne, *A True and Full Relation of the Prosecution, Arraignment, Tryall, and Condemnation of Nathaniel Fiennes* (London, 1644).

[55] *CJ*, 3: 262.   [56] *Ibid.*, 275.

sensitive to any challenge to his authority, but he also may have been trying to protect the Hothams.[57] Many within parliament, including Sir Simonds D'Ewes and John Selden, wanted the sitting court-martial.[58] The war was changing the opinions of those previously opposed to martial law.

A push for a sitting court-martial was made once again in the following spring. The City of London began by petitioning parliament in May 1644 to create a court that would try delinquents and traitors. The House once again debated creating a court-martial for London. Parliament assigned a committee dominated by those who had connections to the city of London to examine the petition.[59] The Commons, however, did not pass the resulting bill. Laurence Whitaker reported that it "was twice read & committed: it being debated bec: it was to establish martiall law, wch in y Peticon of Right had been cryed down."[60] The bill was re-submitted to committee but never returned to the floor of the Commons. The issue only came up again in July after the City of London delivered yet another petition to the Commons that demanded a court to try delinquents. This time the bill passed the Commons on 15 July.[61]

The Lords had their own reservations about the bill. They committed it on 26 July, and the next day, the Earl of Northumberland read the alterations to the Upper House, who approved a proviso that both houses had to be first notified before an execution could take place. The rationale was that the ordinance had given "power only to heare, determyn, Trye Condemne, and Execute, and no power of Mercy, there may be place for mercy to be extended to a fitt subiect wch they conceiue most prop to reserue to the two houses."[62] The alterations led to a fight between the two houses. The Commons disagreed with the proviso on 29 July and demanded a conference on 2 August. The City of London on 3 August delivered yet another petition that demanded a court for the trial of delinquents. After more heated debate throughout August, the Lords finally gave way. On 19 August, parliament authorized through an ordinance a court-martial to sit in London for four months. It would eventually sit through 2 January 1645. While it sat in London, the court had

---

[57] Diary of Laurence Whitaker, BL Add. Ms. 31,116, f. 93; *CJ*, 3: 313.
[58] Diary of Sir Simonds D'Ewes, BL, Harley Ms. 165, f. 210v. Many thanks are owed to Dr. Stephen Roberts for allowing me to see a transcription of this speech.
[59] They had also petitioned in January with no success. *CJ*, 3: 379. LMA Jour. 40 fos. 97v–98. Valerie Pearl, "Oliver St. John and the Middle Group in the Long Parliament: August 1643–May 1644," *EHR* 81:230 (July, 1966): 490–519.
[60] Laurence Whitaker's Diary, BL, Add. Ms. 31,116, f. 138v; *CJ*, 3: 498.
[61] LMA, Jour. 40, f. 102v; *CJ*, 3: 510, 518, 554, 562.
[62] PA, HL/PO/JO/10/1/172, the amendments came from 29 July and were attached to a marked up bill dated 16 August 1644; *LJ*, 6: 646, 648.

jurisdiction over "all causes as belong to military cognizance" in England.[63]

Several changes were made to court-martial procedure in these tribunals. First, parliament designated non-military personnel as well as military personnel to be commissioners. From June 1643 onward, parliament appointed its allies as commissioners of the court-martial.[64] The second major innovation was that parliament often opened the confrontation stage of the trial to the public as early as the summer of 1643.[65] William Prynne's rationale for a public trial in the case against Nathaniel Fiennes, which in this instance failed, was "that there was as great cause to give the Parliament, City, and kingdome satisfaction in this ... it being of as like publike concernment."[66] Third, the crafters of the garrison courts-martial installed a quorum. In all of the ordinances for a garrison court-martial, with the sole exception of a draft ordinance for Hampshire in 1645, parliament named around fifty potential commissioners who could sit on the court, with twelve required to meet the quorum.[67] While it was not unusual to have twelve commissioners at a normal court-martial, it was never necessary. Those who were drafting the orders for the court seemed to want to ensure that the magical number of twelve men sat on a court-martial: the required number for a jury.

Most importantly, the Long Parliament allowed courts-martial to seize property. As we have seen, dating back to the Middle Ages, courts-martial could not seize the property of those they had convicted. This restriction meant that late medieval kings had to use posthumous attainders in order to obtain the property of those they had convicted by a court of the constable and marshal. It also meant that Irish families could successfully defend their titles against Crown commissions at the end of the sixteenth century. Those convicted by martial law in the 1640s, however, were not so lucky. In the court-martial of the Bristol conspirators, for example, the court, after declaring their death sentence, commanded that "all their goodes & estates shalbe forthwth seized to be disposed of according to the order, & appointment of the High Courte of Parliamt."[68] Sir John Hotham, who as we shall see was convicted by a court-martial in 1644, likewise lost his property.[69] Courts-martial had the discretion to seize the property of those they convicted due to the Long Parliament's broader sequestration policies. Any malignant lost their property, while so-called

---

[63] A&O, 1: 487.   [64] Diary of Whitaker, Add Ms. 31,116, f. 59v.
[65] Mercurius Civicus, 3–10 October 1644, 674.
[66] Prynne, A True and Full Relation of the...tryall ... of Nathaniel Fiennes, 12.
[67] CJ, 3: 144; A&O, 1: 486–8, 692–4, 715–6, 842–5; PA, HL/PO/JO/10/1/193, 202.
[68] Bodl. Nalson Ms. 13, f. 376.   [69] HHC, U DDHO 1/46, 48, 61.

milder royalists had to pay a fine, or composition.[70] By proving them guilty of treason, the court-martial also obtained the requisite proof of their malignancy to seize their property due to parliamentary ordinance even though these defendants had not been convicted by a trial by peers. A rule that had been made by parliament could be unmade by parliament.[71]

Along with these changes, parliament authorized seven ordinances of war for the garrison court-martial in London. These were taken from the category which Matthew Sutcliffe framed as "for the Safety of the State, Garrison, and Army."[72] Let us recall that this category outlined the martial law of treason. Specific acts in it included deserting to the side of the enemy, the delivering of a town to an enemy, furnishing the enemy with information or supplies, inciting an enemy to declare war, and breaking an exile. The Earl of Arundel had copied this category into his articles of war of 1639.[73] The third Earl of Essex had done likewise in 1642 but had changed the title of the category to "Of Duties in General."[74] Now the London courts-martial had powers to prosecute any soldier or civilian who broke them.

During the time it sat in London, the garrison court-martial mostly tried those who had committed treason by martial law. On 29 August, the Commons ordered that evidence be heard against the Hothams, Carew, and Waller, who had escaped punishment the previous summer.[75] By early October, the court convicted Thomas Syppens and Francis Pitt for conspiring to betray garrisons to the king.[76] In November, the court, after taking many depositions, convicted Carew of having traitorous intelligence with the enemy and giving over the garrison of St. Nicholas Island to the enemy; after a month's reprieve he went to his death.[77] In late December, the court convicted Captain John Hotham of treason.

---

[70] John Morrill, *Revolt in the Provinces: The People of England and the Tragedies of War, 1630–1648* (2nd ed., Harlow, Essex, 1998), 80–1.

[71] Thus, Jennifer Wells' claim that martial law commissioners could not seize real property is not true of the Civil Wars and Interregnum. Wells, "English Law, Irish Trials, and Cromwellian State Building in the 1650s," *P&P* 227 (May, 2015): 91.

[72] *Sutcliffe*, 310.   [73] *Lawes and Ordinances of Warre* (London, 1639), 7.

[74] *Lawes and Ordinances of Warre* (London, 1642); *Lawes and Ordinances of Warre established for the better conduct of the army, by his excellency the Earl of Essex* (London, 1643).

[75] *CJ*, 3: 610. The slippery Edmund Waller, however, escaped capital punishment yet again. Several bundles of letters were handed over to the judge advocate for the Hothams' trials on 19 October. HHC, U DDHO/1/33.

[76] *Mercurius Civicus*, 3–10 October 1644, 674; Syppens' conviction was examined by the Lords on 12 October and he was respited on 7 November. He had petitioned for a pardon on 12 October. PA, HL/PO/JO/118/1/175. *CJ*, 3: 689; *Mercurius Civicus*, 3–10 October 1644, 674–5. Parliament had referred the case against Pitt to the court-martial: *CJ*, 3: 654.

[77] *Mercurius Civicus*, 14–21 November 1644, 723–5.

His father Sir John Hotham came before the court in late November, and the court convicted him of treason in early December.[78] In all these cases, the court heard an extensive amount of evidence and allowed for detailed defenses.

Some of the preliminary proceedings of Sir John's trial have survived. The famous commander of Hull initially believed himself innocent and had written an impassioned factual defense of his actions.[79] But over time he broke down. He realized, upon viewing the articles the 1644 court was authorized to prosecute, that he might be convicted. Upon this recognition, he shifted from a factual defense to a legal one. In a draft written to the lord president of his court-martial, Hotham pleaded with him to think about his role as a judge and whether it was justifiable to punish a person for a crime by a law published after that act had been committed.[80] Further, Hotham was perplexed by the martial law jurisdiction: "I was employed by ye house before there was any martiall law nay when itt was declared . . . as destructive to ye law of ye land."[81] Hotham had even asked for martial law "upon some necessity," but it was "denied me by ye house."[82] But so much had changed since those days. And while the ordinances postdated his supposed wrongs, they could also have been found in the Earl of Essex' ordinances of war in both 1642 and 1643. Hotham was convicted of treason. Upon hearing the court's verdict, he only replied that "there was another tribunal."[83]

There is one more interesting aspect to Hotham's trial: he was aided in his defense by his son, the lawyer and future radical Durant Hotham.[84] Durant went through his father's entire file. He even wrote a scathing letter to "Mr Saltmarsh" which was attached to his father's summons to appear at his trial as a witness.[85] In a petition sent to the court, Sir John, who had been injured in the fighting and was "lame," asked that he be allowed to sit instead of stand at the bar and that no one else but "himself

---

[78] The abstract of the charges against Sir John can be found in HHC, U DDHO/1/42.

[79] There are several copies of his defense in his archive. See HHC, U DDHO/1/34–8.

[80] Carew had made the same defense. *Mercurius Civicus*, 14–21 November 1644, 725.

[81] HHC, U DDHO/1/40.   [82] *Ibid.*

[83] *The Journal of Thomas Juxon, 1644–1647* ed. Keith Lindley and David Scott (Cambridge, 1999), 69; *Mercurius Civicus*, 19–26 December 1644, 761; *Mercurius Civicus*, 28 November – 5 December 1644, 736–9.

[84] Durant (or Durand) himself examined conspirators for the republican regime in the 1650s. See HHC, U DDHO/1/65. There is also a tract calling for the end of the common law in the Hothams' archive, which was likely Durant's. HHC, U DDHO/1/59. Gordon Goodwin, rev. B.J. Gibbons, "Hotham, Durant (1616/17–1691)," in *ODNB*.

[85] Durant Hotham to Mr. Saltmarsh, 12 November 1644, HHC, U DDHO/1/62. This must be the radical preacher John Saltmarsh, who informed against Hotham to parliament. He was one of the witnesses against him.

and those yt assist him with his papers may haue free room . . . quietly to heare what is spoken."[86] Durant was one of those assistants. Further, while we do not know if Durant helped craft the questions to be asked to the witnesses in the trial, we know he administered them. By special permission of the council of war, he issued the interrogatories toward John's witnesses in his defense, which numbered around ten.[87] A defendant before a court-martial had counsel in 1644.

One of the most interesting cases the court heard was that of Roger L'Estrange, who had been caught in a Lynn tavern trying to overthrow the garrison for the king. On 19 December, the Lords and Commons ordered the commissioners of martial law to try him as a spy. On 28 December, before a sentence was handed down, L'Estrange petitioned Essex. He claimed that he was a soldier with a commission from the king and that there were no precedents "where a person in armes & in employment by commission of his superior, was ever, if apprehended, proceeded against otherwise then as a prisoner of war."[88] In the various defenses he made, L'Estrange pointed out that he was protestant, that he had always been for the king, and that he had a commission, which made his duties of a public, and not of a conspiratorial, nature. To L'Estrange this meant he was not a spy. Prince Rupert, echoing similar arguments, also intervened on his behalf to Essex.[89] The court-martial was not convinced by these arguments and convicted him and sentenced him to death on 28 December.

However, the Lords were not convinced about the sentence. On 1 January, one day before the expiration of the court's jurisdiction, the Lords wanted to certify the sentence against L'Estrange and desired a six-day respite of his sentence.[90] Many within that body became frustrated that they had not been able to save the lives of the Hothams, who went to their deaths on 1 and 2 January, respectively. On 3 January, immediately after the Hothams had been executed, the Commons asked for another continuance for the court-martial. The Lords, who had examined the L'Estrange case the same day, did not immediately agree to a continuation.[91] They stalled for months, and the Commons

---

[86] "Petition of Sir John Hotham," HHC, U DDHO/1/39.

[87] *Mercurius Civicus, 28 November – 5 December 1644,* 738. The interrogatories are in HHC, U DDHO/1/41. The answers are scribbled on a note which survives in HHC, U DDHO/1/43.

[88] Petition of Roger L'Estrange, 28 December 1644, PA, HL/PO/JO/10/1/177; "Certificate of the Commissioners for Martial Law, concerning the case of Roger L'Estrange," PA, HL/PO/JO/10/1/178. Parliament agreed to a trial in London on 19 December 1644. *CJ,* 3: 726–30.

[89] Harold Love, "L'Estrange, Roger," in *ODNB.*   [90] *LJ,* 7: 119–20.

[91] *CJ,* 4: 6–7; *LJ,* 7:121–4.

could never in 1645 obtain a re-authorization of the London court-martial. L'Estrange languished in prison and was eventually exiled.[92] He was saved in the end by the increasing scrutiny of the Lords over the powers of the London court-martial.

The debate over whether or not to grant martial law jurisdiction continued throughout 1645 and 1646. In the one instance where the Lords granted martial law jurisdiction in 1645, the county committee in Kent received martial law powers to punish rebels for four months. But other draft bills for county committees, including Hampshire and the County Palatine of Lancaster, were never made into ordinances. Even Kent could not get its martial law powers renewed after 1645; attempts to punish royalist "rebels" by martial law in the spring of 1648 were refused by parliament.[93] In January 1646, when the Commons seemed to want to secure their garrisons from spies, it passed a bill for a new sitting court-martial.[94] This variation included an amendment that refused any claims to exception, even from Peers of the Realm. The Lords refused to pass the bill, and intense debates between the two houses continued through March. Finally, the Commons relented and removed the amendment from each successive ordinance, ending with London in April 1646. They perhaps did so because of their desire to try William Murray, an agent of Charles I caught coming into the country from France in February.[95]

Garrison courts-martial, for the last time in the war, sat in London, and in many other parliamentary garrisons, throughout the summer of 1646.[96] But this court, unlike its predecessor, only had jurisdiction over those residing in London. Further, it required two eyewitnesses or a confession in order to obtain a conviction. Murray's seems to be one of the few cases the court heard, and he was acquitted because the full proof bar had not been met.[97] The last garrison to receive martial law powers was Kingston-upon-Hull in the summer of 1646. It could also try civilians for treason.[98]

Parliament's use of martial law throughout the 1640s resembled in many ways the experimentation of martial law by the Privy Council in

---

[92] Harold Love, "L'Estrange, Roger," in *ODNB*.

[93] Alan Everitt, *The Community of Kent and the Great Rebellion, 1640–1660* (Leicester, 1966), 141, 231–70. Anthony Welden, in 1648, pleaded with the Commons that a more speedy process that did not rely on the discretion of county jurors was necessary to try royalist "insurgents." Bodl. Tanner Ms. 57, f. 60v.

[94] For more on these garrison courts-martial, see Collins, "Hidden in Plain Sight."

[95] Gardiner, *History of the Great Civil War*, 3: 69–70.   [96] *A&O*, 1: 842–5.

[97] *Mercurius Civicus*, 21 May – 28 May 1646, 2254. A copy of Murray's trial was attached to his 6 July petition for release, PA, HL/PO/JO/10/1/209. While Murray was tried by the garrison court-martial, a special ordinance had to be made to try him, because his crimes were outside of the city of London: *LJ*, 8: 266–7.

[98] *A&O*, 1: 857–61.

the 1590s. Because of perceived intractable legal problems, many MPs wanted to authorize martial law for treason, spying, illegal printing, and other offenses. But many were just as concerned about the power this gave to authorized commissioners and that the authorizations themselves violated constitutional principles. Further, even those who were willing to authorize martial law for a time nevertheless wanted powers to review convictions in order to potentially grant mercy. These opposing desires, on the one hand to use a novel legal remedy to address a pressing problem, and, on the other, to maintain control over it, led to the often serious and protracted debates between the more aggressive Commons and the more conservative Lords. It also led to procedural innovations. Sunset clauses were introduced. Quorums were required. The trials were supposed to be public so that justice could be seen to be done. Even defense counsel was allowed to John Hotham. None of these innovations probably made the tribunals fairer than traditional courts-martial. But they might have appeared fairer to those watching them or reading about them in parliamentary news-books.

The Second Civil War and the regicide

When fighting re-opened in England in 1648, the mood for many within parliament as well as for those within the army had darkened. While English royalists had been conceived of as enemies during the First Civil War, in the summer of 1648, parliament increasingly understood their opponents as rebels. This change did not mean that all who fought against parliament would die by either common or martial law. As Barbara Donagan has shown, the legal classifications parliament and the army made toward its prisoners in this period were rarely that simple.[99] It did mean, however, that the leaders of the royalist forces in 1648 often ended up being tried for treason. In order to make these trials happen, parliament generated hybrid tribunals that were based in part on the adapted courts-martial of parliamentary garrisons during the Civil War.

Throughout the spring and summer of 1648, parliament authorized its commanders to execute by martial law turncoats and commanders of the rebel forces. After Fairfax's victory at St. Fagans on 8 May, the Commons ordered its high command to try by martial law those turncoats and traitors that had been captured in South Wales.[100] Similar orders were sent to commanders in York, Chester, Oxford, and in Montgomery in

---

[99] Donagan, "Atrocity, War Crime, and Treason in the English Civil War."
[100] *CJ*, 5: 556–7.

Wales where turncoats were to face courts-martial.[101] The Lords barred any permanent ordinance from being passed. Parliament had also issued in June orders effectively attainting all who took up arms against it in the summer of 1648.[102] It never followed through with this threat. However, in the aftermath of its victory at Colchester, General Fairfax decided to summarily execute two royalist commanders. They protested that they had neither been convicted at martial law nor a civilian tribunal. Henry Ireton, who chaired the council of war, declared that they were guilty due to parliament's command and because the general was not bound to grant prisoners their lives. They were shot by firing squad and became royalist martyrs.[103]

Many within the New Model Army were furious with the king; they had seen their friends die on the battlefield due to what they perceived to be his deceitfulness. "That man of blood," as they now called him, must pay for his sins. In November 1648, the Army called for Charles' trial. They purged all those in parliament who opposed them to ensure that the king would be brought to justice.[104] The new Purged Parliament in December set out plans to try Charles Stuart.[105] How were they to try the king? There was no precedent in English law for such a trial. In order to create a new court, MPs looked to past courts – both recent and ancient – in order to create a hybrid court. One of these was a court-martial.[106]

One of the central ideas parliament used in the trial was impeachment. Charles Stuart, according to the new legal ideas spun out by the Rump, was no longer a sacred divine-right monarch but an office holder who performed duties for the English state, whose sovereign was the "people." He had abused these delimited powers by levying war against them. The most famous case of this nature was parliament's prosecution of the Earl of Strafford in 1641, but the army had also attempted to impeach members of the Commons in 1647, who, according to Fairfax, had

---

[101] *CJ*, 5: 589–90, 627–9, 632–4, 640–2, 654–7, 659–61, 669–72, 678–9.
[102] *CJ*, 5: 606–8.   [103] Donagan, *War in England*, 363–8.
[104] David Underdown, *Pride's Purge: Politics in the Puritan Revolution* (Oxford, 1971); Patricia Crawford, "Charles Stuart, That Man of Blood," *JBS* 16:2 (Spring, 1977): 41–61.
[105] The Commons created a committee to try the king on 23 December 1648. *CJ*, 6: 102–4.
[106] The most current account is Sean Kelsey, "Politics and Procedure in the Trial of Charles I," *Law and History Review* 22:1 (Spring, 2004): 1–25; this article is part of a corpus arguing that Charles' trial was actually an extended negotiation, Kelsey, "The Death of Charles I," *HJ* 45:4 (December, 2002): 727–54; "The Trial of Charles I," *EHR* 118:477 (June, 2003): 583–616; "Staging the Trial of Charles I," in *The Regicides and the Execution of Charles I* ed. Jason Peacey (Basingstoke, 2001), 71–94. These interpretations have been convincingly challenged by Clive Holmes, "The Trial and Execution of Charles I," *HJ* 53:2 (2010): 289–316. For a historiographical review of those who have written on the trial, see Jason Peacey, "Introduction," in *The Regicides and the Execution of Charles I*, 1–10.

committed various treasons against the army throughout the war.[107] Charles, likewise, was to be prosecuted for abusing his office and, in the process, committing treason. As John Cook concluded the charge against Charles on 20 January, "the said people of England impeach the said Charles Stuart, as a Tyrant Traytor Murderer and a Publick and implacable Enemy to the Commonwealth of England."[108] But the Commons could not try Charles by impeachment procedures because those gave all discretion in both law and fact to the House of Lords, a body that even before it refused to pass the bill that authorized the trial of the king was known to be far more conservative than the Commons.

The three judges of the common law courts were initially included as commissioners. Were they to be separated from a jury? It is possible but the evidence is unclear. They perhaps were simply to be commissioners.[109] Other commissioners included members of the army, parliament, and the London government. By 1 January 1649, the Commons had heard its committee twice and had debated on successive days and had passed the second version of the ordinance to try the king.[110] Twenty were to be

---

[107] For impeachment trials, see Colin G.C. Tite, *Impeachment and Parliamentary Judicature* (London, 1974), 12–23. For the procedures of the trial of Strafford, see Danila Cole Spielman, "Impeachments and Parliamentary Opposition in England, 1621–41" (unpublished PhD dissertation, University of Wisconsin-Madison, 1959), 144–53. Sir Thomas Fairfax, *A Particular Charge or Impeachment in the Name of his Excellency Sir Thomas Fairfax* (London, 1647).

[108] J. Nalson, *A True Copie of the Journal of the High Court of Justice* (London, 1684), 32. For an examination of treason law as it related to the trial, see D. Alan Orr, *Treason and the State: Law, Politics, and Ideology in the English Civil War* (Cambridge, 2002), 171–205.

[109] *Perfect Occurrences of every daies journall of parliament* 29 December 1648 – 5 January 1649, 784. This source got the quorum right (20) and the Moderate Intelligencer confirmed that the judges of the realm and the lords were initially supposed to participate in the trial, *Moderate Intelligencer* 4–11 January 1649, sig., Pppppppppp v. Other sources also took the view that the judges were meant to *be* judges. This interpretation can also be found in *Perfect Weekly Account* 27 December 1648–3 January 1649 (London, 1649), and *Heads of a Diarie* 27 December 1648–2 January 1649 (London, 1649), 39–40; Gardiner has accepted this original plan. *History of the Great Civil War*, 4: 288. For a different view see, S.M. Koenigsberg, "The Vote to Create the High Court of Justice: 26 to 20?" *Parliamentary History* 12 (1993): 281. Other records that predate 6 January make no such distinction. See, Bodl. Carte Ms. 23, fos. 167–8; BL, Add. Ms. 70,006 fos. 51–3v. *Royal Prisoner at Windsor* (London, 1649), 5–6; *The Manner of the Deposition of Charles Stewart King of England by the Parliament and Generall Councell of the Army* (London, 1649); the *Queenes Majesties Letter to the parliament of England* (London, 1649), 5–6; *Mercurius Pragmaticus* 26 December 1648 – 9 January 1649. For an examination of the commissioners of the court, see William Sachse, "England's Black Tribunal: An Analysis of the Regicide Court," *JBS* 12:2 (May, 1973): 69–85; for an examination of potential commissioners before the final version of the Act see Sean Kelsey, "The Ordinance for the Trial of Charles I," *Historical Research* 76:193 (August, 2003): 310–2.

[110] On 23 December 1648 the Commons resolved to form a committee to try the king, *CJ*, 6: 102–3; the first draft of the ordinance was debated on 28 December, a second draft on 29 and on the 30 the Commons ordered the committee to submit another version on 1 January: this version passed the Commons, *CJ*, 6: 105–7.

required for a quorum. Those who accepted were members of the army, radical members of the London government, as well as allies like John Bradshaw and William Steele. Bradshaw had served as a commissioner in the court-martial of William Murray, and Steele had been listed as a potential commissioner on courts-martial since 1644.[111]

On 4 January 1649, the Lords refused to pass the initial act to try Charles Stuart. The judges also refused to participate in the trial.[112] That same day, the Commons passed the ordinance to try the king and secretly engrossed it. One report from the *Kingdome's Weekly Intelligencer* declared that parliament passed the "ordinance for the Triall of the King by a Court Martiall."[113] This gloss was not an attack on the proceedings: the news-book did not refer to the court as a court-martial either before or after 4 January. It is not clear if the report of news-books was accurate. The High Court of Justice ended up being the name for the tribunal.

On 6 January, the Commons published the Act to try the king for treason, having dispensed with the House of Lords.[114] We can glean several clues as to the procedure the Commons envisioned. First, the large body of commissioners with a mandate for a quorum of at least twenty remained. Second, those commissioners would craft the charge; they had the power to "take order for the charging of him the said Charles Stuart with the Crimes and Treasons abovementioned."[115] There would be no bill of indictment proven true by a grand jury. Nor would the Commons craft the charge, as was traditional in treason trials before the Lord Steward in the House of Lords. Third, the commissioners had the powers for the "examination of witnesses upon Oath, which the court hath hereby Authority to administer, or otherwise, and take any evidence concerning the same."[116] While the commissioners needed to prove the guilt of Charles Stuart, they could do so with discretion over how testimony was to be taken. The court, after meeting several times, further clarified its nature. The Commons on 6 January gave the court discretion for naming its own officers. On 10 January, members voted that it would be a presidential council, with John Bradshaw leading the tribunal. All would try both law and fact, with Bradshaw being the first among equals. As its officers, it named Isaac Dorislaus, Robert Aske, William Steel, and John Cook .[117] Dorislaus

---

[111] *LJ*, 8: 267; *A&O*, 1: 486–8, 842–5. For the participants on William Murray's trial see PA, HL/PO/JO/10/1/209.
[112] *LJ*, 10: 641–2; *CJ*, 6: 110–1.
[113] *Kingdomes Weekly Intelligencer* 2–9 January 1649, {1214}. The news-book says it again on 1215.
[114] *A&O*, 1: 1253–5.   [115] *Ibid.*   [116] *Ibid.*
[117] J.G. Muddiman, *The Trial of King Charles I* (Glasgow, 1928), 198; the best source for the trial is the journal of the proceedings of the High Court of Justice taken by the clerks now

had even more training than Steele or Bradshaw in martial law. He had been the judge advocate general of Essex's army.

From the time the Act was passed to the time the king came before the court on 20 January, the court sat in private to make the charge and other arrangements for the trial. These private meetings were commonplace for a garrison court-martial.[118] The private preliminary proceedings were essential because it was here that the lawyers and the commissioners evaluated the evidence from witnesses to see whether or not they had proof for their charges. There was no strict separation at a court-martial or at the trial of Charles I between the prosecution and the judges, as there was at common law or at an impeachment trial at the House of Lords. Even though Charles refused to recognize the court, it still desired to hear eyewitness testimony. It appointed a committee to depose the witnesses, a practice identical to army procedure.[119] Once deposed in private, the witnesses came to court to confirm their depositions publicly on oath.[120] The king refused to acknowledge the court's jurisdiction. But if he had, he could have challenged the witnesses' testimony.[121] The court would have allowed Charles to issue a rejoinder to the charge and to produce his own witnesses to be deposed to contradict the witnesses of the court. Through these procedures, the court tried Charles for levying war against the people of England.[122]

While some of the procedures were consistent between a court-martial and Charles' trial, we should not be blinded to the hybrid nature of the court. The High Court of Justice had blended together procedures from impeachment, courts-martial, as well as clear innovations in order to try the king for treason. It also used a form of proof that signaled other inheritances. Indeed, its very hybridity allowed for onlookers to draw yet another comparison to martial law. Let us return to the Act made on 6 January.

---

in TNA, SP 16/517 which has been transcribed as "Bradshaw's notebook," in Muddiman's *The Trial of King Charles I*; also see Nalson, *A True Copie of the Journal of the High Court of Justice*.

[118] The first meeting of the court took place on Monday, 8 January 1649, Nalson, *A True Copie of the Journal of the High Court of Justice*, 5; Muddiman, *The Trial of King Charles I*, 201–2, 205–6; John Langbein, *Prosecuting Crime in the Renaissance: England, Germany, France* (Cambridge, MA, 1974), 224–8.

[119] Muddiman, *The Trial of King Charles I*, 213. For committees in the army to examine witnesses see LPL, Ms. 709, f. 80 and chapter 3.

[120] Nalson, *A True Copie of the Journal of the High Court of Justice*, 61, 79; Muddiman, *The Trial of King Charles I*, 212. The depositions of the witnesses are on Nalson, *A True Copie of the Journal of the High Court of Justice*, 63–79; Muddiman, *The Trial of King Charles I*, 213–2.

[121] *A&O*, 1: 1253–5.

[122] This charge had been initially levied against him by the army in November. *A Remonstrance of his excellency Thomas Lord Fairfax ... and of the generall councell of officers held at St. Albans the 16 of November, 1648* (London, 1648), 62.

In the opening of the Act, parliament declared,

Whereas it is notorious that Charles Stewart the now king of England not content with those many encroachments which his predecessors had made upon the People in their rights and freedoms, hath had a wicked design totally to subvert the antient and fundamentall lawes and liberties of this nation.[123]

As we have seen, medieval English monarchs had utilized notoriety against "public enemies," criminals who were so well known and dangerous that their guilt was obvious. As we shall recall, notoriety was both the means of bringing a suspect into court and a declaration of that suspect's guilt.[124] The king could thus order the execution of the criminal without proving him guilty.

This was what Edward II had done to Thomas of Lancaster. It was what Edward III and the 1330 Parliament had done to the Earl of March. These were the two most prominent examples Edward Coke gave for martial law both in his speeches in the 1628 Parliament and in his *Institutes*. These two cases did not resemble seventeenth-century martial law practice. However, it was possible that parliament looked for medieval models for their treason trial and either Lancaster or March came up as an example it could selectively follow.

Why use manifest proof and eyewitnesses? In short, the Commons had predicted that Charles would refuse to acknowledge the court. Indeed, rumors that the king would employ this strategy had been circulating since December 1648.[125] Aware of this possibility, parliament authorized the High Court of Justice that "in default of such answer, to proceed to final sentence, according to justice, and the merit of the Cause."[126] But notoriety was a more convincing form of proof than simply convicting the king should he refuse to acknowledge the court. Thus, two tracks were adopted: from the end of December, the *Kingdome's Weekly Intelligencer* was reporting that the Commons was preparing both an act for attainder – which also often used manifest proof – and an ordinance for the trial of the king.[127] This is also why John Cook brought up notoriety during the trial. He declared that "the House

---

[123] *A&O*, 1: 1253.

[124] For notoriety see the prologue. Clive Holmes has been the only historian to notice the significance of the word notorious. "The Trial and Execution of Charles I," 301.

[125] Multiple news books reported the possibility of Charles refusing to plea including *Mercurius Pragmaticus* 26 December 1648 – 9 January 1649, sig., fff3; *The Manner of the Deposition of Charles Stewart, King of England*, 2. The Commons debated this very possibility on 30 December. *Kingdomes Weekly Intelligencer* 26 December 1648–2 January 1649, 1207.

[126] *A&O*, 1: 1253–5.

[127] *The Kingdomes Weekly Intelligencer* 26 December 1648 – 2 January 1649, 1206–7.

of Commons have declared that his treason is notorious and that the matter of fact is true (as in truth it is) my lord, as clear as crystal or as the sun at noonday."[128] President Bradshaw agreed, but in private the court decided it would still depose the witnesses, in spite of the notoriety of the accused, to give "clearer satisfaction of their owne judgments and consciences."[129] Nevertheless, in the end, the Court convicted Charles by his refusal to plea and due to "the Notoreity of the Matters of Fact charged upon him as aforesaid."[130] Manifest proof played an important role in the trial of Charles Stuart.

The High Court was called into action quickly after the execution of Charles to hear and determine treason cases against five royalist leaders of the Second Civil War.[131] The Earls of Cambridge, Norwich, and Holland, as well as Lord Arthur Capel and Sir John Owen, had earned the enmity of the army for their leading roles in the conflict.[132] As in the case for Charles, parliament had considered a variety of different legal mechanisms to punish them. As early as September 1648, the House of Commons had advocated for the attainder of the Earl of Norwich and the impeachment of Lord Capel, the former leaders of the royalists at Colchester. Capel was duly impeached but not tried for his life in October. Meanwhile in November, the Commons considered banishing the Earls of Holland, Norwich, Sir Henry Owen, and Capel, as well as two others.[133] This leniency ended with the Purge. Eventually, the Commons decided to try them by a High Court of Justice.[134]

In many ways, the trials of the five men contained the same hybrid procedural devices found in Charles' trial. While the Commons had not decided in the end to utilize attainder, proof by notoriety was an important device for the prosecution in these cases. The Attorney General, William Steele, argued on 9 February for the "notoriousness of the facts" on the first day of the confrontation stage of the trial for the Earl of Cambridge.[135] Like the trial for Charles, witnesses were also utilized. Similarly, a large body of commissioners – a quorum of fifteen was

---

[128] Nalson, *A True Copie of the Journal of the High Court of Justice*, 56.
[129] Muddiman, *The Trial of King Charles I* (London, 1928), 211.
[130] Nalson, *A True Copy of the High Court of Justice*, 92.   [131] *ST*, 4: cols. 1155–250.
[132] The Earl of Cambridge had led the royalist forces unsuccessfully against Cromwell at Preston. Capel and Norwich were commanding at Colchester. Sir John Owen had a royalist command in Wales. Holland was caught in St. Neots after raising horse for the royalists. Barbara Donagan, "A Courtier's Progress: Greed and Consistency in the life of the Earl of Holland," *HJ* 19:2 (June, 1976): 317–53; Donagan, *War in England*, 397–8; John J. Scally, "Hamilton, James, first Duke of Hamilton," in *ODNB*; Ronald Hutton, "Owen, Sir John," in *ODNB*.
[133] *CJ*, 6: 77.   [134] *Ibid.*, 126, 128, 131.   [135] *ST*, 4: col. 1209.

mandated – determined both fact and law. Close to fifty were present at the opening of the confrontation stage.[136]

This tribunal was just as much about jurisdictional politics as it was about procedural politics. The tribunal crafted by parliament was based on the Civil Power, which prevented the defendants from seeking protection at a court-martial as prisoners of war. Indeed, both Capel and Norwich had been granted that protection when they surrendered at Colchester. However, their surrender did not protect them from civil prosecution.[137] Capel became aware that the High Court, as a hybrid tribunal, offered him the worst of both worlds. He pleaded to be "wholly comprehended by the Martiall Law" that might honor his surrender agreement.[138] Otherwise, he asked, after citing the Petition of Right, to "see his Jury" and to be tried by peers. That jury, he believed, might have mercy in store for him.[139] As he feared, the High Court of Justice, as a hybrid tribunal, proved to be a lethal concoction. He went to the scaffold on 9 March.[140]

For the 1649 High Courts of Justice, some of the procedures of the trial were consistent with a court-martial. They were presidency councils. They had discretion over how they would take evidence. The courts took evidence from witnesses either live, *viva voce*, or by written deposition. There was no distinction between triers of law and triers of fact: the High Court judged both. Army members and Isaac Dorislaus participated as commissioners and as counsel in the trial of Charles I.

It was the actual consistencies with martial law practice as well as the perceptions of what constituted martial law practice that produced comparisons of Charles' trial with a trial by court-martial. Notoriety, as we have seen, was the key form of proof for medieval treason trials that was now associated through Edward Coke's *Institutes* with seventeenth-century courts-martial. It was probably for this reason that Clement Walker, a former judge advocate general, labeled Charles' unusual trial "*in nature a Court Martiall.*"[141] Because it was in a time of peace, Walker, in Cokean fashion, declared that the tribunal had in fact "murdered the

---

[136] *Ibid.*, cols. 1208–9. The tribunal on 5 February called for all witnesses against the defendants to appear before them in private. It heard the witnesses on 6 February.

[137] Donagan, *War in England*, 397–8.

[138] The key word is "might." The Earl of Derby received no such protection by a court-martial after being given quarter when he surrendered to Commonwealth forces in the aftermath of the Battle of Worcester. Barry Coward, "Stanley, James, Seventh Earl of Derby," in *ODNB*.

[139] *ST*, 4: col. 1213.

[140] Capel, Holland, and Cambridge were executed. Norwich and Owen were spared. *CJ*, 6: 159–60.

[141] Clement Walker, *The High Court of Justice or Cromwells Slaughter House*, (London, 1651), 19.

king." An argument initially used to restrain Charles' commissions of martial law was now used to protest his execution. Charles, like Thomas of Lancaster, was executed for notorious treason. Like Thomas of Lancaster, his trial was enormously controversial. Like Thomas, he for many became a martyr.

Martial law, the High Courts of Justice, and the Commonwealth

These hybrid tribunals continued because of the unstable nature of the new regime. Fighting royalists and rebels in Ireland, the Commonwealth was preparing for a new war against its former ally the Scots. Further, royalists still residing in England were plotting the restoration of the Stuart monarchy. Enemies were everywhere. New treason laws had been created that mandated obedience to the Commonwealth. In March 1650, the state considered legalizing martial law so that it could try several royalist conspirators that had recently been entrapped through the efforts of the Council of State.[142] MPs renamed it a High Court of Justice.

It is likely that the treason trial of John Lilburne changed the Commonwealth's mind about authorizing High Courts of Justice. John Lilburne, the leading "Leveller," had consistently attacked the new government. Over the course of 1649, he published numerous attacks on Oliver Cromwell, the Rump Parliament, and the army. He accused Cromwell of treason, declared that the army had illegally purged parliament, and argued that the current government was a puppet to an arbitrary military power.[143] The Commonwealth could not get Lilburne to shut up. It ordered that Lilburne be tried in London for treason according to recent acts that prohibited public polemical attacks against the government. In October, Lilburne was indicted by a grand jury. At his trial, Lilburne argued to the petty jury that it was a trier of law as well as fact, and that he was being tried by bad law. The jury agreed with Lilburne and acquitted him.[144] The Council of State was furious. It had been humiliated by a jury.

Its desire to authorize martial law the following year probably came from the problems that arose in Lilburne's trial. The Council of State

---

[142] *CJ*, 6: 359, 382; Gardiner, *History of the Commonwealth and the Protectorate*, 1: 247–8; David Underdown, *Royalist Conspiracy in England, 1649–60* (New Haven, 1960), 23–30.
[143] See for example, John Lilburne, *An Impeachment of High Treason against Oliver Cromwell* (London, 1649).
[144] Thomas Andrew Green, *Verdict According to Conscience: Perspectives on the English Criminal Trial Jury, 1200–1800* (Chicago, 1985), 153–99.

began considering the possibility of having a court sit in London to prosecute spies in February. On 14 March 1650, a bill was introduced entitled, "An Act for Establishing A Court Martial within the Cities of London and Westminster, and late lines of Communication."[145] We can tell from this title that the crafters of the bill looked to the garrison courts-martial that had operated in London during the Civil War. The ordinance for the 1644 court-martial, for example, was titled "Ordinance for the Establishment of Martial Law within the Cities of London and Westminster and the lines of communication."[146] Meanwhile, the ordinance for the 1646 court-martial was titled "Ordinance for the speedy establishment of a court martial within the Cities of London and Westminster and the Lines of Communication."[147] The change to the title of this new Act was minimal: too minimal, in fact. The Lines of Communication, the ringed fortresses built to protect London during the war, had largely been dismantled in 1647.[148] The only reason why language relating to the Lines of Communication was included was because the makers of the bill were working from a template: the ordinances that legalized the courts-martial in London during the Civil War.

After the first and second readings of the bill, parliament resolved to rename the court to "The High Court of Justice."[149] In deliberations over the next twelve days, MPs inserted two amendments into the bill that altered the court. The first, passed on 21 March, ensured that the High Court of Justice in no way diminished the powers of the Commonwealth's generals and its admirals. Second, on the same day, parliament passed an amendment that required all of the commissioners of the High Court of Justice to take an oath.[150] Most importantly, no amendments were passed that fundamentally changed the procedure of the court. The bill passed on 26 March.[151] In all probability, given the fact that the army still prosecuted rebels by martial law – it also executed the Earl of Derby and several others in the aftermath of the battle of Worcester – the point of the name change was both to hide the authorization of martial law and to present the court as one beholden exclusively to the Civil Power, thus making the courts a symbol of its, and not the army's, sovereignty.[152]

---

[145] *CJ*, 6: 382. Both Blair Worden and Gardiner did not notice that the initial name of this bill was a court-martial. Blair Worden, *The Rump Parliament, 1648–53* (Cambridge, 1974), 222; S.R. Gardiner, *History of the Commonwealth and Protectorate, 1649–56* 4 vols. (Gloucestershire, 1988 ed.), 1: 247–8.

[146] *A&O*, 1: 486.   [147] *A&O*, 1: 842.

[148] For the Lines of Communication in the Civil War, see Victor Smith and Peter Kelsey, "The Lines of Communication: The Civil War Defences of London," in *London and the Civil War* ed. S. Porter (Basingstoke, 1996), 117–49.

[149] *CJ*, 6: 382.   [150] *CJ*, 6: 385.   [151] *A&O*, 2: 364–7.   [152] *ST*, 5: 294–323.

The jurisdiction of the court resembled the 1640s courts-martial and the 1649 High Courts of Justice. Like the 1649 courts, the High Court of Justice was given powers for "examination upon Oath (which the Court hath hereby authority to administer) or otherwise, and taking any other Evidence concerning the same."[153] The High Court of Justice needed to hear evidence when it prosecuted suspects. But the specific presentation of that evidence was left to the court's discretion. The discretion also extended to the making of the charges. The court had the power to "take order for the charging of Offenders with all or any of the Crimes ... and for receiving their personal answer thereunto."[154] There would be no indictment by grand jury. There were other consistencies between the High Court of Justice of 1650 and the garrison courts-martial of the Civil War. First, like the garrison courts-martial, parliament nominated sixty-six commissioners and mandated twelve for a quorum. However, in the courts of the 1650s, almost no military men were nominated as judges. Instead, it would be legal officers of the state and members of London's loyal elite who were to act as commissioners. Parliament's allies sat on the tribunal. Second, in both times that the garrison court-martial sat, in 1644 and 1646, parliament inserted a sunset clause. In 1644, the court-martial was initially authorized to sit for four months. The 1646 court-martial sat for three months. Likewise the 1650 High Court of Justice was authorized to sit for six months, from March 1650 until the following September. The rationale for these limitations was also similar. Many within both the parliaments of the 1640s and the parliament of 1650 were uncomfortable granting permanent jurisdiction. Third, like a court-martial, the High Court of Justice would determine cases by plurality. The High Court of Justice could convict and punish "as the Said Commissioners or the major part of them then present shall judge to appertain to Justice."[155] Unanimity, which was required in trials by jury, was not required at the High Court of Justice.

In the Act, parliament dictated that the High Court could specifically try eight offenses. The first seven articles were consistent to the first seven articles assigned to the garrison courts-martial of the Civil War. The High Court of Justice could punish those who communicated with the "Royal Family"; those who plotted to betray any towns, garrisons, or anything "belonging to this Commonwealth"; those who harbored delinquents; those participating in mutinous assemblies; those who allowed prisoners of war to escape; those taking up arms against parliament; and those who

---

[153] A&O, 2: 367. An identical clause can be found in the act authorizing the 1649 High Court of Justice. Ibid., 1: 1253–5.
[154] A&O, 2: 367.   [155] Ibid., 365.

deserted. The articles thus also derived from the category of wrongs labeled by Matthew Sutcliffe concerning "the safety of the state, garrison, and army."[156] The ordinance authorizing garrison courts-martial during the Civil War weighed heavily on those who brought the 1650 High Court of Justice into being.

The key divergence between the act authorizing the 1650 High Court of Justice and the acts that authorized the garrison courts-martial of the Civil War was the eighth article, which allowed the High Court to have cognizance over five Acts passed by parliament in 1649 that were related to treason.[157] The first made anyone who declared Charles Stuart king guilty of treason. Two others involved the making of scandalous pamphlets and removing "papists" and delinquents from London.[158] The two most important treason acts reframed English treason law away from attacks on the king's personal body.[159] These made offenses like attacks on the Council of State, or the clipping or counterfeiting of money, illegal. But they also included military crimes: mutiny in the army, conspiring with the Commonwealth's enemies, engaging in rebellion, and attempting to seize Commonwealth garrisons were included in both these acts. In other words, the first seven articles in the Act authorizing the High Court of Justice had already been enacted as treason the year before. Why, if parliament had already passed these articles into law, did it list the articles separately in the 1650 Act for Establishing a High Court of Justice?

The answer probably has to do with property seizure. We have already seen that the courts-martial of the 1640s had the powers to seize property due to parliament's sequestration policies. The sequestration committee, which became combined with the committee for compounding, continued to sit through 1653 and "enemies" of the regime continued to have their property seized by non-common law methods. The High Courts of Justice could also have been authorized to seize the property of traitors through the new 1649 treason laws that served as a replacement for 25 Edward III, which because it stated that even imagining the king's death, let alone actually killing him, was treason, was no longer a particularly useful statute for the English Commonwealth.[160] All of these treason statutes passed since the death of Charles I mandated the seizure of the property of those convicted of treason.[161] Because the High Courts now had authorization to execute these new laws,

---

[156] *Ibid.*, 366.   [157] *Ibid.*, 366–7.   [158] *Ibid.*, 1: 1263–4; 2:245–54, 349–54.
[159] *Ibid.*, 2: 120–1, 193–4.   [160] 25 Edw. III stat. 5. c. 2.
[161] *Ibid.*, 2: 120–1, 193–4, 831–5.

they possessed multiple avenues by which they could also seize property of the regime's enemies. With these, the Commonwealth did not need to use common law procedure in order to justify forfeiture.

English citizens were not spared from these procedures. Indeed, the place of one's birth did not matter. Instead, the High Court of Justice had jurisdiction over any "Contrivers or Actors," or more simply, "person or persons."[162] It was to be the act, and not the innate nature of the individual, that was to determine jurisdiction. In this ordinance, then, the Commonwealth not so much altered the subject/enemy distinction so much as it simply ignored it. Thus, like in the Civil War, one's birthplace did not give one birthrights like trial by jury and due process.

Those opposed to the sitting High Court of Justice were alert to the procedural consistencies with a court-martial. Included in this group was Eusebius Andrewes. Andrewes had served Charles I through the surrender of Worcester in 1646. After the Second Civil War, he became ensnared in a ruse designed by the Commonwealth's Council of State to uncover potential royalist conspiracies. He had agreed to a conspiracy to take Ely for Charles Stuart. After tracking Andrewes for some time, the Council of State confronted him in the spring of 1650. A three-person committee led by John Bradshaw, acting in his capacity as president of the Council of State, interrogated Andrewes, who subsequently delivered a written answer to the charge that he had attempted to subvert the government. Andrewes finally came before the court in August 1650, after several petitions he had written had been ignored.[163] His prospects were not good. Not only did the court have all of Andrewes' correspondences about the plot to seize Ely, but it also had his own written answer, where Andrewes confessed to participating in the conspiracy, but that he was only "passively active."[164] The initial answer seemed to be an attempt to induce mercy from a jury.

But upon discovering how he was to be tried, Andrewes denied the validity of a court where he could expect no such mercy. He did so by calling upon his legal and military training. Andrewes was trained in the law. He had been admitted to Lincoln's Inn in 1620 and was called to the bar in 1627. Andrewes also had experience in war. He had served with the armies of Charles I, ending his career with the rank of colonel in

---

[162] *Ibid.*, 2: 364. Thus, in its justification for the trial of six royalists at the High Court of Justice in December 1650, the Commonwealth declared they were members of the "enemies party" in spite of the fact they were all born in England. *An Act for the Tryal of Sir John Stowel etc.* (London, 1650), 914.

[163] *ST*, 5: cols. 8–13; *CSPD*, 1650, 184.   [164] *ST*, 5: col. 8.

1646.[165] He used both of these experiences to attack the court and its procedure. He issued his written response, read by the court in August, which claimed:

> That this Court is (though under a different stile) in nature, and in the Proceedings thereof, directly the same with the Commission Martial; the Freemen thereby being to be tried for life, and adjudged by the major number of the Commissioners sitting (as in Courts of Commissioners Martial was practiced, and was agreeable to their constitution) and consequently against the Petition of Right.[166]

The Petition, according to Andrewes, had affirmed that trial involving life and death for Englishmen could only occur by the laws of the land which he understood to be by either an indictment or presentment and then trial by peers who needed to arrive at a unanimous verdict and not a mere majority. He argued that the martial commissioners were evil, not because of their personal qualities, but through "their proceedings by their own will and opinion, being themselves the Judges and Jury; offices incompatible and inconsistent with the people's liberties." He argued that if the commissioners "read the Act by which you now sit, I am confident you will grant this power to be of the same nature, though not under the same name."[167] A consistent strand of criticism was beginning to emerge. Using the Petition of Right and a narrow reading of clause 29 of Magna Carta, defendants who came before the High Courts consistently denounced them as illegal tribunals.

In spite of these protests, the Commonwealth found the High Court of Justice useful. In the same summer that the High Court heard and determined Andrewes' case, the Commonwealth threatened to use the High Court of Justice to execute six imprisoned royalists as retribution for the murder of Anthony Ascham, the Commonwealth envoy to Spain. It ultimately decided not to execute the six men, holding them hostage as leverage for the safety of its overseas diplomats instead.[168] In December 1650, parliament authorized a High Court of Justice to sit in Norfolk to hear, determine, and punish those who had recently participated in a royalist rebellion, the so-called winter rising, where those sympathetic to Charles Stuart attempted to take Norwich for the exiled monarch. At least eighteen and up to thirty-four men were executed by the High Court of Justice in Norfolk.[169] The High Court continued to

---

[165] J.T. Peacey, "Andrewes, Eusebius," in *ODNB*.   [166] *ST*, 5: col. 21.   [167] *Ibid.*

[168] *CJ*, 6: 434, 436–8; *An Act for the Tryal of Sir John Stowel*. Only one of the six, John Stawell, was tried by the High Court of Justice in December 1650, but his case was referred back to parliament without a verdict given. John Wroughton, "Stawell, Sir John," in *ODNB*; F.A. Inderwick, *The Interregnum, A.D. 1648–1660: Studies of the Commonwealth, legislative, social, and legal* (London, 1891), 259–67.

[169] *CJ*, 6: 504–6; *CSPD*, 1650, 465 *A&O*, 2: 492–3. Accounts of the trials can be found in the correspondence of Thomas Scot, the Commonwealth's spymaster, which were

operate through 1651. In that summer, the court tried the presbyterian minister Christopher Love, John Gibbons, and other London plotters who had been secretly conspiring with the Scots.

All of these defendants received a hearing. The High Court of Justice provided defendants with an opportunity to answer. It often allowed defendants to challenge the charge, obtain counsel, and always sought to examine often weighty evidence. One of the longer cases heard before the High Court of Justice was that of Christopher Love in 1651. After listening to Love's legal defense, it allowed him to bring in Matthew Hale, a young and promising jurist, who vigorously challenged the validity of the charge based upon what he thought was faulty wording and lack of proof. Just as John Hotham had been allowed counsel in his 1644 trial, so now Love was allowed counsel in 1651. However, Hale's and Love's arguments were not effective, in no small measure because they, unlike John Lilburne in 1649, had no jury to convince.[170]

The Commonwealth utilized both courts-martial and the High Courts of Justice in Ireland as well. In Dublin, the Commonwealth granted a martial law jurisdiction for the garrison there. But it extended martial law jurisdiction to include spies and other traitors. As Micheál Ó Siochrú has shown, the Dublin court-martial punished civilians for treason in 1652 if they had made contact with the guerrilla fighters, the "Tory bandits," who were severely disrupting the Commonwealth's attempt at re-conquest.[171] As we have already seen, this court-martial operated by procedures that were very standard in the seventeenth century – even for Irish spies.[172] Further, the Commonwealth adopted a High Court of Justice for the trial of felonies dating back to the 1641 Rebellion. As in England, jury nullification was a chief concern for those making the Irish High Court of Justice.[173] At the High Courts of Justice, the Commonwealth was not embarrassed by juries.

printed in the eighteenth century. *Original Letters and Papers of State Addressed to Oliver Cromwell* ed. John Nickolls (London, 1743), 33–9. Bodl. Nalson Ms. 8, fos. 61–3, 67, 84. *A Perfect Diurnall*, 23–30 December 1650, 725; *A Perfect Diurnall*, 30 December 1650 – 6 January 1651, 737–8; *A Perfect Diurnall*, 6–13 January 1651, 752–3; 27. *A Perfect Diurnall*, 27 January – 3 February 1651, 793. David Underdown, *Royalist Conspiracy in England, 1649–1660* (New Haven, 1960), 43–5.

[170] *ST*, 5: cols 43–294; Inderwick, *Interregnum*, 287–93.
[171] Micheál Ó Siochrú, *God's Executioner: Oliver Cromwell and the Conquest of Ireland* (London, 2008), 213–5.
[172] "Minutes of Courts-Martial held in Dublin in the years 1651–3," ed. Heather MacLean, Ian Gentles, & Micheál Ó Siochrú *Archivium Hibernicum* 64 (2011): 56–164. For this court, see chapter 3.
[173] On jury nullification see Wells, "Irish Trials," 93–4.

Protectorate to restoration

With the transformation in 1653 from a Commonwealth to a Protectorate, the new government made changes to the Commonwealth's treason laws. In a protectoral ordinance passed in January 1654, Oliver Cromwell streamlined the treason acts of the Commonwealth period.[174] The ordinance also revived English statutory treason. It was now treason to "compass or imagine the death of the Lord Protector for the time being" – a clear aping of English statutory treason law, which stated it was treason to "compass or imagine the Death of our Lord the King."[175]

English statutory treason was tried by martial law procedure. In the spring of 1654, a conspiracy had been hatched to murder Cromwell and overwhelm the Protector's garrisons in London.[176] John Gerard, Peter Vowell, and Somerset Fox were accused of being part of a conspiracy to murder Cromwell as he traveled from London to Hampton Court on 13 May. Others were then to take control of garrisons in and around London and proclaim Charles Stuart king of England. The plot failed, and the plotters were captured. On 13 June, a protectoral ordinance authorized the sitting of a High Court of Justice through 20 August. This High Court of Justice had cognizance over all treasons and misprisions of treasons listed in the treason ordinance of January 1654.[177]

For this case, we have a view into the internal proceedings of the court because a written account by its president, John Lisle, has survived.[178] After the establishment of the court, the named commissioners met at the Middle Temple. Sir Thomas Widdrington, a commissioner of the Great Seal, came to administer the oath to each commissioner. Several had reservations about taking it. Justice Atkins of Common Pleas, for example, begged for more time to make his decision before he took the oath. Two days later, he informed Lisle that "he had already taken several oaths as a serjeant and as a judge to do nothing contrary to the laws of England."[179] The connection between the High Courts of Justice, martial law, and the Petition of Right prevented many from participating in the 1650s. In spite of this rejection, Lisle managed to obtain enough men to take the oath to meet the quorum of thirteen mandated by the ordinance.

---

[174] *A&O*, 2: 832–4.   [175] *Ibid.*, 832; 25 Edw. III stat. 5 c.2.

[176] Underdown, *Royalist Conspiracy in England*, 100–2. The plot was described on the opening day of the trial. *ST*, 5: cols. 522–4.

[177] *A&O*, 2: 917–8.

[178] *CSPD*, 1654, 233–40. This record has been briefly discussed by Stephen Black, "*Coram Protectore*: The Judges of Westminster Hall under the Protector Oliver Cromwell," *The Journal of American Legal History* 20:1 (January, 1976): 44–6.

[179] *CSPD*, 1654, 234.

The trial opened in Westminster Hall, which according to Lisle was "very full of people."[180] Like the courts-martial of the 1640s, the High Courts of Justice were open to the public. Fox came first and declared he would confess to his deposition. The other two eventually pleaded not guilty. The court heard eyewitnesses who testified *viva voce* to the suspect's guilt. It then adjourned to the Painted Chamber to deliberate. After reviewing the evidence, Lisle posed two questions to each of the justices: whether the suspect was guilty of plotting to raise forces against the protector and whether the suspect was guilty of compassing the death of the protector. In both cases, the commissioners voted in the affirmative for Fox and Gerard. For Vowell, they only voted on the first question, also finding him guilty. This voting system was consistent with that of a court-martial. The three conspirators went to their deaths shortly thereafter.

The discomfort toward the High Court of Justice felt by Atkins perhaps can also be discerned in parliament. Already by 1653, there is circumstantial evidence that some MPs opposed the sitting of the High Court of Justice. In that parliament, the council of state had recommended a bill on 10 August to legalize a High Court of Justice to punish potential conspirators working for Charles Stuart.[181] But the bill was not introduced until almost the middle of October and then disappeared in committee. Finally, on 21 November, the bill passed, but apparently many were upset with the speed at which the bill was passed through the Commons.[182]

However, we should not overstate opposition to the High Court of Justice. Some scholars have argued that Cromwell's use of common law to try captured rebels in the immediate aftermath of Penruddock's rising – a royalist rebellion in Wiltshire in the spring of 1655 – is evidence that the Protector favored the common law. There is no evidence to support this assertion. Instead, as Stephen Black has noted, he had no other option but to use common law.[183] Under the terms of the Instrument of Government, the written constitution that established the Protectorate in December 1653, Cromwell could issue ordinances only until the meeting of the first Protectorate Parliament. Further, those ordinances would only remain lawful if parliament passed them as statutes. This power allowed Cromwell to issue the new treason ordinance in January 1654

---

[180] *Ibid.*
[181] *CJ*, 7: 297, 353–4; *CSPD*, 1653–4, 82–4; Woolrych, *Commonwealth to Protectorate*, 300–1.
[182] *A&O*, 2: 780–2.
[183] Black, "*Coram Protectore*," 46–7. For the argument that Cromwell had no desire to use the High Court of Justice during the rebellion see Austin Woolrych, "The Cromwellian Protectorate: A Military Dictatorship?" in *Cromwell and the Interregnum: The Essential Readings* ed. David L. Smith (Oxford, 2003), 67–8. Woolrych, *Penruddock's Rising, 1655* (London, 1955), 21–2.

and to authorize a sitting of the High Court of Justice in the summer of 1654. But once the first Protectorate Parliament met in the fall of 1654, Cromwell could no longer make these ordinances. Further, the treason ordinance he had passed was no longer legal. This contentious parliament did not pass a new Act for the sitting of a High Court of Justice.[184] Therefore, Cromwell had to try the rebels at the assizes.

When the next parliament met in the fall of 1656, Cromwell pressed for a new statute that would make it treason to compass the death of the Lord Protector and one that authorized a sitting of a High Court of Justice. The bill was entitled for the "Security of his Highness the Lord Protector."[185] Cromwell and his spymaster Thurloe were well aware that royalists and other disaffected persons continued to plot against the government. Indeed, there had been a plot, unbeknownst to the Protector, to take his life on the first day of parliament, 17 September 1656.[186] After a second reading on 26 September, parliament passed the bill on 9 October. Some MPs had reservations about legalizing a new High Court of Justice but failed in an attempt to mandate that three judges had to participate to make a lawful quorum. The act authorized the Protector to call a High Court of Justice in England, Scotland, or Ireland by a commission of the Great Seal through the last sitting of the subsequent parliament.[187] The Act both expanded and limited the powers of the High Court of Justice. The High Court of Justice could now punish high treason and misprision of treason by the full, traditional method of hanging, drawing, and quartering. In terms of procedure, the Court only had powers to examine witnesses "upon oath . . . or upon confession."[188] The elimination of the court's ability to use written depositions, as we shall see, probably saved John Mordaunt's life.

Cromwell did not use this new iteration of the High Court of Justice until the summer of 1658. That spring, Thurloe had swept up a number of suspected royalist plotters. The three most prominent suspects were Sir Henry Slingsby, who had been in Hull and had been entrapped by military officers pretending to want to give up the garrison to Charles Stuart. The second was Dr John Hewitt, an Anglican minister and leader of a royalist network in London that had been planning an uprising.

---

[184] *The Constitutional Documents of the Puritan Revolution, 1625–1660* ed. S.R. Gardiner (Oxford, 1906), 414. For a discussion of the written constitutions of the Protectorate, see Patrick Little and David L. Smith, *Parliaments and Politics During the Cromwellian Protectorate* (Cambridge, 2007), 12–49. Gardiner, *History of the Commonwealth and Protectorate* 3: 178–252.

[185] The bill was first read on 23 September. *CJ*, 7: 427. C.H. Firth, *The Last Years of the Protectorate, 1656–1658* 2 vols. (London, 1909), 1: 41–2.

[186] Underdown, *Royalist Conspiracy*, 178–93; Firth, *Last Years of the Protectorate*, 1: 31–40.

[187] *CJ*, 7: 429, 431, 435–6; *A&O*, 2: 1038–42.   [188] *A&O*, 2: 1041; *CJ*, 7: 436.

The third was John Mordaunt, the leader of the "new action party" in Surrey, which had also been involved in planning an uprising. The High Court of Justice convicted and killed Slingsby and Hewitt. However, Mordaunt was acquitted, in part due to the fact that the chief witness against him escaped from jail and could not testify *viva voce*, a new requirement that the High Court of Justice was forced to meet. The commissioners split their votes, nineteen to nineteen for conviction and acquittal. The president, John Lisle, voted to save Mordaunt's life.[189] One of the lessons was that Mordaunt was acquitted. But another was that the court almost took his life by a bare majority, had the president decided to vote guilty.

In all these cases, the court heard evidence. It deposed witnesses and it examined the papers and correspondence of the defendants. It attempted to determine fact. It, in short, cared about proving the guilt of those that came before it. The point of the High Court of Justice was not to remove treason cases from the realm of law so that the named commissioners could achieve some pre-determined end. The authorization of the High Court was instead meant to avoid jury nullification and to instill terror. In a report that recalled the Duke of Norfolk's worries about potential jury nullification in 1537, William Lenthal, the speaker of the House of Commons, was told that the Norwich juries in the aftermath of the winter rising "are not apt to find for ye commonwealth."[190] Robert Jermy, a local Norfolk officer, similarly claimed that jurors might be obstinate and it would be "no end to try them by jury, but either to make some exemplary by a martial trial, or by the High Court of Justice."[191] Jermy thought the two to be different but nonetheless related in that they did not use juries. The spymaster Thurloe in 1656 was delighted that parliament had authorized a new High Court of Justice and stated to the diplomat John Pell that it was "thought more safe to try them in this way than by ordinary juries."[192] These views were shared by Cromwell. According to Bulstrode Whitelocke, when he begged the Protector not to try Slingsby and the rest by High Courts of Justice in 1658, Cromwell was "too much in love with the new way and thought it would be the more effectual and would the

---

[189] Underdown, *Royalist Conspiracy*, 209–28; Firth, *Last Years of the Protectorate*, 2: 69–82; Victor Stater, "Mordaunt, John," in *ODNB; ST*, 5: cols. 871–907; *The Publick Intelligencer* 28 June – 5 July 1658, 635–53; *Mercurius Politicus* 1–8 July 1658, [657]–63, 665–70.

[190] Bodl., Nalson Ms. 8, f. 61.

[191] Robert Jermy and others to William Lenthall 4 December 1650, Bodl., Nalson Ms. 8, f. 63.

[192] Thurloe to Pell 9 October 1656, in *The Protectorate of Oliver Cromwell* ed. Robert Vaughan 2 vols. (London, 1839), 2: 37; Firth, *Last Years of the Protectorate*, 1: 41–2.

more terrify the offenders."[193] These rationales were fairly common for justifying martial law.

From the fall of 1658 through 1660, the non-monarchical governments of England did not use the High Court of Justice to punish treason.[194] Charles II, restored in 1660, had no need for the High Court of Justice. At the opening of the treason trials of the regicides in October 1660, Sir Orlando Bridgeman, the presiding judge, declared that if Charles II "will try a man for his father's death, you see he will try them by the laws. The law is the rule and square of his actions."[195] Bridgeman was referring to the regimes of the 1650s. Perhaps, he was also referring to the High Court of Justice. The Interregnum was now over, and jurists once again applied the Petition of Right.

Conclusion

What had been bound by parliament in 1628 became unbound by the parliaments of the 1640s and 1650s. At the outset of the Civil War, the discourses spun by Noy, Selden, and Coke – while divergent from one another – had succeeded to a degree in constraining martial law jurisdiction to the point where Charles had to issue his commanders pardons in 1640. Over the course of the war, parliament authorized martial law jurisdiction: first on soldiers in pay, then on spies and conspirators, and even on rioters. Eventually, giving in to the pressure provided by the City of London, parliament authorized sitting courts-martial in London in 1644 and again in 1646 for all of its garrisons. By 1649, a new government needed new laws and procedures. Martial law was one of the legal strategies the Commonwealth fused together to try Charles I.

The trials of 1649 and the subsequent iterations of the High Court of Justice allowed the Commonwealth and Protectorate governments to prosecute traitors while still avoiding juries. These courts were also meant to show separation from the army even while the procedures the courts utilized stemmed from courts-martial. MPs were embarrassed by overriding the Petition of Right. But they did so nonetheless: not to enable arbitrary power but instead to ensure that discretion remained in the hands of those willing to execute the Commonwealth's, and later the Protectorate's, laws.

The innovations of parliamentary martial law were in some ways consistent with the innovations made by Crown and Council in earlier

---

[193] Quoted in Firth, *Last Years of the Protectorate*, 2: 72.
[194] Underdown, *Royalist Conspiracy*, 286, 254–85; Ronald Hutton, *The Restoration: A Political and Religious History of England and Wales* (Oxford, 1985), 1–118.
[195] Quoted in Howard Nenner, "Bridgeman, Sir Orlando," in *ODNB*.

periods. With every expansion of martial law's ambit – its operation in times of peace, its jurisdiction over civilians, its seizure of property – MPs within parliament likewise installed checks on its power – mandated quorums, the final approval of both houses on a sentence, a full proof bar in 1646, sunset clauses, and, eventually, the banning of written depositions. These parallel innovations produced a variant of martial law that was more controllable. These innovative courts came to an end with the return of the monarchy. In this Restoration, both in England and in its dominions, the Petition of Right's influence on martial law jurisdiction was stronger than in any other period. As we shall see, the globalization of the Petition of Right had unintended consequences for martial law practice.

6　Bound and unbound
Martial law in the Restoration Empire

In 1701, the colony of Nevis, a small sugar island in the Caribbean, had to submit its laws to the Board of Trade so that it could determine if they conformed to England's laws.[1] Upon their submission, the Attorney General Edward Northey warned the Board of Trade that he believed a recently passed act entitled "for the better securing the Island against all assaults" was repugnant because it allowed militia commanders to "take away the lives of such offenders by martial law in a time of peace."[2] One can see why the island government wanted to develop a disciplined militia: the Caribbean was inhabited by Spanish, Dutch, and French outposts. The Board of Trade, however, had no sympathy. It agreed with the attorney general's recommendation and declared the statute repugnant to English law.[3] Yet that same summer, the governor of Jamaica ruled exclusively by martial law. Was Jamaica during this period rife with insurrection? No. Was it being invaded? No. Instead, governor William Beeston had been unable to pass a bill authorizing the billeting of soldiers in civilian houses in the Jamaica legislature. Rightfully worried that aggrieved planters would throw the troops "out of doors," he proclaimed martial law so that the military could command quartering.[4] In both instances, the reversal of the conviction of Thomas of Lancaster was applied to determine martial law jurisdiction. In one instance, it bound martial law. In the other, martial law became unbound.

Those who had crafted the laws of martial law in 1628 had not intended that their arguments be applied in the Crown's overseas dominions. While some of the lawyers who crafted the Petition of Right in 1628 had opposed the Crown delegating martial law jurisdiction to its overseas

---

[1] For repugnancy, see Mary Sarah Bilder, *The Transatlantic Constitution: Colonial Legal Culture and the Empire* (Cambridge, MA, 2004).

[2] Edward Northey to the Board of Trade, 3 September 1701, TNA, CO 153/7, 225.

[3] *Ibid.*, 227–8.

[4] William Beeston to the Board of Trade, 30 July 1701, TNA, CO 137/5, f. 218v (no. 53). The problem was not solved the following spring when the lieutenant governor, Peter Beckford, worried that he might have to proclaim martial law again in order to quarter the troops. Beckford to the Board of Trade, 9 April 1702, TNA, CO 137/5, no. 64.

governors, they did not dwell on it.[5] Nevertheless, by the Restoration, the
Crown lawyers frequently but not always bound martial law jurisdiction
in its imperial dominions temporally. From the Crown's perspective,
martial law was necessary for overseas governance, but it was to be used
rarely. Crown officials supervised martial law jurisdiction, just like all
colonial laws, according to a non-repugnancy test. Using martial law on
civilians during a time of peace was usually considered to be beyond the
boundaries of acceptable adaptation.

It must be stressed that there was not uniformity in the ways that
either the Crown or parliament regulated martial law in England's
empire. Delegated authorities did not always listen to their orders.
And they certainly were not always denied access to martial law in
order to discipline a standing militia in the same way that the colony
of Nevis was in 1701. But governors and governing bodies had to be
careful about ignoring Crown commands for two reasons. First, the
Crown from the 1620s onward flexed its muscle in its overseas dominions in ways that it did not in earlier parts of the seventeenth century.
While never comprehensive, it had an interest in monitoring governors
and reviewing colonial laws.[6] Second, discourses relating to the illegality of martial law circulated around English dominions, which
aggrieved colonists could use in petitions against their governors.
Various boards of trade and parliaments were more than willing to
play referee in these disputes. Governors who wanted to keep both
their masters and their subjects happy had to be very careful in how
they used martial law.

Governors nevertheless utilized martial law to maintain order through
terror in Crown garrisons and occasionally to put down rebellions.
Colonial governments at various moments adapted how they construed
"soldiers," as they often governed their militia in times of war by martial
law. Other governments, most notably the East India Company, decided
to govern their armed forces by martial law even though they had no
explicit authority to do so. None of these governments lived by "martial
rule." But as we have seen, seventeenth-century martial law was not

---

[5] *Proceedings in Parliament 1628*, eds. Robert C. Johnson *et al.* 6 vols. (New Haven, 1977–
83), 3: 433, 612, 618. MPs had stumbled upon the martial law powers of the Muscovy
Company while examining its charter. They protested the Crown's right to issue such
powers to the Company, but only in passing. The issue seems to have been dropped
without any major fight between Crown and Parliament over the Crown's right to delegate
martial law to its overseas governors.

[6] Alison Games, *The Web of Empire: English Cosmopolitans in an Age of Expansion, 1560–1660*
(Oxford, 2008), 255–88. Charles Mclean Andrews, *British Committees, Commissions, and
Councils of Trade and Plantations, 1622–1675* (Baltimore, 1908); Andrews, *The Colonial
Period in American History* 4 vols. (New Haven, 1934–8), vol. 4.

generally used to grant the military unlimited power.[7] Instead, as in England, martial law was one of the many laws governors used to maintain peace and order within English dominions.

The outlier was Jamaica. Governors there had no more power, in theory, to use martial law than governors in other dominions. Indeed, they possessed less formal power than others, like the governors of Tangier, to use martial law. But governors on the island, in order to build fortifications and mandate militia duty, closed the courts down. Instead of the chaos and violence forcing the courts to be closed, governors closed the courts down to create wartime and thus remove legal obstacles to militia duty in order to make public rights claims. The closing of courts was not an effect of wartime. They were its cause.[8] In order to understand how martial law was practised in Jamaica and in other English dominions, let us first examine Crown commissions and charters before we examine martial law practice.

Restoration martial law commissions

Initially after 1628, the Crown expanded martial law jurisdiction for its governors. We shall recall that the Virginia Company and the Plymouth Company received powers identical to those of lords lieutenants in England. By 1632, however, Charles granted powers identical to those of his lord generals to his overseas governors. The 1632 Charter for Maryland, for example, gave its governor powers to exercise "martial law as freely, and in as ample Manner and Form, as any Captain-General of an Army, by virtue of his Office."[9] The governors of Maryland, in other words, could discipline soldiers by martial law as well as execute rebels and invaders by summary martial law: the martial

---

[7] Thus, the debate between Ian Steele and Stephen Saunders Webb over military authority in the Empire, at least as it pertained to martial law, was anachronistic. Ian Steele, "Governors or Generals?: A Note on Martial Law and the Revolution of 1689 in English America," *William and Mary Quarterly* 46:2 (April, 1989): 304–14.

[8] Many thanks to Professor John Harrison for discussions on this point.

[9] "Charter of Maryland, 1632," The Avalon Project: http://avalon.law.yale.edu/17th_cen tury/ma01.asp (accessed 31 August 2014). The Massachusetts Bay charter of 1629 is slightly ambiguous. It does not explicitly invoke martial law although it does grant the Company powers to "incounter, expulse, repell, and resist by Force of Armes" any who attempted to invade or destroy the plantation. However, the charter then goes on to make a strong warning to the Company about not attacking any who were in amity with the Crown. "The Charter of Massachusetts Bay: 1629," The Avalon Project: http://avalon .law.yale.edu/17th_century/mass03.asp, accessed 3 September, 2014. The 1691 Charter explicitly gave the colony martial law powers. "The Charter of Massachusetts Bay, 1691," The Avalon Project, http://avalon.law.yale.edu/17th_century/mass07.asp, accessed 3 September 2014.

law powers granted to lords generals in the early seventeenth century.[10] Others, while also receiving these powers, had martial law powers crafted according to their own specific circumstances. For example, Pennsylvania received powers to utilize the "law of war" upon robbers and pirates because it was "neare many Barbarous Nations."[11] Rhode Island was allowed to array its inhabitants and invade "the native Indians, or other enemyes of the sayd Collony." It could discipline those arrayed according to the "lawe martiall ... only as occasion shall necessarily require."[12] Other governors, like those of Virginia, had implied martial law powers that were similar to those of captain generals.[13] Although there were variations to their powers, most governors throughout the empire possessed powers of martial law.

The 1660s was an important moment in the history of imperial martial law. It was in this decade, more than any other, that the arguments made in 1628 informed the commissions of martial law sent abroad. In order to better understand the influence of the 1628 Parliament, let us examine the commission given to Sir Edward Doyley, the governor of Jamaica, in 1661.[14]

The Crown granted Doyley two powers of martial law. First, Doyley had the power to "fight kill slay represse and subdue all such as shall be in hostile or mutinous manner by insurrection or invasion disturb the peace or attempt the Surprise of or said Island of Jamaica."[15] The governors thus possessed a summary power of martial law. They could execute, *in flagrante crimine*, those invading or committing rebellion. This power was similar to those of lords lieutenants in England. Further, it met the requirements set forth by John Selden on martial law jurisdiction. Second, the Crown commanded that "when the ordinary course of Justice cannot be well and safely attended and applied to that then you the said Edward Doyley doe put in Execution the lawes Martiall

---

[10] See for example the powers granted to the Earl of Leicester, LPL, Ms. 247, fos. 5–8. Also see the commission to the Earl of Arundel in 1639 and the Earl of Northumberland. HEHL, HA Military Box 1 (27).

[11] "Charter of Pennsylvania, 1681," The Avalon Project: http://avalon.law.yale.edu/17th_century/pa01.asp (accessed 31 August 2014).

[12] "Charter of Rhode Island and Providence Plantations, 15 July 1663," The Avalon Project, http://avalon.law.yale.edu/17th_century/ri04.asp, accessed 3 September 2014.

[13] For the Virginia powers of martial law, see *The Records of the Virginia Company of London* ed. Susan Myra Kingsbury, 4 vols. (Washington, D.C., 1906–35), 3: 310, 609–11, 623, 664–65; 4: 105; "Commission to Sir George Yeardley," *The Virginia Magazine of History and Biography* 13 (1905–06): 300. The martial law clauses have been tracked by Wilcomb Washburn in "The Humble Petition of Sarah Drummond," *William and Mary Quarterly* 13:3 (1956): 366. Martial law powers were explicitly granted in the aftermath of Bacon's Rebellion.

[14] "Commission to Sir Edward Doyley," TNA, CO 1/15 no. 10.   [15] *Ibid.*

according to the practize and constitucons of a court martiall vpon soldiers only."[16] In other words, even when the courts were closed, the governor could still only subject his soldiers to martial law. The governor of Bombay, Sir Abraham Shipman, could use martial law in identical ways.[17] These two commissions granted highly restrictive powers of martial law.

This is an essential point given Jamaica's subsequent and notorious history with martial law. The governors had nearly identical martial law powers that the Crown possessed in England and no further powers. Indeed, at least initially there was no substantive difference between these commissions and the martial law jurisdiction that Sir Matthew Hale would grant for England. Although it was a conquered colony, Jamaica was nevertheless not supposed to be ruled by martial law. Instead, the commission combined Selden's discussion of the summary powers of lords lieutenants with the general agreement by Coke and Selden that soldiers could only come before a court-martial if the courts were closed. These discourses, which had been reserved to the journals of parliamentary note-takers, were now imprinted in imperial commissions.

Small changes to those powers, however, made large differences to subsequent uses of martial law. The Crown granted the subsequent governor, Lord Windsor, slightly more extensive powers of martial law. Like Doyley, he possessed a summary martial law power on rebels and invaders. And like Doyley, when the courts were closed, Windsor had powers to punish by martial law. But instead of simply soldiers, Windsor could punish "all notorious offenders."[18] The move from soldiers to notorious offenders would have deeply upset Selden, who would have rightly worried that martial law under this clause could be applied to civilians as well as soldiers. Nevertheless, this adaptation remained in future commissions.[19] Even with this expansion, the governors of Jamaica were still bound in their martial law powers by the status of the courts.

These restrictions were not uniformly issued to all the governors of the empire. Nor were they universally followed. In both Nova Scotia and in Tangier, the Crown issued commissions in the 1660s that allowed governors to use martial law continuously on the soldiers stationed there. Tangier, the courts-martial of which we have already examined, became the largest garrison in the empire during the Restoration.[20] Meanwhile in Ireland,

---

[16] *Ibid.*   [17] Commission to Sir Abraham Shipman, BL, IOR H/48, f. 4.
[18] "Commission of Lord Windsor," TNA, CO 138/1, 10.
[19] "Commission of Sir Thomas Modyford," TNA, CO 138/1, 25. The key is *could*. One could interpret this clause as meaning only notorious offenders *in* military employment.
[20] "Commission to Sir Thomas Temple," TNA, CO 1/16, no. 42. "Commission to the Earl of Peterborough," TNA, CO 279/1 non-folioed. The articles of war for the soldiers are also in this volume.

which also had garrisoned soldiers, the memory of Strafford's treason conviction was still strong in the early 1660s. We shall recall that one of his articles of treason was that he had used martial law upon soldiers in Ireland during "the time of full Peace."[21] Strafford's example worried James Butler, Duke of Ormond, and lord lieutenant of Ireland during the 1660s. Ormond, after having received his commission, wrote to the secretary of state, Sir Henry Bennet, in 1663 and inquired whether his martial law powers included the death penalty.[22] Ormond recalled that Strafford's use of martial law "made parte of the treason vpon w[hi]ch he was condemned."[23] However, Ormond's fears were assuaged enough to try several mutinous soldiers at martial law in 1666 at Carrickfergus.[24] The Crown commands included provisions that were generated during the Petition of Right. But it had enough flexibility to grant more extensive martial law jurisdiction to accommodate its more heavily garrisoned colonies.

Governing soldiers

Whether or not a colony possessed a standing garrison, governors at various moments felt the need to discipline their soldiers by martial law. In these cases, they generally kept a division between those in arms and civilians. This was even true of Tangier. Indeed, rather than being an autocratic "garrison government," as has been described by Stephen Saunders Webb, these militarized towns are more aptly described as governments that also possessed a garrison.[25] The people who inhabited these colonies lived under a jurisdictionally pluralistic legal system, where martial law operated only as a complement to other forms of law, like merchant's law, some variation of English common law, and other, local mayoral courts.

Crown garrisons were few and far between in the Restoration Empire. A garrison was briefly stationed in Dunkirk. A larger garrison at Tangier

---

[21] The article relating to martial law was number five. "The Articles against Strafford," *Historical Collections of Private Passages of State* 8: 1640–41 (1721): 61–101, 186–205. Accessed on British History Online February 2013–September 2015, www.british-history.ac.uk. The attainder made clear that Strafford's trial could not be used as a precedent for further treason trials. 16 Car. I c. 38.

[22] Ormond to Bennet, 13 June 1663, Bodl. Carte Ms. 143, f. 142v.   [23] *Ibid.*

[24] Bodl., Carte Ms. 34, fos. 710, 712, 714, 724, 726; Bodl. Carte Ms. 48, f. 45.

[25] Stephen Saunders Webb in multiple works has argued that the early empire was in fact militarized. The most important of his works is *The Governors-General: The English Army and the Definition of the Empire, 1569–1681* (Chapel Hill, 1979). Webb's work at times is brilliant – and in terms of archival research is always brilliant – but he often overstates his thesis and overlooks English dominions that do not clearly align with his argument. For critiques of Webb, See Richard R. Johnson, "The Imperial Webb: The Thesis of Garrison Government in Early America Considered," *William and Mary Quarterly* 43:3 (July, 1986): 408–30. For a succinct definition of "governor-general," see Webb, *The Governors-General*, 3–6.

of roughly 3,000 men was created in 1662, and it lasted until 1684. In Scotland, the Crown maintained a small army of roughly 1,200 men, which was raised in 1678 during the Bothwell Bridge uprising to around 2,700. Within England, the Crown possessed at the time of Charles II's death in 1685 a force of roughly 8,800 men. In Ireland, the Crown maintained a force of 7,500 men, while in Portugal, due to the marriage agreement between Charles and Catherine of Braganza, the English kept 2,500 soldiers to help the Portuguese fight the Spanish. In the Caribbean during the 1670s, the Crown intermittently kept small forces, never more than 1,000 men, in Barbados, St. Kitts, and Jamaica. The Crown briefly experimented with garrisons in Bombay, New York, New England, Nova Scotia, and Virginia in the aftermath of Bacon's rebellion.[26] By comparison to continental armies, those of the English were small. Most of the court-martial records of these garrisons have not survived.

The notable exception to this rule is Tangier.[27] Tangier came to Charles II as part of the marriage treaty he signed with Portugal. In return for English soldiers who would aid the king of Portugal's war against Spain, Charles received Bombay and Tangier, a Mediterranean port that was surrounded by powerful Muslim polities. To maintain the port, Charles commanded Henry Mordaunt, Lord Peterburgh, to take command and bring with him roughly 3,000 soldiers. In the garrison, from the courts-martial records that have survived, we can tell that the governor sought to try soldiers in pay over disciplinary matters. These courts were brutal but also careful about the taking of evidence. The presidents of the courts also were keenly aware of the boundaries of their jurisdiction. Merchants had their own courts. So too did the town.

The jurisdictional plurality of Tangier, as we have seen in Chapter 3, arose from a desire to keep merchants happy and to lure more mercantile commerce into the city. Crown officials engaged in this strategy because the militarized port was expensive. Many Portuguese and Tangerine merchants departed the port throughout the 1660s because they did not want to be ruled by an English governor and because they felt threatened by the soldiers. The financial problems were compounded by the fact that the Moroccans had successfully isolated the city. The governor of Tangier had no access to grazing land and suffered from shortages of water and other necessaries. In order to raise more money, the Crown, through commissioners it had sent out to examine deficiencies, set out new governing guidelines in 1668 to encourage merchants to return to the city.

[26] The numbers are taken from John Childs, *The Army of Charles II* (London, 1976), 152–61, 196–212. Childs, *The Army, James II, and the Glorious Revolution* (Manchester, 1980), 1–3. The army was increased to over 34,000 by 1688.
[27] BL, Sloane Ms. 1957, 1959, 1960, 1961, 3498, and 3514.

Included in these new provisions were an incorporation of the city and the creation of a mercantile court to handle business disputes. This new jurisdictional plurality replaced an all-encompassing governor's court, which merchants apparently distrusted.[28]

Civilians, while they used martial law to obtain justice against soldiers, were only on the rarest occasions subject to being punished by life and limb at a court-martial. In one instance, Margaret Summerton came before a court-martial in 1664.[29] She had been charged with sedition and attempted mutiny. These were grave offenses and Summerton was ultimately found guilty. However, instead of executing her, the court ordered her whipped at the Parade, imprisoned, and then to be deported from the colony. Another, Robert Barber, was brought before a court-martial in the same year for killing a sailor.[30] He was acquitted. Very few civilians were tried before a court-martial in Tangier.

Tensions between soldiers and civilians certainly existed. However, these battles were usually fought not in the sexy world of crime but instead in the mundane world of debt. We shall recall that by the late sixteenth century garrison governors in English dominions had adopted protections for their troops over non-capital offenses – the petitioning system. Soldiers could not be prosecuted for minor or misdemeanor offenses unless a civilian obtained the permission of the soldier's commanding officer through a petition. This practice was not uniformly followed. But at various moments, we can see this process at work. In March 1667, for example, Sir Thomas Modyford, the governor of Jamaica, declared that militia on active duty could not be sued at law for debts, at least until threats from French privateers had subsided.[31] Further, civilians frequently came before courts-martial in Tangier in order to recuperate debts owed to them by soldiers.[32] These protections naturally at times generated discontent among the civilian populace.

The best evidence of this practice of the petitioning system comes from Ireland during the 1660s and 1670s. If a civilian wanted to take a soldier to court for a non-felony suit, he or she had to write a petition to the lord lieutenant of Ireland, which in the 1660s was the Duke of Ormond. For example, in January 1667, William Basil and his wife petitioned Ormond because they desired to "implead William Lord viscount Charlemount."[33] But they could not do so because

---

[28] E.M.G. Routh, *Tangier: England's Lost Atlantic Outpost, 1661–1684* (London, 1912), 113–32.
[29] BL, Sloane Ms. 1960, fos. 45–6.   [30] *Ibid.*, fos. 46–50.   [31] TNA, CO 140/1, f. 167.
[32] See for example, BL, Sloane Ms. 1957, fos. 40–1, 49; BL, Sloane Ms. 1959, fos. 42–4, 50, 101, 83v, 85v, 1960, f. 4.
[33] Bodl. Carte Ms. 154, f. 62.

Charlemount was "a member of the Army." In a more common petition, John Clignett in February 1669 listed two members of the military indebted to him and asked to be given satisfaction "or els to Admitt yor peticoner to sue them at law."[34] If a civilian prosecuted without first obtaining leave, the lord lieutenant could call the violators before him and possibly imprison them for contempt.[35]

Ormond, or the acting army commander, generally responded to these petitions in one of three ways. First and most commonly, the lord lieutenant ordered one or more of his underlings in the army to investigate the claim. For example, in August 1666, Ormond received a petition from Jane Aylen, a widow from Londonderry. Aylen claimed that Thomas Taylor, a private soldier, had owed her over £80 while stationed in the city and had not paid her before he was relocated to the fortress at Carrickfergus.[36] Ormond ordered Colonel Humphrey Sydenham to examine the widow's claim and to "certifiy vs, what shall appeare vnto him, and thereupon Wee shall giue such further order as wee shall finde to bee fitt."[37] In other cases, Ormond, or his stand in, decided the matter immediately. In the case of John Clignett, for example, the acting lord deputy ordered that the two debtors should satisfy Clignett within two weeks, otherwise Clignett could "take his remedy against them generally by law notwithstanding their Military Capacity."[38] Less often, the acting governor of the army simply allowed the petitioner to find relief at law. In the petition against Viscount Charlemount, for example, Ormond allowed the petitioners to sue at law in spite of Charlemount's military capacity.[39]

In some instances, the commander released cases from martial jurisdiction. In 1668 for example, Henry Hornsworth and his wife Mary accused Sir Arthur Chichester and John Chichester, both officers in the army, of "several violences and misdemenours."[40] The Earl of Ossory, the acting lord deputy, ordered the case to be heard before a court-martial. The judge advocate general investigated diverse informations and deposed witnesses relating to the case. But we then find out that the complainants had already filed suit against the defendants in "several courts": both ecclesiastical and common law.[41] The judge advocate, advising the court, concluded that the charges against the defendants were true but difficult to align with any particular article of war. Further, the petitioners wanted to have their suit tried at common law.

---

[34] *Ibid.*, f. 152v; the petition was here presented to the Earl of Ossory, the Duke of Ormond's son and member of the Irish Privy Council, who was serving as lord deputy of Ireland while his father was in England.
[35] Bodl. Carte Ms. 163, f. 16v.   [36] Bodl. Carte Ms. 154, f. 58.   [37] *Ibid.*
[38] *Ibid.*, f. 152v.   [39] Ibid., f. 62.
[40] Bodl. Carte Ms. 163, fos. 67, 70v. The quotation is on 70v.   [41] Ibid., f. 70v.

Therefore, the court stopped prosecution of the defendants, after the complainants waived their privilege of being remedied at martial law, and allowed them to pursue their cases against the Chichesters' at common law.[42] The petitioning system could certainly be an encumbrance, but from the surviving records in Ireland, it does not seem that the army protected its own soldiers too much from prosecution.

Most of the other areas of the empire did not possess formal garrisons. However, English plantations were often militarized, just not by the Crown's formal armies. The Crown allowed its governors to raise forces, both land and sea, to defend their plantations. In its commission to Sir Thomas Modyford, for example, the Crown allowed him to muster all military forces on Jamaica.[43] Further, the Crown often allowed governors to punish at martial law all those in "military employment," during times when the courts were inoperable, which suggests that colonial militias could at times fall under martial law jurisdiction.[44] By the late seventeenth century, the Board of Trade and Plantations regulated the disciplining of forces according to tracts of time. In war, militia could be governed by martial law. In peace, they could not. But this rule, as with almost every generalization about overseas governance, had exceptions. Some, like the East India Company, always kept their militia supervised by martial law, while other colonies only did so during times of war. Most delegated authorities only punished martial men in arms during times of war.

Both Massachusetts and Virginia utilized martial law when they comprehended their plantation to be in wartime. For example, Massachussetts' General Court adopted articles of war for its forces at the outset of King Philip's War in October 1675.[45] Like most articles of war, the Massachusetts code included the death penalty, to be determined by the General Court, acting as a court-martial.[46] Likewise, the House of Burgesses in Virginia adopted twenty-six articles of war for the governance of its "army" in March 1676 during its campaigns against Native Americans.[47] The House stipulated that commanders could execute the articles with the exception of any offense involving life and limb. Those accused of capital offenses were instead to be tried before a council of war that the House had appointed to coordinate the war effort.

---

[42] *Ibid.*   [43] TNA, CO 138/1, f. 25.   [44] *Ibid.*

[45] Kyle Zelner, *A Rabble in Arms: Massachusetts Towns and Militiamen during King Philips' War* (New York and London, 2009), 40–43.

[46] Massachusetts General Court, *Severall Lawes and Ordinances of War Past and Made the 26th October, 1675* (Boston, 1675).

[47] *Hening's Statutes at Large: Being a Collection of all the Laws of Virginia, from the First Session of Legislature in the Year 1619*, 13 vols. (Torrence, 2009), 2: 331–36. An example of a court-martial can be found from 1673, during the Third Anglo-Dutch War. See "Miscellaneous Colonial Documents," *The Virginia Magazine of History and Biography* 20 (1912): 28–9.

The East India Company likewise used martial law on its "soldiers." Upon taking over Bombay from the Crown in 1668, the Company issued articles of war to govern its militia stationed in the settlement.[48] Nevertheless, many believed that the Company did not have powers of martial law. The Company imprisoned one militia officer, Henry Gary, for telling his soldiers that they could not be punished by martial law.[49] Gary was technically right: the Company did not have martial law powers in its charter to punish its soldiers by martial law. Nevertheless, by 1674, some company factors made full use of martial law. In August of that year, the governor and council of war in Bombay uncovered a plot made by a group of soldiers to overthrow the Company's government.[50] The following month, the governor and his council decided upon using martial law because the soldiers had engaged in mutiny. Martial law would also provide "discouragemt of such villanous persons & for the future security and quiett of the Island it would be farr better to trye them by a Court martiall."[51] After a long, drawn-out procedure, where the council of war deposed many witnesses, and where the governor and council further debated whether or not they should actually execute the capital sentence required of a guilty verdict for mutiny, the governor decided to execute several soldiers. He argued once again that it was necessary for the future order and security of the polity. Several were condemned to death and forced to roll dice to see whose life would be spared.[52] Given that they had no explicit martial law powers, these acts could have gotten the East India Company in trouble had they come to light in Westminster.

Nevertheless, the Company's leadership in London approved of these severe measures and encouraged the use of martial law on company militia throughout its domains after it received some formal powers of martial law in its new 1683 charter. The Company in the Charter was allowed to

Execute and use, within the said Plantations, Forts and Places, the Law, called the Martial Law, for the Defense of the said Forts, Places and Plantations, against any foreign Invasion, or domestic Insurrection or Rebellion.[53]

It is unclear even here, however, if it had martial law jurisdiction over its soldiers outside of times of invasion or rebellion. Nevertheless, after 1685, the Company was sending "martial law books" to all of its governors in South Asia and in St. Helena.[54] These books were probably

---

[48] BL, IOR H/49, 71–91.   [49] BL, IOR G/3/1, 54.   [50] BL, IOR G/3/1, 73.
[51] *Ibid.*, 95.   [52] *Ibid.*, fos. 94–106.
[53] *Charters Granted to the East India Company, from 1601; also Treaties and Grants, made with, or obtained from, the Princes and Powers in India* (London, 1773), 121.
[54] BL, IOR E/3/90, fos. 205, 256, 284; BL, IOR E/3/91, fos. 2–4, 7, 23, 31, 33, 38, 58, 193–95.

reproductions of James II's pamphlet on military discipline meant for his army in England.[55] The Company encouraged its factors to use martial law to maintain order and discipline and to terrify soldiers into obedience. There are no surviving courts-martial records that would allow us to discover how extensively capital punishment was employed in India through courts-martial. What seems more clear is that prior to 1685 the Company's governors did not utilize the jurisdiction on its civilian inhabitants. The governor of Surat, for example, declared that it "would reflect much on the Company's honour" to punish civilians by the articles of war.[56] In India, as in Virginia and Massachusetts, local officials maintained a distinction between men in arms and civilians.

Controversies arose over the use of martial law on militia in certain areas of the empire. We have already examined the controversy in Nevis. Likewise, in Carolina controversy erupted over the use of martial law in peacetime. The governor of Carolina, Peter Colleton, had arrived there in 1686 in the aftermath of the Spanish sack of Stuart Town, the new Scottish plantation in Carolina. He also, like every English governor, had to worry about French attacks in the aftermath of the Glorious Revolution. After failing several times to get a militia act passed through the Carolina legislature, Colleton passed ordinances of war to govern a militia in order to instill more discipline into a force that needed to better defend the colony.[57] A group of planters who opposed him and his brother, who was a proprietor, claimed that Colleton was trying to use martial law to control the Indian trade. But their more effective argument against Colleton ended up being that he had "published certain Articles of War [yet], still permittinge preposterously the courts of Common Law to be kept open."[58] Colleton was replaced.[59]

---

[55] My guess for the book is the English army's *Abridgement of the English Military Discipline Printed by Especial Command for the Use of his Majesties Forces* (London, 1685). The guess is based upon the company's 1685 command to its factor on Pryaman (Sumatra) to train its troops "with the order and exercise of all sorts of arms compiled into one book and printed by his maties order ... " BL, IOR E/3/91, f. 4v. The articles of war could have been created by the East India Company, based on the ones used in Bombay in 1668 or could have been taken from the king's articles of war for his troops in Ireland. *Rules and Articles for the Better Government of His Majesties Army in this Kingdom* (Dublin, 1685).

[56] Quoted in Sir Charles Fawcett, *The English Factories in India: The Western Presidency, 1670–1677* (vol. 1) (Oxford, 1936), 35.

[57] John Stewart to William Dunlop, 27 April 1690 in *The South Carolina Historical and Genealogical Magazine* 32 (January, 1931): 10–11, 27.

[58] This claim was made in the petition to Seth Sothell by several planters. Sothell eventually replaced Colleton as governor. This protest has been printed in William James Rivers, *A Sketch of the History of South Carolina, to the close of the proprietary government by the revolution of 1719* (Charleston, 1855), 423.

[59] For the proprietors' agreements that Colleton should not have used martial law, see TNA, CO 5/288, 182.

Through this short example, we can see that the reversal of the conviction of Thomas of Lancaster could be invoked in faction fights. While the Crown desired to restrain martial law jurisdiction, latitude was given for it over the governance of martial men. What governors had to fear was a backlash from their subject populations, who could deploy the law of martial law to censure or even remove undesired governors by petitioning supervisory bodies in England.

Martial law and civilians

Unlike early Virginia or Ireland in the sixteenth century, Restoration governors used martial law to discipline civilians rarely. Nevertheless, in Ireland, Virginia in the aftermath of Bacon's Rebellion, and in St. Helena, an island controlled by the East India Company, delegated authorities used martial law to punish severe threats to their authority. These actions often aroused considerable controversy.[60]

In Ireland, powers of summary martial law became circumscribed to the punishment of those who resisted arrest. For certain offenses, the government used it as part of an enhanced policing power as a substitute for the unreliable *posse comitatus*. For example, lords lieutenants gave their military and local sheriffs powers of summary execution in certain cases that involved "tory" bandits.[61] These para-military gangs were a consistent problem throughout the late seventeenth century. In order to stop them, lords lieutenants commissioned warrants to their soldiers to arrest the gangs and to bring them to justice. For example, in 1667, the Irish Privy Council sent out a warrant to their soldiers to track down "Neill oge o Neale" and several others for burglaries, murders, and a variety of other wrongs. The soldiers had powers to bring the bandits in to justice. If they resisted, they could be "cut off by the sword."[62] Usually, these soldiers only had powers to execute tory bandits if they resisted arrest.[63] The words martial law, which had been used in all the commissions and proclamations of the sixteenth century, were omitted.

---

[60] In Jamaica, particularly in 1685, the governor and planters could have tried slaves at martial law for their roles in various rebellions. But they seemed to have only tried them at regimental courts-martial. TNA, CO 140/3, f. 90v. For an account of the 1685 rebellion, see TNA, CO 138/5, 87ff. Orlando Patterson, "Slavery and Slave Revolts: A Socio-Historical Analysis of the First Maroon War Jamaica, 1655–1740," *Social and Economic Studies* 19:3 (September 1970): 289–325.

[61] S.J. Connolly, *Religion, Law, and Power: The Making of Protestant Ireland, 1660–1760* (Oxford, 1992), 203–09.

[62] Bodl. Carte Ms. 163, fos. 23v–24.   [63] *Ibid.*, f. 3v.

Summary martial law powers survived in Ireland even though its name did not.

The largest number of executions of civilians by court-martial took place in the aftermath of Bacon's Rebellion in late 1676 and early 1677 in Virginia.[64] Over the course of the rebellion, the septuagenarian governor William Berkeley used powers of martial law to try, convict, and execute fourteen of Bacon's followers.[65] The first five trials took place in Accomack in the autumn of 1676, when Berkeley had captured some of Bacon's officers charged with taking the then fleeing governor. The final eleven trials took place in January 1677. On 11 January, Berkeley convened a council of war on a ship in the York River and tried four men for treason and rebellion. All four confessed, were found guilty, and were subsequently hanged. On 20 January, Berkeley charged William Drummond, one of Bacon's key supporters, with treason and convicted him before a council of war at Middle Plantation, where he was subsequently hanged. Finally, on 24 January, Berkeley brought another five men before a council of war at his home at Green Spring. They were all convicted of treason. Two escaped and the other three were hanged. Taken together, Berkeley used martial law on non-military personnel more than any other governor in the Restoration.[66]

Three commissioners arrived in Virginia in February 1677 to investigate the causes of the rebellion. They brought an army of 1,000 men to subdue the uprising that had already been subdued.[67] The leader of the commission was the newly minted lieutenant governor Herbert Jeffries who also commanded the English forces on their way to Virginia. While technically subordinate to the governor, the commissioners from February 1677 were in charge of the reconstruction of the colony. They declared Virginia to be in a state of peace, and while more men were to be tried for treason, they could no longer be tried by martial law:

Although wee rather commend what before hee might bee forced to doe in Furore Belli by a martiall power considering how the face of affaires then looked ... that

---

[64] For Bacon's Rebellion, see Wilcomb E. Washburn, *The Governor and the Rebel: A History of Bacon's Rebellion in Virginia* (Chapel Hill, 1957) and James Rice's new account: *Tales from a Revolution: Bacon's Rebellion and the Transformation of Early America* (Oxford, 2012).

[65] A list of those executed can be found in Peter Force, *Tracts and Other Papers Relating Principally to the Origin, Settlement, and Progress of the Colonies in North American: from the Discovery of the Country to the Year 1776* 4 vols. (Gloucester, MA, 1963), 1: no. 10.

[66] Records of the courts-martial are extant from 11 January 1677 onwards in Hening, *Statutes* 2: 545–48.

[67] Two commissioners, Francis Moryson and Sir John Barry sailed in November. Herbert Jeffries the third commissioner, sailed in December. Washburn, *The Governor and the Rebel*, 92–113.

the lawes might returne to their owne proper Channell and that all future proceedings of his might bee by a Jury.[68]

Subsequently, in March, the commissioners tried and executed another
nine men for treason before a jury.[69] Once the time of war had ended, jury
trials resumed.

The story did not end there. In the fall of 1677, Berkeley having died in
the summer, family members from two of those executed by the late
governor sent petitions to the Board of Trade and Plantations challenging
the legality of Berkeley's use of martial law. The first petition came from
Sarah Drummond, the widow of William Drummond, who had been
executed at Middle Plantation that January, and had been posthumously
attainted by the House of Burgesses.[70] She claimed that Berkeley had
illegally executed her husband and confiscated his property to the detri-
ment of Sarah and her children. The language of the petition shows that
Sarah, or her legal aid, knew well the parameters of martial law. It also
shows that either Sarah or her lawyer was familiar with English debates
over what constituted a time of war:

That your Petitioners said husband was, after late rebellion there, taken, stript,
and brought before sir W. Berkley then Governor there, who immediately (tho' in
time of peace) was, without laying anything to his charge, sentenced to die by
Martial law (although he never bore arms or any military Office).[71]

Drummond framed the charge against Berkeley with an understanding that
in the empire those who possessed military office were often subject to
martial law in times of war. However, she claimed that neither standard had
been met in her husband's case. Why did Drummond frame the argument
in this way? Possibly she wanted to argue that because her late husband had
been executed in the middle of January, after the most tumultuous period
of the insurrection, he should have been tried by a jury. Given that Berkeley
was dead, her goal was not to get him in trouble. Rather the petition was
meant to inflame the passions of members of the board in an attempt to get
them to reverse Berkeley's decision to seize Drummond's property through
an act of attainder after he had been executed by martial law.[72]

[68] Quoted in Washburn, *The Governor and the Rebel*, 110.
[69] These trials, which had both grand and petty juries can be found in Hening, *Statutes*, 2:
548–58. Washburn, *The Governor and the Rebel*, 119.
[70] Hening, *Statutes*, 2: 370, 375, 377. Washburn, "The Humble Petition of Sarah
Drummond," 354–75. The petition is in TNA, CO 5/1355, 186–88.
[71] The petition has been reprinted in Washburn "The Humble Petition of Sarah
Drummond," 355–56.
[72] It is unclear if Drummond was deprived of all her husband's property which was
extensive or simply a leased plantation in James City that belonged to the
Commonwealth and could be revoked, see *Ibid.*, 370–2.

Given the response of the Board, the tactic worked. The Lords of Trade and Plantation called the proceedings "deplorable" and stated that "ye estate of those that dye by martial law does not escheat but descend to their heirs."[73] However, Berkeley had not escheated property at martial law but had done so through an act of attainder, a maneuver that had been common in medieval English law. Nevertheless, the Lords condemned the act of attainder, which they wanted repealed, stating that it was meant to "iustify and indemnify" the dead governor.[74] The idea of using martial law in a time of peace planted by Sarah Drummond had created a controversy over Berkeley's usage of martial law. She recovered all of her dead husband's estate.[75]

The outcry by the Lords of Trade and Plantation toward Drummond's petition was not replicated, nor did it provide any precedent for ending martial law. The Lords of Trade and Plantations' suspicions were aroused only a month after Drummond's petition when the descendants of a much better-known traitor, William Carver, delivered a similar petition to the Board.[76] This time eyewitnesses from Virginia were on hand to confirm that Carver had attacked Berkeley on Accomack and was deeply involved with the rebellion.[77] Carver's attempts were unsuccessful. Further, the Crown continued to delegate martial law jurisdiction to its governors of Virginia. Herbert Jeffries, in 1676, received powers to execute martial law "during times of war ... where the ordinary Course of Justice cannot be well and safely attended and applied to."[78] In 1682, the new governor, Thomas Lord Culpepper, received similar powers. Nevertheless, the petitioning powers of Virginia's civilians would have made these men think twice about using martial law, especially in ways that could be seen as being beyond their commissioned powers.[79]

The only other major case of delegated authorities employing martial law on civilians came in 1685, in the East India Company controlled island of St. Helena. The Company, since acquiring the island in 1658 as a way station for its ships, had encouraged plantation in an attempt to

---

[73] TNA, CO 391/2, f. 129.   [74] TNA, CO 391/2, fos. 129–30.

[75] Wilcomb Washburn, "The Petition of Sarah Drummond," 371–2.

[76] TNA, CO 391/2, f. 146; Washburn "The Petition of Sarah Drummond," 359; the petition has also been abstracted in "Virginia in 1677 (continued)" *The Virginia Magazine of History and Biography* 23 (1915): 24–5.

[77] "Virginia in 1677 (continued)," 25.

[78] "Virginia Colonial Records. Culpepper's Administration (Continued)." *The Virginia Magazine of History and Biography* 14 (1907): 357.

[79] "Virginia in 1682 (continued)" *The Virginia Magazine of History and Biography* 26 (1918): 262.

emulate English Atlantic holdings. This policy led to the foundation of the capital Jamestown and the growth of the population to nearly one thousand soldiers and planters, the largest population in any of the East India Company's holdings.[80] However, once in St. Helena, the planters became unruly, particularly over the Company's taxation policies. Between 1679 and 1684, groups of dissatisfied soldiers and planters had staged four riots in protest, culminating in the fall and winter of 1684, when they conspired to overtake Jamestown and remove the governor.

The Company had already been encouraging more severe measures against mutineers and, as we have seen, had obtained from the Crown in 1683 martial law powers to maintain order within their various dominions. Nevertheless, the governor of St. Helena, John Blackmore, initially hesitated to use martial law on the mutineers in St. Helena, even those that were soldiers. Instead, in December 1684, Blackmore tried four Company soldiers, the supposed ringleaders of the conspiracy, for mutiny by a jury packed with soldiers.[81] Why not try the four soldiers by a court-martial? The answer is probably that the governor was confused over his legal powers. In 1682, the Company had sent a missive telling the governor that in any case involving life or limb, he had to use a jury.[82] Blackmore seemed hesitant to execute them even after the jury had convicted the men, which suggests he was worried either about causing a new insurrection or that he might be tried back home for executing the mutineers.[83]

When the Company leaders in London learned of the attempted mutiny on St. Helena, they obtained from James II a special commission to try the mutineers by martial law.[84] The Crown had been informed of the ringleaders through the information of members of the Company, who had set sail for England shortly after the riots had taken place on the

[80] Stephen A. Royle, *The Company's Island: St. Helena, Company Colonies and the Colonial Endeavor* (London, 2007), 44–126; Philip J. Stern, "Politics and Ideology in the Early East India Company-State: The Case of St. Helena, 1673–1696," *The Journal of Imperial and Commonwealth History* 35.1 (March, 2007): 1–23.

[81] For a description of the trial see BL, IOR G/32/2, f. 588, which not only mentions the word "jury" but also "foreman," two words never used at a court-martial. I thus hesitantly disagree (he has looked at records in St. Helena that I have not examined) with the assessment of the trial made by Royle, *The Company's Island*, 114–19. Further, the mother of one of those condemned, Dorothy Bowyer, petitioned Parliament on 16 May 1689, and did not refer to the proceedings against her son as a court-martial, a claim which would have been very helpful to her case. *CJ*, 10: 135. Many thanks to Philip Stern for helping me with this case.

[82] BL, IOR G/32/1, f. 27.   [83] Royle, *The Company's Island*, 118–19.

[84] The commission is strange not least because there is no record of it in the Crown Office Chancery records at the National Archives (C66), and there was no trace of it there in 1689 either, when the Commons investigated the commission on 25 May, see *CJ*, 10: 151. The Commons obtained a copy of the commission from the "Privy Council Books" although I have not found the commission in TNA, PC 2/71. See *CJ*, 10: 152.

island. James ultimately granted the Company the commission because he had "byn credibly informed yt there has byn formerly a Treasonable Rebellion and insurrection made in our Island of St. Helena."[85] James did not grant the Company powers to execute anyone it deemed guilty of treason. Instead, he specified that only those guilty by "due proof" could be executed. He also exempted all the planters other than the supposed ringleaders from martial law jurisdiction. The fact that the Company sought out a special commission shows the limitations of its martial law powers. Their desire for James' approval also reveals that the Company leaders knew what they were about to do was controversial.

In November 1685, members of the Company returned with the commission and tried and convicted fourteen St. Helena planters. The commissioners hanged five men immediately. These men had all been named by James in the commission as those the Company could potentially execute by martial law.[86] One planter named George Shelton, who according to the aggrieved petitioners was stifled to death in prison, had not been named. Potentially, Shelton had been murdered. The other eight still remained jailed on the island in 1689, in no small measure because the Company could not execute them according to the commission. It did not place the whole island under martial law.

As in the aftermath of Bacon's Rebellion, surviving family members on St. Helena submitted petitions in 1689 that declared the courts-martial to be illegal. These complaints, however, were not heard by the Board of Trade but instead by the sitting parliament. This parliament, further, was no friend to the East India Company. During 1689 and continuing throughout the 1690s, many who supported free trade or an alternative company to operate in the East Indies attacked the privileges of the East India Company. They found a receptive ear among many in parliament who were also concerned about the Company's political autonomy in Asia.[87] The relatives of those executed at martial law in 1685 made good use of this window. Indeed, it is likely that they stumbled upon the best possible political climate for their cause.

The first petition arrived in May. On the sixteenth day of that month, Martha Bolton and Dorothy Bowyer, relatives of men executed on St. Helena in 1685, delivered a petition to parliament. They argued that

---

[85] The commission has been printed in *Extracts from the St. Helena Records* ed. Hudson Ralph Janisch (St. Helena, 1908), 30.
[86] Royle, *The Company's Island*, 118–19. The relatives of the deceased also gave an account of the tribunals. *The Most Deplorable Case of the Poor Distressed Planters in the Island of St. Helena under the cruel oppressions of the East India Company* (London, 1690).
[87] Philip Stern, *The Company State: Corporate Sovereignty and the Early Modern Foundation of the British Empire in India* (Oxford, 2011), 142–64.

the East India Company had murdered their relatives, one at a "pretended court martial," the other at the jury trial in December 1684, and had then illegally seized their property.[88] Bolton prayed that "those concerned in the taking away her said Husband's Life, may be brought to condign Punishment; and to receive Redress for herself and Children."[89] The Commons took the two petitions very seriously and notified the East India Company that it would be investigating the matter further. Many thought this was the beginning of the end for the East India Company.[90]

In the resulting investigation, the Commons condemned the acts of the governor and lieutenant governor, John Blackmore and Captain Holden, and sought a further investigation into those who instructed them to use martial law. Beginning on 25 May, the Commons investigated the powers of martial law granted through the Company's charter as well as its commission from James to use martial law. The Commons examined both a narrative of the supposed uprising and a journal of the court-martial proceedings. It also called in witnesses and interrogated both Blackmore and Holden. Based on the investigation, parliament decided to exempt all East India Company men from pardon who had either sought out the martial law commission or who had taken part in writing instructions for how it should be executed.[91]

The controversy had not ended. On 6 November of that year, the daughters of the late John Colson, one of the men executed at martial law, delivered a petition to the House of Commons. The petition called upon specific legal language taken from Sir Edward Coke. The daughters opened the petition by stating that they

Humbly presented to the Charitable Consideration of the Honourable, the knights and citizens and burgesses in Parliament assembled By Elizabeth, Martha, Grace, and Sarah, the mournful daughters of John Colson, who was one of those that were Murthered by a Pretended COURT-MARSHAL at that place.[92]

The last line of the opening harkened to Coke's *Institutes*, where the oracle of the common law had argued that any execution by a court-martial while the Courts of Westminster were open was murder.[93] The Commons agreed. They declared that "John Colson and the rest of the Persons who

---

[88] *CJ*, 10: 135.   [89] *Ibid.*
[90] Henry Horwitz, "The East India Trade, the Politicians, and the Constitution, 1689–1702," *JBS* 17 (1978): 2.
[91] *CJ*, 10: 151, 155, 167–68.
[92] *The Most Deplorable Case of the Poor Distressed Planters in the Island of St. Helena under the cruel oppressions of the East India Company*, 1.
[93] Sir Edward Coke, *The Third Part of the Institutes of the Laws of England* (London, 1644), 52.

were executed ... were put to Death contrary to law, and murdered."[94] The Commons made a request to the Crown that Blackmore and Holden be sent over in custody to answer the charge of murder. They also formed a committee of inquiry to examine who obtained the commission in the first place and who wrote the instructions for its execution.[95]

Parliament's decision made the Company and its lawyers incredulous. William Atwood, a reasonably famous lawyer known for his imperial apologetics, had initially been employed by the Company to argue its case in front of the committee. Later, he produced an apology for its actions.[96] Atwood claimed that the Petition of Right did not apply to St. Helena because the Petition of Right was only concerned with England and therefore did not ban martial law in cases of treason committed overseas. He crafted his argument around the Crown's ability to grant powers of martial law in its commissions to delegated authorities. After all, the Company had sought and received a commission from James II to execute martial law.[97] Further, hostile juries on St. Helena, according to Atwood, might refuse to convict defendants. This was a standard justification for martial law.[98] Atwood's protests, however, fell on deaf ears from those sitting in parliament. The committee to examine the East India Company's actions issued its report in November 1690. They declared that those who had sought the commission from James II had indeed committed "murther."[99]

The Crown and its council probably thought differently in all likelihood because the East India Company gave generously to William III.[100] While Atwood's arguments were unconvincing to those sitting in parliament, they were in all likelihood more convincing to William III and his ministers who cared about preserving the Crown's prerogative powers. We do not know exactly what the Crown thought of Holden or Blackmore's actions.[101] Other Company officials were not tried for murder. The Crown did not re-issue any special commissions authorizing martial law for specific crimes. But in its new charter to the East

---

[94] *CJ*, 10: 280.   [95] *Ibid.*

[96] William Atwood, *An Apology for the East-India Company with an account of some large prerogatives of the Crown of England* (London, 1690). For Atwood see Charles Ludington, "From Ancient Constitution to British Empire: William Atwood and the Imperial Crown of England" in *Political Thought in Seventeenth Century Ireland* ed. Jane Ohlmeyer (Cambridge, 2000), 244–71.

[97] Atwood, *An Apology*, 25.   [98] *Ibid.*, 26.   [99] BL, Add. Ms. 22,185, f. 29.

[100] William A. Pettigrew and George William Van Cleve, "Parting Companies: The Glorious Revolution, Company Power, and Imperial Mercantilism," *HJ* 57:3 (September, 2014): 631. Also see James Bohun, "Protecting Prerogative: William III and the East India Trade Debate, 1689–1698," *Past Imperfect* 2 (1993): 63–86.

[101] Royle, *The Company's Island*, 119. Blackmore died from a fall in London. It is unclear what Holden did with his life after 1690.

India Company in 1693, the Company received all the powers it had possessed previously. Further, the Company declared to its residents on St. Helena in 1711 that it still could use martial law if it deemed it necessary.[102]

Nevertheless, the Company had learned a painful lesson from its experience with parliament. In 1693, another mutiny broke out in St. Helena. Company officials refrained from using martial law and instead opted for jury courts.[103] In choosing this more conservative option, the governor of St. Helena adopted a typical stance of most governors in the empire during the late seventeenth century: martial law was often too dangerous and too controversial to use. Their planters did not like the jurisdiction. Moreover, they could come back to England and appeal the governor's decision. The only way governors could get away with extensively using martial law was if the law of martial law itself could be made to justify its use. The governors of Jamaica did just that.

Martial law and Jamaica

Jamaican governors closed their courts frequently during the Restoration. In these times, they used martial law traditionally. They disciplined soldiers and "sailors" who broke the commands issued in articles of war that diverged little from English practice. But they also used the closing of the courts for other purposes. Governors made public rights claims on property – usually in the form of mandatory labor from both planters and their slaves. Jamaicans got away with using martial law so frequently because they had adapted English legal discourses – most notably the reversal of the conviction of Thomas of Lancaster – to expand martial law jurisdiction. They did so, of course, by closing the courts down. But they did not need to close them down due to war. Instead, they closed them down based on public or "eminent" danger, a tract of time that was activated by rumors and threats of conspiracies and invasions, as well as actual rebellions and invasions. In order to understand why this legal innovation happened, we need to first briefly examine the origins of English rule on the island.

Jamaica was a consolation prize. The English invasion force that entered the Caribbean in 1655 was under orders from Lord Protector Cromwell to capture Hispaniola as a first step in a planned conquest of all

---

[102] *Charters of the East India Company*, 143; Philip Gosse, *St Helena, 1501–1938* (London, 1938), 396–7.
[103] Royle, *The Company's Island*, 122–25.

Spanish New World possessions, dubbed the "Western Design."[104] After failing miserably in their attempts to capture Hispaniola, the expedition, led by General Robert Venables, fell upon the island of Jamaica – a large but sparsely inhabited Spanish possession in the south Caribbean. The expedition seized the capital quickly and sent word to Cromwell of their "victory." The Lord Protector was inconsolable. The mighty "Western Design" was a catastrophe.

In order to salvage something from the wreckage, the high command on Jamaica attempted to build a plantation in and around Cagway, the southern port that would be renamed Port Royal in 1660. Plans were afoot to persuade mercantile interest in the new colony and to attract settlers from England and Scotland as well as other English Caribbean settlements. The remaining soldiers who had survived the campaign and the "starving time" on the island were encouraged to become planters.[105] The nature of the government of Jamaica, however, remained martial. The council of war headed by the governor ruled the island. Courts-martial disciplined the soldiers. Soldiers in turn built the fortifications around the garrison and the town. In November 1655, for example, Edward Doyley proclaimed that a portion of the regiment "doe attend to work make capp and finnish the palisades about the garrison of the towne"[106] They were to receive a double allowance for their efforts. The governor's court also adjudicated mercantile cases, which involved Jamaica's growing contraband trade. By 1660, many feared that the governor was going to rule solely by martial law. In commenting upon Jamaica in 1657, Cromwell's colonial committee noted that the plantation "looks only like a great garrison, and rather an Army than a Colony."[107] The Restored monarch, Charles II, and his council in 1661 agreed with this assessment and sought to transform Jamaica into a civil polity.

By the Restoration, the discretionary powers of the governors became constrained by Crown order. In 1661, Charles II sent Sir Edward Doyley a commission that ordered him to create an elected council who with the governor would create civilian courts that could administer justice based

---

[104] The classic account of the invasion of Jamaica is S.A.G. Taylor, *The Western Design: An Account of Cromwell's Expedition to the Caribbean* (Kingston, 1965). Also see Timothy Venning, *Cromwellian Foreign Policy* (New York, 1995), 71–90; Webb, *Governors General*, 158–67.

[105] One of the proclamations from the period, for example, is that those who ate the horses would suffer the pains of death. "Col. Edward Doyley's Journal," BL, Add. Ms. 12,423, f. 7v–8.

[106] "Doyley's Journal," BL, Add. Ms. 12,423, f. 2.

[107] Quoted in Webb, *Governors-General*, 200.

upon a non-repugnancy principle.[108] By the time of his successor, Lord Windsor, Jamaican planters demanded to live under all the laws of England.[109] Under this new government, as we have seen, Jamaican governors had martial law powers similar to the ones the Crown possessed in England.

The problem, however, was that Jamaica was more vulnerable to attack than the Crown's other plantations. The privateering enterprises of the Jamaicans earned them enemies. Further, England was still officially at war with Spain, and during the Restoration would be at war with both the Dutch and the French. The Spanish, French, and Dutch were all nearby and could retaliate with relative ease against their tormentors. Many would have known well the lesson of Providence Island, the English Caribbean plantation that had been destroyed by the Spanish in 1641, in part due to its weak defenses.[110] Like that failed enterprise, Jamaica had weak fortifications. And like Providence Island, Jamaicans had little hope of aid from other English plantations or from the English navy. Further, maroon communities on Jamaica also posed threats to the newly founded polity. Drastic measures were necessary for the preservation of Jamaica.

One of the first differences between Jamaica and other plantations was that the Jamaican Assembly granted extensive martial law powers for the governance of the militia. In November 1664, it passed the first militia act.[111] The act stipulated that due to the island being in the "midst of a Subtile rich & potent Enemy" it needed to have a well-trained militia.[112] When the men were "up in arms," all of the articles of war could be applied to them, including those that prescribed capital punishment. When they were not in arms, commanders could only imprison or fine their soldiers according to the ordinances of war.[113] This act went into effect the following year when the "Varmahaly Negroes" began to "rob and kill." "Put in a posture of Warr," the militia regiments were to be governed by a "court marshall."[114] Articles of war were then issued. This perhaps was a violation of the Jamaican commission. But the Jamaicans

---

[108] TNA, CO 1/15, f. 20. The instructions also told Doyley to construct an Admiralty court. *Ibid.*, f. 22.

[109] Lord Windsor had proclaimed that the laws of England were in force on the island, a proclamation the Crown and Lords of Trade later regretted. A.M. Whitson, *The Constitutional Development of Jamaica, 1660 to 1729* (Manchester, 1929), 18.

[110] Karen Ordahl Kupperman, *Providence Island, 1630–1641: The Other Puritan Colony* (Cambridge, 1993), 188–90.

[111] TNA, CO 139/1, fos. 49–51.   [112] *Ibid.*, 49.

[113] *Ibid.*, 50. This would involve punishments like "riding the horse." TNA, CO 140/1, 184.

[114] TNA, CO 140/1, 135.

could have argued that the courts were impeded during the rebellion at least for the militia in the field. The militia act was re-passed by the Assembly in 1671 after some debate over whether the Act of 1664 was still in operation.

The use of martial law was common enough that by 1667 the island had a permanent judge advocate general.[115] Jamaican governors used this martial law power to discipline their soldiers on several occasions in their fights against maroon communities and during slave rebellions. In 1676 and in 1685, for example, articles of war were issued for the island's militia during internal wars. The process for 1676 can be delineated. That year, the governor Lord Vaughan ordered that the colonels of each regiment "publish the Articles of war."[116] Each regiment had a court-martial that would supervise punishment for breaches of these articles, and even planters not participating in the militia could be fined by the court for not providing enough men.[117] This was an aggressive use of martial law, but one that was not that divergent from the other examples that we have seen. Clearly, the colony on Nevis attempted a similar law that provided a strong militia in 1701 which was denied by England's attorney general. The Jamaicans, however, got away with not requiring the courts to be closed during these internal wars. The supervision over martial law was inconsistent.

Jamaican governors also used martial law to discipline sailors in their "navy." By the time of Sir Thomas Modyford, who became governor in 1664, governors were also vice-admirals.[118] Later Jamaican governors were explicitly given martial law powers over their sailors.[119] During times when they wanted to raid the Spanish, governors created a navy, effectively privateers, and nominated an admiral to lead it. In 1670, for example, Modyford nominated the infamous buccaneer Sir Henry Morgan to lead the Jamaican "navy" in its raid on Panama. Morgan obtained powers to "execute martial law, according to the Articles of Warre already made, or which hereafter shall be made by his Excy the same having been first published to them."[120] Martial law was just as useful for disciplining pirates as it was for disciplining soldiers or sailors. But both for its militia and for its navy, martial law was so far only used for disciplinary purposes.

---

[115] For the advocate see TNA, CO 140/1, 155.   [116] TNA, CO 140/3, 453–70.

[117] This was ordered by Hender Molesworth, the governor in 1685, TNA, CO 140/4, f. 90v. But the practice predates Molesworth's reign as planters complained about excessive fines in 1679. TNA, CO 1/43, f. 234v.

[118] TNA, CO 138/1, 25.

[119] See for example the commission to the Earl of Albemarle in 1686, TNA CO 138/5, 235.

[120] TNA, CO 138/1, 48.

Closing courts and building forts

In 1667, Thomas Modyford ordered the courts closed. French privateers had been attacking the Jamaicans. As he reported to his patron, the Duke of Albemarle, he and his council "vnanimously concluded necessary to put this iland in a military posture of defence & to silence all our comon law courts."[121] He declared martial law and published ordinances of war, 44 forty-four articles long, to govern Jamaica. All of the ordinances were unexceptional except the first, which declared that the common law courts be,

after this next sitting adjourn'd without D[el]ay & not to be reasum'd without new & express orders from his Excellency and that in lieu thereof Courts Marshal shall be held within the Precincts of every Regiment and a General Court Marshal.[122]

Part of what Modyford was doing was using martial law to govern his militia as had been done in August 1665. But it seems like the civilian courts had remained open then. Why close the courts in 1667? Modyford claimed it was to avoid defeat by a foreign design.[123] A more plausible reason was to prevent the courts from jailing his militiamen for debts. Most importantly, with the courts closed, he could force planters and their slaves to help work on the fortifications. In other words, he was using martial law to make public rights claims. In order to better understand why this should be so, we need to more closely examine controversies relating to property seizure in early Stuart England.

In England, some accepted the idea that the monarch through his or her prerogative could take anything that was necessary for the preservation of the commonwealth. In the early seventeenth century, this power was referred to as the Crown's absolute prerogative. In peacetime, the Crown executed the laws of the realm, dubbed its "ordinary" prerogative. However, in times of emergency or distress, the Crown, as Paul Halliday has phrased it, could work miracles upon the law.[124] What does this have to do with the closing of the courts? In order to better understand the connection, we need to examine how jurists attempted to bind the absolute prerogative through the reversal of the conviction of Thomas of Lancaster.

[121] Sir Thomas Modyford to the Duke of Albemarle, 14 January 1667, TNA, CO 1/21, no. 5.
[122] "Lawes Military for the Island of Jamaica published by his Excellency Sir Thomas Modyford," BL, Add. Ms. 12,429, f. 72v. Another copy of the ordinance can be found in TNA, CO 140/1, f. 136.
[123] Modyford to Albemarle, 14 January 1667, TNA, CO 1/21, no. 5.
[124] Ken MacMillan, *Sovereignty and Possession in the English New World: the Legal Foundations of Empire, 1576–1640* (Cambridge, 2006), 17–48; Paul D. Halliday, *Habeas Corpus: From England to Empire* (Cambridge, MA, 2010), 68–9.

The first attempt was in 1610 in debates over the legality of impositions. Impositions referred to the extra-parliamentary raising of customs
duties on certain overseas imports.[125] In 1606, the Levantine merchant
John Bate failed or refused to pay the levy and had his case heard before
the chief justices of the realm sitting in Exchequer chamber. The case was
decided for the Crown but did little to assuage the anger of those who felt
that the king's policies were arbitrary. In the summer of 1610, after James
had continued the policy of impositions, the House of Commons debated
their legality. Those in favor of the Crown's position argued that his
decision to raise the customs revenue fell under his absolute prerogative,
which was mysterious and beyond the powers of lawyers to understand.
In response, a young lawyer by the name of Heneage Finch declared that
while the monarch had prerogative powers, the common law understood
and bounded those powers, and lawyers through their professional reason
could understand them.

This comprehension included what constituted wartime. For Finch,
war "at home" or internal to the realm was when the "judges cannot sit at
Westminster."[126] This was a clear allusion to the reversal of the treason
conviction of Thomas of Lancaster. When this state of shuttered courts
existed, the common lawyers had no cognizance over property, and those
things which took place in times of war did not alter previous agreements.
Through a reading of Bracton, Finch argued that a "descent into a state of
war" did not take away a presentment or any other agreement that was
made during a state of peace. Nor did any action taken during war alter
agreements made in peace. His example came from an *elegit* case, which
involved debt, where a tenant was not exempted because he was disturbed
by war.[127] In wartime, the courts slept.

This line of argumentation arose again during the Ship Money disputes. Ship money referred to a power the Crown had to command
coastal towns to provide a ship so that the Crown could maintain its
rights over the sea against its enemies.[128] Charles I claimed he was
using the levy in 1634 to combat pirates, which constituted a "time of

---

[125] G.D.H. Hall, "Impositions and the Courts, 1554–1606," *Law Quarterly Review* 69
(1953): 203–4.

[126] *Proceedings in Parliament, 1610* ed. Elizabeth Read Foster 2 vols. (New Haven, 1966),
2: 236.

[127] Here, Finch cited a case from the reign of Edward II which can be found in
Anthony Fitzherbert, *Graunde Abridgement* (London, 1516), "Execution" no. 246.

[128] Christopher W. Brooks, Law, *Politics and Society in Early Modern England* (Cambridge,
2008), 201–08. The most comprehensive discussion of Ship Money can be found in
Nicola Penelope Perkins, "The Judiciary and the Defence of Property in the Law Courts
during the Personal Rule of Charles I," (unpublished PhD diss. University of Cambridge,
1997).

war" and of danger to the realm. He also had concerns about maintaining control over the English Channel. The Crown levy was controversial because it required funds for the maintenance of ships, not *actual* ships. Further, it became much more pervasive than earlier medieval ship money practices, as all counties of England eventually had to pay the levy, and not just coastal towns. The levy, especially by 1637, seemed to be something more akin to a permanent tax, as it had been ordered by the Crown each year since 1634.[129] Its controversial nature led Charles to ask his judges for an opinion on the levy's legality in February 1637. They concluded that it was legal. However, continued unhappiness over Ship Money by August 1637 finally forced Charles to allow the judges to hear a case over its legality. That month a writ was issued against John Hampden, a man who had refused to pay the levy. The fundamental issue in the case was the Crown's claim to the property of its subjects when it deemed that property necessary for the safety of the kingdom. The argument laid forth by the Crown's lawyers was successful. The Ship Money levy was ruled legal and the Crown continued to employ it through 1640.[130]

However, the losing argument of Oliver St. John remained influential and is important for our understanding of what took place on Jamaica. St. John did not question the Crown's right to protect its subjects.[131] But he did claim lawyers could discern which channels it needed to go through depending on the tract of time the kingdom was experiencing. There were two tracts of time for St. John: imminent danger and war.[132] For the first, which involved apprehension of a future threat to the realm (like a plot or a conspiracy), the king had to go through parliament. For the second, which involved a present threat to the realm, he could take actions alone. Let us handle the second first.

For all the lawyers in the case, property was a human creation that was protected by the courts. This attitude was generally true of early modern jurists.[133] For St. John, in emergencies, "all things are again resolved into the common principles of nature."[134] Citing the reversal of the conviction of Thomas of Lancaster, St. John declared that wartime—a temporal state

---

[129] The arguments for why the levy was controversial are clearly elucidated by Henrik Langelüddecke "I finde all men & my officers all soe unwilling:" the Collection of Ship Money, 1635–40," *JBS* 46 (July, 2007): 509.

[130] Ship Money was eventually overturned by the Long Parliament.   [131] *ST*, 3: col. 859.

[132] For the difference between apprehended danger and real danger, see Perkins, "The Judiciary and the Defence of Property," 24–8.

[133] Brooks, *Law, Politics and Society*, 423–24.

[134] *ST*, 3: col. 904. Nicola Perkins has rightfully warned against using the printed reports of the trial as opposed to the abundant manuscript literature. However, her reading of St. John is similar to my own. The real problems with the printed sources relate to the judgement given by Sir George Croke. Perkins, "The Judiciary and the Defence of Property in the Law Courts during the Personal Rule of Charles I," introduction.

where property once again became common – existed only when the Courts of Westminster were closed or when the king raised his standard on a battlefield. During these periods, the Crown could appropriate the property of its subjects, burn the property down, or do anything else necessary for the survival of the kingdom. In these times, the Crown, or even subjects could commandeer property. Along with the same justifications made by Heneage Finch, St. John also connected this boundary with the Roman idea of *iustitium* which was declared during a *tumultus*.[135] In these periods, Roman magistrates could seize what was necessary for the preservation of the commonwealth.

Second, St. John admitted there were times of "imminent danger." While jurists disagreed on its exact definition, imminent danger generally had a lower bar for justifying extraordinary action. Crown lawyers and St. John agreed on this. Danger could be a rumor or a plot to undermine the government. It could be information of foreign plans of invasion or of preparations of invasion. For Sir John Bankes, the Crown's attorney general in 1637, the king hardly needed "Hannibal *ad portas*" in order to take extraordinary action. For St. John, however, danger meant that only the king in parliament could take extraordinary action, not the king and his council or the king on his own. It was in parliament during times of imminent danger that the king could take pre-emptive actions in order to preserve his subjects from ruin.

The Long Parliament adopted and deployed the tract of time known as imminent danger frequently to justify the extraordinary acts it made beginning in 1641. But let us explore only one example that was sufficiently similar to the problems the Jamaicans faced over twenty years later. In November 1642, due to threats from royalist armies, Exeter was in danger of falling. The Commons authorized the mayor to melt the bells of the city and to pick men from his militia to serve with the trained bands for the city's defense.[136] The Commons also demanded that all within the city give up whatever property that was necessary for the defense of the city. This was because "in Times of common Danger ... when the Publick Peace and the Safety of each particular Man is equally threatened and concerned" and because "the Benefit of Preservation and Safety ... doth redound and come unto all" every inhabitant of the city of Exeter needed to provide for the upkeep of the defenses.[137] Because of the time of imminent danger, private property protections came to an end, and the parliamentary commanders could seize what they would, tax who they would, and imprison those who resisted. These orders by parliament had nothing to do with martial law. The Courts of Westminster, further,

---

[135] *ST*, 3: cols. 904–05.   [136] *CJ*, 2: 863–64.   [137] *Ibid.*, 863–64.

remained open. The overriding of common law property protections was based on the power of parliament, not on martial law jurisdiction.

Most colonies similarly authorized emergency measures through their legislatures. These produced statutes that mandated material, labor, and other services from colonists for the protection of the colony during times of war and distress. The House of Burgesses in Virginia, for example, passed a statute in February 1644 that created a council of war for the purpose of administering the colony's military efforts against Native Americans.[138] It ordered that the three counties charged with fighting, Isle of Wight county and Upper and Lower Norfolk counties, form a council of war. This body had powers to "leavie such and soe manie men, arms, ammunition and other necessaries as emergencie of occassions shall require."[139] Ultimately the governor, his council, and the House of Burgesses had jurisdiction over the council of war. Colonists could petition these bodies if they thought that the council of war had abused its powers. In Massachusetts, the General Court similarly issued orders, including mandating labor through the impressment of men and material for the colony's war efforts. In 1675, for example, during King Philip's War, the General Court made orders for the impressment of men throughout the summer.[140] Legislatures could take emergency actions.

The problem for Modyford and for other Jamaican governors was that Jamaica's assembly was riven with faction.[141] Little could get done at all, let alone quickly. Modyford by 1667 certainly had no desire to resort to it. The Assembly had from its outset desired to control taxation and many within the body opposed privateering and wanted peace and trade with nearby Spanish settlements. A faction of plantation owners emerged within the assembly, led by William Beeston, Samuel Long, and Sir Thomas Lynch, that supported this more peaceful stance. This group fought vigorously with Modyford, who had since his arrival in 1664 been promoting war and privateering. The Assembly thus only met once during Modyford's tenure in the winter of 1664/1665, when the governor attempted to pack the body with his own supporters. He unsuccessfully attempted to try Samuel Long for treason.[142] He also removed Lynch from his position as chief justice and provost marshal. The Assembly might block any emergency measure. Further, law courts controlled by his rivals might also get in the way.

---

[138] Hening, *Statutes*, 1: 292.   [139] *Ibid.*   [140] Zelner, *A Rabble in Arms*, 40–43.
[141] It was first formed in 1663. Whitson, *The Constitutional Development of Jamaica*, 22.
[142] Nuala Zahedieh, "Modyford, Sir Thomas," in *ODNB*; Whitson, *The Constitutional Development of Jamaica*, 32–7.

Fortunately, for Modyford, he did not necessarily need to go through his assembly. Modyford's commission gave him powers to build fortifications and promised funds for that purpose.[143] The governor also possessed powers to destroy. The Crown allowed Modyford and his council to "disfurnish, sleight, raze or otherwise howsoever to alter as shall be most for the safety and good of our said island."[144] With these powers, Modyford was supposed to protect the island. Further, it provided £500 worth of tools for the building of forts.[145] However, when it came to how Modyford was to coerce the planters to labor on forts, the governor's accompanying instructions simply stated that the forts would be built at public charge.[146] This command was of little help help to the governor. Forcing all the planters on the island to give up their time, capital, or property required legal authority. The closing of the courts and the declaration of martial law generated a time that allowed him to make such commands. No members of the assembly could challenge him. No members of the judiciary could challenge him. No courts were open to protect private property. In wartime, all became available for the public good.

Once made, Modyford's successors, even those who had opposed him during his regime, found Jamaican martial law useful. We can track how often his successors used this tactic through a report made by the assembly of Jamaica to the governor-general, the Earl of Carlisle, in 1679. The assembly was opposing the Crown's and thus Carlisle's attempts at centralized reform.[147] But for our purposes what is intriguing about the document is that it included a history of martial law on the island from the moment Jamaica became a civil polity in 1661. Surprisingly enough, the planters were not complaining about its usage. Rather, they claimed that their endurance of martial law showed their loyalty and willingness to sacrifice their own private gain for the good of the English Crown. They recalled how in the winter of 1667 under Modyford, the "whole island was putt vnder law Martiall."[148] The courts were closed until May, when

---

[143] TNA, CO 138/1, 25.   [144] *Ibid.*

[145] *Ibid.*, 29. At least according to Henry Morgan, in 1678, the Crown had not kept up with granting annual payments for the upkeep of the forts. Morgan to Henry Coventry, 9 Apr. 1678, Longleat House, Coventry Ms. 75, f. 242v.

[146] TNA, CO 138/1, 31.

[147] TNA, CO 1/43 no. 157 II. For the constitutional conflict between the Jamaican Assembly and the Crown see Whitson, *The Constitutional Development of Jamaia,* 70–109; Webb, *The Governors-General,* 151–326.

[148] TNA, CO 1/43 no. 157 II; the planters actually say 1665 and 1666; it is possible that the courts were closed in 1665 but I have found no evidence the courts were closed; by 1666 they were referring to their own system of dating where the new year did not begin until 25 March.

Modyford, due to complaints from planters, reopened them.[149] Sir Thomas Lynch in 1673 declared martial law again. Sir Henry Morgan, the lieutenant governor and famed pirate, declared martial law in 1678. Finally, under the Earl of Carlisle, martial law was the only law of the island for three months in 1679. The closure of the courts had become normative.

Modyford and his successors used martial law to commandeer labor, both slave and free, to build and repair fortifications. As the planters noted in their petition to Carlisle in 1679, under martial law, they had used "our Servants, Negroes Horses even all that we have to your Majestys service."[150] Under martial law, Jamaican planters had enclosed Fort Charles, which was near Port Royal, and had made breast works around Port Royal under Modyford. Under Lynch, they had built Fort James, another citadel near Port Royal, and had thrown up defenses around the city's harbor. In 1678, they had built Fort Rupert and Fort Carlisle, both again to protect Port Royal, and made new lines at Fort James. In 1679, yet another fort was built under martial law, this time named after the infamous privateer and lieutenant-governor Sir Henry Morgan.[151] William Beeston described the imposition of martial law in 1678, upon pretext of a war with France:

Accordingly the Council of Warr met where it was concluded that on the 10th Inst., the Civil and Common Law should be lay'd by & the Articles of Warr to be in force 20 days & the Island in a Military Posture & that in that time all possible Industry should be us'd to fortifie all parts of the Island for the doing of which every tenth Negroe in the Country & every fourth Negroe at Port Royal were to Labr on the publick works & accordingly the 10th day it was put in Execution & every one apply'd themselves heartily to their business.[152]

In a letter to Henry Coventry, a secretary of state, Morgan, acting as lieutenant governor in 1678 upon the departure of Lord Vaughan, explained how this process worked. Because of the threats to the island, Morgan had closed the courts. Regimental courts-martial convened throughout the island where Morgan's militia officers sent out orders for the repair of fortifications. Morgan had apparently issued earlier orders as well for the repair of forts. According to Morgan, his plans for the upkeep of the fortifications were met with approval so the planters

---

[149] On 27 March 1667 Modyford declared that the courts would reopen in May of that year. TNA, CO 140/1, fos. 166–7.

[150] BL, Add. Ms. 12,429, f. 94v. This was another petition by the planters protesting their loyalty and commitment to Jamaica to the governor.

[151] *Ibid*; for an overview of the fortifications of Port Royal, see Michael Pawson and David Buisseret, *Port Royal, Jamaica* (Oxford, 1975), 37–42.

[152] Journal of William Beeston, BL, Add. Ms. 12,430, f. 35v.

agreed "[t]hat the labour of the Negroes in all Places might be continued vntill the tenth of June next, and in the meanetime the fortification and security of the island to bee only regarded."[153] "Extraordinary" things were done in that June, when Morgan could command the slaves to labor on public works.

Not everyone, as Morgan tendentiously claimed, was happy with these periods of martial law. Those who were planting were often struggling in the first decades and deeply resented the periods of martial law. John Style, a self-styled "poor planter," wrote to Sir William Morrice, one of Charles II's secretaries of state in January 1669, to report the "tyranny" of the governors of Jamaica.[154] Style described how Modyford had forced planters "to come down 20 and 30 miles to keep guard, not one Christian must be left at home." Style blamed Modyford's actions on the old soldiers, presumably he meant former Cromwellian officers now living in Port Royal, who used martial law to "ruin" their neighbors by not allowing them to work on their own crops.

The use of martial law was probably not a conspiracy to ruin the planters, but it was a mechanism to commandeer labor. In 1679, the Earl of Carlisle recorded in a letter to the Privy Council in July that the council had decided to declare martial law for thirty days: "I being very glad of this opportunity to carry on soe necessary a work, which otherwise would have gone on very slowly and now is a great satisfaction and encouragement to their resolution to defend the place."[155] After the thirty days had expired, the council decided to extend martial law, which relieved Carlisle because "without continuing it some days longer the new Battery would not have bin finished."[156] Wartime was becoming a convenient way to finish public works projects.

While some like Style opposed martial law, the elite in Jamaica generally assented to the emergency measures. Indeed, during the late 1670s and early 1680s, the Jamaican assembly vigorously defended Jamaican autonomy from any attempts by the Lords of Trade to constrain them.[157] Beginning in 1676, the Lords of Trade had decided to reign in the Assembly's legislative powers and attempted to pass a bill through the Assembly that mirrored Poynings' Law in Ireland. Poynings' Law allowed the English Privy Council to inhibit any original bills from being produced by the Irish legislature.[158] Everyone outside the Board

---

[153] Sir Henry Morgan to Coventry, 30 April 1678, Longleat House, Coventry Ms. 75, f. 247.
[154] John Style to Sir William Morrice 14 January 1669 TNA, CO 1/24 no. 8.
[155] TNA, CO 138/3, f. 171.   [156] *Ibid.*, f. 172.   [157] TNA, CO 1/43, f. 234v.
[158] For Poynings' Law in Ireland, see James Kelly, *Poynings' Law and the Making of Law in Ireland, 1660–1800* (Dublin, 2007).

of Trade and Plantations, including the current and former governors of Jamaica, thought the plan ill-advised because Jamaica was too far away from England. In this period of crisis, the Privy Council, with the help of the Earl of Carlisle and Sir Thomas Lynch, who was now in England, attempted to pass a new militia bill for the island. The Assembly refused to pass it. Initially their intransigence was part of a strategy to avoid the precedent of the Lords of Trade making bills for Jamaica. But after the Lords of Trade abandoned its attempt to enforce Poynings' Law in 1680, the Assembly still debated the passage of the bill. One of the complaints was that courts-martial possessed too much discretion in how much they could fine those who presumably did not provide labor or report for militia duty. But the planters did not oppose on principle the closing of the courts.

Indeed, the "Act for settling the Militia," which was accepted by the Crown and Council and printed in 1684, reflects the practices begun in the previous decades.[159] The law stated that when the courts were closed, martial law was in force. The governor with his council could shut the courts down and declare martial law "upon every apprehension and appearance of any Publique danger or Invasion."[160] Under this jurisdiction the governor and his council of war could "[c]ommand the Persons of any of His Majesties Leige People, as also their Negroes, Horses, Cattle, for all such services as may be for the Publick Defence."[161] The commander could also seize timber, "pull down houses . . . command ships and Boats" and anything else he or the council of war thought necessary for the preservation of the island.

The rationale for the Jamaican planters to accept these provisions likewise rests in the act. The common law courts of Jamaica did not recognize the seizures. Thus, when "the Common law revives" all those materials taken from the subjects on the island had to be returned to them as before. Further, if any property had been damaged in the fighting, the governor and his council had to recompense the planters for their losses.[162] Island residents could expect to receive "reasonably valued" compensation for the damages to their property, what or whichever that was, either out of the public revenue or by act of assembly. Property was still protected even if for a time the governor had absolute power over it.

---

[159] The act was passed by the Jamaica Assembly in 1681 under Sir Henry Morgan. But the Lords of Trade did not approve of it until the spring of 1684 after Sir Thomas Lynch had successfully passed a new revenue bill more amenable to the Lords of Trade through the Jamaican legislature. It is printed as *The Laws of Jamaica* (London, 1684), 64–72.

[160] *Ibid.*, 67.   [161] *Ibid.*, 68.

[162] Thanks to Professor Lee Wilson Ghowanlu for pointing this out to me. *Laws of Jamaica*, 68–69.

The records of these compensations survive. While most of the declared accounts for English colonies do not survive for the seventeenth century, some of those for Jamaica do. They reveal that planters received compensation for their efforts during times of emergency. Let us begin with the most detailed description of the costs of a Jamaican fort: that of Fort Charles.[163] This came from the reports of Sir Charles Littleton, who acted as governor when Lord Windsor had left the island. In these reports of the building of the fort, which was *not* under martial law, Littleton claimed expenses for the wages of "negroes that wrought at the fort." Presumably, the wages were given to the owners of these slaves. Even the "pottatoes" fed to the slaves were listed in the account of the fort. After the forts began to be built in times of martial law, little changed. While Sir Thomas Modyford's accounts provide too few details to be of any use, those of Sir Thomas Lynch make similar expense claims as those of Littleton.[164] Lynch listed the "wages of labourers & negroes" who helped repair forts during his tenure. Much more interestingly, Lynch listed the accounts for one Captain Reginald Wilson, entitled "for Moneys by him disbursed for service done and Goods taken up in the tyme of an Alarum the year 1673."[165] Captain Wilson was in charge of Jamaica's Admiralty Court. So it is likely that he took the funds from prizes seized at admiralty and reimbursed planters from the Crown portion for labor and other property seizures taken when the courts were closed in 1673. Jamaican martial law required labor, but property losses were compensated.

It was definitely not convict labor. This had been the strategy deployed by the governors of Tangier. In that city, the governors often punished soldiers who had transgressed the articles of war by forcing them to work in the "king's works," which often meant helping build or repair the fortifications around the city.[166] They did so without pay and had to return to jail after their labors had ended for the period mandated by the court. As we have seen, on rare occasions, the court-martial indefinitely enslaved the convict and forced him to work only on public works until the governor granted him his liberty.[167] The Jamaicans did not follow this example. They were

---

[163] TNA, AO 1/1274/250.
[164] Modyford's declared accounts are TNA, AO 1/1274/252. Lynch's are TNA, AO 1/1274/253.
[165] TNA, AO 1/1274/253.
[166] BL, Sloane Ms. 1957, fos. 27–9, 42, 57–8, 71; BL, Sloane Ms. 1959, fos. 48, 107; BL, Sloane Ms. 1960, fos. 26–8, 30, 35.
[167] BL, Sloane Ms. 1960, fos. 25–6.

not using convict labor to build forts. Instead, courts ordered planters and their slaves to work only on fortifications during wartime. Failure to heed such commands resulted in a fine.

In granting powers to proclaim martial law, the planters of Jamaica maintained expectations that those powers were nevertheless delimited. The constraints – both for when martial law could be declared and how the governor could use it – remained and the obligations of the governor to follow the rules and procedures of martial law had not been lifted. For example, when Sir Henry Morgan declared martial law in the spring of 1678, the first action he took was to issue the ordinances of war. After his declaration, Morgan wrote into his order book the oaths that those sitting as judges had to take before sitting on a court-martial. Each had to swear to "promise before God vpon his Gospell that I both will and shall judge uprightly according to ye Laws of God, our Nacon and these Laws of Warre."[168] The judge could not take bribes nor decide in anger; he was bound to see justice done. Their discretion was extensive but not unlimited.

The closing of the courts meant the vacation of all other forms of law. However, even in this theoretically legal vacancy, normativity guided action. Modyford in 1667 had issued the ordinances of war and had closed the court down with the first article. Sir Thomas Lynch and Sir Henry Morgan had done likewise. By the 1680s, the governor's ability to close the courts during times of distress became enshrined in statute.[169] In 1667, it was unclear that Jamaican militia officers could appropriate or destroy property. In 1671, Lynch through proclamation clarified that they could take such measures. By the 1680s, the Militia Act authorized these actions.[170] By the late 1660s, Modyford ordered slaves and other workers to build forts when the courts were closed. Later governors turned this innovation into a custom, making the work expected. By the 1680s, this activity was authorized by statute.[171] Further, planters could expect compensation for the destruction of their property. Reaction to crisis generated law which became customary and which eventually generated a statute, normalizing and regulating activities to some extent in even the most chaotic of circumstances. All-encompassing martial law was not simply unlimited power. Jamaicans through a creative reading of their martial law commissions

---

[168] TNA, CO 140/3, f. 648.
[169] TNA, CO 140/1, f. 159; the unwritten laws of war governed legal cases not determinable by the ordinances. BL, Add. Ms. 12,429 f. 75; TNA, CO 140/3, 648; Lynch, *The Laws of Jamaica*, 67.
[170] TNA, CO 140/1, f. 260; Lynch, *The Laws of Jamaica*, 67–8.
[171] TNA, CO 1/43, no. 57 II; TNA, CO 140/3, 651; Lynch, *The Laws of Jamaica*, 68.

had not created the suspension of law. They instead had created a wartime normative order that allowed them to build and maintain their fortifications.

Jamaican martial law out of control

Bad precedents begin as measures good unto themselves.[172] This was the case for Jamaican martial law. By 1685, the acting governor of the island, Hender Molesworth, declared that under martial law his power was "absolute and uncontrollable."[173] Four years later, its practice came under intense scrutiny. By the eighteenth century, governors were using the shutting of courts for all kinds of purposes that generated hostility among the inhabitants of the island. To show how this happened, let us return to Jamaica's Militia Act.

A key divergence can be found between the Crown commission and the Militia Act. Whereas the Crown allowed the governors of Jamaica to use martial law when the courts were impeded in times of rebellion or invasion, the Jamaican Militia Act allowed the governor to declare martial law "upon every apprehension and appearance of any Publique danger or Invasion."[174] First, the governor only had to apprehend danger. It did not need to appear. What was danger? There were, of course, multiple definitions. But commonly, as we saw with Oliver St. John's argument, public or "eminent danger" involved a plot or conspiracy and not necessarily an outright declared war. This new phrase, depending on how one interpreted danger, granted the governor far more discretion as to when he could close the courts down and declare martial law than the original Crown commissions.

In England, as so many scholars have noted, the supposed plots that generated claims to imminent danger involved some kind of papist Catiline, who was attempting to overthrow the Protestant religion and the English government. The Long Parliament in particular claimed its knowledge of a plot to declare a time of imminent danger and authorize a variety of emergency measures.[175] On Jamaica, plots were frequently used to justify martial law in the eighteenth century, as well. As Jason

---

[172] Sallust, *The War with Catiline* trans. J.C. Rolffe, rev. John T. Ramsey (Cambridge, MA, 2013), 114–15.

[173] So said Hender Molesworth, the acting governor of Jamaica in 1685 in his letter to James II and his council that informed them of a slave rebellion and Molesworth's subsequent declaration of martial law. TNA, CO 138/5, f. 91.

[174] Lynch, *Laws of Jamaica*, 67.

[175] See for example 16 Car. I, c. 7; *LJ*, 4: 384–5, 424–7.

Sharples has so wonderfully demonstrated, in the Caribbean, the plots did not involve papists but instead slaves, who, remarkably, also supposedly had plans similar to those of Catiline.[176] By making claims to such a plot, the governor could shut the courts down. Embedded within imminent or common danger, in other words, was a doctrine of preemption.

Discontent about martial law increased in the eighteenth century. But even as early as 1688/89, planters began to protest what they believed to be cynical uses of martial law. In those years, the lieutenant governor Sir Francis Watson found martial law useful to maintain power in an increasingly bitter faction fight on the island. Watson had been lieutenant to the 2nd Duke of Albemarle, who had arrived in Jamaica in 1685, and had immediately aligned himself with the faction around Sir Henry Morgan. Morgan had been displaced from his post as lieutenant governor by Albemarle's recently deceased predecessor Sir Thomas Lynch, who had aligned himself with the less adventurous and increasingly wealthier planter faction on the island.[177] Along with Morgan, Lynch had removed Morgan's followers, including one of the most notorious men on the island, the lawyer Roger Elletson. During Albemarle's reign, the fortunes of the Morgan faction were reversed, and by 1688 Elletson had gained the prestigious post of chief justice. All of the men under Lynch's faction, now led by the planter Hender Molesworth, had been removed from power. The only problem for the faction in power was that Albemarle had died in October of that year and it was unclear who would replace him.

That autumn, James II ordered those purged to return to office and declared to Watson that Hender Molesworth would return to Jamaica and rule as lieutenant governor.[178] In a later missive in December, the Crown ordered Roger Elletson to be removed from office. By now, William of Orange had invaded England. He eventually would topple James. The regime change did not help Watson and his faction. In February 1689, the new king repeated James' commands to remove

---

[176] Jason T. Sharples, "Discovering Slave Conspiracies: New Fears of Rebellion and Old Paradigms of Plotting in Seventeenth Century Barbados," *American Historical Review* 120:3 (June, 2015): 811–43; Sharples, "The Flames of Insurrection: Fearing Slave Conspiracy in Early America, 1670–1780" (unpublished PhD diss. Princeton University, 2010), 180–96.

[177] Immediately after Lynch's death, Hender Molesworth assumed command of the island until Albemarle's arrival in 1687. Lynch had banned Elletson from practicing law. See Blathwayt to Lynch, 28 June 1684, Colonial Williamsburg Foundation, Blathwayt Papers. Hender Molesworth to Blathwayt 8 September 1684, Colonial Williamsburg Foundation, Blathwayt Papers. Albemarle named Elletson as his chief justice, reversing his ban on practicing law, in February 1688. TNA, CO 140/4, f. 204.

[178] The King to Deputy Governor Sir Francis Watson, 30 Nov. 1688, TNA, CO 138/6, fos. 71v–2v.

Elletson from office, after petitioners in Jamaica had once again complained about Watson's "arbitrary" rule.[179] Upon receiving this new
command, Watson refused to comply, arguing that the command had
not been stamped with the Great Seal. The faction out of power became
furious. In order to quell the uproar, Watson in a letter told the Crown
that he proclaimed martial law in response to worries about the Spanish
and the French.[180]

In his justifications, Watson explained that martial law had been necessary to put the island in a posture of defense.[181] As in other times of
martial law, the lieutenant governor had ordered citadels to be repaired
with new lines of defense being added to Fort Charles. However, many
within the island believed that Watson's use of martial law was a desperate
attempt to hold on to power. In March 1689, the attorney general of the
island likened Elletson to Empson and Dudley. He also claimed that
Watson used martial law in order to help Elletson and another named
Colonel Needham, who were deeply in debt, to escape from the island.[182]
In May 1689, Smyth Kelly, the former deputy provost marshal who had
been deposed by the Albemarle faction, wrote to William Blathwayt, the
former and future secretary of war, and claimed that Watson and his
council of war had kept the planters oppressed under martial law. They
were in arms "night and day."[183] Watson, who was only supposed to be
acting as president of the council, had taken the title of governor. His
council of war, according to Kelly, was full of indebted, lowly men.
Further, Watson ruled by the sword, and "court marshalls are held in
all ye parishes of ye island ye offices being most of them ye meanest
tradesmen."[184] As it was useful in building forts, so was martial law useful
in faction fights.

From the perspective of the planters, Roger Elletson was the chief
architect of this desperate attempt to stay in power. When Watson finally

---

[179] The King to the President and Council of Jamaica 1 December 1688, TNA, CO 138/6,
72v-3. Petition of Planters and Traders of Jamaica in London to His Highness the Prince
of Orange 11 January 1689, TNA, CO 137/2, no. 1; The King to the President and
Council of Jamaica, 22 February 1689, TNA, CO 138/6, fos. 78v–81.

[180] Sir Francis Watson to Lords of Trade and Plantations, 15 March 1689, TNA, CO 137/
2, no. 2.

[181] Francis Watson to William III, 6 June 1689, TNA, CO 137/2, fos. 22v.

[182] The Attorney General of Jamaica to Lords of Trade and Plantations, 12 March 1689,
TNA, CO 137/44, no. 1.

[183] Mr. Smyth Kelly to William Blathwayt at Whitehall 27 May 1689, Colonial
Williamsburg Foundation, Blathwayt Letters; Blathwayt had been replaced as secretary
of war in April 1689 for John Temple, but was subsequently reappointed, Barbara
C. Murison, "Blathwayt, William" in ODNB.

[184] Mr. Smyth Kelly to William Blathwayt at Whitehall, 27 May 1689, Colonial
Williamsburg Foundation, Blathwayt Letters.

succumbed to pressure and re-opened the courts in June 1689, the assembly called for Elletson to be tried for treason.[185] They jailed him and issued a long treason impeachment, which included 25 charges. The twenty-fourth article accused Elletson of contriving to rule the island by the sword.[186] The planters accused Elletson of betraying the stipulations for using martial law outlined in the Militia Act and in the king's commission to the governor. Elletson had declared martial law in spite of the fact that "no appearance or apprehension of any enemy abroad or Insurrection or rebellion at home" had taken place. This unprovoked decision was a "manifest subversion of the English laws Rights Libertyes and Propertyes" of the great planters.[187] The indictment claimed it could call the governor and his council to account for abusing claims to danger.

Nothing more came from this charge. Indeed, we do not know what the English parliament thought about these arguments, or if it ever heard them. Elletson seems to have been deported without trial in 1692.[188] We can learn from this incident that while the governor had discretion to close the courts down, he did not have unlimited discretion.

Nevertheless, Jamaican governors' power was extensive. The closing down of the courts gave them so many opportunities for creativity – many called it abuse – that went beyond trials by court-martial. We have already seen Jamaican governors close the courts so they could billet soldiers and use martial law during so-called slave "conspiracies." Throughout the eighteenth century, Jamaican governors continued to employ this strategy, declaring martial law so they could force men into militia duty. Other governors followed the Jamaica paradigm. The governor in Antigua in 1736 closed the courts down and declared martial law during a slave conspiracy. The governor of Bermuda in 1761 did likewise. The governor of Montserrat did likewise in 1768.[189] Merchants often complained, but governors continued to close the courts down.

The reversal of the treason conviction of Thomas of Lancaster was the key law that governed Jamaican martial law practice. William Noy's interpretation of a state of war – that it could be used by a commander of an army in the field confronting an enemy whose banner was raised – was not as influential in the empire. Selden's – that martial law was simply the right of execution on those rebels and invaders in a time of wrong – was important but not as consequential as Coke's initial interpretation of martial law. Lancaster's reversal – and its relationship to martial law – was

---

[185] They first petitioned the king about his illegal activities, TNA, CO 137/2 no. 16.
[186] TNA, CO 137/2, fos. 107–108v.   [187] *Ibid.*
[188] Whitson, *The Constitutional Development of Jamaica*, 132.
[189] Sharples, "Flames of Insurrection," 180–96.

influential in part because the *Institutes* of Sir Edward Coke used it. It was also communicated through the commissions the clerks of the Crown Office wrote for some delegated authorities. We shall recall that both MPs and the St. Helena petitioners had mimicked Coke in their attacks on the East India Company's use of martial law in 1689. South Carolinians protesting martial law also used the claim of the courts being open in their protest. Jamaican martial law was likewise based on the closing of the courts.

Thus a new page had been written in the history of the reversal of the conviction of Thomas of Lancaster. Once used to overturn a conviction upon record due to the notoriety of the offense in the fourteenth century, the status of the courts became frequently used in the early seventeenth century to restrain the monarchical prerogative. If the courts were open, claimed Heneage Finch, the Crown could not mandate new impositions. If the courts were open, claimed Sir Edward Coke, the Crown could not use martial law to discipline soldiers. If the courts were open, claimed Oliver St. John, the Crown could not mandate Ship Money from its subjects. If they discerned danger, claimed Jamaican governors, they could close the courts and do all of the above. One can only wonder what early Stuart lawyers would have thought about Jamaican martial law.

Conclusion

Pressure on governors to refrain from using martial law came from both the people they governed and governing bodies in England. While the Petition of Right was not law in the colonies, the law of martial law associated with it nevertheless provided a discursive tradition that colonists could use to combat innovative usages of martial law. The Crown's willingness to hear petitions from aggrieved colonists both at the Board of Trade and Plantations and later at parliament provided a forum for redress, which colonists used to their advantage. Governors apprehended these potential consequences from the beginning of the Restoration. By 1689, experience had proven that using martial law to punish civilians was indeed dangerous. When governors actually employed martial law, it was usually to discipline soldiers and seamen. Governments from the Massachusetts General Court to the East India Company adopted these measures. However, delegated authorities used martial law rarely on civilians in part because of the restricted nature of their commissions.

Governing bodies in London and Westminster wanted to intervene. The law of martial law allowed them to supervise their delegated authorities and act as a referee between governors and subjects when controversies arose over martial law jurisdiction. These enhanced their authority. The Board of Trade and Plantations, which was unhappy with the governance of Virginia, got to intervene through Lady Drummond's petition. The English parliament seized the opportunity provided by the distressed planters on St. Helena to intervene in the affairs of the East India Company. And the Proprietors of Carolina intervened in the governance of the plantation through the petitions protesting governor Colleton's use of martial law on the militia. Just as the Privy Council had increasingly monitored martial law use in Ireland in the 1580s, so did imperial governing bodies monitor its use in the Restoration Empire. Martial law was useful for imperial governance. Supervision over martial law jurisdiction was likewise useful.

This monitoring did not end innovation. The Jamaican example makes that clear. The Jamaican polity used the reversal of the treason conviction of Thomas of Lancaster to create a martial law jurisdiction that was just as interested in property as it was in using courts-martial that had powers to take life and limb. While it would become known in the nineteenth century for the summary executions of political dissidents, this all-encompassing jurisdiction had initially been created to help the nascent Jamaican polity defend itself from attacks by Spanish and French invaders, hostile maroons, and conspiratorial slaves. Its history in the empire had only begun.

On 28 January 1716, Thomas Marritt came before a court-martial sitting in the Great Chamber at the Horse Guards. His regimental commander had accused him of deserting his regiment, the First Regiment of his Majesty's Foot Guards, in the past fall. Apparently after deserting, Marritt falsified his name to "John Williams" and re-enlisted the ensuing January in the Third Regiment of his Majesty's Foot Guards. Once again he deserted. Peter Wright, a private in the Third, discovered Marritt hiding at his mother's house, who lived just beyond Hackney. Marritt, after being dragged down the stairs by Wright, "denied that he ever had been in the Army, and made resistance."[1] Perhaps Marritt knew what was awaiting him. Instead of facing a jury of his peers, Marritt faced a court-martial. On 28 January, it convicted him of desertion and sentenced him to death.

In spite of the fact that this court-martial took place on English soil, and in spite of the fact that the Courts of Westminster were open, those who sentenced Marritt to death did not face murder charges. They had parliament to thank for it. Starting in 1689 in response to mutinying soldiers, MPs began to empower the use of martial law on soldiers, which had the effect of suspending the Petition of Right.[2] That the Revolutionary Parliament – the same parliament that passed the Bill of Rights – expanded martial law jurisdiction caused consternation among English historians and legal scholars working in the eighteenth and nineteenth centuries.[3] These early historians insisted that the makers of the Mutiny Act could not have overturned the Petition of Right. In order to execute this sleight of hand, they argued that the Mutiny Act had not

---

[1] "At A Gen. Court Martial Held in the Great Chamber at the Horse Guards. 28 January 1715/16," TNA, WO 71/122.
[2] 1 Gul. & Mar. c.5.
[3] The Revolutionary Convention passed the "Declaration of Rights" that was accepted by William III in February 1689. The Declaration of Rights passed as a statute, "the Bill of Rights," in December 1689. For their history, see Lois G Schwoerer, *The Declaration of Rights, 1689* (Baltimore, 1981).

authorized martial law. Instead, the writers of the Mutiny Act authorized "military law."[4] This interpretation has been called into question by more recent scholars.[5] We will confirm the more recent view that the Mutiny Act was really the authorization of martial law. We will do so by showing that parliament suspended the Petition of Right for soldiers in the same way that it occasionally suspended Habeas Corpus for plotters. By 1715, the suspension of the Petition of Right became more or less permanent for soldiers for certain offenses.

The Mutiny Act was but one way in which the parliaments of the post-1689 period aided the rise of martial law. In 1715, parliament was concerned about the potential for an uprising over the Hanoverian succession. To combat unrest, it passed the Riot Act, which allowed Justices of the Peace to convict rioters summarily. It also allowed them to execute those who resisted arrest. The same powers embedded in the proclamations against retaining in Ireland and rioting in England in the sixteenth century were now authorized against rioters in England in the eighteenth century. The innovations that resulted in the Mutiny and Riot Acts meant those living in the eighteenth century would experience martial law jurisdiction far more often than their seventeenth-century predecessors.

"Not a [jurisdiction]"

In order to understand how this came to be, we must first examine the reaction against martial law jurisdiction during the Restoration. This will help us sharpen the contrast between the pre- and post-1689 worlds while also helping us better understand the dilemmas post-1689 governments faced when they attempted to discipline their soldiers. Sir Matthew Hale was a part of this reaction, and his discussion of martial law has been much quoted and almost always misunderstood. Let us turn to him first.

Hale lived and worked in an environment of suspicion toward military power. The instability of the Civil Wars led many jurists to want an end to the practice of keeping a standing army in England.[6] And yet a small standing army remained in order to prevent a new civil war. Larger garrisons existed outside of England. Many thought these forces might return England to the chaos of the 1650s. Many also by

---

[4] For these older interpretations, see C.M. Clode, *Administration of Justice under Military and Martial Law* (2nd ed., London, 1874), 19–21; William Winthrop, *Military Law and its Precedents* 2 Vols. (2nd ed. Boston, 1896), 47–50.

[5] John Childs, *The British Army of William III, 1688–1702* (Manchester, 1987), 86–7. Also see David E. Engdahl, "Soliders, Riots, and Revolution: The Law and History of Military Troops in Civil Disorders," *Iowa Law Review*, 57 (1971): 1–73.

[6] Lois Schwoerer, *No Standing Armies! The Antiarmy Ideology in Seventeenth Century England* (Baltimore, 1974).

the 1670s worried that they might become "slaves" to a military power and be ruled exclusively by martial law.[7]

Hale's biographer, Gilbert Burnet, depicted Hale as virtuously standing against these threats to English liberties. He told a story about how Hale had upheld the common law throughout the 1650s in the face of what he considered to be the martial polity of Cromwell. Hale had accepted Cromwell's offer to ride circuits on the Crown Side, which meant he would hear felony cases. But Hale, according to Burnet, often used his powers to undermine the military regime. In 1653, he arraigned two soldiers for the death of "one of the king's party." The soldiers had attacked the man because he, contrary to proclamation, was carrying arms. The jury convicted one of manslaughter and the other of murder. Their commander, Colonel Whalley, made a scene in the courtroom and declared the soldiers were only following orders. Hale was unmoved and had the murderer immediately executed so that he had no chance to obtain a reprieve. Burnet's moral of the story was clear: through Hale, the law triumphed over military power.[8] In this context of opposition to martial power, Hale discussed the history and jurisdiction of martial law in his now famous *The History of the Common Law of England.*[9]

First, before we discuss Hale's much more famous comments on martial law, let us discuss his lesser known discussion of martial law in his section on the "Analysis of the Law" that comprised notes on a variety of topics discussed in the history.[10] This included a discussion of the "king's rights of dominion or power of empire."[11] In it, Hale divided the king's powers over his own subjects by time: "[t]imes of peace. Times of war."[12] In a time of war, the king possessed these powers over his own subjects: "[h]e may raise men to suppress their insurrections by force. He may punish them by martial law during such insurrection or rebellion, but not after it is suppressed."[13] This claim was similar but not identical to the

---

[7] *Ibid.*, 95–136. J.G.A. Pocock, "Machiavelli, Harrington and English Political Ideologies in the Eighteenth Century," *William and Mary Quarterly* 3rd ser. 22:4 (October, 1965): 560.

[8] Gilbert Burnet, *The Life and Death of Sir Matthew Hale, knight* (London, 1683), 25–6.

[9] For an intellectual biography of Hale, see Alan Cromartie, *Sir Matthew Hale, 1609–76: Law, Religion and Natural Philosophy* (Cambridge, 1995).

[10] This section was at times excluded from publication. The modern edition, for example, does not include it. Sir Matthew Hale, *The History of the Common Law of England* ed. Charles M. Gray (Chicago, 1971). I have used Charles Runnington's fourth edition of Hale's work, published in 1779. The only scholar I know who has discussed this aspect of Hale's work on martial law is Matthew Warshauer. Warshauer, *Andrew Jackson and the Politics of Martial Law: Nationalism, Civil Liberties, and Partisanship* (Knoxville, 2006), 179.

[11] Hale, *The History of the Common Law of England*, pt. 2, 8.   [12] *Ibid.*

[13] *Ibid.*, pt. 2, 12.

one made by Selden in the Petition of Right Parliament. The king could execute a rebel or invader *in flagrante crimine*, but once the tumult had ended, or once the rebel was taken prisoner and the insurrection over, the common law needed to return. However, Hale did not make clear here whether a rebel could be tried by a court-martial while the general insurrection was taking place. Selden would have disallowed such an action, but Hale, in admittedly draft notes, might have allowed monarchs a slightly more expansive power of martial law.

Before we turn to Hale's more famous argument on sitting courts-martial, or plenary martial law, we first need to examine William Blackstone. We need to do so because Hale's precise argument has been obscured by the eighteenth-century jurist, whose *Commentaries on the Laws of England* borrowed heavily from Hale's work. For Blackstone, martial law "is built upon no settled principles, but is entirely arbitrary in its decisions, is, as Sir Matthew Hale observes, in truth and reality no law, but something indulged, rather than allowed as a law."[14] For Blackstone, indeed, martial law was outside of the realm of law because of its arbitrariness. And it is true that Hale had declared about martial law that "in truth and reality it is not a law, but something indulged, rather than allowed, as a Law."[15] However, Hale never stated that martial law had no settled principles. Nor did he argue for the arbitrariness of its decisions.

When Hale declared that martial law was not really a law, he was claiming that it was not really a law of England, not that it failed to meet an abstract definition of law. We must remember that his discussion of martial law came in his section on jurisdiction called "*Concerning the* lex non scripta i.e. *the common or municipal law of this Kingdom.*"[16] This section is divided into two: the common law based on immemorial custom and statute and the "*leges non scriptae*, and by those particular laws I mean the laws ecclesiastical, and the civil law."[17] Why were laws based on Roman Civil Law unwritten? Because, according to Hale, their jurisdiction was not based upon imperial authority but instead upon the customary practices of the English realm. These courts included the High Court of Admiralty, the ecclesiastical courts, and the Court of the Constable and the Marshal. According to Hale, all of these laws, and not just martial law, were merely "indulged according to that reception allowed them."[18] He then went about discussing their various jurisdictions. The only difference between martial law and the other courts was that it was bound temporally. It did not exist on a day-to-day basis. It was

---

[14] *The Commentaries on the Laws of England of Sir William Blackstone in Four Books* ed. Edward Christian 2 vols. (London, 1818), 1: 412.
[15] Hale, *History of the Common Law of England*, 34.   [16] *Ibid.*, 23   [17] *Ibid.*, 26.
[18] *Ibid.*, 27.

not allowed by custom. Nor, at least in his time, was it allowed by statute in England. Instead, "[t]his indulged law," as he framed it, was only applicable because of necessity during times of war.[19] Hale certainly hated martial law because it was associated with the standing army: an institution he wanted eliminated. However, like the other Civil Law traditions, he believed it needed to be indulged in certain moments.

Hale recognized both the substantive and procedural traditions of martial law. He was well aware of the ordinances of war that he recovered from reading the medieval black book of the admiralty. He was also well aware of the procedures of courts-martial: "the Civil Law has been used and allowed in such Things as belong to their Jurisdiction."[20] Unless he believed the Roman Civil Law to be outside of the realm of law and justice, it is impossible to think that Hale believed martial law to be contrary to an abstract definition of law. Instead, martial law was not a law *in England* at all except in times of war.

Hale's reading of martial law in his *History of the Common Law* is admittedly confusing. However, his discussion of martial law is actually quite clear in his lesser known *Prerogatives of the King.*[21] In this more extensive discussion, Hale recognized the dual role of the marshal, who served as a judicial officer in both the Court of the Verge and the courts of the constable. In times of peace the marshal participated in the Court of the Verge. However, in times of war the constable and the marshal and, by the seventeenth century, a council of war made law for the army. For Hale this was necessary because "the laws framed for the government of a society in war are not nor cannot be applied to the government of an army, that power therefore warrants the raising of an army warrants the providing of law for that army."[22] The power to make and provide law for the army, for Hale, "is properly martial law." Martial law was a jurisgenerative power. Its product was the articles of war written to govern soldiers on any given campaign.

Hale would not have understood our modern distinction between military and martial law. He believed that martial law was *the law* of the army. He also would have been enormously confused by subsequent interpretations of his work. Martial law was not extra-legal nor was it arbitrary in his view. Instead it was precisely *because* armies needed substantive law and procedures crafted for war that made martial law jurisdiction necessary. Martial law was not a law of England at all because it

---

[19] *Ibid.*, 35.   [20] *Ibid.*, 36.
[21] *Sir Matthew Hale's Prerogatives of the King* ed. D.E.C. Yale (London: Selden Society, no. 92, 1976), 117–32.
[22] *Ibid.*, 119.

was the law of the army and, for Hale, a standing army should not exist in England except in times of necessity. Only then should martial law be indulged. An entire historiographical tradition is founded on a misreading of Hale.

Hale's jurisdiction for martial law was highly restricted. Building upon the works of Sir Edward Coke, Hale argued that martial law could not be used in England except during wartime, where it only could be used on soldiers. He defined wartime as the courts of Westminster being closed. In order to prove this, Hale, like Coke, relied on the reversal of the conviction of Thomas of Lancaster, which he incorrectly described in the *History of the Common Law* as the reversal of the conviction of Edmond, Earl of Kent.[23] Hale quoted the reversal of Lancaster's conviction at length, and included the portion where the 1327 Parliament stated that one definition of wartime was when the king's standard was raised. Hale, like Coke, did not mention this definition of wartime, opting instead for the more restrictive status of the courts. Hale thus granted martial law jurisdiction over soldiers in wartime as well as a summary power of execution of rebels and invaders. As we have seen, the commissions of martial law abroad granted very similar jurisdictions. Hale, like those commissions, included in his definition of martial law the substantive law of the army as well as the procedures associated with courts-martial. What, if any, role Hale played in the making of those commissions is unclear.

Martial law in Restoration England

This restrictive boundary was enforced by the Crown's legal officers, often to the frustration of Charles II. The Crown resorted to issuing articles of war that only gave its commanders powers to discipline for misdemeanor while in England.[24] The Duke of Albemarle, the lord general of Charles II's army, ordered in 1663 that if "any person is to suffer the paines of death no tryall execution or proceedings be made therupon but according to the

---

[23] Hale noted that "Edmond Earl of Kent; who being taken at Pomfret [Pontefract], 15 Ed. 2. the King and divers lords proceeded to give sentence of death against him, as in a kind of military court by a summary proceeding; which Judgment was afterwards in 1 Ed. 3 reversed in parliament ... " *Ibid.*, 35. However, Edmond Earl of Kent was convicted because of the notoriety of his offense by parliament in the third year of Edward III's reign and not in 15 Edw. II. Scott L. Waugh, "Edmund [Edmund of Woodstock], first earl of Kent," in *ODNB*. He was later posthumously pardoned by Edward III. Lancaster, however, was executed in the fifteenth year of Edward II's reign and his conviction was posthumously reversed in the first year of Edward III's reign. Hale clearly meant Thomas of Lancaster and not the Earl of Kent. He provides the correct citation in *Prerogatives of the King*, 121.

[24] Childs, *The Army of Charles II* (London, 1976), 78.

knowne lawes of the land . . . "[25] Albemarle then issued a shortened code to govern the army, which contained no punishments of death or loss of limb. This code was the primary source for military discipline within England until 1685. For sailors, the Restoration Parliament was more accommodating in passing legislation that authorized martial law jurisdiction. But it still refused to grant martial law jurisdiction *in* England. Instead, naval commanders could punish their sailors who were on board their ships at sea.[26] Attempts by the Crown to authorize the use of martial law for soldiers in England in both the Second and Third Anglo-Dutch War failed. The Lord Keeper Orlando Bridgeman, for example, refused to authorize commissions of martial law for Charles' generals in 1672.[27] His stance successfully barred martial law jurisdiction from English soil, although it perhaps cost him his position in the government.[28] The Crown was thwarted whenever it desired to find an alternative to common law to discipline soldiers. Restoration England was preserved from martial law jurisdiction.

Just because it was deprived of a key tool of fear and coercion did not mean that the Crown stopped deploying the law as a means of terror. As Tim Harris has shown, in the aftermath of major political rioting, the so-called bawdy house riots of 1668 – attacks by dissenting protestant apprentices on the brothels of London in order to protest the licentiousness of the court – Charles and his legal officers had the leading rioters tried for treason at common law.[29] The old way to terrify apprentices was to issue proclamations that threatened execution by summary martial law if the rioters refused arrest or refused to disband. This option was no longer available to the king and his council during the Restoration. So they threatened rioters with treason prosecutions instead.

---

[25] "Militarie Orders and Articles made by his Majestie," 17 March 1663, TNA, SP 29/69, f. 81ff. Powers of life and limb were only granted to generals during expeditions abroad. See TNA, C 66/3205, m. 1–2d; TNA, C 66/3201, 7d. The printed articles of war reflect this distinction. Contrast the articles sent to the governor of Tangier and the general of the 1678 expedition to Scotland, and the articles of war that governed soldiers stationed in Ireland with those issued in 1663 for soldiers in England. TNA, CO 279/1; *Articles and Rules for the Better Government of his Majesties Forces by land during this Present War* (London, 1673); *Articles and Rules, for the better Government of his Majesties Forces in Scotland* (Edinburgh, 1678); *Rules and Articles for the Better Government of his Majesties Army in this Kingdom* (Dublin, 1685).

[26] 13 Car. II. c.9.

[27] TNA, SP 104/77, fos. 59v, 92v. Bridgeman claimed that martial law commissions violated the Petition of Right. Apparently there was some dispute on this point, and that others examined the commissions Charles I granted his generals during the Bishops' Wars.

[28] Childs, *The Army of Charles II*, 77; K.H.D. Haley, *The First Earl of Shaftesbury* (Oxford, 1968), 304–5.

[29] Tim Harris, *London Crowds in the Reign of Charles II: Propaganda and Politics from the Restoration until the Exclusion Crisis* (Cambridge, 1987), 82–91.

When it came to enemies, however, the Crown still used martial law as a strategy of terror. Gerbrandt Zas and William Arton, two men commissioned by the Prince of Orange to convince members of Charles' government to make peace in 1672, found out this fact the hard way.[30] During the height of the Third Anglo-Dutch War in December 1672, Zas and Arton were ordered by the Crown to depart from Harwich because Charles' informant networks had learned that these two men had been spying in England. Zas left in December 1672.[31] But he returned shortly thereafter on instructions to use up to one million guilders to convince Charles' government to make peace.[32] On 16 January, they were taken in Harwich, and examined by Crown officers. The Privy Council ordered their arrest, and interrogated them before they were interrogated again in the Tower on 27 January.[33]

On 14 February, Charles and his ministers decided that they would try Zas and Arton by a court-martial.[34] Charles' attorney general, Heneage Finch, advised they be tried by martial law for spying.[35] Military officers served as commissioners. John Russell, the colonel of the Cold Stream Guards and the son of the Duke of Bedford served as president. Three lawyers trained in Civil Law attended the court. Charles empowered this tribunal, which sat in the Tower, to hear and determine all things against the two alleged spies. They had powers to torture the spies – provided that they did not take their lives or limbs – into revealing what their plans were in England and on what information they had obtained.[36] They had to seek the king's approval before they convicted the men of life or limb. The commissioners recorded that they asked, over and over again in the month of March, three questions: what were their instructions; who gave them their instructions, and what were they planning on doing with the money they had been authorized to spend when Crown officers detained them.[37] It is likely that the two were

---

[30] For this episode, see K.H.D. Haley, *William of Orange and the English Opposition, 1672–4* (Oxford, 1953), 67–87.

[31] A passport was issued to Zas on 12 December. He was required to leave England within 24 hours. *CSPD*, 1672–3, 270. It was reported that he left by 19 December. Silas Taylor to Williamson, 19 December 1672, *CSPD*, 1672–3, 293.

[32] Haley, *William of Orange*, 76.

[33] Silas Taylor to Williamson, 16 January 1673, TNA, SP 29/332, f. 123. They were examined in the Tower on 27 January. TNA, SP 29/332, f. 299. Haley, *William of Orange*, 84.

[34] The commission for the trial is in TNA, C 66/3152, 9d and TNA, SP 30/F, f. 541. The orders for the trial can be found in BRO, D/ED/056. These instructions are in the papers of the Trumbull family.

[35] Haley, *William of Orange*, 84–5.

[36] Alan Marshall, *Intelligence and Espionage in the Reign of Charles II, 1660–1685* (Cambridge, 1994), 128; James Heath, *Torture and English Law: An Administrative and Legal History from the Plantagenets to the Stuarts* (Greenwood, CT, 1982), 172–9.

[37] The examination records are in TNA, SP 29/334, fos. 277–83. Haley, *William of Orange*, 84–6.

tortured by the commissioners seeking these answers. It is unlikely that Charles or his council ever seriously considered killing the two men. Already by the end of March, the Privy Council was in negotiations with the Dutch for a prisoner exchange.[38] The negotiations dragged on for a year before Zas was finally exchanged in March 1674. Enemies like Zas were the only ones subject to martial law in England during the reign of Charles II.[39]

Supervising the army: The war office

While martial law was used rarely, legal problems nevertheless arose between the army and civilian legal officials. Our understanding of these issues stems from the extant records from the War Office, the new if small bureaucratic corps that had developed out of the English Civil War to monitor Crown soldiers. It is worth our time to briefly explore its development.

Record keeping in matters of discipline had slowly gotten better since the sixteenth century. Especially after the procedural transformation of courts-martial that took place in the early seventeenth century, the clerks and judge advocates maintained records of the courts-martial proceedings so they could deliver the findings of the court to the lord general of the army. He could then examine the court's findings and sign the warrants that executed the prescribed punishments, mercies, and acquittals of the councils of war. During the Civil War secretaries to the lord general kept detailed records of the business of the army. John Rushworth, the first secretary and his assistant, William Clarke who eventually became George Monck's secretary in Scotland, kept extensive records of the army's business.[40] The survival of these records was still a matter of luck, however, as no centralized administrative body desired to maintain them.

But by the latter half of the seventeenth century these records became a part of the institutional archive of the War Office. When Charles II was restored in 1660, he did not re-establish the Council of War – the body that had supervised soldiers during his father's reign. Instead, the administration of the army ran through the lord general, George Monck, the Duke of Albemarle. The general had as his aide William Clarke, an experienced secretary of war, and he also employed a permanent judge advocate general who possessed the office for life, a commissary general,

---

[38] Sir J. Barckman Leyenbergh to Williamson, 16 May 1673, TNA, SP 29/335/2, f. 68.
[39] A warrant for Zas' release is dated 12 April 1674. TNA, SP 44/28, f. 111. Arton escaped from the Tower in the autumn of 1673. Haley, *William of Orange*, 86.
[40] For the duties of the secretary of the general see BL, Add. Ms. 15,856 f. 54v.

a paymaster general, and a muster master general.[41] These officers deposited more archival material than their predecessors.

The secretary of war became increasingly powerful over time. James II's secretary William Blathwayt oversaw the army's expansion. He archived all of the warrants he issued in the name of the general.[42] These records included troop movements, correspondence, and most importantly for our purposes, written evidence relating to military discipline. The War Office also kept records of individual courts-martial that arrived from the field, a calendar of courts-martial, and eventually manuscript histories of English and European courts-martial.[43] The creation and development of the War Office also meant the creation of its archive, which kept track of courts-martial records much better than the Council of War, the Privy Council, or of individual judge marshals or advocates. It also kept track of the many disputes between James' army and the civilian population during his reign. Let us turn to those now.

Martial discipline under James II

James II succeeded his brother to the throne in 1685.[44] He attempted to maintain a much larger standing army than his predecessor. At the beginning of his reign, James inherited an English army of around 8,800 men. In the spring of his first year a major rebellion broke out in the west of England – now known as Monmouth's Rebellion. James raised a considerable number of men to put down the rebellion, and continued them in pay after the rebellion had ended. By the end of 1685, he had increased this army to around 20,000. By November 1688, when William of Orange's invasion force landed at Torbay, James had increased his army to just over 34,000 men.[45] This experiment exacerbated several legal problems involving the army that had already existed in Charles' reign. We will examine three of them: trials by court-martial that involved life and limb, the legality of punishing soldiers for desertion, and finally punishing soldiers for misdemeanor.

In spite of his arbitrary reputation, James and his legal counsel used martial law to prosecute by life and limb in a manner somewhat consistent

---

[41] Childs, *The Army of Charles II*, 90–111.   [42] TNA, WO 26/1–6.

[43] The courts-martial records can be found in TNA, WO 89/1; WO, 26/6; and in WO 71/121. A partial calendar of all courts-martial conducted in the late seventeenth century survives. TNA, WO 92/1.

[44] The most comprehensive treatment of military-civil relations in this period is Steven Pincus' several discussions on the matter in *1688: The First Modern Revolution* (New Haven, 2009), 118–78. I am here only trying to focus on what I believe to be the most pressing legal problems related to James' standing army.

[45] John Childs, *The Army, James II, and the Glorious Revolution* (Manchester, 1980), 1–3.

with some early Stuart interpretations of the Petition of Right. The army generally did not punish by life and limb by martial law except when there was an enemy army in the field: Noy's interpretation of wartime was still prevalent at the end of the seventeenth century.[46] The majority of legal evidence that we have of courts-martial punishing with death during James' reign comes from the summer of 1685, during James' campaign against the Earl of Monmouth. During the rebellion, James' military commanders arraigned soldiers before courts-martial on several occasions. At the opening of the court, the president justified the proceeding by stating it was enforcing "The rules and articles for the better government of his Majesty's land forces in pay during the present rebellion," which gave the court powers to try by life and limb.[47] This usage was consistent with the idea that an army "chasing enemies or rebels" could be disciplined by martial law even though it made no reference to the enemy's banner. After the rebellion had ended, James sent out general directions to his commanders about the punishment of soldiers. All cases involving life or limb were now to be handled at common law.[48] Wartime had come to an end.

James' interpretation of martial law jurisdiction exempted civilians from being tried for life and limb at courts-martial. Soldiers and only soldiers were to be tried by martial law for felony. In a robbery case in August 1685, for example, William Blathwayt ordered a colonel to hand over two men accused of the crime because one was not a soldier in pay.[49] Further, if a soldier had committed a felony against a civilian, he could not be tried at martial law.[50] This line of demarcation kept civilian courts in charge of meting out justice on civilians for felony. This included rebellion. Coke, Selden, Hale, and most common law jurists opposed martial law jurisdiction on prisoners who were English subjects. James and his legal counsel followed this prescriptive advice in 1685.[51] This reservation did not mean that the rebels got off with their lives. It simply meant that the Crown was forced to strategically utilize common law procedures to ensure the maximum number of convictions.

---

[46] In 1688, James issued articles of war to his soldiers stationed in England in anticipation of the Dutch invasion that prescribed the death penalty. *Rules and Articles for the Better Government of his Majesties Land Forces in Pay* (London, 1688). Even this code stressed that "no punishment amounting to the loss of Life or limb, be inflicted upon any offendour in time of Peace." *Ibid.*, 35. Noy's interpretation can also be found in lieutenancy notes on martial law. "Notes on Martial Law, 1696," SHC, 371/14/J/15.

[47] TNA, WO 89/1, f. 86. *Rules and Articles for the Better Government of his Majesties Land Forces in Pay during this Present Rebellion* (London, 1685).

[48] TNA, WO 4/1, 12.   [49] *Ibid.*, 15.   [50] *Ibid.*, 47. Also see *Ibid.*, 15, 56–7.

[51] For the punishment of the Monmouth rebels, see John Tutchin, *The Bloody Assizes* (Toronto, 1929).

The suspected rebels came before the chief justice of King's Bench, George Jeffreys, who heard and determined the treason trials. The summary executions of traitors by martial law of the sixteenth century were not an option for James II.

Soldiers during times of peace were tried at common law for felony. Many within the army were not happy about this policy. Since the Restoration, many within the armed forces believed themselves fully exempt from civilian law. This attitude of defiance in turn caused consternation among the leading lights of the Restoration legal regime. In 1663, only three years after the Restoration, Orlando Bridgeman, the chief justice of Common Pleas, complained to the Earl of Clarendon, the lord chancellor of England, that a soldier accused of rape was being protected by his commander, the Earl of Oxford.[52] Clarendon intervened on behalf of the civilian authorities. James' government continued Clarendon's policy. In December 1686, a soldier stationed in Loughborough was accused of murdering a townsman. After he was arrested, his comrades helped him escape from jail. His commander then protected him from being caught by putting him under military guard. Blathwayt, on orders from James, reprimanded the commander for failing to punish those who had helped break the soldier out of prison and then instructed him that the soldier needed to be caught and returned to the civil authorities.[53]

The major point of contention between James and common lawyers was over the punishment of desertion.[54] From the middle of the fifteenth century, English parliaments had granted common law courts jurisdiction over deserting soldiers. Soldiers and sailors in pay who had run away from wars abroad were guilty of felony without benefit of clergy. In successive reigns from Henry VI to Edward VI, parliaments made statutes authorizing common law to punish desertion as a felony.[55] However, from a seventeenth-century perspective, all of these desertion statutes were problematic. Those made in the reign of both Henry VI and Henry VII contained language that suggested that only soldiers who had departed England could be tried for desertion. In the reign of Henry VIII, parliament passed a more extensive statute, which declared that any soldier in pay or pressed to serve the king "upon the sea, or upon the land, or beyond the sea" could be prosecuted for

---

[52] Bodl. Clarendon Ms. 80 f. 176-v; *The Autobiography of Sir John Bramston, K.B.* ed. Thomas William Bramston, ESQ (London, 1845), 126–7.

[53] TNA, WO 4/1 42–43.

[54] Sir William Holdsworth, *A History of English Law* 12 vols. (London, 1922–38), 6: 227–9.

[55] 18 Hen. VI c. 19; 7 Hen. VII c. 1; 3 Hen. VIII c. 5; 2&3 Edw. VI c. 2. The Edwardian statute was repealed by 1 Mar. c. 1 and revived by 4&5 P. &M. c. 3.

desertion.[56] However, all of the statutes regarding felony made in the reign of Henry VIII were overturned by the first parliament of his son, Edward VI. Elizabeth's parliaments never re-passed a statute as extensive as that of 3 Henry VIII.[57] Could one punish a soldier stationed in England for desertion at law in the seventeenth century?

The answer varied depending on the jurist. In 1601, the chief justices of the realm debated the issue. The chief question was whether or not soldiers meant to go to Ireland to serve in Elizabeth I's wars against Irish rebels could be punished for desertion if they abandoned the army after they had received pay but prior to embarkation.[58] The judges in what came to be called the "Case of Soldiers" focused on the statutes made in the reigns of Henry VII and Henry VIII, which according to Edward Coke, were "all of one and the same effect, and penned in the same words."[59] Because these two statutes were effectively the same, according to Coke, the statute of Edward VI that declared all statutes made in the reign of Henry VIII relating to felony null and void did not apply to the desertion statute. Thus the Crown could punish deserters who had not departed England at common law for felony. However, the issue was not resolved. For Restoration jurists disagreed with the decision made in *The Case of Soldiers*. Sir Matthew Hale argued that Henry VIII's desertion statute was different from that made in the reign of his predecessor because this statute applied to men serving in England and abroad, and not just abroad.[60] Therefore, for Hale, the desertion statute of Henry VII remained in force: men deserting the Crown's armies after being sent abroad could be punished at law for felony. But no statute remained in force that allowed for deserting soldiers stationed in England to be punished at law for felony.

In 1684, the last year of the reign of Charles II, the regime contemplated these varied interpretations. It did so after a soldier named James Walden was caught after he had deserted his regiment stationed at Windsor the year before. William Blathwayt was confused about what to do with Walden, and submitted the details of his case to the attorney general, Robert Sawyer. Sawyer argued that Walden could be tried at law for desertion according to 3 Henry VIII. His reasoning was that the statute "extends to Retainers for land Service within the Realm, as beyond

---

[56] 3 Hen VIII c. 5.   [57] 5 Eliz. c. 5

[58] Co. Rep. 6: 27. There was an earlier case, in 1596, that also established that legal officers could prosecute soldiers in England. See, HEHL, Ellesmere Ms. 1686.

[59] Co. Rep 6: 27.

[60] Sir Matthew Hale, *Historia Placitorum Coronae: The History of the Pleas of the Crown* (London, 1778), 671–8.

the Sea which the statute of 7 Henry VII Cap: 19 doth not."[61] Sawyer thus agreed with Hale that the two statutes were different, and unintentionally gave those in opposition to the regime an easy case to make that soldiers could not be punished at common law for desertion.

Throughout James' reign, he and his lawyers interpreted 3 Henry VIII to be in force during times of peace. On 25 July 1685, the king sent a missive to his garrison commanders, who had notified the king of multiple desertions in their ranks. James ordered them to keep caught deserters in custody "to the end they may be punished according to law."[62] That summer, the Old Bailey heard two desertion cases against the soldiers Samuel Anderton and John Somerset. In both, the soldiers were found guilty by a jury and sentenced to death.[63] Desertion was punishable at common law in England.

This practice soon became controversial. By 1686 James seemed tempted to remove military discipline completely into the hands of courts-martial. According to an anonymous news-book, James in June 1686 ordered that soldiers accused of desertion should be tried at courts-martial, "his Majesty finding rather encouragement given to than justice done upon, deserters by the judges at Common Law."[64] Another news-book reported that a soldier in September 1686 was executed for desertion at martial law in Plymouth.[65] It is possible that this jurisdiction switch was made because certain judges refused to hear cases involving desertion. This certainly happened in London that same September. The new recorder of the City, Sir John Holt, doubted whether a soldier could be tried for desertion.[66] Holt informed the lord chancellor, Baron Jeffreys, who called in nine justices to make a determination. All but Holt declared it was legal for the soldier to be tried. Ultimately a jury found the soldier guilty and he was executed. Three others were executed at the Old Bailey for desertion shortly thereafter.[67] Holt was dismissed from service. In January 1687, William Blathwayt responded to legal questions raised by one of James' garrison commanders by instructing them that all soldiers who deserted their colors were to be tried at law.[68] The matter seemed to be at an end.

The issue, however, was not entirely resolved. In April 1687, the attorney general for James brought a case relating to desertion before

---

[61] TNA, WO 26/6, f. 7.   [62] Ibid., 55.
[63] Old Bailey, July 1685 trial of Samuel Anderton (t16850716-20) and trial of John Somerset (t16850716-35).
[64] CSPD, 1686–87, no.149.   [65] Ibid., no. 961.
[66] Ibid., 1686–7, no. 962; The Autobiography of Sir John Bramston, 245–6.
[67] CSPD, 1686–7 no. 962.   [68] TNA, WO 4/1, 45.

King's Bench. A soldier, William Dale, had been convicted for desertion at the Reading assizes.[69] However, he had been reprieved because the Crown wanted him to be executed before his regiment in Plymouth, not at the site of his conviction. Through a writ of Habeas Corpus, Dale was brought before King's Bench, where the legality of 3 Henry VIII was once again debated.

The case came at a time of intrigue between the very powerful lord chancellor of England, Baron Jeffreys, and his former protégé, the current chief justice of King's Bench, Sir Edward Herbert. Aligning himself with the Earl of Sunderland, James' secretary of state and one of Jeffreys' chief rivals on the Privy Council, Herbert had attacked Jeffreys earlier in the year by "laying open his bribes and corruption" from when he had presided over the bloody assizes.[70] It was even rumored that Herbert would soon replace Jeffreys as lord chancellor. That spring, in response to this threat from his younger colleague, Jeffreys attempted to have Herbert removed, and replaced by Sir Robert Wright. Herbert sustained this initial attack and remained on King's Bench, while Wright was named chief justice of Common Pleas.[71] Jeffreys was not satisfied, and still sought the ouster of Herbert.

Herbert would not survive Jeffreys' next attack on his position. On 15 April, Dale was brought before King's Bench. The attorney general made a motion that the court should order the defendant to be executed in Plymouth. According to several reports of the case, Herbert, "in some heat," responded that the motion was highly "irregular, for the prisoner was never before the Court."[72] In one account of the proceedings, an anonymous correspondent told one of James' envoys, the Marquis D'Albeville, that Herbert shouted at the attorney general that "difficul-tyes were throwne upon the Court on purpose to embarrasse them by people that had cinical ends."[73] Presumably, Herbert believed that Jeffreys was responsible for this case being heard at King's Bench because he knew he would not side with the king's demands, and that his position on desertion was not to the king's favor. One of the deputy justices, Sir

---

[69] There are four reports of this case. *Modern Reports, or Select Cases adjudged in King's Bench, Chancery, Common Pleas, and Exchequer since the Restoration of Charles II* (hereafter *Mod. Rep.*) ed. Thomas Leach, 12 vols. (London, 1793), 3: 124; Sir Bartholomew Shower, *The Reports of Cases adjudged in the Court of King's Bench: during the reigns of Charles the Second, James the Second, and William the Third*, 2 vols. (London, 1794) 2: 653–4; Harvard Law School, Ms. 1071, f. 9v; Lincoln's Inn, Ms. 375, f. 43. There is also correspondence to James' diplomat the Marquis D'Albeville, probably from Robert Yard. 15 April 1687, LL, D'Albeville Ms. Sometimes the reports name the soldier William Beal. Others claim his name is William Dale.

[70] Quoted in Jeffrey R. Collins, "Herbert, Edward" in *ODNB*.

[71] Anonymous to D'Albeville, 15 April 1687, LL, D'Albeville Ms.

[72] *Mod. Rep.* 3: 124.   [73] Anonymous to D'Albeville 22 April 1687, LL, D'Albeville Ms.

Francis Wythens, also became enraged over the proceedings. Observers speculated that he was incensed by the advancement of Wright to chief justice of Common Pleas. The justices refused to hear the case against Dale.

Eventually, this personal rivalry produced disagreements over the legality of desertion prosecutions. Three days later, the Attorney General brought in the prisoner through a writ of Habeas Corpus. The records of Dale's trial were brought in for review through Certiorari. The justices now were willing to hear the case, but they refused to side with the king. Both Herbert and Wythens insisted that Dale could not be executed at Plymouth. He had to be executed either in Berkshire (of which Reading was the county seat) or in Middlesex by the prerogative of King's Bench.[74] More importantly, during the hearing both expressed reservations about whether desertion could be punished at common law. In the end both refused to answer the question, instead demurring. The king was incensed by their actions. The following day, he removed Herbert to Common Pleas and installed Wright as chief justice of King's Bench. He also removed Wythens from the bench.[75] Citing numerous precedents, Wright approved the transfer of the execution site to Plymouth. Dale would die in front of his former colleagues so "that by this example other souldiers might be deterred from running from their Colours."[76] Herbert did not take his new position well. One observer noted that "my lord chancellor has got the ascendant ouer the Ch. Justice Herbert which does not a little mortify the latter."[77]

Uncertainty over the legality of punishing soldiers for desertion continued. As late as the summer of 1688, juries in London convicted soldiers of desertion at the Old Bailey.[78] But we also have some evidence of resistance: in at least one other desertion case, the grand jury refused to find a true bill.[79] More importantly, very serious legal minds – who in other instances agreed with James' policies – did not think desertion was punishable at law. Hale, Holt, and seemingly Herbert and Wythens, all disagreed that 3 Henry VIII was a valid authorization to punish desertion as a felony.

There were other tensions between the army and the civilian legal apparatus. Conflicts over jurisdiction frequently arose over misdemeanor

---

[74] *Mod. Rep.* 3: 124.
[75] Anonymous to D'Albeville 22 April 1687, LL, D'Albeville Ms.; *Mod.Rep.* 3: 125.
[76] *Mod. Rep.* 3: 125.   [77] Anonymous to D'Albeville 3 May 1687 LL, D'Albeville Ms.
[78] *Old Bailey*, May 1688, trial of Simon How (t16880531–14).
[79] *The Autobiography of Sir John Bramston*, 276. A judge also attempted to reprieve a soldier for desertion in August 1687 but the king refused to pardon him. Anon. to the Earl of Huntington, 20 August 1687, HEHL, HA Ms. 6999.

offenses. By the 1670s, Charles II had re-introduced the petitioning system, which required that civilian authorities ask permission before they prosecute soldiers for misdemeanor.[80] Charles made his policy regarding misdemeanor clear through a Royal Proclamation issued in 1672 during the Third Anglo-Dutch War. He declared that his subjects, "when and as often as they shall receive any kind of Injury or Abuse from any of the Souldiers under his Majesties Pay, forthwith to make their Complaints unto the Officer or Officers under whom such Souldiers shall serve."[81] At the outset of James' reign, the new king issued a nearly identical proclamation.[82] This petitioning system meant that the army officers stood as gatekeepers for any non-capital suit against soldiers.

We can see how the petitioning system worked during the reign of Charles II through a case heard at the Old Bailey in 1678. In December, two soldiers were indicted for misdemeanor riots.[83] They had attempted to break their friend named Sparks out of a London jail. The two defendants accosted the Constable who had arrested Sparks and told him he was not allowed to arrest a soldier. The constable declared that he did not think Sparks was a soldier and demanded to see the imprisoned man's name on a muster roll. The defendants then flew into a rage, gathered ten of their friends, and threatened to burn down the jail. The constable alerted the Court of Alderman of London. They in turn contacted the lord general, the Duke of Monmouth, who cashiered the twelve men and allowed them to be prosecuted at law. The men were fined £50. However, they were only prosecuted after Monmouth had *given* the London magistrates permission.

In James' reign a more centralized war administration heard and determined petitions made against soldiers. Let us look at an example from Chester to understand this legal procedure better. In 1688, a long-running feud between a quartermaster, John Eames, and a constable of the town boiled over. In January, Eames with two of his soldier friends ambushed and brutally beat the constable of the town. The governor made a formal complaint to the king through William Blathwayt. James examined the case, and on 14 February, Blathwayt reported to the commanding colonel, the Earl of Huntington, that James had made a decision. Eames was suspended without pay for 15 days, and 30 shillings of his pay was ordered to be given to the injured constable. But

---

[80] The only scholar who has noted the Petitioning System is John Childs, and only for the reign of Charles II. Childs, *The Army of Charles II*, 78–80.

[81] *By The King. A Proclamation for Prevention of Disorders which may be committed by Souldiers* (London, 1672).

[82] *By the King: A Declaration* (London, 1685).

[83] *Old Bailey*, December 1678 (16781211).

before the deal could be accepted, "releases are to be given on all sides, that no further prosecution be had att the Quarter Sessions or else where in relation to this business."[84] Common law had been circumvented.

The chief officer of Eames' regiment had also been circumvented. Through the officer's response, we can understand why the governor bypassed him, and why the War Office ended up handling many of these misdemeanor cases. About a week before Blathwayt informed the Earl of Huntington of the decision against Eames, the acting commander of the regiment, Henry Hastings, complained that he had been left out of the process: "I extremely wondered how a complaint of that kind should happen and I know nothing of it." Hastings then expressed his disapproval that Eames was being prosecuted at all. According to Hastings, the constable had been shouting expletives out of the window at him and had not revealed that he was an officer of the law.[85] Apparently, this omission justified the beating he ended up receiving. Had the matter simply been left to his commander, the constable would not have received justice.[86]

The supervision over military-civilian conflicts often involved detective work. In the spring of 1687, for example, William Blathwayt sent Edward Sackville, a brigadier in the army, on a mission to Salisbury.[87] The town government had complained to Westminster on several occasions about outrages committed by the soldiers stationed in the city against its citizens. Sackville was to "use the best ways and means for the discovery of the truth in relation to any complaint that shall be brought to unto you concerning Our forces in those parts."[88] Sackville was to return with enough information so that James or one of his advisors could resolve the disputes. In other cases, the Crown allowed prosecutions to continue at common law. For example, in January 1686, William Blathwayt informed Lord Dunbarton, the commander of a regiment stationed in Exeter, that upon "information given to his Matie of an assault" made upon a citizen by a lieutenant and nine soldiers, the king commanded that the ten men face trial at law. The lieutenant was to take a recognizance to appear at the next assizes, while the nine soldiers were to be tried at the Mayor's Court.[89] Even in this instance, where soldiers were to be tried at law for misdemeanor crimes, it was this process of inquiry that decided it. Law could only function against soldiers when the king or his ministers allowed it.

---

[84] Blathwayt to Huntington, 14 February 1688, HEHL, HA Ms. 837.
[85] Hastings to Huntington 8 February 1688, HEHL, HA Ms. 5622.
[86] The soldier was punished. See Peter Shakerly to William Blathwayt, 15 February 1688, BL, Add. Ms. 38,694, f. 115.
[87] TNA, WO 26/6, 112.   [88] *Ibid.*   [89] TNA, WO 4/1, 26.

What happened when civilians refused to ask permission to prosecute soldiers? In the reign of Charles II, his Privy Council heard cases where civilians had arrested soldiers without permission after having them apprehended for contempt.[90] During the reign of James II, the number of cases of civilians arresting soldiers without permission rose dramatically. While the total tally is unclear because colonels in regiments probably handled at least some of these cases locally, we know for certain that the War Office issued warrants – which have never been examined before – to apprehend no fewer than 145 men and women for arresting soldiers without permission.[91] But what happened once the warrant was issued?

The warrants reveal little about the process of adjudicating these disputes. They always commanded one of James' chamber messengers in ordinary to apprehend between one and five people who had been involved in an arrest of a soldier. It usually commanded the messenger to apprehend the suitor and those that had actually arrested the soldier: the bailiffs or constables involved. It commanded the messenger to bring those named "before us to answer for their contempt."[92] We do not know, with one exception, where the alleged crime took place. And we do not know how the civilians were punished for arresting the soldier, although we can guess, as they were being punished for contempt, that they served a short time in jail.[93] It is likely that many of these soldiers had been arrested for debt. We only have one record of an actual hearing taking place as a result of civilians being apprehended. In December 1687, a messenger in ordinary apprehended Samuel Harper, who was eventually brought before the king in council to answer for arresting Robert Meldrum, a servant in Colonel Hamilton's regiment.[94] The Privy Council decided that Meldrum, because he was only a servant of the regiment, was not exempt from prosecution, leaving us to ponder how someone guilty of illegally arresting a soldier would have been punished.

The final problem with the warrants is that they end abruptly in the spring of 1688. However, the final warrant reveals a potential reason for why they end. On 12 April, the Earl of Sunderland issued a warrant for the king's messenger in ordinary to apprehend John Wilks, a bailiff, for arresting a soldier without leave of his commanding officer and carrying

[90] TNA, PC 2/64, f. 394.
[91] For a locally handled case, see for example, Ingram to Carlisle 4 July 1687, HEHL, HA Ms. 6998. The apprehension warrants can be found in TNA, WO 26/6.
[92] See, for example, TNA, WO 26/6, 73.
[93] We can make this guess because the Privy Council imprisoned civilians for other crimes against soldiers, like taking their horses for brief periods of time. See TNA, PC 2/71, f. 434.
[94] TNA, WO 26/6, 117; TNA, PC 2/71, f. 565.

him to Newgate.[95] The warrant also stated that Wilks and "all Justices of the Peace" were to attend a court-martial at the Horse Guards. This is the one and only warrant that references a court-martial. It appears that these cases were now going to be heard by a sitting court-martial in London. The judge advocate, or the presiding officer of the court, now probably issued the warrants of apprehension.

We have almost no records of this court.[96] But we do know that it was formed in March 1688. The judge advocate general of James' reign, George Clark, mentioned in his autobiography that all legal issues involving the army from that period forward were heard before the Horse Guards court-martial.[97] This claim was not strictly true. John Bramston, in his memoirs, reported that the court-martial only had powers to hear and determine all "misdemeanors of Officers and Souldiers; as also to heare and determin all petitions or compleints that shall be brought before them by any other person."[98] Felonies, like desertion, remained in the purview of common law courts. Judging from the warrant issued by Sunderland in March, the court-martial had the powers to punish those who had arrested soldiers without leave of the commanding officer. Further the court would make all recommendations for civilians seeking redress against soldiers, which would ultimately be decided by James. From a civilian perspective, this must have been chilling to have to attend a court-martial, and potentially be punished by it.

The response to the petitioning system was mixed. As we have seen, some obeyed it. Others made it clear that they believed the petitioning system was at best informal. In Michaelmas 1674, for example, a captain of one of Colonel Russell's companies stationed in London and his sergeant came before King's Bench, of which Matthew Hale was chief justice. In this "Case of Captain C," the soldiers were accused of rescuing one of their colleagues who had been imprisoned for debt.[99] When asked to answer for his actions, the captain argued that a civilian officer could not arrest a soldier without "leave of his officer."[100] With every justice reportedly agreeing with him, Hale replied that "every officer and soldier is as liable to be arrested as a tradesman or any other person

---

[95] TNA, WO 26/6, 123.

[96] The only record for this court-martial is a warrant from the lord general to the judge advocate general to convene a court-martial to try misdemeanor offenses in July 1688. BL, Add. Ms. 9760, f. 7.

[97] "The Autobiography of George Clark," in *HMC* Leyborne-Popham MS (London, 1899), 265.

[98] *The Autobiography of John Bramston*, 306; Narcissus Luttrell, *A Briefe Historical Relation of State Affairs from September 1678 to April 1714* 6 vols. (Westmead, Farnborough, Hants., 1969), 1: 434; Childs, *The Army, James II, and the Glorious Revolution*, 91–2.

[99] "The Case of Captain C," I Ventris 25 Chas. II, 167–8.   [100] *Ibid.*, 168.

whatsoever."[101] Irate, Hale scolded the soldiers, and declared that Charles' proclamation was at best "a civility" between civilian and military authorities.

The justices of King's Bench during James' reign also had reservations about the petitioning system. In the spring of 1686, King's Bench heard a request from James to commit a constable who had arrested a soldier without permission from the king.[102] The king assured the chief justice that "he would not protect any one of his guards against the course of the law no more than the meanest of his Subjects." But the constable had attempted to arrest the soldier in one of the king's parks, outside his jurisdiction. The report is unclear on what happened after this assurance. In another instance, the justices of the King's Bench refuted the legality of the warrants of apprehension issued by the War Office. In Michaelmas 1686, Samuel Corbett sued for a writ of Habeas Corpus.[103] The War Office had issued a warrant of apprehension for him on 8 October for arresting John Brooks, a soldier in Werden's regiment of horse.[104] King's Bench reviewed the apprehension warrant. The justices bailed Corbett and ruled that the warrant was not legally valid because "the warrant was under the king's own hand, without seal, or the hand of any secretary or officer of state, or justice."[105] Others apprehended also sued for Habeas Corpus. That same term, Charles Wilson, John Latham, Edward Sommers, William Armstrong, and Elizabeth Bayly all sued for Habeas Corpus.[106] A warrant of apprehension had been issued for all five of them on 6 October for being involved in the arrest of George Hule, the master gunner of Chepstow Castle.[107] It is unclear whether the justices bailed the prisoners. Wilson, one of the arresters, continued to pursue legal action against Hule. The next year, Wilson sued an outlawry against Hule for assault and battery. Once again the War Office issued an apprehension warrant for Wilson.[108] He was ordered to appear before king and council. As always, we have no record of what happened to Wilson during this hearing.

There was no outright revolt by the judiciary in the reign of James II but his army clearly generated legal tensions. In many ways, his reign resembled the 1620s where the real controversies over soldiers were related to but not identical with martial law practice. Whether desertion was legal

---

[101] *Ibid.*   [102] Harvard Law School, Ms. 1071, fos. 6v–7.
[103] TNA, KB 21/29/145/HC (Michaelmas, 1686). Many thanks to Professor Paul Halliday for helping me with these references.
[104] TNA, WO 26/6, 101.   [105] Sir Bartholomew Shower, *Reports*, 2: 638.
[106] TNA, KB 21/29/145/HC (Michaelmas, 1686).Two others, Charles Fisher and Robert West, also sued Habeas Corpus after having been apprehended. TNA, WO 26/6, 99; TNA, KB 21/29/145/HC (Michaelmas, 1686).
[107] TNA, WO 26/6, 101.   [108] TNA, WO 26/6, 113.

or not had to in the end be decided by the sacking of judges and their replacement by those more friendly to the king. Civilians were obstructed from trying soldiers even if they had at the very least a mechanism to bypass local officers who wanted to shield those under their command from prosecution. It is likely that some in 1688 came before courts-martial to answer for arresting soldiers without permission. Many of these same problems awaited the victors of the Glorious Revolution.

Making the Mutiny Act

James' reign did not last long.[109] His policies of religious toleration toward Protestant dissenters and Catholics alienated many of the conservative Tory Anglicans who had supported him early on in his reign. By 1688, the ecclesiastical establishment was in full revolt against the king. Seven Anglican bishops issued a pamphlet explaining why they refused to proclaim James' Declaration of Indulgence – a proclamation that set aside the penal code against Catholics and dissenters. James charged them with seditious libel. But he could not gain a conviction. On the day the bishops were acquitted, seven alienated nobles sent a letter to William of Orange that invited him to invade England. Several months later, William obliged, in no small measure because English resources would help him in his war effort against Louis XIV of France. Many officers within the army abandoned James, who quickly fled.[110] By February 1689, a convention parliament had named William of Orange and Mary king and queen of England. As part of the deal, William and Mary agreed to the Declaration of Rights, which among other demands asserted that no standing army could exist in England without the consent of parliament. With this newfound power over England's military forces, parliament now also had the responsibility over its discipline.[111]

MPs quickly discovered the difficulties that came from controlling an army. Throughout the winter, English soldiers mutinied and deserted in large numbers. On 1 March, the MP Hugh Boscawen spoke against the depredations committed by soldiers who had deserted their regiments. Bands had killed a man in Cornwall. Many soldiers were fleeing to Scotland.[112] On 13 March, MPs ordered a committee to draft a bill that

---

[109] The best narrative history of the Glorious Revolution is Tim Harris, *Revolution: The Great Crisis of the British Monarchy, 1685–1720* (New York, 2006). For a new interpretation of the Revolution, see Pincus, *1688*.

[110] For the conspiracy among army officers against James, see Childs, *The Army, James II, and the Glorious Revolution*, 138–67.

[111] Childs, *The British Army of William III, 1688–1702*, 86.

[112] Anchitell Grey, *Debates of the House of Commons from the Year 1667 to 1694* 10 vols. (London, 1763), 9: 131.

would legalize punishment for mutineers and deserters. The Commons delegated the responsibility of crafting this bill to some of its most important MPs.[113] Four names in particular stand out. On the committee sat Sir John Holt, William Sacheverell, Sir William Williams, and Sir Thomas Lee. Holt, we will recall, had refused to convict a soldier of desertion at the Old Bailey in the fall of 1686. His obstinacy eventually led to his resignation as Recorder of London. Lee, Sacheverell, and Williams were part of the opposition to Charles II's policies in the 1670s. All three had been vociferous opponents of Charles' standing army.[114] These three had argued for disbanding the army and replacing it with a militia. They had also argued that soldiers should be subject to common law, not to martial law. On 15 March, the Commons learned of a major mutiny in Lord Dunbarton's Regiment at Ipswich. Many MPs became more urgent about the passing of a Mutiny Act. On 19 March, the bill was read a second time and recommitted to a slightly different committee. Holt, Lee, Williams, and Sacheverell remained. On 28 March, parliament passed the Mutiny Act, which legalized the punishment of life and limb by court-martial for desertion, mutiny, and sedition.

In spite of the fact that we know little about its making, we can nevertheless understand the provisions in the Mutiny Act by contextualizing it with the background of James' reign and through the Suspension of Habeas Corpus Act, which had also recently been passed. We have already addressed the former. Let us now examine the latter.

The first act that suspended Habeas Corpus, passed in early March 1689, was actually a statute that empowered legal officers to detain prisoners arbitrarily.[115] The Act through its empowerment of local officials had the effect of suspending the Habeas Corpus Act of 1679.[116] Hence, it was actually named "An Act for Impowering his Majestie to Apprehend and Detaine Such Persons as He shall finde just Cause to Suspect are Conspireing against the Government."[117] The act claimed that because the realm was in a "[t]ime of Imminent Danger," the Crown could detain without bail suspected plotters against the government. Supposed plots and conspiracies by nefarious enemies necessitated arbitrary imprisonment. Finally, the Act had a sunset clause. It would expire on 17 April and then the Habeas Corpus Act of 1679

---

[113] *CJ*, 10: 47. The members of the committee are briefly discussed in Schwoerer, *No Standing Armies*, 152.

[114] Schwoerer, *No Standing Armies*, 96.

[115] 1 Gul. & Mar. c. 2. As Paul Halliday has noted, the word "suspension" was never inserted into any Suspension of Habeas Corpus Act. Halliday, *Habeas Corpus: From England to Empire* (Cambridge, MA, 2010), 248.

[116] 31 Chas. II c. 2.   [117] 1 Gul. & Mar. c. 2.

would once again become law. Parliament would re-empower the king to imprison without bail twice more in 1689.[118] The Habeas Corpus Act was set aside so that the king could preserve the realm from harm.

The Mutiny Act was likewise a suspension through empowerment. The makers of the act began by asserting that a standing army was only legal in England if it was authorized by parliament. Just as the Suspension Act declared the Habeas Corpus Act to be the law of the land, so the Mutiny Act made clear that the Petition of Right's ban on martial law was ordinarily law. But, because of the "time of Danger" and the "Exigence of Affaires," where the "Common safety of the Kingdome" and the "Protestant Religion" were threatened, soldiers needed to "be brought to a more Exemplary and speedy Punishment than the Usuall Formes of Law will allow."[119] Like the act that suspended Habeas Corpus, the makers installed a sunset clause that limited martial law jurisdiction in England to six months. Parliament had suspended the Petition of Right's ban on martial law by empowering military commanders to use martial law on soldiers. The Mutiny Act was a suspension act.

The jurisdiction was circumscribed in several ways. Martial law could only be used on soldiers defined as those who had voluntarily signed up for the army, who had taken the oath of a soldier, and who had the articles of war read to them. If these qualifications had not been met, a court-martial could not try someone.[120] None of these stipulations were new. As we have seen, armies employed them regularly throughout the seventeenth century. The inclusion of mutiny was a direct result of the mutinies by soldiers in the previous months. The crime of false musters was a constant problem for military officials throughout the seventeenth century and thus was also included. The makers of the Mutiny Act included desertion because of doubts over whether soldiers in England could be punished at law for it. Given that Holt was an influential MP, it seems likely that his interpretation that common law had no cognizance over desertion had prevailed with the 1689 Parliament. Martial law, albeit for temporary periods, now had jurisdiction over desertion. In the end, the Mutiny Act might as well have been called the "Desertion Act" as that was the wrong tried most frequently by courts-martial in early eighteenth-century England.[121]

The crafters of the Mutiny Act seemed to have wanted to bring an end to the Petitioning System. Within the Act, the makers declared that

---

[118] 1 Gul. & Mar. c. 7, c. 19.   [119] 1 Gul. & Mar. c. 5.

[120] In our first complete set of courts-martial records in England, from the reign of George I, the court always asked the defendant if they were a soldier in pay, and if they had taken the oath. TNA, WO 71/122.

[121] TNA, WO, 71/122. False musters was included in the Mutiny Acts beginning in 1 Gul. & Mar. sess. 2 c. 4.

"nothing in this Act contained shall extend or be construed to Exempt any Officer or Soldier whatsoever from the Ordinary Processe of Law." However, the Mutiny Act failed to remove the petitioning system completely. While the warrants of apprehension cease in William's reign, commanding officers still expected to be notified before a civilian magistrate arrested a soldier for misdemeanor.[122] Tensions over misdemeanor crimes committed by soldiers continued in the 1690s. The Mutiny Act probably aided civilians in their quest to seek justice from soldiers, but it was not a cure-all for civil-military relations.

Like when the Long Parliament adapted martial law jurisdiction during the Civil War, the Revolution Parliament adapted courts-martial to make conviction more difficult and to make outside supervision easier. The Act mandated that all courts-martial contain at least thirteen members and that in cases involving life and limb, the court-martial needed nine votes for conviction. Those who made the Mutiny Act wanted to ensure that at least twelve men heard and determined a trial. Courts-martial might not have been common law, but it could now be construed as a trial by peers because more than twelve men heard a case. Both of these stipulations suggest the discomfort the makers of the Mutiny Act had toward martial law procedure. But discomfort did not lead to dissuasion. Over time the Mutiny Act was transformed from a stop-gap measure into the normative way soldiers would be governed.

Beyond 1689

The Mutiny Acts were eventually expanded to include more of the articles of war – articles similar to the ones that had so shocked Edward Coke in 1628. Further, by 1715 government officials had powers of summary execution through the Riot Act that strongly resembled the summary martial law powers of sixteenth century London provost marshals.

The temporal claims for the passage of the Mutiny Act were broadened over time.[123] Parliament eventually removed the Mutiny Act from any temporal constraints whatsoever. Beginning in November 1689, parliament stopped justifying the passage of the Mutiny Act because of a "time of danger." It instead justified the Mutiny Act because of a "time of warr."[124]

---

[122] BL, Add. Ms. 9,760, fos. 7–9.

[123] There were still gaps when the Mutiny Act was not in force in England in the 1690s. 11 November–20 December 1689, 21 December 1691–9 March 1693, 2 March 1695–9 April 1695, 11 April 1698–20 February 1702. In Anne's reign, it was continually in force. See Clode, *The Administration of Justice under Military and Martial Law*, 20–7.

[124] 1 Gul. and Mar. sess. 2, c. 4.

But wartime was not defined by the closing of the courts or by the raising of the banner. Instead, it was defined by England's declared war with France. Throughout the 1690s, this much broader definition of wartime was used to justify the Mutiny Act. In the last Mutiny Act passed in William's reign, the suspension of the Petition of Right was simply "judged necessary," while in Anne's reign the renewed war against France and Spain was used to justify suspension. In the first year of the reign of George I, rebellion became the justification. Then, it simply became necessary for the safety of the realm.[125] Necessity became perpetual.

The Mutiny Acts also expanded the cognizance of courts-martial within England. During the reign of Anne, the makers of the Mutiny Acts experimented with incorporating the articles of war into the common law. Common law courts had powers to prosecute desertion beyond the seas, and, eventually, re-direct cases to courts-martial. Further, by 1709, common law courts could try soldiers for felony for active disobedience to their officer, sedition and mutiny, and the refusal to obey an officer.[126] Courts-martial could also try these offenses as mutiny began to be understood more and more broadly. Slowly, martial law powers under the Mutiny Act expanded.

The Mutiny Act allowed a wider jurisdiction abroad. By 1720, commanders began claiming that their cognizance was widened provided that the civilian courts were closed, un-cooperative, or non-existent. According to article of war 44, if civilian courts abroad refused to try a soldier within eight days, the commander could try him by martial law. Quickly, the eight days provision was dropped. After 1722, in the garrisons of Minorca and Gibraltar "or in other places beyond the Seas" commanders had powers to put their troops to trial by martial law for those wrongs usually reserved for common law prosecution because civilian jurisdictions were not in operation.[127] It is not difficult to trace where this came from: the reversal of the conviction of Thomas of Lancaster. The courts being out of operation, or non-existent, martial law became an acceptable alternative to civilian jurisdiction. Commanders with powers derived from the Mutiny Act, especially abroad, possessed an extensive martial law jurisdiction.

Terror through exemplary justice was not exclusively reserved for soldiers. In 1715, parliament passed the Riot Act so that local justices of

---

[125] The claims for the legality of the Mutiny Act have been traced in Clode, *The Administration of Justice*, 23–4.

[126] 7 Anne c. 4.

[127] Frederick Bernays Wiener, *Civilians under Military Justice: The British Practice since 1689, especially in North America* (Chicago, 1967), 14. The number of the article changed with each new printing of the articles of war.

the peace could suppress disorders similar to ones that had taken place immediately preceding and succeeding George I's coronation in 1714.[128] In order to maintain the peace, the makers of the Act declared that for the "more speedy and effectual punishing" of rioters, JPs, constables, and mayors among other legal officers were authorized to demand those congregated in groups of twelve or more to disperse. The demand was made formal through the recitation of a short proclamation.[129] If, after an hour, the congregants had not dispersed, they could be punished as felons without benefit of clergy. For our purposes, it was the Act's authorization of enhanced policing powers that are most worthy of study. For just as provost marshals in earlier periods possessed the right to execute by martial law those who resisted the course of justice, so any legal officer under the Riot Act had a pre-emptive pardon should they kill or maim resistors of arrest. Let us compare the two side by side. For example, provost marshals in London in 1598 had powers to execute "all such as shall not be readily reformed and corrected by the ordinary officers of justice."[130] Effectively, this was a threat to get riotous "vagabonds" to submit to justices of the peace and willingly re-locate back to their home county. Likewise, the Riot Act threatened those who would not disperse with summary execution. In this case, the many legal officers empowered by the Riot Act would be "free discharged and indemnified" if any rioter happened "to be killed, maimed, or hurt, in the dispersing, seizing, or apprehending, or endeavoring to disperse, seize, or apprehend them."[131] Parliament granted powers of execution in a different way than the Privy Council had granted it in the 1590s. But the effect was the same. Those who put down riots were free from any worry should they kill or injure their suspects. By the end of the eighteenth century, this power had become militarized.

The Riot Act would not always be understood as granting a martial law power. Given the diversity of opinions on martial law, it would have been strange if that had been the case. But for those who followed Selden's line of thinking, that martial law was a power of execution against those who willfully stood outside of the king's peace, the Riot Act could be understood as a martial law power. While Selden had not contemplated riot, he

---

[128] 1 Geo. st. 2 c. 5.
[129] *An Act for Preventing Tumults and Riotous Assemblies, and for the More Speedy and Effectual Punishing Rioters* (London, 1715), 243.
[130] *TRP*, 2: no. 796.
[131] Julius Ruff, *Violence in Early Modern Europe, 1500–1800* (Cambridge, 2001), 191. Anthony Babington, *Military Intervention in Britain: from the Gordon Riots to the Gibraltar Incident* (New York, 1990).

was invested in the idea that individuals while committing a wrong had entered into a time of war. In this time, common law process was unavailable and officers of the peace could if necessary maintain the peace with force. Should they take the person committing a wrong into their custody, a time of peace returned and they had to prosecute the suspect through the common law courts.

Conclusion

Neither the Mutiny Act nor the Riot Act replaced preexisting martial law jurisdiction. They were simply added alongside them. Jurists continued to believe, and in the Caribbean practice, that should the courts close or should the army be in the field against an enemy, martial law was perfectly legal. Thus, into the eighteenth century, there were both prerogative and statutory claims to exercise martial law. This meant that in places where governors were more powerful, as in Jamaica, they exercised their right to discern danger, close the courts, and declare martial law. Meanwhile, in British dominions where parliaments held more sway, the Mutiny Act or colonial replicas of the Mutiny Act allowed commanders to punish their troops by martial law. Because of this combination, martial law was used more often in the eighteenth century than it was in the seventeenth century.

MPs in the 1628 Parliament had attempted to bind martial law to wartime. These efforts were overturned at various points during the Civil War and Interregnum. With its new charge to take command of the army in 1689, MPs, within months, likewise suspended the Petition of Right, even though many of them had fought to prevent the legalization of martial law during the reigns of Charles II and James II. Slowly, through the re-passages of the Mutiny Act, imminent danger became declared war. War became peace. Thomas Marritt in the end was convicted of desertion and sentenced to death under a jurisdiction that had been generated, expanded greatly, and made permanent in just less than 27 years. Innovation, to paraphrase the 1628 MP Robert Mason, comes in gently at first and grows strong by degrees.

Conclusion

Using ideas from the Middle Ages, European armies, Roman history, and from their own experiences, Crown officers, MPs, and jurists made and re-made martial law. In the sixteenth century, Tudor officers took the language from a commission of *oyer and terminer* and combined it with the procedures used to govern medieval hosts – which in all likelihood were adapted from the criminal process of the Court of the Verge – in order to discipline the Crown's armies and to try and convict the impoverished who had risen over religious and economic grievances. Very soon after, the Crown adopted a new variant of martial law. In order to threaten religious dissenters, notorious traitors, and abettors of pirates, the Tudors made summary martial law process, where commissioners could convict and execute through manifest proofs. In Ireland, under the Earl of Sussex, this summary variant of martial law became the normative means to punish poor vagrants, poor illegal retainers, poor notorious suspects, and poor traitors. Meanwhile, in the English armies in the Low Countries, generals and their assistants transformed martial law once again. A court of the marshal became a council of war, where discretion was spread throughout the increasingly large officer corps. A judge advocate started many of the actions against the soldiers. He, or by the end of the seventeenth century, his clerk, also recorded the evidence. These courts in general cared deeply about either eyewitness testimony or a confession before they convicted any within the martial polity of a capital offense. They were very different from the actions of the martial law commissioners in Ireland. The same two words, "martial law," encompassed different practices.

This re-fashioning continued throughout the seventeenth century. In the 1620s, the Crown adapted martial law once again, this time allowing local authorities like deputy lieutenants, mayors, and others martial law jurisdiction in combination with the military officers stationed in the county. With a quorum of three, the Privy Council allowed them to punish soldiers and other dissolute persons by martial law. These innovations continued during the English Civil War when parliament began trying traitors in its garrison towns. Eventually, the Long Parliament mandated a quorum of twelve, which often included members of the local militia or influential parliamentary lawyers. Civilian spies were tried for treason at these adapted tribunals. The Commonwealth and Protectorate governments used this adapted court-martial as a model for their "High Courts of Justice" that tried conspirators in England throughout the 1650s. In this variant, the High Court's sentences allowed the state to seize the property of those convicted. The innovations did not end there. In 1689, the Revolutionary Parliament passed the Mutiny Act, which suspended the Petition of Right in order to authorize the use of martial law on soldiers for mutiny, desertion, and false musters. This act, like the acts of the Long Parliament, mandated a quorum, this time of thirteen commissioners. Parliament on multiple occasions transformed martial law.

As with its process, Crown authorities adapted and innovated in the substantive laws of martial law. In the sixteenth century, the creativity of Crown authorities was mostly related to its experimentation with allowing martial law commissioners to prosecute various statutory wrongs by martial law. By the end of the sixteenth century, however, generals and their assistants transformed the articles of war by selectively imitating classical and European martial law codes as well as generating new laws based on the perceived needs of the campaign or garrison. Matthew Sutcliffe, in his enormously influential work on martial laws, catalogued these ordinances. They were eventually incorporated into the ordinances of war for the English armies in the Bishops' Wars, the Civil War, the garrison in Tangier, and for the Jamaican militia. The navy incorporated a shorter version to govern its sailors from the 1640s onward. At various moments, authorities adapted this martial lawmaking tradition for the supervision of colonial ventures. Both the authorities of the Roanoke colony of 1585 and the Jamestown Plantation, in the much more famous *Lawes Diuine Morall and Martiall*, used martial laws for governance. Civilians were sometimes subject to these laws both abroad and in England and Ireland. Both the Long Parliament and the governments of the 1650s adapted the ordinances for the safety of the garrison to punish civilian spies and traitors. By the early eighteenth century, the parliaments of Anne incorporated some of the ordinances into the common law tradition while also including them in the Mutiny Act. The articles of war, like martial law process, were dynamic.

Like its procedures and its substance, the jurisdiction of martial law also underwent transformations. Courts of war in the Middle Ages disciplined the host when the banner was raised by the customs of the constable and marshal. In times of war, signified by the banner raised or the courts being shut, Crown authorities could likewise punish traitors through manifest proofs like notoriety. The sitting Court of Chivalry, meanwhile, handled cases relating to heraldry as well as treason cases overseas. By the sixteenth century, many still wanted the 12-mile circumference around the banner to demarcate martial law jurisdiction. But quickly the banner became turbulent times in general. Eventually, the Crown began targeting specific offenses to punish by martial law. Like in so many other areas of law, authorities used martial law creatively in the sixteenth century.

This creativity generated a strong reaction by those who wanted more stability within the legal order. The first serious and prolonged attempt at the circumscription of martial law began in Ireland. Crown authorities in the 1580s first made the argument that martial law was merely a power to execute rebels, invaders, and those who resisted arrest *in flagrante crimine* in order to restrain summary martial law. Once a person had been taken prisoner, according to this interpretation, authorities were required to use common law process. In the same decade Sir James Crofts attempted to delimit martial law to the host during turbulent times. Similar, if more elaborately constructed, arguments were made during the 1628 Parliament. Using part of the reversal of the conviction of Thomas of Lancaster, Sir Edward Coke argued that martial law was only legal when the Courts of Westminster were closed. John Selden, on the other hand, argued that martial law was merely a power to execute rebels and invaders *in flagrante crimine*. William Noy, meanwhile, argued that if the enemy's banner was raised in the field, then a commander could punish his soldiers by martial law. A time of war, variously interpreted, became the most important justification for martial law jurisdiction.

These separate arguments were often combined in the Restoration as clerks sent them across the globe through commissions and charters. Sir Matthew Hale allowed, like Selden, commanders to execute rebels or invaders in the field. For soldiers, he argued that sitting courts-martial should only be allowed when the courts were closed. These stipulations were put into many of the commissions for English governors abroad. In Virginia, St. Helena, the East Indies, and most importantly, the Caribbean, debates over martial law jurisdiction were replayed anew. Some authorities blatantly ignored restrictions on martial law. Others followed them. Various petitioners used Hale and Coke's understanding of martial law to contest the convictions of their relatives at courts-martial. Governors in Jamaica, however, used these jurisdictional rules to their advantage, often with the consent of the prominent planters of the island. By closing the courts down, the governors mandated labor for the construction of defenses throughout the island. They used the same process to mandate militia duty, billeting, and other services that the legislature ordinarily would not have allowed. In all of these places, arguments that attempted to circumscribe martial law were only partially effective.

An increasingly complex state apparatus monitored martial law jurisdiction. In the Middle Ages, the organization of the king's war machine was primarily the duty of his household officers, who oversaw the host, its courts, and its discipline. By 1600, the Privy Council, which had emerged in the latter half of the sixteenth century, monitored the delegation and use of martial law jurisdiction. It had been the Privy Council that initially wanted to restrain martial law practice in Ireland by the 1580s. By the seventeenth century, the houses of parliament, in 1628 but especially after 1641, took on the role of authorizing and monitoring the execution of martial law jurisdiction. The Long Parliament often reviewed controversial cases heard before courts-martial. The Glorious Revolution Parliament did likewise when it debated the legality of the East India Company's uses of martial law. By the Restoration, the Lords of Trade monitored controversial uses of martial law in the empire. Meanwhile, the increasingly sophisticated War Office kept courts-martial records and attempted to regulate disputes between civilians and soldiers. The Secretary of the Navy likewise monitored naval courts-martial. In order to maintain discipline, resolve disputes over a controversial jurisdiction, and assert its authority over an increasingly far-flung empire, the multipronged English state was usually more than happy to play referee over proper martial law practice.

Out of all of these institutional bodies and state officials, arguments to restrict martial law to wartime were least effective against determined MPs even if they often forced them to simultaneously curb the powers of martial law commissioners. These men in the Commons and the Lords often overrode the restrictions on martial law through ordinance and statute. Authorized for the disciplining of soldiers and then of spies and traitors, the Long Parliament used martial law even when the traditional badges of wartime were not to be found. These authorizations continued throughout the 1650s. But most importantly, the 1689 Parliament and many of its successors believed it necessary to authorize martial law for the disciplining of soldiers through the Mutiny Acts and summary martial law through the Riot Act. Along with these authorizations came restrictions in the form of quorums, sunset clauses, and even in one instance a requirement for full proof by Roman Civil Law standards before conviction. Nevertheless, more than any other authorization, parliamentary statute allowed for martial law to remain one of England's laws.

From a historical perspective, the centrifugal forces of martial law appear strong. But from a more human perspective, martial law would not have appeared so splintered. Jamaicans knew that martial law meant militia duty or that their slaves were required to work on forts. In England in the 1620s, soldiers knew that if they rioted or deserted they might be executed by martial law. Suspected traitors in both the 1640s and 1650s had a hearing either at an adapted court-martial or at a High Court of Justice. Soldiers were informed through attendance at the Parade which punishments were handed down to their peers. Martial law was dynamic but it was not arbitrary. In any given setting, martial law commissioners put forth settled principles. Indeed that was the point. The arguments that martial law did not have a substantive law tradition, that its procedures were capricious or even non-existent, or that it was detached from the legal order itself are wrong.

This is particularly true of the seventeenth century, when martial law practice was not differentiated from military law. Instead of allowing the military's high command, or anyone else who possessed martial law jurisdiction, to remove themselves from the legal forms of the court-martial and the ordinances of the army or navy, the Crown, its governors, and various parliaments mandated that those procedural and substantive laws be followed both in the field and upon suspected conspirators, spies, and traitors. The only exceptions to this were rebels and invaders who could be executed *in flagrante crimine* and, in Ireland, tory bandits who resisted arrest. As admittedly problematic as some seventeenth-century martial law practices were, rules nevertheless restrained martial law commissioners from engaging in arbitrary practices. When this was not the case, the closest examples from this work are the summary martial law commissioners' actions in sixteenth-century Ireland, violence and abuse of power followed. The very modern division between martial law – as some kind of state of exception – and military law has made it more likely for such catastrophes to occur as it has tended to grant commanders authority to abandon legal forms in a state of emergency. Understanding the history of martial law on its own terms might nevertheless lead us to contemplate whether the separation of martial law from military law in modern times is useful or necessary.

Far from being incompatible with the English legal tradition, martial law – unlike so many of the other laws on William Fleetwood's list – survived because it was such an alluring alternative to trial by jury. As long as grand and petty juries possessed discretion to determine verdicts, as long as common law process was understood as being too slow or too obstructive, and as long as common law was thought to be too lenient, Crown officers, MPs, and colonial governors were tempted to employ martial law either as an all-encompassing replacement to common law or as a complement to common law process for certain offenses. The granting of discretion to the juror in turn created the desire to prevent the delegation of that same discretion in certain times. Martial law in its various guises was too useful as a tool of governance to be completely abandoned.

By mostly ignoring martial law, scholars have missed out on an important and extremely controversial component of the English legal order that went global in the seventeenth century. The dynamism and vernacular nature of its tradition meant that it could be exported to a wide range of English holdings. Martial law can be found at America's founding, in India, Jamaica, Tangier, Ireland, as well as England itself. This tradition was highly creative, and accounted at different moments for different enemies, different treatments of civilians, as well as different treatments of soldiers. Recognizing that this dynamic tradition was a part of the English legal order will hopefully encourage scholars to re-evaluate the relationship between law and war in the Anglo-American and even pan-European traditions. Traditional citations of Grotius, Vattel, and Lieber not only do not sufficiently account for legal practice during war but they also only account for a small proportion of juristic thought.

Remembering how martial law was made and re-made, why it was used, and how – and how successfully – it was circumscribed has shed new light on England's legal culture. Rather than seeing martial law as being unique, we should instead understand that England's laws were dynamic, its legal culture politicized, and that its growing empire shaped both domestic and imperial legal practice. Indeed, recovering the history of martial law helps us better understand the complex, multi-jurisdictional, and multi-procedural legal order it operated in. This divisive, competitive, and politicized legal culture fought over martial law's frame but these fights were not always played out in the binary Crown versus parliament or absolutism versus ancient constitutionalism models that have been traditionally used to describe early modern English constitutional politics. This work encourages scholars of seventeenth-century English politics and culture to once again examine England's multipolar legal culture.

II

The Mutiny Act went global in the eighteenth century. From England to Minorca to Gibraltar and eventually to North America, British soldiers were disciplined through the successive passages of the statute. Along with its official passage, colonial assemblies passed replicas of the Act in their legislatures so that they too could discipline soldiers through martial law.[1] Many by the middle of the eighteenth century believed that martial law *was* the Mutiny Act. Judge advocate generals by 1765, in the aftermath of British occupations in West Florida and in Quebec, determined that the Mutiny Act only governed soldiers.[2] But these controversies only concerned military generals, not those who also had powers of martial law as governors of colonies.

By 1775, governors in Colonial America began to examine the martial law powers within their charters and commissions that had been made in the seventeenth century more carefully. Because of the political upheavals of the time, Massachusetts fell under martial law. Quebec was to follow shortly after, when the governor Sir Guy Carlton believed it necessary to force his colonists into militia duty. Then, in perhaps the most surprising twist in a story that has contained so many of them, Lord Dunmore, the governor of Virginia, declared martial law in November 1775. Ousted from the capital, Dunmore raised the Crown's banner, the ancient signifier of wartime, at Kemp's Landing. He likewise declared the courts to be shut. Normally so watchful over their enslavement, the courts were fast asleep as Dunmore offered emancipation to the slaves of rebels should they serve the British imperial nation. Through yet another innovative use of the reversal of the conviction of Thomas of Lancaster, martial law became linked with emancipation.[3]

The Caribbean strategy of closing the courts down in order to make public rights claims became a pan-imperial one. Further, the Riot Act, which had been used frequently in England, was transported throughout English dominions, giving governors powers traditionally associated with summary martial law. Imperial governors at the end of the eighteenth century and into the nineteenth century commonly used martial law as a form of judicial terror to the extent that English jurists demarcated their usage from the military law that continued to discipline soldiers. R.W. Kostal has painstakingly charted its use in this period:

"martial law" had been proclaimed numerous times (including in Barbados 1805, 1816; Ceylon 1817, 1848; Demerara 1823; Jamaica 1831–2; Cape Colony 1835,

---

[1] Leonard Woods Labaree, *Royal Government in America: A Study of the British Colonial System before 1783* (New Haven, 1964), 397–8.

[2] Frederick Bernays Wiener, *Civilians under Military Justice: The British Practice since 1689, Especially in North America* (Chicago, 1967), 37–63; Douglas Hay, "Civilians Tried in Military Courts: Quebec, 1759–64," in *Canadian State Trials: Law, Politics, and Security Measures, 1608–1837* ed. Frank Murray Greenwood (Toronto, 1996), 115–27.

[3] James Corbett David, *Dunmore's New World: The Extraordinary Life of a Royal Governor in Revolutionary America – with Jacobites, Counterfeiters, Land Schemes, Shipwrecks, Scalping, Indian Politics, Runaway Slaves, and Two Illegal Royal Weddings* (Charlottesville, 2013), 95–110.

1846, 1850–1; Canada 1837–8; Cephalonia 1849; India 1857–8; St. Vincent 1862) ...[4]

Finally, Governor Edward John Eyre proclaimed martial law in Jamaica in October 1865. In order to put down a riot in Morant Bay, Eyre had closed the courts down in Surrey County excluding Kingston Parish. Well after the "rebellion" was crushed, Eyre executed at least 439 black Jamaicans.[5] Included in the death tally was George Gordon, a fierce political opponent of the governor who was actually forcibly moved into Surrey County where the courts were closed so that his execution by martial law was justified. Once again, the most "poor and afflicted people" living within British dominions called for "help and comforte."[6]

In extensive arguments over the course of late 1865 and 1866, those appalled by Governor Eyre's acts sought to hold him accountable. He argued that the courts were closed and that he had a right as governor to put down rebellion. His opponents, consistent with Edward Coke, believed the governor had committed murder because he had unlawfully used martial law. Consistent with John Selden, one of their main arguments was that the executions had not been done upon those *in flagrante crimine* but instead had been performed after the supposed rebels had been taken prisoner. Consistent with the general history of martial law, the results of the inquiry were deeply disappointing for those who sought justice for the victims of its violence.[7]

While A.V. Dicey claimed that England knew no martial law in his famous constitutional history of England, and while Maitland claimed that there were no substantive rules to martial law other than the government's right to preserve itself, martial law practice persisted throughout the British Empire. From South Africa at the end of the century to England itself through the Defense of the Realm Act at the opening of World War I, martial law continued to be re-made to fit new circumstances. It remained one of England's laws.

---

[4] R.W. Kostal, *A Jurisprudence of Power: Victorian Empire and the Rule of Law* (Oxford, 2006), 201.

[5] *Ibid.*, 13.

[6] Sir James Crofts, "A Discourse for the Reformacons of Ireland," NRO, Fitzwilliam Ms. 67 (Irish), f. 12v.

[7] Kostal, *A Jurisprudence of Power*, 193–257.

Manuscript bibliography

Berkshire Record Office, Reading

D/ED/O56: Papers of William Trumbull

Bodleian Library, Oxford

Carte
Ms. 23, 34, 48, 143, 154, 163: Papers of James Butler, 1st Duke of Ormond

Clarendon
Ms 80: Papers of the Earl of Clarendon

Firth
Ms.C4: Lord Lieutenants Book for County Essex

Nalson
Ms. 8, 13: State Papers, c. 1640–60

Rawlinson
Ms. A 171, A 181, A 295, A 314, C 972:
Papers of Samuel Pepys

Tanner
Ms. 57: Correspondence from the Committee of Kent, c. 1640s
Ms. 103: Thomas Audley's "An Introduction . . . to the Wars"

The British Library, London

Additional Ms.
4,159: Legal Tracts on Martial Law, c. 1640s
4,786: Tracts Relating to Irish Affairs
9,760: Blathwayt Papers
12,423: Journal of Col. Edward Doyley
12,429: Jamaica papers
12,430: Journal of William Beeston
14,286: Journal of William Clarke

21,922: Deputy Lieutenant Book of Sir Richard Norton
22,185: Johnson Papers
23,971: Thomas Audley, "A Treatise on the Art of War"
29,974: Civil War Papers
30,170: Articles of War (1585–6)
31,116: Whitacre's House of Commons Proceedings
37,536: Irish State Papers, c. 16th Century
38,139: Articles of War (1585–6)
38,240: Liverpool Papers
38,694: War Office and other Correspondence
41,613: Misc. Legal Papers c. 1600–10
61,336: Blenheim Court Martial Records
64,890: The Papers of Sir John Coke
70,006: Correspondence of Sir Robert Harley, 1647–52
72,422: The Papers of William Trumbull
72,545: The Papers of William Trumbull

Cotton Ms.
Titus C.1: Papers relating to the office of Earl Marshal and Constable
Vespasian C.XIV: Papers relating to the office of the Steward, Earl Marshal, and Constable

Egerton Ms.
784: Whiteway's Diary
2,087: Papers Related to Dover, c. 16th–17th Centuries

Harley Ms.
164–5: The Journals of Sir Simonds D'Ewes
168: A Collection of Small Tracts, and Papers of State matters, mostly written by the Hand of Mr. Ralph Starkey
444: Minutes of the Council of War, 1588
519: The Institution and Dyssepline of a Soldier, temp. Elizabeth
703: A book written (as it seems) by Sir Walter Covert, Kt, 1583–1627
847: Historical Papers, temp Elizabeth
980: Thomas Gibbons Collections
2,057: Papers relating to the City of Chester, c. 1600
3,638: A Book containing a Variety of Historical Papers, temp. Chas. I
4,191: A Book Directing the Choosing & Ordering of the Army & Making War
4,602: Sir William Throckmorton, "Commentaries on Caesar," 1655
5,109: Misc. Papers relating to the Military
6,008: William Throckmorton's "A Brief Treatise of War," 1649
6,068: A Collection of Records Concerning Wales
6,802: Papers of Edward Walker, Royalist Secretary of War
6,844: Misc. Papers relating to Military Affairs
6,851: Papers of Edward Walker relating to Civil War
6,852: Papers of Edward Walker relating to Civil War
6,991: Letters of considerable persons, 1571–4
7,018: Accounts relating to the army and the navy

India Office Records
E/3/90–91: East India Company General Correspondence
G/3: Bombay Factory Records
G/32: St. Helena Factory Records
H/48–9: Records relating to Bombay

Lansdowne Ms.
59, 62, 66, 70, 78: Papers of Sir William Cecil, Lord Burghley
155: Miscellaneous State Papers, 16th Century

Sloane Ms.
1,957, 1,959, 1,960 (bound together): Courts Martial Records, Tangier, 1661–9
1,961: Records relating to Courts-Martial, Tangier c. 1671–3
3,498: Minute Book of Courts-Martial, Tangier, 1661–79
3,514: Records of John Luke, Judge Advocate General, Tangier, 1661–79

Cambridge University Library, Cambridge

Ms. Kk.I.15: Irish State Papers, 16th Century
Add. Ms. 6,998, 7,002: Papers of Sir William Maitland

Chester and Cheshire Archives and Local Studies Service, Chester

M/MP: Mayor's Military Papers, c. 1570–1600

The Churchill Archives Centre, Churchill College, Cambridge

Earle Ms. 4/8/1–2: Courts Martial Records, Ireland, c. 1700

Colonial Williamsburg Foundation, Williamsburg, VA

Papers of William Blathwayt

Derbyshire Record Office, Matlock

D1232: Sanders Ms.

Devonshire County Record Office – Exeter

ECP BK: Exeter City Quarter Sessions Records
L290: Ancient Letters
Misc. Rolls: Commission of Martial Law

Durham University Library, Durham

Bowes Ms. 534: courts-martial records, 1570

Folger Shakespeare Library, Washington, D.C.

V.b.142: Papers Relating to the 2nd Earl of Essex

Gloucestershire Archives, Gloucester

GBR 2/2: Gloucestershire Lieutenancy Book, c. 1620s
GBR G3/SO7: Abstract of Quarter Sessions, Recognizances and
Orders, 1675–90

Hampshire Record Office, Winchester

44M69: Jervoise Family of Herriard Park Ms.
5M50: "Southampton Marshall Business"

Harvard Law School Library, Cambridge, MA (examined on microfilm at the University of Virginia Law Library)

Ms. 1,071: Case Reports, late 17th century

Hatfield House

(examined via the Cecil Papers: http://cecilpapers.chadwyck.com at the
Folger Shakespeare Library, February 2013)
Cecil Papers 63/108, 64/67, 168/64, 215/13: The Papers of William and
Robert Cecil

Henry E. Huntington Library, San Marino, CA

Ellesmere Ms. 1,686: Case report relating to desertion statutes
Ellesmere Ms. 1,700: Papers relating to Ireland. c. 16th century
Hastings Ms. 837, 5,622, 6,998, 6,999: Correspondence of Theophilus
Hastings, Seventh Earl of Huntington
Huntington Ms. 30,881: The Letter Book of the Earl of Huntington,
c. 1580s

Hertfordshire Record Office, Hertford

Verulam Ms. XII: Papers of Sir George Croke

Hull History Centre, Hull

U DDHO 1/31–62: Hotham Ms.

Isle of Wight Record Office, Newport

OG/BB: Oglander Ms.

Lambeth Palace Library, Lambeth

247: Papers relating to the Army
597, 608, 614, 616: Carew Ms.
709: Shrewsbury Ms.
943: Laud Ms.
3,470: Fairhurst Ms.
3,474: Hale Ms. (Misc.)

Lilly Library, Indiana University, Bloomington IN

D'Albeville Ms.

Lincoln's Inn, London (Examined on microfilm at the University of Virginia Law Library)

Ms. 375: Case Reports, late 17th century

London Metropolitan Archives, London

Jour. 22, 40: Journals of the Common Council
Rep. 23, 25, 59: Repertories of the Court of Aldermen
QQ: Mayor's Letter Books, c. 1640s

Longleat House (Viewed on Microfilm at the British Library)

Coventry Ms. 75: Correspondence relating to Jamaica

The National Archives, Kew

(State Papers Ireland and Domestic viewed through State Papers Online: http://gale.cengage.co.uk/state-papers-online-15091714.aspx at the Folger Shakespeare Library and the National Archives, Kew, November 2011–July 2015)

Accounting Office
1: Audits of the Imprest and Commissioners of Audit

Admiralty
1/5253: Naval Courts Martial Records

Chancery
66: Patent Rolls
82: Warrants for the Great Seal
193/142: Precedent Book of William Porter

Colonial Office
1: Privy Council, America and West Indies
5: Board of Trade and Secretaries of State: America and West Indies,
    Original Correspondence
137: Jamaica, Original Correspondence
138: Entry Books, Jamaica 17th Century
139: Jamaica, Acts
140: Jamaica Sessional Papers
153: Leeward Islands, Entry Books
279: Board of Trade, Tangier Correspondence
391: Board of Trade Minutes

Exchequer
39/93/15: *Placita Exercitus* temp. Edward I
351: Declared Accounts of the Army

King's Bench
21: Crown Side, Rule Books

Privy Council
2/64: Privy Council Registers, 1673–5.
2/71: Privy Council Registers, temp. James II

State Papers
1: State Papers Domestic, Henry VIII
9: Williamson Collection
10: State Papers Domestic, Edward VI
11: State Papers Domestic, Philip and Mary
12: State Papers Domestic, Elizabeth I
14: State Papers Domestic, James I
15: State Papers Domestic, Addenda, Edward VI–James I
16: State Papers Domestic, Charles I
24: Papers of the Committee of Indemnity
29–30: State Papers Domestic, Charles II
44: Secretaries of State: Entry Books to 1782
59: State Papers: Border Papers
60: State Papers Ireland (temp. Henry VIII)
62: State Papers Ireland (temp. Philip & Mary)

63: State Papers Ireland (temp. Elizabeth I–Charles I)
104: State Papers, Foreign Entry Books

War Office
4/1: Secretary of War, Out-Letters
26/1–6: Warrants, War Office
55/1939: Governor of Berwick Entry Book of Correspondence, 16th Century
71/121: Courts Martial Records c. 17th Century
71/122: Courts Martial Records c. 18th century
89/1: Courts Martial Records c. 17th Century
92/1: Calendar of Sentences of English Courts Martial, c. 17th Century
93/5: Manuscript history of the Court of the Constable and Marshal
93/6: "Description of Courts Martial Proceedings in Several European Countries"

National Library of Ireland, Dublin

d. 2,687: Martial Law Commission, 1562
d. 2,688–9: Commission of Martial Law, with Instructions temp. Henry Sidney
d. 3,106: Martial Law Instructions, 1584–5
d. 3,181: Inquisition taken at Rappellegh, 1592
d. 3,261: Commission of Martial Law, 1597
3,319: Legal Tract on Ireland, c. 1600
8,066/2: Letter Patent to Walter, Earl of Essex
18,768: Colclough Ms.
29, 711: Inquisition taken at Co. Wexford, 1591

Northamptonshire Record Office, Northampton

Fitzwilliam Ms. 67 (Irish): Papers of Sir James Crofts

Parliamentary Archives, London

HL/PO/JO: House of Lords Main Papers

Staffordshire Record Office, Stafford

D593: Leveson Ms.

Surrey History Centre, Woking

371/14/J/15: Rough Notes on Martial Law, 1696
6729: More Family of Loseley Park Ms.

William Andrews Clark Memorial Library, UCLA, Los Angeles, CA

Army Account Book, 1692

Worcester College Library, Oxford

Clarke Ms. 21: Dundee Court Martial Records

Index

1549 Rebellion, 62–3

Lightning Source UK Ltd.
Milton Keynes UK
UKHW020644220520
363663UK00011B/1815

9 781107 469488